Offenders, Deviants, or Patients?

Offenders, Deviants, or Patients?

An Introduction to the Study of Socio-Forensic Problems

HERSCHEL PRINS

Tavistock Publications

First published in 1980 by
Tavistock Publications Ltd
11 New Fetter Lane, London EC4P 4EE
Published in the USA by
Tavistock Publications
in association with Methuen, Inc.
733 Third Avenue, New York, NY 10017

© 1980 H.A. Prins

Typeset by Inforum Ltd, Portsmouth
Printed in Great Britain by
Richard Clay (The Chaucer Press) Ltd,
Bungay, Suffolk.

ISBN 0 422 76800 6   (hardback edition)
ISBN 0 422 76810 3   (paperback edition)

British Library Cataloguing in Publication Data

Prins, Herschel Albert
    Offenders, deviants or patients?
    1. Insane – Commitment and detention – Great
    Britain 2. Insane, Criminal and dangerous –
    Great Britain 3. Mentally ill – Care and
    treatment – Great Britain
    1. Title
    365'.64   HV8742.G7
    ISBN 0-422-76800-6
    ISBN 0-422-76810-3 Pbk

Contents

Acknowledgements   vii
1 Introduction and rationale   1
2 Criminal responsibility and related matters   8
3 Mental disorder and criminality   41
4 Psychiatry, the courts, and the penal system   102
5 Psychopathy – concept or chimera?   138
6 Are such men dangerous?   163
7 Fire-raising and fire-raisers   195
8 Sexual behaviour and sexual offending   213
9 Alcohol, other drugs, and crime   263
10 Female offending   297
11 Conclusions and some thoughts on reforms   330
   Name index   352
   Subject index   360

Acknowledgements

Many people have contributed to my understanding of 'offender/patients' and the problems associated with their management. A decision, taken early on in life, to become a probation officer, was probably determined quite strongly by a background of a family heavily involved in various aspects of social welfare, particularly the welfare of those labelled as offenders.

Many fine teachers have contributed much to my personal and professional understanding of offenders, but I would like to place upon record a special debt of gratitude to two of them. First to the late doctor Hermann Mannheim, for many years Reader in Criminology in the University of London; it was he who first generated my enthusiasm for the subject matter of criminology. Second to the late Doctor Peter D. Scott, with whom I had the privilege of working for some time. It was Peter Scott who stimulated my interest in mentally abnormal offenders and in socio-forensic problems more generally. Doctor Scott's tragic death at a comparatively early age robbed forensic psychiatry of a gifted clinician, teacher, and writer. My debt to both these men is considerable and it seems fitting to record it here.

It is of course invidious to single out individuals for special mention, but there are many other teachers, colleagues, and friends – too numerous to mention here – who have enriched my understanding in this field. Indeed, it would be difficult at some points to disentangle those ideas expressed in this book which are theirs and those which are my own; for any unintended plagiarism I beg their forgiveness. I have acknowledged permission to quote at length from the specific work of others or to reproduce some of my own work at appropriate places in the text, but, should any reader find that he or she has been quoted without due acknowledgement, I hope my oversight will be forgiven. The multi-disciplinary nature of this work has meant that I have had to engage the specialist subject matter of both law and psychiatry. I am especially grateful to four people who have offered me very constructive advice and criticism in these areas: to John Finch, of our Faculty of Law for help with Chapter 2; to Doctor Douglas Leslie, Consultant Psychiatrist, Glenfrith Hospital, Leicester and Clinical Teacher, Faculty of Medicine, Leicester University, for help with Chapter 3; to Professor Harvey Cleckley, Georgia, USA for very helpful comments on Chapter 5; and finally to Doctor N.J. de Ville Mather, formerly Lecturer in Forensic Psychiatry, Manchester University, for advice on Chapter 8. However, I must take responsibility for any errors or omissions that remain in these chapters.

My sincere thanks are also due to Janet Kirkwood who typed numerous and barely decipherable drafts of the manuscript with such patience and skill. Finally, my special thanks are due to my wife Norma, who did much to correct infelicities of style and grammar, and to Helen and Jeremy, who have tolerated my absences from domestic pursuits with such good grace. It is to all of them that this book is affectionately dedicated.

University of
Leicester, 1979

CHAPTER ONE

Introduction and rationale

If a man will begin with certainties, he shall
end in doubts, but if he will be content to
begin with doubts, he shall end in certainties.
                              FRANCIS BACON

The rationale for this book has emerged as a result of a general
interest developed over many years concerning the understanding and treatment of offenders. Recently, I have come to
be particularly interested in the borderland area between mental disorder and criminal behaviour and in the relationships
between the many disciplines and professions that struggle to
confront the problems inherent in these relationships. Thus,
psychologists, sociologists, psychiatrists, lawyers, police scien-
tists, social administrators, geneticists – to name but a few –
have all made contributions to this field. It is truly a multi-
disciplinary area and as Gibbens (1968) has pointed out:'Any
claim to specialisation [in this area] must lie in being able to
cross . . . social and administrative boundaries, as well as in the
specialised studies of particular mental conditions . . .'
    A number of fairly recent reports – for example, that of the
Committee on Mentally Abnormal Offenders (Home Office
and DHSS 1975), the MIND (NAMH) report (Gostin 1977),
and the Government White Paper on the Review of the Mental
Health Act, 1959 (DHSS *et al*. 1978) have all drawn attention to
some important current issues in this field – some of which will
be referred to again in the final chapter of this book. At this
point it is important to emphasize that many of these issues

present a number of challenges to and dilemmas for the social work, legal, penal, police, nursing, psychological, and psychiatric professions. For me, these concerns have been attested to more specifically in the interest shown by a number of our students in Leicester University's School of Social Work, who, in recent years, have opted to undertake my special course on *Mentally Abnormal Offenders*. More recently, a further group of interested professionals has enrolled for similar courses in our Department of Adult Education. The membership of these latter courses has been very catholic, including representatives of all the professions and disciplines alluded to above; it is encouraging to note that further courses have been requested.

I hope, therefore, that this book will appeal to a very wide range of professional readers. I hope also that it will be of interest to the concerned lay person because, through the media, the general public is being alerted more frequently and often very dramatically to the many problems in this area. It is my intention to examine certain specific problem areas and offender/patient groups in a way that will, I hope, not only assist the wide range of practitioners already referred to in their day-to-day work, but also will be of value to those whose occupations are more academic and who have teaching and training responsibilities. Since the field is such a very broad one, any selection of topics must be somewhat arbitrary. However, I have made my particular choices for the following reasons. First, because they are of special interest and concern to me; this seems in itself to be a not unreasonable justification. Second, because the literature on these topics is very widely scattered and not readily available to those who could most profitably draw upon it. Third, because I believe that some of the offender/patients to be discussed in this book are not considered attractive to work with by many in the medical, social work, and other 'caring' professions. They are, in the words of the late Doctor Peter Scott the 'unrewarding, degenerate, "not nice" offender(s)' (Scott 1975). We shall see, at various places in this book, how the system 'shunts' them in various directions, sometimes labelling them as offenders, sometimes as patients, and sometimes as deviants. The 'labels' frequently serve to offload real responsibility and are a convenient means of rationalizing our discomfort, ambivalence, and non-involvement. These 'shunting' exercises are of course compounded by our reluctance to face up to issues of treatment versus punishment. They also illustrate some of the dilemmas inherent in distinguishing between normality and abnormality, sickness and sin, care and control. At the present time such problems seem to me to be highlighted because established values appear to many people to be in a state of flux, and there is an acknowledged difficulty in deciding how to set appropriate limits to behaviour – both in society at large, and more specifically within those professional groups charged with the management of certain individuals labelled variously as offenders, deviants, or patients.

The problem of who should care for the more dangerous of these mentally disordered offenders was emphasized recently in the cases of *Robert John Mawdsley* and *Barry Williams*. The circumstances surrounding both cases were reported in *The Guardian* in some detail and are worth quoting here since they illustrate graphically some of the problems referred to above. They also serve to set the scene for some of the matters to be discussed later in this book.

(1) Robert John Mawdsley, described by Mr Barry Mortimer QC prosecuting, as 'one of the most dangerous and determined killers held in prison in this country', pleaded guilty to murdering two prisoners at Wakefield Prison, and was sentenced to life imprisonment on each charge.

The killings took place when Mawdsley was already serving a sentence of life imprisonment for murder. The two men killed by Mawdsley had cells on the same landing. The motives for the killings were uncertain but about two months before the killings Mawdsley had told another prisoner that he was considering 'doing someone in' because he was sick of Wakefield and he would be certain to get moved to another prison.

On the morning of 28 July Mawdsley had obtained a fearsome weapon from somewhere unknown. It was a dagger made out of a piece of steel which he tucked into his trousers. Sometime before exercise, (first victim) came into Mawdsley's cell. Mawdsley took the knife out and attacked (first victim), stabbing him about the back and head. During the course of the struggle he fell on to a bed and Mawdsley took a length of cord from his pocket and he garrotted this man by tying a ligature tightly round the neck.

After exercise, Mawdsley was walking round the landing and saw (second victim) in a cell. He was on his bed and Mawdsley took out the knife and launched a terrifyingly violent attack on (second victim) stabbing and penetrating his skull, and stabbing his chest through to the stomach. He then caused some fearful violence to the side of his head probably by banging his head against the wall.

In June 1974 Mawdsley had been convicted of manslaughter by reason of diminished responsibility after he had stabbed a man with whom he had a homosexual relationship. A hospital order had been made without time limit: Mawdsley was then held in Broadmoor Hospital.

On 26 February 1977, Mawdsley and another prisoner took a fellow prisoner hostage in Broadmoor. After hours of negotiations with the staff Mawdsley suggested that the hostage should be exchanged for a doctor. After torturing the victim, Mawdsley and another man strangled him by fastening a ligature around his neck. Mawdsley was convicted for murder, and remained in Broadmoor until his transfer to Wakefield.

At the trial for the Wakefield killings, Mr Mortimer said of Mawdsley that, 'He is a man who may be said to have little to lose'. Mr Justice Cantley told Mawdsley: 'I make no recommendation about the minimum period of your detention because I see no point in doing so. At present, I see no reason why you should ever be released, but it may be that something will happen which will enable you to be released at some time.' (Source: *The Guardian* 17 March 1979.)

(2) Barry Williams, aged 34, armed with a gun in both hands, ran amuck and killed three of his neighbours and two other

people. He was finally caught after a police chase through
Derbyshire. At Stafford Crown Court on 26 March 1979 he
pleaded guilty to manslaughter on the grounds of diminished
responsibility and was ordered to be detained indefinitely in
Broadmoor. Williams, a foundry worker, was said to be an
introvert, with an intense and irrational hatred of his allegedly
noisy neighbours. He thought that they were against him and
that they made noises to upset him deliberately. In October
1978, after drinking nearly half a bottle of whisky, he launched
an attack on them, shooting two of the male members of the
Burkitt family who were outside the house repairing a car. He
then shot at Jill Burkitt as she came out of the house; when
another neighbour came out to investigate the noise she was
shot in the chest and shoulder. He then drove off in his car,
throwing a home-made bomb and firing six more shots at
neighbouring houses. Later, in the course of his escape he
killed two members of staff of a nearby petrol filling station.
When, after a long chase, he was subsequently overpowered by
the police, he is alleged to have said: 'You don't understand.
You would have shot them if you had been me. They were not
human beings. They were just things.' At his trial, it was
alleged that Williams was in legal possession of various
firearms, but enquiries made during the investigation of the
case revealed that he had been involved in a number of incidents that would most likely have prevented him from being
granted a firearms certificate had they been known to those
issuing it. Staff at one of the rifle clubs to which he belonged
said he was never interested in orthodox target shooting and
had once been ordered off the range for dangerous behaviour.
Other incidents included two occasions when Williams made
unprovoked attacks on persons he considered had been making a noise near his house. Seven days before the multiple
killings, he is alleged to have threatened to exterminate his
neighbours. Described as an introvert – 'a shadowy figure', 'a
mister nobody' – his phobia about noise was compounded by a
sense of persecution. He is alleged to have told the police that
he thought his neighbours had been laughing at him and that
local people thought he was a 'poof' because he was quiet and

had few girlfriends. It was suggested at his trial that he had also been contemplating his own death, for he had taken out an insurance policy which would have given his parents £6,000 if he had died. Like Mawdsley, he too may have considered he had nothing to lose. (Source: *The Guardian* 27 March 1979.)

These two cases illustrate, if in somewhat extreme form, a number of the issues referred to earlier. In addition, they illustrate the problems involved in trying to assess degrees of dangerousness – a matter to be dealt with at some length in a subsequent chapter. In Mawdsley's case, it became clear that not even the high security of Broadmoor could contain him. In such cases as that of Williams, the court would almost certainly receive evidence that he was suffering from a mental disorder that might, in time, respond to treatment. His case also illustrates vividly the dangers that can arise when individuals are allowed to have easy access to weapons of destruction.

In summary then, this book opens with an examination of some general issues of criminal responsibility and the problematic nature of the relationship between mental disorder and criminality. I shall then examine some particular offender/patient groups with special reference to the anxieties they cause to those who have to care for them. It could be argued that there are general methods of treatment that can be applied 'across the board' to offender/patients as a group. It is my contention (and this contention will be supported by the evidence I adduce later in the book) that one can apply generic principles of treatment to a limited extent, but that care and management are based best upon an in-depth understanding of the complex aetiology of particular clinical groups. It is for this reason that I have chosen to look at certain offender/patient groups in some detail in the hope that armed with such knowledge, the efforts of those in the caring and containing professions may not only be better informed, but hopefully be more rewarding and successful.

References

DHSS, Home Office, Welsh Office, Lord Chancellor's

Department (1978) *Review of the Mental Health Act, 1959*. Cmnd. 7320. London: HMSO.

Gibbens, T.C.N. (1968) The Task of Forensic Psychiatry. *Med. Sci. Law* **8**: 3–10.

Gostin, L.O. (1977) *A Human Condition (Vol. 2)*. London: MIND(NAMH).

Home Office and DHSS (1975) *Report of the Committee on Mentally Abnormal Offenders (Butler Committee)*. Cmnd. 6244. London: HMSO.

Scott, P.D. (1975) *Has Psychiatry Failed in the Treatment of Offenders? The Fifth Denis Carroll Memorial Lecture*. London: ISTD.

CHAPTER TWO

Criminal responsibility and related matters

The Law is the perfection of reason . . .
                              LORD COKE

The Law is a ass – a idiot.

                                   DICKENS

The problems to be discussed in this chapter are complex and interrelated. They cannot be fully understood without some knowledge of ethics, law, psychiatry, and to a lesser extent, theology. These problems are further complicated by the manner in which certain terms are used, sometimes synonymously, sometimes not, by a wide range of people. Thus, it will be necessary to offer some definitions of words such as 'responsibility', 'capacity', 'culpability' etc. For, often folk are not unlike Lewis Carroll's Humpty Dumpty who, it will be remembered, said: 'When I use a word, it means just what I choose it to mean – neither more nor less.'

My main purpose in this chapter is to provide a map which will give an outline of the main contours of this area. It may be likened to one of those large road maps that are provided by the motoring organizations and which are deliberately devoid of the finer detail. For this, the traveller must turn to the more detailed charts provided by the Ordnance Survey or similar organization. It is hoped that the references made in this chapter to more substantial sources of information will, by analogy, serve this latter purpose. The material to be surveyed in this outline map will include first of all some consideration of the terms used in discussions of responsibility. Second, I shall provide a short account of the development of concepts of responsibility and allied matters; third, a description of the manner in which the law makes various special provisions for what I shall choose to call the 'erosion' of responsibility. (The choice of this word will be the subject of later comment.) Finally, some brief consideration will be devoted to the relationship between mental disorder and crime in the light of recent proposals for reform.

A question of semantics

The lay person may well use terms such as responsibility or guilt in less precise fashion than would the lawyer or student of jurisprudence. Thus, the former, if asked to define responsibility, would come near to the dictionary definition, which in the *Concise Oxford Dictionary* reads: 'Liable to be called to account, answerable to, *morally* accountable for actions, capable of rational conduct.' The important point to be noted here is in the emphasis I have added. The law is not necessarily concerned with morally reprehensible conduct. My colleague John Finch puts this argument very well and I am most grateful to him for allowing me to quote him at length.

> 'Clearly the spheres of law and morals do not necessarily coincide, though legal and moral exhortations may coincide in certain cases. Many crimes exist which are generally regarded as offensive to morals. Such is the crime of murder. Similarly one ought not to steal, and stealing is also thought to be immoral, though some cases may be regarded as less immoral than others, and stealing in general may be thought less immoral than murder. Opinions may, however, vary on both counts. Second, there are crimes (of a species proliferating in modern times) which are of a regulatory nature, such as parking offences and penal provisions in statutes of an administrative nature, and which are contrary to legal but not to moral stipulations. But even in relation to such penal offences, it might, however, be

thought that any crime, however technical, is immoral – though the reasonableness of such a belief might decrease in the light of the plethora of strict liability offences under our law, the doubt being engendered more by the absence of mental conditions for responsibility than simply by the number of such offences. Thirdly, there are activities widely held to be contraventions of morality but which are not the subject of legal penal prohibitions, the notable example in our own legal system being adultery.'   (Finch 1974)

The Wolfenden Committee in their report on *Homosexual Offences and Prostitution* (1957) made a further important distinction between *private* and *public* morality: 'Unless a deliberate attempt is to be made by society, acting through the agency of the law, to equate the sphere of crime with that of sin, there must remain a realm of private morality and immorality which is, in brief and crude terms, not the law's business.' Not all jurists however would accept the limitations suggested by the Wolfenden Committee. The extent to which the criminal law *should* concern itself with matters of private morality has been cogently argued by Lord Devlin in his Maccabean lecture *The Enforcement of Morals* (Devlin 1959). For the purpose of this chapter, I shall use the term responsibility in a restricted sense, namely one of *liability to come within the purview of the criminal law and to be dealt with by the systems that operate for its enforcement.*

Lay people may use the word 'irresponsible' to denote legal lack of responsibility. 'Irresponsible' for our purposes can be said to mean simply lack of legal responsibility and is not used here in any pejorative sense.

Hart, whose book *Punishment and Responsibility* (1968) is a seminal contribution to this field, draws attention to the 'diverse application of the word "responsibility" '. He suggests that responsibility really means 'answerable to' and that only with the passage of time has the 'liability–responsibility' element been introduced. He states 'that though some sense of "answer" is connected with all the main meanings of responsibility, it is not that of answering questions and the connexion, though systematic, is indirect'. It is of interest that Hart does not deal with this most important etymological issue in the main part of his text, but deems it sufficient to deal with it in the section entitled 'Notes' at the end of the book.

The word 'culpable' is found not infrequently in the literature on responsibility and allied matters. For our purposes, it is taken to mean blameworthiness in the criminal sense. However, if we do use it in this way, we must acknowledge a moral quality creeping into its usage. 'Capacity' is sometimes used as a synonym for legal competency. Thus, in legal terms, it would seem to denote some quality existing within the individual – for example, to form an intent to act in a certain way. We shall consider the matter of intent itself a little later. The term 'liability' is sometimes used as being synonymous with responsibility. The COD defines it as being 'legally bound, answerable for; under an obligation to do something'. As far as the law is concerned liability can certainly go beyond responsibility in the sense of moral culpability. There are many offences, notably those of 'strict liability' (sometimes called 'absolute liability'), for which a person may be punished even though he is not aware of the existence of facts which make his conduct a criminal offence. An example is that of the shopkeeper found to have purveyed contaminated meat or other foodstuffs. In recent years, the House of Lords has given indication that there should be some restriction on the interpretation of offences of strict liability. A leading case for further reference is that of *Sweet* v. *Parsley*.* This concerned a young woman who was originally convicted of being concerned in the management of premises (she being the tenant of a farmhouse in Oxfordshire which she sublet to various other tenants) in which the prosecution alleged cannabis was being smoked. Her conviction, after appeal, was eventually overturned as a result of a decision of the House of Lords. Those wishing to follow up this and other aspects of strict liability should read Hogan's erudite yet witty inaugural professorial lecture entitled *Criminal Liability Without Fault* (Hogan 1969). Hogan's central thesis is that 'strict liability is justified only to the extent that its imposition may be shown to prevent the occurrence or recurrence of harm beyond that which would be prevented by

* [1969] 1 All ER 347.

the imposition of liability for intentionally reckless or negligent conduct'. (For further consideration of this and allied matters, see also Jacobs 1971.)

There are one or two additional terms that we must attempt to clarify at this point. It has been well stated that an act does not make a person *legally* guilty unless his mind is also legally blameworthy. In this connection, we should note what has already been said about the difference between legal blameworthiness and moral turpitude. Lawyers denote this concept of legal guilt through the use of the latin term *mens rea*. Simply put, this means of legally guilty intent, or more precisely having the intention to commit an act that is wrong in the sense that it is legally forbidden (Hart 1968). We should note also that there must be an *act* or *omission*. Lawyers call this the *actus reus*. An omission is a *failure* to do something; a simple example would be failure to give precedence to pedestrians on a 'zebra' crossing.

But what of more complex and emotive situations in which a person may be charged with a failure to do something which amounts to more serious negligence? A negligent act causing the death of another can of course lead to a charge of manslaughter. In the case of *R. v. Bateman* in 1925, the court held that:

> 'in order to establish criminal liability the facts must be such that, in the opinion of the jury, the negligence of the accused went beyond a mere matter of compensation between subjects and showed such disregard for the life and safety of others as to amount to a crime against the State and conduct deserving punishment.'

Criminal liability for manslaughter may thus be incurred through a negligent act. In another instance the courts have held (in the case of *R. v. Senior* (1899)) that failure to seek medical aid, as for example in the case of a sick child, may result in a finding of manslaughter. In a much more recent case (*R. v. Stone* (1977)) it was held that all that need be proved by the prosecution is gross negligence in the sense of a *reckless* disregard of danger to the health and welfare of an infirm person under the care of the accused.

In such instances (as in strict liability) the question of intent does not necessarily arise. But in cases where the law requires that we did *intend,* for example, to cause bodily harm or to rob a person's house there are as we shall see later, various 'excusing' or 'exculpating' conditions or situations that can be put forward. (See also Hart 1968.) A recent report produced by the Law Commission has dealt in some detail with the semantic considerations involved in determining the legal and judicial meaning of terms such as 'wilfully', 'recklessly', 'maliciously', 'with intent', 'knowledge' etc. *Paragraph 6* of their summary of recommendations is worth quoting in full.

'(a) A Court or jury, in determining whether a person has committed an offence, should decide whether –
  - (i) he intended a particular result of his conduct,
  - (ii) he was reckless as to such a result,
  - (iii) he foresaw that such a result might occur,
  - (iv) he knew that a particular circumstance existed, or
  - (v) he was reckless as to the existence of such a circumstance, by reference to all the evidence, drawing such inferences from the evidence as appear proper in the circumstances; and
(b) it should be a relevant factor –
  - (i) for the purpose of (a) (i), (ii), and (iii) above that the result was a natural and probable consequence of that person's conduct,
  - (ii) for the purpose of (a) (iv) above that a reasonable man in his situation would have known that the circumstances existed, and
  - (iii) for the purpose of (a) (iv) above that a reasonable man in his situation would have realised that there was a risk of the circumstances existing.'

(Law Commission 1978)

The definition of a 'reasonable man' will of course rest upon moral assumptions and sentiments that will change over time. The 'reasonable man' may, like the chameleon, take on the characteristics of his social and cultural surroundings.

A brief excursion into history

Generally speaking, the present day view is that men and women are to be held responsible for their acts and are capable of exercising control over them. As Clarke (1975) puts it: 'Unless it can be shown that (and there are a limited number of acceptable defences) [a man] was not so capable, he is punished for breaking the law in accordance with the gravity of the offence.' History shows that matters have not always been so clear cut and it is therefore worthwhile making a brief excursion into the past at this point.

In societies with legal systems less sophisticated than our own it was normal for punishment to be imposed for the commission of a criminal act regardless of the mental state of the person concerned; indeed early common law gave priority to the need to preserve law and order. Guttmacher (1968) points out that the writings of the Old Testament give indication of mainly severe forms of justice without mitigating features being much in evidence. However, if the crime was unintentional, some mitigation of penalty was available as, for example, through the provision of a city of refuge for those who killed unintentionally. In addition, minors, imbeciles, or deaf mutes were amongst those who were specially singled out for less harsh treatment. He points out that in the *Talmud* we find the use of the Hebrew word *shoteh* which was intended to describe the mentally ill and defective person though only in very general terms. In Roman times we see the beginnings of an attempt to introduce some idea of diminishment of responsibility and Walker (1968b) has traced the attempts to mitigate the harsher penalties of the law in the Saxon era. In the thirteenth century, it seems to have been generally held that neither the child nor the madman should be held liable; this was the view of Bracton, author of what is generally regarded as the first major treatise on English law. In respect of the madman, we should note Bracton's statement, *'Furiosus non intelligit quod agit, et anima et ratione caret, et non multumdistas a brutis'* – 'an insane person is one who does not know what he is doing, is lacking in mind and reason, and is not far from the brutes.' (But today we might well take exception to an insane person being likened to a brute.) Both Walker (1968b) and Jacobs (1971) have drawn attention to an apparent error of translation in another of Bracton's statements. This is worth quoting because it illustrates some of the problems inherent in tracing the evolution of legal concepts. Bracton is alleged to have stated: 'And then there is what can be said about the child and the madman (furiosus) for the one is protected by his innocence of design, the other is excused by the misfortune of his *deed* [my italics].' It is not at all clear from this text why the madman is not to be held responsible. Bracton took his text from a translation of the work of Modestinus. In its original form, this referred not to the misfortune of his deed (infelicitas *facti*), but to the misfortune of his fate (infelicitas *fati*). This makes more sense, for in Roman Law, there appears to have been an assumption that an insane offender was sufficiently punished by his madness *(satis furore ipso punitur)*. After Bracton, the law treatises seem to contain little, if anything, on the subject of criminal responsibility until the mid-seventeenth century, though if we searched the original sources thoroughly enough we might find examples from the period between Bracton and Grotius, who 'taught not to pay attention in punishing to what had happened but to the future results of the treatment'. Reprisals which do not have implications for future behaviour he called 'purposeless self gratification' *(triumphum et gloriam animi)*; punishment by reprisals he called no legal punishment but a hostile act *(poena non est, sed factum hostile)* (Scott 1962). Sir Edward Coke (1644) seemed content to follow Bracton, contending again that the madman is punished sufficiently by his fate. Sir Matthew Hale (in a treatise published in 1736, some sixty years after his death) wrote what may be regarded as the first authoritative socio-legal treatment of the subjects of idiocy and madness and their relationship to criminal responsibility. Hale tried to distinguish total from partial insanity; the latter would not exempt from criminal responsibility: 'The best measure I can think of is this; such a person as labouring under melancholy tempers hath yet ordinarily as great an understanding, as ordinarily [a person] of fourteen

hath, is such a person as may be guilty of treason or felony . . .'
(Jacobs 1971: 27).

It is probably safe to assume that these early writers in
considering what states of mind might have bearing on
responsibility and liability to punishment had in mind only the
most seriously insane persons – 'the raving lunatics'. However,
in the eighteenth century, there were a number of cases which
seemed to demonstrate a willingness to recognize broader
interpretations of mental disorder. It needs to be remembered, however, that almost without exception these cases
under consideration were those of murder or at least of murderous assault. For example, in Arnold's case, in 1724, the
judge suggested that 'if a man be deprived of his reason, and
consequently of his intention, he cannot be guilty . . .' (Jacobs
1971: 27). Similarly in 1760, when Lord Ferrers was tried
before the House of Lords, emphasis was placed upon the
possession or otherwise of reason and the degree to which this
might exculpate the accused from responsibility. It should be
noted that both the cases of Arnold and Ferrers led to what are
described as *special verdicts* under the Common Law. (There
was, as we will see later, no statute law that granted exemption
from responsibility at this time.)

Both these cases helped to pave the way for a more liberal
interpretation of 'excusatory' criteria. This was clearly evident
in a case that has become almost as famous as that of Daniel
M'Naghten – namely that of James Hadfield. This case has
been very well documented by many writers – for example, by
Walker and Jacobs, so that the story need be told but briefly
here. Hadfield was tried in 1800 for shooting at George III. He
suffered from a delusion that he was called upon to sacrifice
his life for the salvation of the world. Not wishing to be guilty of
suicide, he chose to commit his crime for the sole purpose of
being executed for it. The case is of interest from two points of
view. First, because it was probably the earliest occasion in
which brain damage as such had been advanced as a relevant
factor (Hadfield had received very severe sword wounds to the
head during war service). Second, because his brilliant counsel, Erskine, was probably able to capitalize upon the develop-

ing community interest in insanity and secure an acquittal without much difficulty. For it should be remembered in the context of Hadfield's case, that George III suffered from recurrent attacks of so called mental illness, although the cause and exact nature of his malady have never been adequately established. Despite the uncertainty about the diagnosis Hadfield was certainly acquitted at a time when the King's 'malady' had helped focus increasing attention on insanity. However, not all cases were brought to such a satisfactory conclusion as was Hadfield's. A similar plea in the case of Bellingham who, in 1812, shot the Prime Minister, Spencer Perceval, was unsuccessful and he was condemned to death. And, as Walker (1968a) reports, a contemporary of Bellingham's (an epileptic farmer called Bowler) who had – presumably on grounds of his epilepsy – been found to be insane by a civil commission of lunacy was executed for shooting a neighbour with intent to kill him.

The case of Daniel M'Naghten in 1843 is of vital importance because this first instance in which a legal test of insanity was formally promulgated remains the law relating to insanity up to the present day. However, other tests of mental disorder have since been introduced which have significantly reduced insanity as a defence as such. M'Naghten, a Scot, seems to have suffered from what we would describe today as paranoid delusions. As a result of these delusions, he attempted to kill the Prime Minister, Sir Robert Peel, but not knowing what Peel looked like, M'Naghten shot and killed his secretary, Drummond, by mistake. At his trial, a number of medical men testified to his unsoundness of mind and he was found 'not guilty by reason of insanity'. Queen Victoria, who had been the subject of several attempted assaults upon her person by numerous people alleged to be of unsound mind, was not pleased with the verdict. It may be that her displeasure, and the interest she and her Consort took in this and other cases, was more than a little influential in the decision of the House of Lords to call the Judges before them to answer certain questions arising from M'Naghten's case.

Two of the answers given by the Judges have come to be

known as the 'M'Naghten test'. This states, in effect, that:

> 'the jurors ought to be told in all cases that every man is to be
> presumed to be sane and to possess a sufficient degree of
> reason to be responsible for his crimes, until the contrary be
> proved to their satisfaction; and that to establish a defence
> on the ground of insanity, it must be clearly proved that, at
> the time of the committing of the act, the party accused was
> labouring under such a defect of reason, from disease of the
> mind, as not to know the nature and quality of the act he was
> doing; or, if he did know it, that he did not know what he was
> doing was wrong.'

Once one has disentangled the somewhat archaic language, it
is possible to see that there are two 'limbs' (as some lawyers
choose to call them) to the M'Naghten 'Rules' as they have since
come to be known. A man has a defence first, if he did not
know the nature and quality of his act or second, if he did know
that, but did not know that it was wrong. It is not hard to see
why these rules have been the subject of continuous criticism
almost from the day they were posited. In the first place, they
were framed at a time when pre-eminence was given in the
developing science of psychology to cognitive faculties (i.e. the
faculties of knowing, reasoning, and understanding) as distinct from emotional or volitional factors. We shall also see how
this concentration on cognitive aspects played its part in the
development of the concept of psychopathy (see Chapter 5).
Second, two further problems have arisen. First, the interpretation of the word 'wrong' in the Rules. It has been established
(in the case of *R.* v. *Windle* in 1952) that 'wrong' means wrong
in law and not morally wrong. (Though the Australian courts
have refused to follow this interpretation.) The second problem concerns the use of the words 'disease of the mind'. It
should be noted that the Rules were formulated at a time when
the study of psychiatry was also in its infancy and when organic
explanations for mental disorders were being sought. How is
one to distinguish disease in this sense from other less exclusively mental diseases, as for example, in the case of epilepsy, in
which a person may be unable to control his behaviour in

certain situations? The resolution of problems arising from involuntary behaviour of this kind will be discussed later. Third, under the Rules, there must be established a *causal* connection between the mental abnormality and the commission of the offence. This is frequently very difficult to prove.

In view of all these apparent defects in the Rules, it is remarkable that they have survived for so long, though as we will see later, their invocation has been far less frequent since the introduction of the Homicide Act of 1957 and since the abolition of the death penalty for murder. However, various attempts have been made to broaden or clarify them. The Atkin Committee (1923) wished to see a major amendment of the Rules to allow for the inclusion of the term 'irresistible impulse', but this concept has never found much support in English Law, though, again as we will see later, the expression of so called 'irresistible impulses' seems to have been taken into account by Judges in their charges to juries and in their actual sentencing practices. In the United States, where the M'Naghten Rules were adopted early on, there have been a number of modifications – notably the Durham Rule, which states succinctly that an accused person is not to be held to be criminally responsible if his unlawful conduct was the product of mental disease or defect. (However, its very succinctness has led to as many difficulties of interpretation as existed before its introduction.) Similarly, Commonwealth countries have made modifications in the light of the M'Naghten experience. The whole matter was examined again in the *Report of the Royal Commission on Capital Punishment* in 1953. Partly as a result of this re-examination and borrowing also from Scottish precedent, the concept of diminished responsibility was introduced in the Homicide Act of 1957.* The advantage of this Act is that it reduces what would otherwise be murder to manslaughter and it also enables the courts to take into consideration a far wider range of disorders than those covered by the M'Naghten Rules. Murder is now reduced to manslaughter if the accused

---

* Unless stated otherwise, I refer in this chapter to the law and its interpretation in England and Wales. Scottish law and practice is different.

'was suffering from such abnormality of mind (whether arising from a condition of arrested or retarded development of mind or any inherent cause or induced by disease or injury)' as substantially impaired his mental responsibility (*Section 2*). We shall proceed to a more detailed examination of diminished responsibility a little later.

More recently, the *Butler Committee (Report of the Committee on Mentally Abnormal Offenders)* (Home Office and DHSS 1975) has made proposals for clarifying the application of the M'Naghten Rules and the Homicide Act further (such as introducing a refinement in the definition of mental illness and outlining new procedures through which the courts should deal with such disordered persons). These will also be the subject of later comment.

The object of the foregoing section of this chapter has been to sketch in some historical pointers. The choice of these and the manner in which they have been presented may seem to be somewhat arbitrary. It would, for example, have been possible to trace the historical background of some of the concepts now to be discussed *seriatim*, but this would, in my view, have made for a rather repetitious presentation. In the foregoing brief sketch, I hope I have shown some of the ways in which the law has had to gradually take into account knowledge derived from developments, first in psychology and subsequently in psychiatry, in trying to estimate the degree of criminal responsibility that should be attached to the actions of men and women.

Erosions of responsibility

A word of explanation is necessary in relation to my use of this phrase. To the best of my knowledge, it does not appear in any of the textbooks and I have introduced it here merely for convenience and with some hesitation. It is meant to serve as an umbrella term for those situations, states of mind, being, or attributes that may cause a person to be held non-responsible in law or for his responsibility to be severely diminished in a variety of ways. Let me deal first of all with the clearest example of the law holding that a particular group of persons shall not be held to be responsible in law – namely that of children below a certain age.

CHILDREN

Jones and Card in the eighth edition of the legal manual *Cross and Jones' Introduction to Criminal Law* (1976) state that: 'It is irrebuttably presumed that no child under the age of 10 years can be guilty of an offence.' Children of this age and below are said to be *doli incapax* (not capable of crime). From the age of ten years, and below fourteen years, they are also presumed to be incapable of committing an offence. However, this presumption may be rebutted by proof that the child knew that what he was doing was wrong. In practice, this means that a child between the ages of ten and fourteen can only be found guilty if the prosecution is able to prove that he committed the *actus reus* with *mens rea*. Namely if such a person in this age span can be said to have what the law describes as 'mischievous discretion'. It is also worth noting that boys under the age of fourteen are irrebuttably presumed to be incapable of sexual intercourse and thus cannot be convicted of the offence of rape; but they can be convicted of the lesser charge of sexual assault. As Jones and Card point out, it seems somewhat strange where evidence is produced showing a boy of fourteen *capable* of performing the act of intercourse that this irrebuttable presumption of incapacity should still exist. This *may* be because the special exemptions in relation to children have their origins a long way back in history and, as we saw earlier, the law at a very early stage in its development created special exemptions concerning the responsibility of children. We should perhaps also note in passing, that the law also tries to *protect* children from a curiously assorted variety of dangers. Scott (1962) lists some of these; for example, from suffocation from drunken bed-fellows, from intoxicants, dangerous performances, possessing gun-powder, from certain sexual acts, from peddling wares, and a number of others.

INVOLUNTARY CONDUCT AND AUTOMATISM

Before proceeding to examine the way in which the law takes account of certain abnormal mental states in determining the degree of responsibility that should be attached to an action or omission, we need to consider some matters concerning the nature of voluntary conduct and the nature of the state known as automatism. (See also Chapter 3.)

Earlier in this chapter, reference was made to the notion of intention. Implicit in this notion is the assumption that the act complained of should have been voluntary; that is, within the control of the person. An act or omission to act is considered to be involuntary where it can clearly be shown to be beyond the control of the person. A case often cited in legal texts is that of *Hill* v. *Baxter*** in which it was alleged that the defendant had contravened the Road Traffic Act, 1930 by driving dangerously. He pleaded that he had become unconscious and that he remembered nothing of the alleged incident. This plea was accepted by the magistrates on the grounds that severe loss of memory must have been caused by the sudden onset of illness which had overcome him. The Divisional Court, however, did not accept this, suggesting that he might just have fallen asleep. However, in expressing their view in this particular case, they did agree that there might be some states of unconsciousness, or even clouded consciousness, such as those due to a stroke or an epileptic fit, which might exclude responsibility in similar cases. One of the Judges hearing the appeal suggested that similar exculpation from responsibility might have arisen if, for example, a man had been attacked by a swarm of bees and because of their action he had lost directional control of the vehicle. It is true that such cases come before the courts infrequently and hypothetical examples are usually given by the judges in the course of their commentaries on particular cases. Hart (1968) has made a very useful distinction between circumstances 'where the subject is conscious and those where he is unconscious'. His distinction, with some paraphrasing by me, is worth quoting in full.

* [1958] 1 Q.B. 277. (Jones and Card 1976: 83).

(a) *Conscious*
  (i) Physical compulsion by another person.
  (ii) Muscular control impaired by disease; e.g. in the case of St Vitus Dance or Chorea.
  (iii) Reflex muscular contraction;
  e.g. in the case of the hypothetical swarm of bees mentioned previously.
(b) *Unconscious*
  (i) Natural sleep at normal time. He quotes the example of a woman taking an axe and killing her daughter while sleepwalking.
  (ii) Drunken stupor. As for example in the case of a woman in a drunken state 'overlaying' and thus killing her child.
  (iii) Sleep brought on by fatigue. As for example in the case of driving referred to previously.
  (iv) Loss of consciousness involving collapse. For example in cases of epilepsy or hypoglycaemia.

We can see that many of these states mentioned might lead successfully to a plea for negation of responsibility. The problem is that the courts have to interpret such pleas according to individual circumstances so that no general ruling can be found in the law reports which will apply automatically in all cases. For example, if I fall asleep at the wheel of my car and cause an accident, am I to be considered to be exempted entirely from responsibility or will the court suggest (as it did in the case of *Kay* v. *Butterworth*)* that I must have known that drowsiness was overcoming me and that because of this, I should have stopped driving and thus averted an accident.

AUTOMATISM

Sometimes, an accused will plead excuse from responsibility because it is alleged on his behalf that he was in a state of automatism. This means being in a state capable of action but not being conscious of that action. The Court of Appeal has

* (1945) 173 L.T. 191. (Jones and Card 1976: 83).

held that such a state can be a defence because 'the mind does not go with what is being done'. It is customary to distinguish between insane and non-insane automatism. In the latter case the accused must be acquitted. An example of this would be where the accused could show conclusively that the automatism was caused by a blow on the head or by a state of somnambulism. In the former case, if the accused is shown to be suffering from a defect of reason due to disease of the mind (per M'Naghten) because of insane automatism then he will be found 'not guilty by reason of insanity'. When one examines the various cases that are cited, it appears that the decision as to whether insane or non-insane automatism will be invoked or accepted by the courts is somewhat arbitrary. (Readers wishing to investigate the medico-legal aspects of automatism should consult Blair's excellent paper (Blair 1977).) The Butler Committee, in reviewing such defences, has suggested that these should normally result in an absolute acquittal since it would be wrong to describe such persons as mentally disordered. (They had in mind, for example, persons suffering from concussion or from hyperglycaemia as a result of not taking insulin.) However, the accused will have to bear the burden of adducing evidence of non-insane automatism; his claim must be buttressed by adequate medical evidence. It is not sufficient to state 'I just blacked out', or 'I can't remember what took place'. (For a more detailed discussion of the relationship between epilepsy and automatism see Fenton (1975) and Chapter 3.)

INTOXICATION

Voluntary or self-induced intoxication by means of alcohol or other drugs may be adduced as a defence only if it can be shown to have caused a disease of the mind in M'Naghten terms. Thus, it could be advanced as a defence if an accused was found to be suffering from alcoholic dementia as a result of prolonged alcohol indulgence. The other situation in which it can be adduced as a defence is if *specific intent* is an essential ingredient of the offence and that because of intoxication the accused lacked the capacity to form such intent.

This has been held in one or two well-known cases; for example those of *Bratty* and *Lipman* (see Jones and Card 1976: 85 for a further discussion). In Bratty's case, it was stated that in crimes such as murder, where proof of a specific intent was required, this might be negated by drunkenness and the accused might be convicted of a lesser charge; for example one of manslaughter or of unlawful wounding. Similarly, in the case of Lipman, the accused, who was under the influence of the drug LSD was convicted of manslaughter and not of murder. His defence was that he must have killed the girl he was sleeping with whilst under the influence of the drug. Part of his defence consisted of the claim that he was being attacked by snakes; the immediate cause of his bedfellow's death was asphyxia caused by having part of a sheet stuffed into her mouth. For the most part, the law has always seen intoxication as an aggravating rather than a mitigating factor and normally the rule is that voluntary intoxication is no defence. Moreover, a plea of diminished responsibility under the Homicide Act cannot be based on drunkeness itself though, as pointed out in Jones and Card, it is likely that a permanent injury to the brain produced by drink would be held to be an 'injury' within the meaning of the Act. In cases where an accused person is in a state of involuntary drunkenness, he may well have a defence. An example of this would be where the accused had been deliberately drugged or had had intoxicants poured into a non-intoxicating beverage without his knowledge. Similarly, the unexpected side effects of taking medically prescribed drugs may be a successful defence. Such a defence will not be available however if the defendant takes alcohol against medical advice after using prescribed drugs, or if, for example, he fails to take regular meals while taking insulin for a diabetic condition (that is in crimes not requiring evidence of *specific intent*).

As already mentioned, the degree to which voluntary intoxication mitigates or exacerbates a criminal act has always been a controversial issue and it was one which exercised the minds of the Butler Committee. They suggested (as others have done – see for example, Samuels (1975)) that a new offence be created, namely that of being voluntarily drunk and dangerous. Thus it would be an offence for a person whilst voluntarily intoxicated to do an act or make an omission that would amount to a dangerous offence if it was done or made with the requisite state of mind for such an offence. The new offence of being 'drunk and dangerous' would not be charged in the first instance but the jury would be directed to return a verdict on this offence if intoxication was being raised successfully as a defence. The Committee include a definition of a 'dangerous offence' – namely that of involving injury to the person or death, or consisting of a sexual attack on another, or involving the destruction of or causing damage to property so as to endanger life (Home Office and DHSS 1975: paras. 18.53–9).*

Mental disorder and criminal responsibility – further considerations

I have inevitably made considerable reference already to some aspects of the ways in which mental disorder may have a bearing upon the alleged responsibility of an accused. It is now necessary to consider some aspects of this more fully, though a more detailed description of the legal and administrative processes involved will be given in subsequent chapters. It is convenient to divide the subject matter in the following way and in so doing, I have adopted (with some modifications) the outline followed in the *Butler Report*:

(1) pre-trial action, i.e. the decision to prosecute;
(2) disability in relation to the trial (fitness to plead);
(3) the Special Verdict;
(4) diminished responsibility and infanticide.

(1) Pre-trial action – the decision to prosecute

In considering this matter, we should be mindful of the fact

* See also the more recent decision in *R.* v. *Majewski* [1977] A.C. 443.

that the prosecuting authorities – mainly the police, but sometimes the Director of Public Prosecutions and more rarely, the
Attorney General – are given wide discretionary powers in
relation to the initiation of prosecutions. We know that this
discretion is exercised in various ways by the police, but
detailed information as to its actual extent is not so readily
available. Some of the factors that operate in the exercise of
this discretion are well documented by Walker (1968b). It is
highly probable that a number of persons afflicted by a variety
of mental disorders may well be screened out of the judicial
process through the exercise of police discretion. For example,
it is frequently the case that in areas where there are large
psychiatric or subnormality hospitals, patients occasionally
abscond and during their absconsions, they may commit
offences, usually of a minor kind. Rather than launch a prosecution, the police will normally return such patients to the
hospital. I know of cases where hospitalized subnormal
patients have committed minor acts of shoplifting when out
shopping; they have usually been informally cautioned rather
than prosecuted. I have described elsewhere (Prins 1973: 23)
the case of a man convicted of an offence of indecent exposure
who had successfully completed a period of probation coupled
with psychiatric treatment. Some years later, he was again
reported for (and admitted to) a similar offence. He was found
to have been going through serious recent stress and the
police, following consultation with the psychiatrist who had
treated him originally and on the understanding that he would
see him again, agreed not to bring a further prosecution. We
should note also that Section 136 of the Mental Health Act,
1959 enables the police to take persons found in a place to
which the public have access and who seem to them to be
seriously mentally disordered, to a place of safety and detain
them for up to seventy-two hours so that they may be
examined with a view to being hospitalized. In a number of
these cases, it is clear that this procedure may obviate the need
for prosecution for such offences as breach of the peace,
threatening behaviour, or even a variety of minor assaults. The
Butler Committee considered in some detail this question of

relief from prosecution in relation to those who were considered to be mentally disordered. They concluded that 'where
any apparent offender is clearly in urgent need of psychiatric
treatment and there is no risk to members of the public, the
question should always be asked whether any useful public
purpose would be served by prosecution'. They recommended
that Chief Officers of police should review their policy and
practice in such cases and that further guidance should be
given by the Director of Public Prosecutions. The tenor of the
Butler proposals seems to indicate that they would wish for a
more liberal approach to these matters. Unnecessary prosecution is not only expensive in the consumption of the time and
energies of all concerned, but may be positively damaging to
the patient. The Committee indicated that this more liberal
approach might be taken even in respect of more serious cases.
However, it seems that the Director of Public Prosecutions
tends to prosecute in *all* cases where serious harm is involved
and one must have some doubts whether the public would
accept all that readily what might be seen by some as a further
erosion of criminal responsibility. Finally, as we shall see when
we examine the question of 'fitness to plead', we should always
provide opportunities for people to be able to deny their
complicity in an offence if that is their wish, and/or is the view
of those advising them.

(2) DISABILITY IN RELATION TO THE TRIAL (FITNESS TO PLEAD)

In reviewing certain of the historical aspects concerning the
determination of responsibility, we have seen that in the cases
of some of the accused, there seems to have been no doubt that
they were 'mad by any standards'.* Now sometimes this 'madness by any standards' may be highly relevant to the determination of the accused's responsibility at the time of the offence,
but at others, it may only be in issue at the time of the trial and it
is this matter we must now consider. By tradition, the court has
to satisfy itself that a man's mental abnormality is so severe that

* A phrase attributable I think to the late Dr P.D. Scott.

he cannot even be tried. This means in effect, can he understand the charge, can he challenge jurors, can he follow the evidence, and can he instruct counsel? These elements used to constitute the components of being declared 'insane on arraignment', nowadays the term used is 'unfitness to plead'. The Butler Committee suggest the use of the words 'under disability in relation to the trial' or 'under disability' as being more in keeping with modern thought and practice. The issue of fitness to plead is not raised very frequently; mainly because a person has to be very seriously disabled psychiatrically to satisfy the relevant criteria. I know of two cases, however, which fulfill these particular criteria quite well. In the first instance, a man was suffering from such serious delusions that in the course of them, he killed his wife. He was still suffering from these at the time of his trial and subsequently. In another instance, a young man was found to be so subnormal in intelligence and understanding, that he too, was found unfit to plead.

In most cases then, the defendant will be shown to be suffering from very serious mental illness or subnormality. An accused claiming to suffer from amnesia, for example, (as in the case of Podola in 1959) would not normally satisfy the strict criteria laid down, for one can be amnesic yet still be quite able to follow the trial itself. The consequences which flow from such findings can be very serious for the defendant and as the Butler Committee pointed out, are productive of some anxiety concerning civil liberties. If found to be unfit to plead, the accused will currently be detained without limit of time in one of the Special Hospitals under Section 65 of the Mental Health Act. This means in effect, that the accused may be detained without ever having had the chance to rebut the charges that have been brought against him; moreover, he will have been sentenced to custodial treatment in a hospital for an indefinite period. The Butler Committee made certain recommendations both in relation to law and practice. They suggested that the existing criteria for determining whether a defendant is 'under disability' should be brought up-to-date and that they should in future consist of:

(1) whether he can understand the course of the proceedings at his trial so that he can make a proper defence;
(2) whether he can understand the substance of the evidence;
(3) adequately instruct legal advisers;
(4) plead with understanding to the indictment (charges).

They make a major proposal concerning procedure and one which would help to obviate the possibilities of the injustice referred to above. They recommend that the question of disability should be decided at the outset of the trial, or as soon as it is raised as an issue. Where disability has been found and where the medical evidence suggests prospect of early recovery, the judge should be given power to adjourn the trial for up to three months in the first place with renewal for a month at a time up to a maximum of six months. If the accused recovers within the six months' period, the normal trial should proceed immediately. A *trial of the facts* (that is, the substance of the case) should take place either as soon as disability has been found and there is no prospect of the accused recovering, or as soon as during the six month period as he may prove to be unresponsive to treatment or he recovers. If the accused is *found to be under disability*, there should nonetheless be a trial of the facts at the appropriate time. If a finding of not guilty cannot be returned, the jury should be directed to find that the 'defendant should be dealt with as a person under disability'. This new form of verdict would not count as a conviction nor, say the Butler Committee, should it be followed by custodial punishment; the court should have wide discretion as to what penalty should be imposed. The procedures outlined earlier and the Butler recommendations apply only to the Crown Court at present, but the Committee suggests that magistrates' courts should, in future, also have the power to determine and act upon the issue of disability.

These new proposals attempt to safeguard the interests of accused persons who are considered to be 'under disability'. On the one hand, we would wish to protect them from harsh penalties and on the other, give them opportunities for the evidence against them, as to the acts they are alleged to have committed, to be tried and tested publicly in a court of law. Even though there are only a very small number indeed of such cases dealt with in the course of a year in England and Wales we should remember that they are illustrative of some of the most fundamental dilemmas in the administration of justice.*

(3) THE SPECIAL VERDICT

In the foregoing section, I considered the position of persons who were held not to be responsible by reason of serious mental disorder *at the time of the trial*. We now have to consider the situation that arises when an accused claims that he should not be held responsible because he was suffering from mental disorder at the time of *the offence*. The court has to decide, not only whether the offender 'did the act or made the omission charged', but also whether he was so insane at the time as not to be responsible in law for the action. We have seen how the M'Naghten Rules were promulgated in order to deal with this kind of situation and it remains true today that they are the *only* test when insanity is being pleaded as a defence. That the Rules are invoked in only a handful of cases in the course of any one year is due mainly, as we have seen earlier, to the introduction of the concept of diminished responsibility and, at a later stage, to the abolition of the death penalty for murder. As we saw also, a much wider range of abnormalities can now be introduced as a result of this more recent legislation. Moreover, as we shall see subsequently, the Mental Health Act, 1959 makes provision for the courts to deal with such cases with a good deal of flexibility, for example, through the use of hospital orders with or without restrictions.

Even though the number of 'special verdicts' will be very small in the course of any one year, it is worth considering, albeit briefly, some of the recommendations made by the

---

* It is of interest to note that in Scotland the finding of 'disability' (insanity in bar of trial) is used about ten times more frequently than in England and Wales. It appears that nearly all psychotic offenders are found to be under disability. (Chiswick 1978).

Butler Committee in relation to these. The Committee concluded that the M'Naghten Rules were not a satisfactory test nor did they feel they could suggest the adoption of American codes of practice (for example, the *Durham* rule referred to earlier in this chapter). They suggested a new formulation of the Special Verdict, namely, 'not guilty on evidence of mental disorder'. The grounds for this would comprise two elements.

(1) A *mens rea* element, approximating to the first 'limb' of the M'Naghten Rules. That is the jury would find that the accused did the act but did not have the *mens rea* – i.e. did he know what he was doing? The jury would then return a verdict of not guilty on evidence of mental disorder. There must be in this latter instance, as in the case of the M'Naghten Rules, a clear *causal* connection between the mental disorder and the absence of *mens rea*.

(2) A second element which would provide for specific exemption from conviction for defendants suffering from *severe* mental illness or *severe* subnormality at the time of the act or omission charged. This element would need a substantial amendment to the existing law. Under the Mental Health Act, 1959 severe mental *subnormality* is defined as a state of arrested or incomplete development of mind, which includes subnormality of intelligence, and is of such a nature or degree that the patient is incapable of living an independent life, or of guarding himself against serious exploitation, or will be so incapable when of an age to do so. By contrast, severe mental illness (and for that matter, mental illness itself) is not defined in the Act. The Butler Committee propose a definition of severe mental illness which would be contained in a new or amending statute. It is worth quoting this definition in full since it provides us with a useful statement of serious mental illness as it relates to criminal responsibility. 'A mental illness is severe when it has one or more of the following characteristics:

(a) Lasting impairment of intellectual functions shown by failure of memory, orientation, comprehension and learning capacity.

(b) Lasting alteration of mood of such degree as to give

rise to delusional appraisal of the patient's situation, his past or his future, or that of others, or to lack of any appraisal.

(c) Delusional beliefs, persecutory, jealous or grandiose.

(d) Abnormal perceptions associated with delusional mis-interpretation of events.

(e) Thinking so disordered as to prevent reasonable appraisal of the patient's situation or reasonable com-munication with others.' (para. 18.35. See also Appen-dix 10 of the Report.)

The Committee's proposal in respect of this second 'limb' is also controversial in another respect. It is clear that unlike the M'Naghten requirement, there need to be no *causal* connec-tion between the mental disorder and the criminal behaviour; all that needs to be demonstrated is that the accused person was suffering from severe mental illness or severe subnormal-ity at the time he did the act in question. However, the Commit-tee seem to think that a causal connection can be assumed in view of the criteria of severity contained in their proposed definition.

The likely results of implementing the Butler proposals would be twofold. First, to broaden the range of cases that can now be dealt with under the M'Naghten ruling. Second, the Judge would be given a wide discretion as regards sentence; this might include anything from a hospital order to an abso-lute discharge. It must be recognized, however, that the degree to which a much wider range of persons would in future gain exemption from criminal responsibility may not win immedi-ate acceptance from the public. The latter so often seem to think that the adoption of a more reasoned and humane approach in what after all, are still a handful of cases each year, may open the floodgates of licence and 'mayhem'.

(4) DIMINISHED RESPONSIBILITY AND INFANTICIDE

We saw earlier how the statutory notion of Diminished Responsibility was introduced by the Homicide Act, 1957, as a defence to a charge of murder. We also noted that it was introduced to reduce liability for murder to manslaughter. The accused now has to satisfy the court that at the time of the offence he was suffering from an abnormality of mind which substantially impaired his mental responsibility. The advantage (some perhaps would say the disadvantage) of this enactment is that it enables a wide range of mental and other conditions to be taken into account. In the case of Byrne – a psychopath – in 1960, abnormality was construed as 'a state of mind so different from that of ordinary human beings that a reasonable man would term it abnormal'. But, one may ask, who is to define a 'reasonable man'? The advantage of a successful plea of diminished responsibility is that it gives the judge the opportunity to use a wide range of penalties – from imprisonment at one end of the scale, to absolute discharge at the other. Such a defence, however, raises a number of problems. What in the context of the Homicide Act is an 'abnormality of mind' and how is 'substantial' to be defined? If abnormality of mind is taken to include also failure to exercise control (the old chestnut of the irresistible impulse again) then where are we to draw the line? As Samuels (1975) cogently points out:

> 'Judges strive to prevent what might be described as character defects from masquerading as evidence of diminished responsibility, e.g. bad temper, jealousy, hatred, rage, drug taking, low intelligence, poor judgement, racial characteristics, political fanaticism and similar unfavourable personal failings.'

Samuels also points out the temptation to offer extenuations such as provocation or mercy killing as evidence of diminishment of responsibility.

Psychopathy is perhaps a good case in point; in itself it is probably insufficient for pleading diminished responsibility as it is not seen as mental illness proper, and for its use in such a plea it needs to be linked with other extenuating factors. However, as we shall see in Chapter 5, some authorities (Henderson 1939; Cleckley 1976) have suggested that psychopathy should be seen as a true mental illness. Samuels points out some curious and disturbing facts in relation to diminished responsibility.

'If a defendant just kills his victim for what appears to be a very ordinary motive such as greed or jealousy, diminished responsibility stands little chance of being established, but if the defendant has a history of mental trouble, goes in for perverted sexual practices with the victim before and after death, mutilates the body, cuts it up, sends it through the post, sends cruel postcards to the relatives, mutilates himself, swallows razor blades, inserts nails into his urethra, endeavours to commit suicide ... then the more horrible the killing the more likely diminished responsibility will be established, because the *further removed from normal behaviour the behaviour of the defendant, the more he appears to be mentally ill,* or so the submission runs [my italics]. The jury, however, may tend to reject the defence and to go for murder, in view of the horrible nature of the circumstances, though the trial judge will endeavour to prevent this and the Court of Appeal will quash a murder verdict if the jury does not listen to the trial judge.'

These comments by Samuels are of interest because they seem to go to the heart of the matter of diminished responsibility. For although psychiatric experts may be able to suggest that someone's responsibility is diminished by an 'abnormality of mind', it will be for the juryman – that ordinary man on the 'Clapham omnibus' so beloved of lawyers, to endeavour to determine what seems reasonable in all the circumstances. Bizarre behaviour may well seem beyond our 'ken' but it does not necessarily follow that it should be equated with, or be due to, an abnormality of mind in a strictly psychiatric sense. For after all, may not some people be plainly evil? It is all too easy to embrace the more comfortable notion that 'he must have been *mad* to behave in such a fashion'.

The Butler Committee are in no doubt that the present provisions relating to diminished responsibility are unsatisfactory. They suggest that the provision is needed only because the offence of murder carries a mandatory life sentence. They also reject the suggestion made by some people that it should be extended to offences other than murder. They recommend instead that the mandatory life sentence for murder be abolished; consequently the provision of diminished responsibility would be unnecessary. The courts would be able to apply a range of penalties according to the circumstances in individual cases.

Infanticide

The special offence of infanticide was introduced in order to relieve women who had caused the death of their children from the mandatory life sentence for murder.* It is an interesting creation in that it gives statutory recognition to a specific state of mind in a woman who causes by any wilful act or omission the death of her child under the age of twelve months when the balance of her mind is disturbed by reason of not having fully recovered from the effect of giving birth to a child or by reason of the effect of lactation consequent on the birth. The Act was passed at a time when more emphasis than was probably justified was placed upon what were thought to be the adverse effects of childbirth upon a woman's mental state. Moreover, when one looks into these comparatively rare cases, there are usually significant factors operating other than psychiatric abnormality arising directly as a result of the birth (for example, severely adverse domestic conditions or severely stressful personal situations that do not necessarily amount to mental abnormality). The present defence of diminished responsibility covers virtually the same ground and the Butler Committee's proposal that the special offence of infanticide could be abolished seems sensible.

Concluding comments

In this chapter, I have tried to demonstrate the range of situations and conditions that may serve to exculpate an accused from responsibility for crime and how some of these have developed over time.

There are many conflicts of opinion within this field. There

* Infanticide Act, 1938. (The offence was originally created by the Infanticide Act of 1922, but amended by the Act of 1938.)

are, for example, the age-old arguments over the differences between what behaviours should be considered crimes as distinct from acts of moral transgression; what should be regarded as sickness and what as sin? How much emphasis should be placed upon the protection and cure of the individual – particularly if he is clearly severely deranged – and how much emphasis should be placed upon the protection of the community at large? It is not difficult to see that the law may seem to be a somewhat clumsy instrument for trying to meet all these conflicting purposes – many of these being not only finely poised but also highly emotive. I shall be considering later in this book some of the issues involved in deciding upon what may be regarded as treatment, as distinct from punishment. It is merely necessary at this stage to point to the curious paradox by which a man may be found 'not guilty by reason of insanity', yet can be ordered to be detained without limit of time in a Special Hospital under conditions which may appear to him and his family to be hardly different from those of imprisonment. Other offender/patients may be detained in hospital, ostensibly in their 'best interests', for periods of time far beyond those for which their depredations would normally be punished by fixed sentences of imprisonment. In effect, we seem to be saying that because a man may be deemed to be mad, he may be *doubly* punished – a far cry apparently from the Roman law referred to earlier – which it will be recalled held that a man visited by madness who committed crime was punished enough by his condition without the law adding to his punishment. There is also an assumption that one must be either 'mad' or 'bad' and that the two states are mutually exclusive. We shall see later that the two conditions *can* coexist and that it is this coexistence that has led to controversies concerning the best management of such offender/patients.

In reviewing the question of responsibility (amongst other matters) the Butler Committee seem to have adopted a fairly liberal approach. The Committee were probably very mindful of the need to 'carry' public opinion with them rather than to present proposals that were too radical. Proposals for reform that are too radical so often have the effect of defeating their

objectives; they may, contrary to the intentions of those concerned, merely have deleterious consequences for those for
whom the proposals were intended to offer help. It seems that
the Butler Committee tried to get the balance right and in so
doing, bore in mind the conflicts implicit in determining the
best interests of the offender on the one hand and the protection of society on the other. In Chapter 3, the possible relationships between specific mental disorders and criminal
behaviour will be considered in some detail.

References

Atkin Committee (1923) *Report of the Committee on Insanity and
    Crime* Cmnd. 2005. London: HMSO.
Blair, D. (1977) The Medicolegal Aspects of Automatism. *Med.
    Sci. Law* **17**(3): 167–82.
Chiswick, D. (1978) Insanity in Bar of Trial in Scotland: A
    State Hospital Study. *Brit. J. Psychiat.* **132**: 598–601.
Clarke, M.J. (1975) The Impact of Social Science on Concep-
    tions of Responsibility. *Brit. J. Law and Society* **2** (1): 32–44.
Cleckley, H. (1976) *The Mask of Sanity* (5th edition). St Louis:
    The C.V. Mosby Co.
Devlin. Lord (1959) *The Enforcement of Morals.* Oxford: Oxford
    University Press.
Fenton, G.W. (1975) *Epilepsy and Automatism*. In T. Silverstone
    and B. Barraclough (eds) *Contemporary Psychiatry*. Ashford,
    Kent: Headley Bros.
Finch, J. (1974) *Introduction to Legal Theory* (2nd edition). Lon-
    don: Sweet and Maxwell.
Guttmacher, M.S. (1968) *The Role of Psychiatry in Law.* Illinois:
    Charles C. Thomas.
Hart, H.L.A. (1968) *Punishment and Responsibility. Essays in the
    Philosophy of Law.* Oxford: Clarendon Press.
Henderson, D.K. (1939) *Psychopathic States.* New York: W.W.
    Norton.
Hogan, T.B. (1969) *Criminal Liability Without Fault.* Leeds:
    Leeds University Press.

Home Office and DHSS (1975) *Report of the Committee on Mentally Abnormal Offenders (Butler Committee)*. Cmnd. 6244. London: HMSO.

Jacobs, F.G. (1971) *Criminal Responsibility*. London: London School of Economics/Weidenfeld and Nicolson.

Jones, P.E., and Card, R.I.E. (1976) *Cross and Jones' Introduction to Criminal Law* (8th edition). London: Butterworths.

Law Commission (1978) *Report on the Mental Element in Crime* H.C. Paper 499. London: HMSO.

Prins, H.A. (1973) *Criminal Behaviour. An Introduction to its Study and Treatment*: London: Pitman.

Royal Commission on Capital Punishment (1953) Cmnd. 8932. London: HMSO.

Samuels,A. (1975) Mental Illness and Criminal Liability. *Med. Sci. Law* **15** (3): 198–204.

Scott, P.D. (1962) Age and Development. Responsibility for Crime. *Med. Sci. Law* April: 212–220. Quoting Von Hentig, H. in *Punishment: Its Origins, Purpose and Psychology* (1937: 123). London: Hodge.

Walker, N. (1968a) *Crime and Insanity in England (Vol. 1)*. (Especially Chapters 1–5). Edinburgh: Edinburgh University Press.

—— (1968b) *Crime and Punishment in Britain*. Edinburgh: Edinburgh University Press.

Wolfenden, J. (1957) *Report of the Committee on Homosexual Offences and Prostitution* (Chairman: Sir John Wolfenden) Cmnd. 247. London: HMSO

FURTHER READING

Books

Flew, A. (1973) *Crime or Disease?* London: Macmillan. (Chapter 2).

Glueck, S. (1966) *Law and Psychiatry: Cold War or Entente Cordiale?* Baltimore: Johns Hopkins.

Hoggett, B. (1976) *Social Work and Law: Mental Health*. London: Sweet and Maxwell. (Chapter 7).

Jeffery, C.R. (1967) *Criminal Responsibility and Mental Disease.*
    Illinois: Charles C. Thomas. (Chapters 1 and 3).
West, D.J. and Walk, A. (1977) *Daniel McNaughton: His Trial
    and the Aftermath.* Ashford, Kent: Gaskell Books (for the
    Royal College of Psychiatrists).
Wootton, B. (1959) *Social Science and Social Pathology.* London:
    Allen and Unwin. (Chapter 8).

Articles

Bleechmore, J.F. (1975) Towards a Rational Theory of Crimi-
    nal Responsibility: The Psychopathic Offender. *Melbourne
    University Law Review Part 1* **10**: 19–46 and 207–224.
Briscoe, O.V. (1975) Assesment of Intent – An Approach to
    the Preparation of Court Reports. *Brit. J. Psychiat.* **127**:
    461–65.
—— (1975) Intention at the Moment of Crime . . . Beyond
    Reasonable Doubt. *Med.Sci.Law* **15** (1): 42–6.
O'Connor, D. (1975) The Voluntary Act. *Med.Sci.Law* **15** (1):
    31–6.
Power, D.J. (1977) Memory, Identification and Crime.
    Med.Sci.Law **17** (2): 132–39.

CHAPTER THREE

Mental disorder and criminality

Hearken ye judges!
There is another madness besides and it is
before the deed, Ah,
Ye have not gone deep enough into this soul!
NIETZSCHE

In Chapter 2 reference was made to certain forms of mental
disorder and their possible relationship to questions of criminal responsibility. Such references were made perforce in very
general terms. In this chapter, which is divided into two parts, I
shall discuss mental disorder and its possible relationship to
criminal behaviour in more detail.* First, I shall give a brief
account of a number of studies that have been undertaken in
which attempts have been made to indicate the degree of
association or otherwise between mental disorder and crime.

* The term mental disorder is used here, as it is used in the Mental Health Act,
1959, namely to include mental illness, mental subnormality, psychopathy,
and any other disorder or disability of mind. This enables a broad range of
disorders and so-called illnesses to be discussed under one fairly all-embracing
title. I am aware that there are certain semantic risks that may flow from such a
choice. I choose to use the term 'disorder' rather than 'abnormality' for reasons
similar to those that influenced the Butler Committee, namely, that as they say,
'there are people who can be said to be mentally abnormal, in the sense of
diverging from the statistical norm of mental functioning, although not necessarily disordered.' However, I agree with their conclusion that the use of the
term 'mental abnormality' does also have some advantages (particularly from
the viewpoint of this book) since it enables one to 'discuss the problems raised
by offences committed under the influence of alcohol and other drugs without
begging the question whether such offences involve *mental* disorder.'

These studies have been made, almost exclusively, of already identified criminal populations. Rarely have they examined the extent of criminality in psychiatric hospital patients. In the second part, I shall outline, briefly, a classification of the main psychiatric (mental) disorders, go on to discuss their manifestations in more detail, and attempt to indicate the circumstances in which they may have relevance to criminal conduct. Some of the matters to be discussed in the latter part of this chapter will serve as a lead in to Chapter 4 in which the roles of psychiatrists in the courts and the penal system are discussed briefly. Some so-called mental disorders – for example, psychopathy, those involving sexual deviation and offending, the abuse of alcohol and other drugs – are only mentioned here as they are the subject of more detailed treatment in subsequent chapters.

Part one

An important problem arises in trying to establish any causal connections or relationship between mental disorder and criminality, namely that of attempting to make connections between very divergent behaviours. The substance and definition of mental illness has been open to much challenge and dispute in recent years; there are commentators such as Szasz (1962) and Laing and Esterson (1964), who see current definitions of mental illness largely as ploys by which the state and its agents seek to control those whose behaviour is seen by them as merely different and socially unacceptable. This summary statement may seem to be somewhat unfairly dismissive of some very useful points that have been made by proponents of the so-called 'anti-psychiatry' school.* Even if we tend to dismiss some of the more polemical writing on mental disorder, it is only fair to state that there is considerable divergence of opinion amongst contemporary psychiatric practitioners as to the precise nature of mental illness and its causes. Gunn (1977a) states the problem succinctly from the psychiatrist's

---

* The books by Clare (1976) and Wing (1978) listed under further reading provide cool appraisals of the current scene.

point of view: 'Yet most of us believe that somewhere in the confusion there is a biological reality of mental disorder, and that this reality is a complex mixture of diverse conditions, some organic, some functional, some inherited, some learned, some acquired, some curable, others unremitting.' The question of causation and classification is dealt with in more detail later in this chapter.

Similar problems arise when we consider the nature of criminality. For, at its simplest, crime is merely that form of behaviour defined as illegal by the criminal law. We know that at various times in our history, acts judged as criminal have been redefined, or even removed from the statute books. In a sense, crimes 'come and go' according to changes in public opinion (see Prins 1973). The fact that the crimes of attempted suicide, and homosexual acts in private between adult consenting males have been removed from the statute book are two illustrations of this phenomenon. New offences are also created, particularly in times of war or of serious crisis; moreover, our increasingly complex society has necessitated the introduction of all manner of laws and regulations to govern aspects of our conduct. Croft has summarized the position very well.

'Not only has crime been defined variously at different periods in history but the opprobrium which crime attracts, and the degree of gravity with which particular crimes are regarded, has also changed. No doubt this has something to do with the prevalence of certain sorts of crimes and the reaction of society (more precisely, the reaction of those responsible for the enforcement of the law) to them but an assessment of the frequency of some particular form of behaviour is not of course synonymous with the definition of that behaviour as criminal. Indeed, it is safer to assume that we are all criminals, or at least have the potential to be criminals given the right conditions, and to take courage from the fact that some people at least are not apparently regular offenders. If such a view seems unduly cynical, it is because the breaking of the rules and conventions which regulate human behaviour is widespread and it becomes an issue of policy, even of political philosophy, to determine whether the criminal law, as distinct from the many other formal and informal methods of controlling conduct, should be invoked to regulate certain sorts of activities.'

(Croft 1978: 2)

Since much 'criminal behaviour' is thus somewhat arbitrarily defined and there is serious disagreement as to the existence and definition of mental disorder, it is hardly surprising that we find difficulties in trying to establish connections between these two somewhat ill-defined and complex forms of behaviour. Nevertheless, it would seem worthwhile to attempt some examination of their possible relationships, acknowledging that any conclusions must be tentative and seen against the background of the inherent difficulties referred to above.

STUDIES OF PENAL AND OTHER POPULATIONS

Over the years, various efforts have been made to estimate the prevalence of mental disorder in criminal and penal populations. I have already made reference to two of the difficulties involved in such attempts, namely the problem in defining both crime and mental disorder and the difficulties in drawing satisfactory links between the two conditions. Moreover, nearly all the studies that have been carried out have been of inmates of penal or correctional establishments or specialist court clinics. Thus, one is bound to be drawing conclusions from highly selected populations. This fact has important implications. For example, it is quite likely that imprisonment itself may well exacerbate certain underlying psychiatric conditions, or the impact and effects of such imprisonment may be so severe as to precipitate mental disorder in certain individuals. Feldman (1977) speculates that it may also be the case that those who are in fact in some way mentally disordered may be less skilful in crime and thus caught more easily. He also suggests that the police may tend to charge some of these offenders more readily and that in addition pleas of 'guilty' may be more frequent. It is difficult to substantiate any of these speculations, but certainly one must be very careful in drawing firm conclusions as to the relationships between mental disorder and crime from studies of such highly selected groups. Scott (1969) has suggested that even if we allow for the high degree of selectivity in penal populations the proportion of clearly identifiable psychiatric diagnoses is something in the region of 15 to 20 per cent. More recently, Gunn *et al.* (1978) have estimated that about one third of the sample of 629 prisoners they studied could have been regarded as requiring psychiatric attention at the time of interview. This does not mean that all would have been diagnosed as suffering necessarily from a formal psychiatric illness.

In order to show some of the disparities that exist I have taken examples for comparative purposes from various studies that have been undertaken in the last fifty to sixty years (see *Table 3(1)*). To make assimilation more easy I have classified the information by nature of disorder and tried to indicate the size of the sample surveyed (where such information was available). Unless stated to the contrary, the populations were drawn from penal institutions or court clinics.

Table 3(1) *Prevalence of psychiatric disorders in penal populations*

nature of disorder	percentage	size of population	author(s) of study and date
Psychosis	12%	608	Glueck (1918)
(e.g. schizo-	0.6%	1,380	Thompson (1937)
phrenia,	26%	100	Oltman and Friedman (1941)
affective			
disorders)	1.5%	10,000	Bromberg and Thompson (1947)
	15%	66 (homicides)	Gillies (1965)
	12%	50 (homicides)	Tupin, Mahar, and Smith (1973)
	10%	100	West (1963)
	0.5%	149 (Approved School boys)	Scott (1964)
	2%	300	Bluglass (1966)
	10%	289	Guze (1976)
	3%	75	Faulk (1976)

mental	28%	608	Glueck (1918)
subnormality	2.6%	1,380	Thompson (1937)
	16%	100	Oltman and Friedman (1941)
	2.4%	10,000	Bromberg and Thompson (1947)
	2.4%	91	Woddis (1964)
	14%	300	Bluglass (1966)
	6%	not given	Gibbens (1966)

psychopathy	19%	609	Glueck (1918)
(sociopathy)	5.6%	1,380	Thompson (1937)
	14%	100	Oltman and Friedman (1941)
	6.9%	10,000	Bromberg and Thompson (1947)
	60%*	149 (Approved School boys)	Scott (1964)
	27%	66 (homicides)	Gillies (1965)
	13%	300	Bluglass (1966)
	70%	289	Guze (1976)

* personality disorder

psycho-	3.0%	100	Oltman and Friedman (1941)
neurosis			
(neurosis)	6.9%	10,000	Bromberg and Thompson (1947)
	7.9%	304 (boys in detention centre)	Banks (1964)
	2.0%	300	Bluglass (1966)

alcoholism/ excess/heavy drinking	51%	500 (traffic offenders)	Selling (1940)

50%	not given	Banay (1942)
80%	not given	Cramer and Blacker (1963)
55%	66 (homicides)	Gillies (1965)
56%	50 (discharged male offenders)	Maule and Cooper (1966)
11%	300	Bluglass (1966)
40%	404	Gibbens and Silberman (1970)
37%	90	Gunn (1973)

Notes

(1) The term *prevalence* is borrowed from the field of epidemiology and is used here to mean the number of persons suffering from a particular disorder at any given time. It should be distinguished from *incidence*, which is generally taken to mean the number of examples of a disorder which begin during a *specified* period.

(2) Concerning alcoholism, we should note that almost all studies indicate a significant association between alcoholism or excessive drinking, and criminality (see for example Edwards, Hensman, and Peto (1971), Tinklenberg (1972), Nicol *et al.* (1973)). As we shall see later in this book, the precise nature of this association is far from clear.

(3) Prevalence of *organic* disorder has not been included, mainly because of the very small percentages usually reported. In certain circumstances its presence can be very important and further reference is made to this later in the chapter.

PREVALENCE OF CRIMINALITY IN PSYCHIATRIC POPULATIONS

Reference has already been made in the preceding discussion to the numerous difficulties that occur in attempting to draw specific conclusions from studies of mental disorder in penal and similar populations. In order to offer conclusive evidence of association or lack of it we would need to show the prevalence of criminality in psychiatric hospitals and similar samples. To date, very little work has been done on this, largely, as Gunn (1977a) points out, because of the ethical difficulties involved in investigating the criminal backgrounds (if any) of hospitalized psychiatric patients. However, a few studies have attempted to investigate this area, and these are now reported upon. Walker (1968) has estimated on the basis of various epidemiological studies, that about 12 in every 1,000 of the population will suffer from some kind of identifiable psychiatric disorder. Gunn (1977a) on the basis of calculations made by McClintock and Avison (1968) suggests that approximately 1 in 3 of the male population and 1 in 12 of the female population would be convicted of a 'standard list' (fairly serious) offence in their lifetime. In the light of these combinations of figures, it would be surprising (as Gunn suggests) if psychiatric hospitals did not contain an appreciable number of persons with criminal records. Guze (1976) examined a population of some 500 patients attending a psychiatric clinic in the United States. He found that 4 per cent had a history of the commission of a serious offence. (The offences included robbery, burglary, and sex offending.) Guze also quotes another American study by Brill and Malzberg (undated report) in which the arrest records of 5,354 male ex-patients from New York State Mental Hospitals were examined for the period 1946–1948. The authors concluded that 'patients with no record of crime or arrest have a strikingly low rate of arrest after release', and that 'patients who have a prior record of arrest have a rearrest rate which compares favourably with figures available for persons in the general population who have an arrest record . . .' Guze also quotes studies by Ashley (1922), Pollock (1938), and Cohen and Freeman (1945) which indicate a lower arrest rate for former psychiatric in-patients than is found in the general population. However, he also reports contrary findings by Rappeport and Lassen (1965, 1966) indicating that 'women with a history of psychiatric hospitalisation are more likely to be arrested for aggressive assault than are women in the general population . . .' and that males had 'a significantly higher arrest rate . . .' for robbery than did the general population. Unfortunately diagnostic criteria are not described altogether adequately so that it is difficult to draw too many firm conclusions from these apparently conflicting results. Gunn (1977a) reports a study made by Tidmarsh and Wood (unpublished) of persons using London's largest Reception Centre. (Such centres being the successors to the old 'casual wards' and providing accommodation for persons without a settled way of life.) Of 4,000 persons who had been at the centre at some time in the past, they estimated that 79 per cent had previous convictions and 58 per cent had been in prison. Tidmarsh made psychiatric assessments and found about 1,200 men had been diagnosed as mentally ill or subnormal. Only just over one quarter were said to have no psychiatric disorder. Gunn reports three other findings by Tidmarsh and Wood which are of particular interest from our point of view. First, men with no psychiatric abnormalities were the least likely to have had convictions. Second, most of those without prison sentences had not been in psychiatric hospital. Third, most of those who had not been in psychiatric hospital had not been in prison either, while 'conversely those who had been in either type of institution had usually been in both'. This study seems to support the view of psychiatrists such as Rollin (1969) that there is a 'stage army' of persons who drift in and out of each type of institution. He came to this conclusion as a result of an almost unique study of patients admitted to one of our large psychiatric hospitals in the Home Counties (Horton Hospital). The catchment area included part of the Metropolitan District of London. Rollin found that some 83 per cent of his sample were diagnosed as suffering from schizophrenia. He examined the records of those admitted without recourse to a court (that is, under Part IV of the Mental Health Act, 1959 – and sometimes through the use of Section 136 – referred to in Chapter 2). Of seventy-eight such cases, he found the following distribution of offences: *sex offences*, 10 per cent; *violence*, 13 per cent; *stealing*, 9 per cent; *public order offences*, 57 per cent. When he enquired into the records of such non-prosecuted patients he found that 40 per cent had a criminal record, 36 per cent of them being persistent offenders. He also examined the prosecuted group; that is, those admitted for psychiatric treatment under the relevant sections of Part V of the Act (see also Chapters 2 and 4) finding that 63 per cent had previous convictions and that 44 per cent had previously been subject to a custodial sentence. Thus, it is not hard to see that there is a considerable degree of overlap between the two groupings. However, to be able to offer more precise data as to possible causal or associative factors one would need not only to examine substantial samples of psychiatric hospital patients, but also cohorts of offenders appearing before the courts. As far as I am aware this has never been carried out and the ethical objections referred to by Gunn are of course considerable. Some authorities, such as Penrose (1939), have stated that the populations of prisons and psychiatric hospitals are inversely related. Penrose attempted to demonstrate that before the Second World War, those European countries with a large psychiatric hospital population had a small penal institution population and vice versa. Penrose's so called 'law' might well be cited today since our prison staffs are complaining that they are having to cope with too many mentally disordered offenders and our psychiatric hospitals seem for their part very reluctant to take them – not infrequently in the face of the express wishes of High Court judges and other sentencers. Some of these problems and the policy issues arising from them are the subject of comment in the final chapter of this book.

Part two

CLASSIFICATION OF MENTAL DISORDERS –
INTRODUCTORY NOTE

Before proceeding to the question of classification, brief reference will be made to the question of causation of mental disorder. It is not possible to go into this in detail here; readers interested in this aspect should consult some of the books listed as recommended reading for this chapter. Suffice it to say at this stage that, apart from organic conditions (to be discussed later) there are considerable divergences of opinion as to the weightings to be given to various supposed causative factors in all other major mental disorders. If there are divergencies of opinion concerning causation, there are even greater divergencies of opinion concerning the lines of demarcation between mental health and mental ill-health. However, it is worth attempting a brief perspective on this matter and the words of Menninger (in Jahoda 1958) are apposite in this context. He defines mental health:

> 'as the adjustment of human beings to the world and to each other with a maximum of effectiveness and happiness; not just efficiency, or just contentment, or the grace of obeying the rules of the game cheerfully, *but all of these together* [my italics]. It is the ability to maintain an even temper, and an alert intelligence, socially considerate behaviour and a happy disposition.'

In this book, we are particularly concerned with the question of 'socially considerate behaviour' and the extent to which a lack of it should bring penal or quasi-penal sanctions into play. Although it is difficult to define mental ill-health (mental disorder) I think it is important to make my own position clear. I take it to be a term to be applied to those people who, for psychological and other reasons, are frequently unable to fulfil their lives to their own satisfaction or (frequently) to the satisfaction of others. In addition they may, from time to time, become so disturbed as to require some form of psychiatric or other intervention. I am aware that the term 'disturbed' is contentious and that some people can be contained within, and supported by, their social environments, while others require specialist help outside it. It follows, therefore, that the terms I am using suffer from a certain degree of imprecision and a wide range of interpretation. Wing (1978) has alerted us to the fact that some of the confusion seems to arise because the term 'illness' is used in two quite different ways. 'In one usage, people are regarded as sick, or regard themselves as sick, because of some experience or behaviour that departs from a standard of health generally accepted in the community.' Wing agrees with Mechanic (1968) that this is rightly called 'illness behaviour', and that standards for the designation of this kind of illness vary very widely not only from community to community but also over time. In respect of the second use of the term, Wing reserves this for notions of 'disease' proper:

'a limited and relatively specific theory about some aspect of psychological or biological functioning (that) is put forward because it is thought to be relevant to the reduction of some recognizable impairment which causes disability or distress.' Wing suggests that these 'two usages represent different types of theory. Over the centuries, the second usage has become more and more precisely differentiated from the first, but has also become more restricted.' Wing further suggests that this has meant that much 'illness behaviour' cannot helpfully be explained in terms of disease theories. Although Wing is making these statements in a paper primarily about schizophrenia – a condition, he says, which can be explained medically, socially, and psychologically – they have a more general applicability. They also support my earlier contention that the understanding of mental disorders is facilitated by a multi-causal (explanatory) and multi-disciplinary perspective in which boundaries will inevitably be blurred. For those who have devoted themselves to the study of the phenomena of mental disorders, this multi-causal and multi-disciplinary approach presents at one and the same time a dilemma and a stimulating challenge.

I have referred to causal factors only briefly, but a few words by way of elaboration are necessary. Trethowan (1973) puts it well when he states that: 'Mental disorder arises not from the operation of any single aetiological factor but from many. Broadly, these factors fall under two headings: 1) *endogenous* including genetic and other constitutional factors; 2) *environmental* (or 'exogenous') factors which may be physical, psychological or social or a combination of these.' Trethowan goes on to emphasize that the two categories are not mutually exclusive and there is always overlap. Cobb (1948) provides us with a concise and at the same time comprehensive four factor framework for aetiology (causation), which is presented in modified form below.

(1) The role of inheritance in the development of illness, which can be subdivided into the genetics of the illness itself and the inherited predisposition towards illness.

(2) The effect of chemical changes or their lack. 'By definition this would have to be ruled out if the chemical agent led to visible lesions, or if emotional stress was the immediate cause of the chemical change.'
(3) Structural alterations of the central nervous system.
(4) The effect of stresses within the personality.

The difficulties inherent in attempting to ascribe mental disorders to a single source or cause have been very well summed up by Valentine (1955) in the form of the following analogy.

'Suppose we are studying an apple's fall from a tree; gravitational attraction, of course, is the single 'cause'. But gravity is operating all the time; why didn't the apple fall before? Because the stalk only gradually becomes brittle enough to permit it to fall. But here is another apple, with an equally brittle stem; why didn't it fall? Because it was a little higher; or wasn't exposed to the breeze as the other one was.'

Valentine discusses the relative ease by which experiments could be designed to ascertain which cause was effective in the case of the apples, but points by way of contrast to the extreme difficulty in designing experiments to show why people develop psychiatric disorders. For, he says:

'we have only a rough idea of what the variables are, and only a rough idea of how to measure them. If we study the person, we have difficulty in knowing how much of his history has contributed towards the disease; if we study the disease, we have corresponding difficulty in knowing how much of it may have been modified by the personality in which it arose; there is no easy cross reference method to return a quick answer.'

There may, as Valentine suggested, be no *quick* answer, but in the twenty-five years since he wrote the extract quoted above, some progress has been made in trying to measure and define more accurately the impact of the mentally disordered person's social environment. A notable example is the recent work on depressive disorder in women by Brown and Harris (1978). In this study the authors were able to develop quite rigorous devices with which to measure the impact, time scale, and perceived personal significance of events thought to be crucial to the development of depressive disorder in women. This book is worthy of the most careful study because it provides a remarkable combination of sociological and clinical analysis.

An outline classification

Mental disorders have been classified in a variety of ways and there is no universal acceptance of any one classification, although from time to time the World Health Organisation has endeavoured to introduce uniformly acceptable classifications and definitions. The following is a simplified classification accompanied by some explanatory comment (see *Table 3(2)*).

Table 3(2)   *Outline Classification*

The functional psychoses	the affective disorders schizophrenic illnesses
The neuroses (psychoneuroses)	mild depression anxiety states hysteria obsessional states
Mental disorder as a result of infection, disease, metabolic disturbances, and trauma	(including epilepsy)
Mental disorder due to the ageing process	(for example, the pre-senile and senile dementias)
Abnormalities of personality and psycho-sexual disorders	
Alcohol and other drug addictions	
Mental subnormality (deficiency, handicap, retardation	(including chromosomal abnormalities)

The remainder of the chapter is devoted to a more detailed account of each of these disorders and their association or otherwise with criminal behaviour.

The arbitrary nature of the above classification will become very apparent when we consider each grouping in more detail. We shall then discover that not only is there a considerable degree of overlap, but also disagreement as to the extent to which some of the conditions described should even be regarded as mental disorders. Some disorders listed in the classification will not be considered in *detail* at this stage as they will be dealt with more comprehensively later in the book. They are merely included at this point in an attempt to give an overall classificatory and descriptive picture as a framework for further discussion.

THE FUNCTIONAL PSYCHOSES

The term functional psychoses is used for that group of 'severe mental disorders in which no evidence of underlying organic brain dysfunction has been proved to exist' (Munro and McCulloch 1975). It would probably be more true to assert that the phrase 'not *yet* been proved to exist' would be preferable since there is a substantial body of opinion indicating that for these particular mental disorders there is the possibility of a clear biochemical cause. The two illnesses subsumed under the heading functional psychoses are (1) the affective disorders (manic-depressive illness) and (2) schizophrenia (or the schizophrenias as some would prefer to describe them). The affective disorders will be considered first; in so doing, we again need to be mindful of the fact that it is only possible to give the barest outline here. The underlying characteristic of an affective disorder is a basic disturbance of mood; in cases of *mild* depressive disorder (see later) the disturbance of mood (or affect as it is sometimes called) may be quite slight and may often be almost unnoticeable to those quite close to the person. In *severe* affective disorder, the mood disturbance is much more pronounced; a useful 'aide memoire' is that the main characteristics are those of 'loss' — of energy, of libido (sexual drive and energy), weight, appetite, interest in oneself and one's surroundings. Such features of loss may be so marked in severe cases that the patient is quite unable to perform normal daily functions and routines; he may indeed present as a person in a state of abject misery and tearfulness. The older term *irrational melancholia* describes these particular features very well. Other characteristics are varying degrees of tension, feelings of guilt, lack of concentration, irritability, marked disturbance in sleep patterns, and preoccupation with what are believed by the sufferer to be disordered bodily functions (for example the patient believes he has an incurable cancer or that his insides are rotting away). Some forms of depressive disorder are sometimes characterized by agitation, restlessness, hand wringing, or severe retardation in all spheres of activity. Suicidal thoughts are often prominent, and may occasionally be put into effect. It should be noted that when the patient is in a severe state of depression, the degree of retardation will generally preclude suicidal action. As recovery takes place, however, and the patient emerges from this severe state, such thoughts may again become prominent and the patient may then put them into action. It is therefore crucial for the patient's mental state to be carefully monitored at this time and relatives and friends warned of the dangers of seeking premature discharge.

At the other end of the spectrum of the affective illnesses we should note that periods of depressive disorder may be interspersed with occasional attacks of mania – a condition in which the patient develops grandiose ideas, may become uncontrollably excitable, overactive, and socially disinhibited. In addition, insight may be entirely lacking and any attempt to interfere with the patient's activities may be strongly resisted – sometimes to the extent that severe physical violence will be used. Mania in its extreme form is a comparatively rare illness, but just occasionally the behaviour of severely manic individuals may bring them into conflict with the law – sometimes in bizarre circumstances. We should note also that the illness may present in less severe form. This illness, hypomania, may bring the patient into only slightly less dramatic confrontation with the authorities – as we shall see later.

Psychiatrists tend to be divided in their views as to the classification and aetiology of the affective disorders. Some hold the view that two types of affective disorders can be discerned – *endogenous* (that is where no clear precipitating factors can be seen) and *exogenous* (or reactive). In such cases it is held that fairly clear precipitating factors can be seen; for example a particularly stressful recent life event or situation. In practice, it is often difficult to discern such precise demarcations since precipitating factors may not always be immediately apparent and they may have operated in a very subtle manner. In addition, people's thresholds for stressful events vary considerably. We shall consider these thresholds in more detail when we examine mild (neurotic) depressive illness. Finally, it should be noted that severe depressive illness is sometimes referred to as psychotic depression, and when it appears in later life it may be described as involutional melancholia. When states of depression alternate with episodes of mania the term manic-depressive psychosis is used; some authorities refer to the depressive phase of this particular illness as 'bipolar' depression, using the term 'unipolar' depression for those cases in which mania has not previously been present.

From a treatment point of view, it appears to be the case that *endogenous* depression sometimes seems to respond best to physical treatments such as ECT (Electro-Convulsive Therapy), and *exogenous* depression may respond best to medication and the various forms of psychotherapy (the reasons for this are not altogether clear). For those who wish to pursue this topic further, the work of Mendels (1970) is strongly recommended; it offers a clear and concise account of classification, aetiology, and management.

SEVERE AFFECTIVE DISORDER AND CRIME

Depressive illness

From time to time, we find cases in which it has been alleged that a person charged with a serious offence (murder for example) was suffering from a severe depressive disorder at the time of the commission of the offence. West (1965) made a study of cases of *Murder Followed by Suicide*. He was able to show from his very careful case histories that a substantial number of these particular murderers were suffering from serious mental illness – in particular depression. He says that sufferers from psychotic depression may,

> 'become so convinced of the helplessness of their misery that death becomes a happy escape. Sometimes before committing suicide, they first kill their children and other members of the family . . . Under the delusion of a future without hope and the inevitability of catastrophe overtaking their nearest and dearest as well as themselves, they desire to kill in order to spare their loved ones suffering . . .'
>
> (West 1965: 6)

Such attitudes have a delusional quality to them and are of course quite irrational. Schipkowensky (1969) has also commented upon the patterns and depths of the delusional systems in such cases. This author emphasizes the extent to which 'The patient feels his personality is without value (delusion of inferiority). His life is without sense, it is only [one of] everlasting suffering . . .'; and also the patient's feeling that he 'deserves to be punished for his imaginary crimes . . .' (pp. 64–5).

It is of interest to note that of West's seventy-eight 'murdersuicide' offenders, twenty-eight (seven male: twenty-one female) were classified by him as suffering from severe depressive illness (as compared with four suffering from schizophrenia; two from morbid jealousy; four from psychopathy; seven from marked neurosis or instability; and thirty-three who were judged to be 'relatively normal').

I know of a young man in his early twenties who became so convinced that the world was a terrible place in which to live that he attempted to kill his mother and his sister and then himself. Only swift medical intervention saved the lives of all three of them. Following his court appearance he was made the subject of hospital care. He responded well to physical treatment (ECT) for his depressive disorder and made a good recovery. As far as I know (some twenty-five years later) he has not again come to the attention of the courts or authorities. The task of estimating the extent and duration of a depressive illness and its relevance to serious offences such as homicide is a very difficult one. Gunn *et al.* (1978: 35) put the case very well:

'. . . it is very difficult to establish *unless several helpful informants are available* [my italics] whether a depressed murderer is depressed because he has been imprisoned for life, depressed because of the conditions in which he has been imprisoned, depressed by the enormity of his crime, or whether he committed murder because he was depressed in the first place . . .'

The comment Gunn and his colleagues make about the value of informants is a very significant one for social workers because they can play a most important part in ensuring that a *comprehensive* social history of the offender/patient is obtained. Often, it is only when this vital information has been gathered that one can see the individual against the background of his social milieu, and any stresses that have arisen within it. Moreover, glimpses of his life style against this social background may provide important diagnostic and prognostic clues. The importance of the social context is stressed by Woddis (albeit by implication) in his paper on *Depression and Crime* (1957). He suggests on the basis of many patients observed by him, that three groups of cases need to be recognized.

'(1) Cases in which the depressive state had not been recognized because its possibility had never been considered.
 (2) A few cases in which a tendency to repeated offences had been 'cured' by treating a depressive illness.
 (3) A small number of cases, particularly those of a violent nature, in which 'all the clinical signs of depression may disappear as if the explosive nature of the act had worked as a cathartic and the patient had "cured" himself.'

The significance of severe depressive illness in other types of violence is also commented upon by the same author in a subsequent paper (Woddis 1964).

Manic episodes

Some of the significant characteristics of mania and hypomania have been alluded to already. From time to time, persons suffering from varying degrees of mania will come to the attention of the courts and allied authorities because of their outrageous and potentially dangerous or disruptive behaviour. A colleague and I (McCulloch and Prins 1978), have described in some detail the case of a car-salesman aged twenty-three. This young man initially impressed his employer with his energy and enthusiasm. However, it was not long before his ideas and activities quickly took on a grandiose and highly unrealistic quality. For example, he sent dramatic and exaggerated letters daily to a wide range of motor manufacturers. His social behaviour began to deteriorate rapidly, he lost weight through not eating (he 'never had time') and he hardly ever slept. One night, in a fit of pique directed towards his employer, he returned to the garage showrooms, smashed the windows, and also caused extensive damage to a number of cars. He subsequently appeared in court and was made the subject of a Hospital Order under the Mental Health Act, 1959. (See Chapter 4.) The attributes of this type of manic offender/patient are worth re-emphasizing since such a person justifies the 'illness' label very clearly. 'He thinks himself omnipotent and becomes convinced that his wildest ideas are in fact very practical. Because his memory is unimpaired, he is capable of giving rationalised arguments and explanations to support his proposed actions . . .' (McCulloch and Prins 1978). Additionally, the patient may actually become hallucinated. For example, the young man just described alleged that he 'saw' the motor manufacturers reading his letters to them; when questioned about their alleged reactions to his unsolicited overtures to them he replied: 'I saw them, didn't I?' Sometimes, the manic episode will be followed by a 'swing' into a depressive illness. Neustatter (1953) describes the case of a man who became involved in quite extensive frauds and thefts during a manic episode. He responded quite well to treatment when eventually persuaded to accept the need for it. However, some time after, he came to Neustatter's attention again following a suicide attempt while in a depressed state. Finally, it is worth repeating that manic patients are very difficult to treat. They resist the idea that there is anything wrong with them. They lack insight, but are often deceptively lucid and rational. Moreover, they can be very hostile and sometimes physically aggressive towards those they think are obstructing them in their desires and intentions.

The relationship between milder forms of depressive disorder and criminality will be examined under the general heading of neurotic conditions, although the arbitrary nature of this distinction has already been acknowledged.

Schizophrenic illness(es)

It is customary to use the term schizophrenia in the singular when describing what seem to be a wide range of illnesses. Moreover, it has become clear in recent years that although the illness has certain basic characteristics there are in fact many variants of it, so that it is probably more accurate to use the descriptive term schizophrenic *illnesses* or the *schizophrenias* (Fulcher 1975).

There has always been controversy concerning aetiology and classification. At the present time, it can be stated that although environmental and social factors may play a significant part in the onset and of course of such illnesses, there are certainly likely to be genetic and biochemical factors which determine the origins of the disease in the first instance. The simple (yet complex) truth of the matter is that we do not know with any real degree of certainty what *causes* schizophrenic illnesses.

The most important single characteristic feature of schizophrenic illnesses is the disintegration and (in some cases) apparent destruction of the personality. It should be noted here that the term schizophrenia is frequently used incorrectly in two ways. First of all, lay people tend to use the term to denote the state of being in 'two minds', no doubt a derivation from the old descriptive term – 'split mind'. Second, people sometimes use it to describe *Jekyll and Hyde* characteristics – being sane one minute and mad the next. Both interpretations are quite erroneous; in the schizophrenic illnesses we are dealing with what can best be regarded as a splintering of the mind – 'the personality shatters and disintegrates into a mass of poorly co-operating components rather than into a neat division into two parts. In particular, there is incongruity between thoughts and emotions' (McCulloch and Prins 1978: 77). The main signs and symptoms of schizophrenia fall under the following broad headings though they will not be present of course in every case, but as we shall see later, some manifestations of the illness will be of more importance than others from a socio-forensic point of view.

(1) *Disorders of thinking.* Delusions are common. For example, the patient may believe that his thoughts are being stolen by others.

(2) *Disorders of emotion.* These may range from anxiety, perplexity, and a flattening of mood (sometimes interrupted by severe outbursts of rage) on the one hand – to complete incongruity of affect on the other – for example, the tendency to giggle or laugh at something sad.

(3) *Disorders of volition.* The key characteristic here is likely to be apathy and a consequent withdrawal from social intercourse. The patient may also behave in a very negative fashion – a condition known technically as *negativism*.

(4) *Psycho-motor symptoms.* Periods of complete lack of motion or a stuporose state may be interspersed with outbursts of unpredictable violence.

(5) *Hallucinations.* In the schizophrenias, these are mostly of an auditory nature. They may consist of voices which tell the patient to do certain things, or alternatively the patient may state that his thoughts can be heard by others or controlled by them. Occasionally, a patient may think that he is being interfered with sexually and this feeling may

result in unprovoked assaults on quite innocent bystanders. Sometimes a schizophrenic patient will suffer from an *illusion*. This needs to be distinguished from an *hallucination*. In the case of an illusion, the stimulus may be a real one, but the patient will misinterpret it. For example, a jacket draped over a chair may take on the property of some frightening monster intent upon harming the patient.

Psychiatrists (with varying degrees of agreement) classify the schizophrenic illnesses in the following fashion.

(a) *Simple schizophrenia*. In these cases, the onset is fairly gradual, occurs in early adult life, and the initial signs and symptoms may be unrecognized. Such patients are not commonly hallucinated or deluded, but there may be emotional 'blunting' or shallowness.

(b) *Hebephrenic schizophrenia (Hebephrenia)*. The onset, which occurs most frequently in late teenage or early adult life, is often quite dramatic and accompanied by delusions and hallucinations. The patient may deteriorate fairly rapidly, and the prognosis is frequently not favourable.

(c) *Catatonic schizophrenia*. Classical presentations of catatonic schizophrenia seem to be seen fairly rarely these days, due no doubt to the early use of certain drugs helpful in this particular condition. Some psychiatrists describe two forms of the illness – depression and excitement. For our purposes, we can simplify matters and take the two together. The illness tends to be more common in females in their mid-twenties. The patient may be difficult to rouse, will be unresponsive to social intercourse and overtures of help; in some cases the limbs may be rigid and board-like. In others, they take on a curious characteristic known as *flexibilitas cerea* (waxy flexibility) in which the limbs can be placed and then left in the most awkward positions almost indefinitely. The non-responsive and mute behaviour of the catatonic schizophrenic may be interspersed by unpredictable and violent outbursts – sometimes these may be of considerable ferocity. It should be noted, however, that such cases are rare; these and cases of acute mania probably account for most of the very small number of incidents of serious violence indulged in by psychiatric patients.

(d) *Paranoid schizophrenia and paranoid states*. In these cases the keynotes are irrational over-suspiciousness and ideas of self reference. The patient may be convinced that people are continually talking about him, or accusing him of sexual indiscretions such as persistently associating with prostitutes. Ideas of a persecutory nature are also frequently present. These are not only quite impervious to all attempts to remove them by rational means; in addition, almost always they will be long lasting.

The above outlines have been greatly oversimplified. No reference has been made to those illnesses on the 'borderland' of schizophrenia and the so-called schizo-affective disorders. Readers requiring more detailed information are advised to consult one of the specialist text books referred to at the end of the chapter.

Schizophrenic illnesses and crime

The schizophrenic illnesses do not feature significantly from a numerical point of view in the causation or explanation of criminality. Woddis (1964) discussing ninety-one cases thought to be suffering from some form of mental abnormality and referred to him by the courts for reports diagnosed nine of his cases as schizophrenic. Kloek (1969) reporting upon 500 cases seen by himself and colleagues at a Dutch forensic observation clinic found only one case in which they could confidently ascribe a clear diagnosis of schizophrenia. In thirty other cases the diagnosis of schizophrenia was considered a possibility but had to remain in doubt. West (1965) in his study of seventy-eight murder-suicide offenders (a highly selected sample) found only four (two males, two females) classified as schizophrenic, and two others (males) were classified as suffering from 'morbid jealousy'. More recently, Faulk (1976), in his study of seventy-two men in Winchester prison, assigned a diagnosis of schizophrenia to only two cases;

in order to do this he used very rigorous criteria of symptomatology.

Despite their numerically small representation, it is worth
looking briefly at some of the situations in which schizophrenic
illness may play a causal or explanatory part in criminal acts. I
would wish to stress here that from time to time, the onset and
course of such an illness and its possible relationship to a crime
may have been overlooked – sometimes with tragic consequences; we shall examine this aspect in more detail in
Chapter 6.

(1) *Schizophrenic illness and violent crime.* As has already been
observed, the patient suffering from catatonic schizophrenia
may occasionally erupt into violence and 'lash out' at those
around him, but the circumstances in which such behaviour
will bring about a confrontation with the law are comparatively
rare. Persons suffering from delusions of one kind or another
may act upon these; we saw (in Chapter 2) how McNaghten
acted in this way. Some years ago, John Ley – a former
Australian senior law officer – was convicted of murdering a
man whom he deludedly believed to have seduced his wife. Ley
refused to have insanity pleaded as a defence at his trial;
however, although convicted he was not executed, but found
to be suffering from a paranoid illness and sent to Broadmoor.
And much more recently, Ian Ball was ordered to be detained
in a special hospital as a result of his elaborate (and yet highly
delusional) plans to kidnap Princess Anne. I know of less
'notorious' cases; for example, the man who stood his trial on a
charge of murder because he felt compelled to 'beat the devil'
out of his father, and of another who was compelled to kill his
wife because she was 'evil'; he felt that her sins could only be
purged by killing her. The seriously *paranoid* individual is quite
likely to appear to be sane and intelligent in all other respects.
To the unwary and inexperienced interviewer, the delusional
system may be so well encapsulated that it may not emerge
unless the matters upon which the system has fastened are
broached in the examination. The severely paranoid and the
morbidly jealous individual can be a very dangerous person

indeed – probably one of the most potentially dangerous that the penal and hospital systems have to cope with. The ideas and preoccupations of such persons are so fixed and long-lasting that they may persist in pursuing their alleged unfaithful spouse or other subject of their delusions from one part of the country to the next despite all attempts at intervention. No form of rational persuasion to get them to alter their beliefs seems to be effective in such cases.

(2) *Other offence behaviour*. In schizophrenic illness of insidious onset there is often, as we have seen, an accompanying decline of social functioning and competence. In such cases, the individual may well succumb to temptations (sometimes prompted by others) that he would have well resisted had he been in normal mental health. We sometimes find cases of shoplifting or other thefts being committed in these circumstances.

(3) *Schizophrenic illness, vagrancy, and kindred offences*. In cases of persons suffering from so-called simple schizophrenia we have seen that the deterioration may take the form of a steady diminution of social functioning accompanied by a withdrawal from society. Such persons may come to the attention of the courts for offences such as begging, breach of the peace (insulting words and behaviour), or vandalism (wilful damage). Rollin (1969) found a very high proportion of such cases in his Horton Hospital 'stage-army' sample. Such an offender/patient who is shunted between hospital, prison, and community, can best be described as a social nuisance rather than as a social menace. Just occasionally, however, such a person may commit a serious crime as a result of 'hearing the voices'; arson being one such example, as we shall see in Chapter 7.

(4) *Schizophrenic illness and the bizarre crime*. Occasionally a crime is committed which shocks the community because of its ferocity or depravity. Such offences may be committed by persons who seem to have behaved with senseless and quite appalling cruelty. They show a lack of feeling for their victims which seems quite incomprehensible to most of us. In such cases, it is sometimes found that a schizophrenic illness of insidious onset

has occurred, but its presence has been overlooked. It seems probable that some cases of sadistic sexual murder may be committed by such a schizophrenic though it is sometimes very difficult to differentiate the diagnosis in such a case from a similar offence committed by the cold and callous psychopath. An example of this difficulty can be found in the case of Neville Heath who not only killed two young women but severely mutilated them during a state of sexual frenzy. (See also Chapter 5.) This severe lack of feeling can be important in other ways. It has been suggested by Topp (1973) that some self-immolators may be able to destroy themselves in this way because they have been able to split off feeling from consciousness, this making them well-nigh impervious to the pain of death by fire. (See also Chapter 7.)

Although, as we have indicated, the incidence of the schizophrenic illnesses in relation to crime is apparently very low, it is likely to be of considerable importance in *particular* cases; it is for this reason that I have sought to emphasize some of these. For those who may have professional involvement with the person concerned (for example, social workers, general practitioners, personnel officers, the police) it is as well to be aware of the significance of even slight changes in behaviour, but more importantly of *a-typical* behaviour. These may give clues (along with other evidence of course) to the possibilities of an underlying schizophrenic illness. Intervention at an early stage may, as I have already suggested, help to avert a tragedy.

THE NEUROSES (PSYCHONEUROSES)

The terms neuroses or psychoneuroses (which are for the most part synonymous), when used correctly, describe a wide range of conditions which are characterized by certain fairly specific mental and physical symptoms and signs; they usually have as their origin the existence of some mental conflict of which the sufferer may frequently be quite unaware. The neuroses are usually regarded as being less severe in nature than the psychoses mainly because the sufferer is not likely to be out of touch with reality, is less floridly ill and behaves quite rationally in most respects. However, many neurotic conditions (particularly the obsessive states) are severely disabling and some psychiatrists prefer not to make too sharp a distinction between some forms of neuroses and the functional psychoses – depressive disorder being a good case in point. (See earlier discussion.)

Although there is no absolute consensus of opinion concerning classification, the following seems to be acceptable to most people:

> mild depression;
> anxiety states;
> hysteria;
> obsessional states.

For present purposes it will be useful to concentrate upon mild depression, anxiety, and hysteria, making less detailed reference to the obsessive disorders. It should be noted that although these disorders are grouped in the way I have suggested, there is frequently an overlapping of symptoms so that it is unwise to see them as discrete entities.

A special problem arises in any discussion of the neuroses. Many of us show – albeit in varying degrees – a number of 'neurotic' traits. For example, how many of us do not show a high level of anxiety in certain unfamiliar or threatening situations, become mildly depressed when things go badly, or have certain obsessional traits which enable us to carry out some tasks more effectively? This may be especially relevant in those employments where meticulous attention to detail is required. One professor of psychiatry of an earlier generation is said to have described obsessionals as 'the salt of the earth'! We not only need to distinguish between (a) common 'neurotic' traits, (b) more serious neurotic traits or reactions, and (c), fully developed neurotic illnesses, but to remember that there will be overlap between all three categories. (For some discussion of this see the classifications suggested by Slater and Roth (1969).) Few people would disagree with the view that the specific label of neurotic illness should be reserved for those instances where the patient/sufferer is seriously disabled and where although he may have a degree of insight into his condition he is powerless to do anything about it. Neurotic illnesses in their classical presentation do not feature significantly amongst the ranks of criminals. Woddis (1964) found only three cases of psychoneurosis and two dissociated states in his sample of ninety-one offender/patients; Faulk (1976) only found one. Despite this small proportion, the relevance of these conditions (in common with those described earlier) may be of considerable importance in specific cases. I shall deal with mild depression first.

Mild depression

Instances of mild depression may not always be recognized immediately because the behaviour of the individual concerned may depart only marginally from the norm. In mild depression, we may see many of the symptoms of major depression but in less severe form. People suffering from this disorder tend to become morbidly preoccupied with areas of everyday life; for example, they may become very concerned about their self-esteem, their self image, their competence, and their health. Increasing irritability may be an important diagnostic sign, as may a tendency to unpredictability in a hitherto highly organized and predictable individual. In states of mild depression, the sufferer may well depart from usual and expected modes of behaviour. I have described elsewhere (McCulloch and Prins 1978), the case of a married woman of sixty, of impeccable previous character, who, for no apparent reason, stole a tin of soup from a supermarket. This isolated offence seemed so entirely out of character that the court sought a psychiatric report. This indicated quite clearly that she had been suffering from a neurotic depressive illness for some time. The court made a probation order with a requirement for psychiatric treatment as an out-patient. Her depression cleared up quite quickly following treatment and she did not re-offend. Woddis (1957) cites several cases in which stealing occurred against a background of depressive illness. Most of his examples were of middle-aged or late middle-aged women, but he also cites the case of a young man of twenty-one charged with the persistent stealing of motor cars. He had a history of recurrent depressive attacks which seemed to be clearly associated in time with his car thefts. Abreactive treatment using the drug pentothal revealed that the offences had started at the time his father had been burned to death in a lorry. The young man had intense feelings of guilt at not having got to his father quickly enough. When these matters were brought more clearly into consciousness and clarified, the stealing stopped. He was reported to be crime free on a five-year follow up. Gibbens and Prince (1962) found that a significant number of the shoplifters they studied could have been regarded as depressed; in addition the significance of the menopause and of pre-menstrual tension was also noted. (These last two aspects will be considered more fully in Chapter 10.) Neustatter (1953) makes the point that in cases of mild depressive illness it may be that 'the pleasure of acquisition helps to overcome the depression, and it is really an anti-social form of the normal impulse to cheer oneself up by going shopping when low spirited.' Unfortunately he does not go on to say whether or not the courts should excuse or mitigate culpability in such cases. Clearly, other evidence of a true depressive disorder would be needed.

From time to time, I have come across cases of young adult males who have stated that they had embarked upon a series of offences because they felt 'low' or 'fed-up'. Sometimes, their past and recent histories revealed a number of depressive elements but it would have been difficult to have ascribed the clinical label 'neurotically depressed' to most of them. Such cases do highlight the need for us to be precise in our use of descriptive terms. In discussing such cases we should clearly not use the term 'depressed' in the clinical sense when we merely mean just 'miserable' or 'fed-up'. A clearer perspective upon the matter and the relative importance of depressive factors may be obtained when the antecedent history is examined carefully. (See also Woddis 1957.)

Anxiety states

True anxiety neurosis is usually characterized by a 'morbid or pervasive fear or dread' (McCulloch and Prins 1978). It may occur as a single symptom or in conjunction with other psychiatric conditions – particularly in cases of depressive illness. In the sense in which psychiatrists use the word it goes well beyond reactions to normal fear and worry. Often the anxiety can be seen to be associated with some specific environmental situation or stress, but in other cases it is said to be 'free-floating' – a nameless and non-specific dread. Symptoms may include palpitations, giddiness, nausea, irregular respiration, feelings of suffocation, excessive sweating, dry mouth, and loss of appetite.

Anxiety states as such do not often account for criminality, but a morbidly anxious individual may feel so driven by his anxieties that he may commit an impulsive offence. This seems particularly likely to happen in males who feel, for whatever reason, that their self-image or masculinity have been threatened. We also find that such cases may occur in individuals where the anxiety state is accompanied by or associated with an obsessive and perfectionist personality. I know of a young man who made a serious and unprovoked attack upon an innocent passer-by in the street. As the defendant put it, 'I just exploded. I don't know why; the tension I had been feeling recently just became unbearable.' Subsequent psychotherapy over many months revealed a very vulnerable personality accompanied by a lack of self-esteem and a compulsive need to work in order to keep unnamed anxieties at bay. Later in psychotherapy, it became apparent that many of his problems were associated with a relationship with his father which bordered on hatred. The innocent bystander *happened* to look just like his father and therefore the assault was in many respects no mere accident.

Finally, I should emphasize that anxiety has been discussed here in a very specific and narrow sense. I am not referring to situations where an offender is apparently almost pathologically anxious in the context of his present predicament (for example, facing a court hearing or being detained in prison). Gunn's comments quoted earlier in relation to depression are equally relevant here.

Hysteria

The clinical condition of hysteria was defined by the late Professor Fish as, 'the presence of mental or physical symptoms for the sake of some advantage, *although the patient is not fully aware of the motive*' (quoted in McCulloch and Prins 1978). As with schizophrenia, the term is often used quite incorrectly by lay folk. It is not to be equated with 'having hysterics' or acting histrionically (highly dramatically) though both these characteristics may be shown by hysterics in certain situations. Furthermore, it needs to be differentiated from hysterical personality. Hysterical symptoms can be classified briefly as follows.

(a) Those associated with the senses – for example, deafness or blindness.

(b) Those associated with motor symptoms – paralysis, spasms, or tremors.

(c) Those where mental symptoms present, such as memory loss (which may sometimes be associated with a fugue or wandering state), pseudo-dementia, Ganser Syndrome, stupor, hysterical phobias. These may also present as anxiety and depressive states in which the patient may react in difficult or unpleasant situations with symptoms of these latter illnesses. The key-notes in all of these disorders are symptoms of conversion or of dissociation. Conversion symptoms may occur, for example, in hysterical states in the form of fits which may be superficially similar to those produced in epilepsy due to organic causes. Dissociation arises when the individual has a conflict which produces anxiety, but the latter is overcome by some manifestation of physical or mental illness which submerges the real anxiety. Because of the processes at work, one frequently notices in hysterical individuals that the emotions which should accompany events or memories of them are often inappropriate; thus an account of an incident given by an hysteric, which one would expect to produce sadness, may be told with a bland smile on the face. Such a phenomenon is frequently described as 'la belle indifference' – sublime (beautiful) indifference. From our point of view, hysterical amnesia, fugues, and the Ganser syndrome are of the greatest importance and I shall now consider these in a little more detail. Amnesias due to *organic* disorders or disease will be dealt with under the section concerned with these states; but again, there are obvious areas of overlap.

In some cases it is difficult if not impossible, to distinguish a genuine hysterical illness from simulation or malingering. Very careful elicitation of the facts is required to resolve this issue, but it is possible to state some quite useful generalizations.

(1) In malingering the motivation is more or less at a conscious level. The symptoms are usually of sudden onset and have some connection with situations the malingerer is keen to avoid. In wartime, psychiatrists become very familiar with such cases. (For examples see Neustatter 1953.)

(2) The malingerer's symptoms are usually over-acted and exaggerated. During his trial it was alleged that Haigh – the 'acid bath murderer' – had feigned insanity in order to avoid the death penalty. He produced most bizarre evidence in support of his claim – stating for example that at various times he had drunk both blood and urine. However, the signs and symptoms reported by him bore no relation to any symptomatology known to psychiatrists and not surprisingly his insanity defence was rejected. It is of significance that one of the first questions he is alleged to have asked the police when arrested was 'How long does it take to get out of Broadmoor?' (Neustatter 1953). In summary, malingerers who attempt to feign mental illnesses tend to present the kind of symptoms they believe an insane person would present. (See for example the remarks made earlier in this chapter concerning lay interpretations of schizophrenia.) One should add of

course that some chronic mental hospital or clinic attenders become very adept at picking up psychiatric signs and symptoms and it is not unknown for even highly experienced observers to be misled occasionally.

(3) The symptoms may only be present when the malingerer is being observed. This is important from a socio-forensic point of view, as a true picture of the supposed malingerer may only emerge after fairly lengthy and close observation. Thus remands to prison or psychiatric hospitals may be necessary so that as complete a picture as possible can be established.

(4) The symptoms tend to be made to order. For example, if the person examining the suspected malingerer suggests that a certain symptom of the illness being feigned is absent in the individual's presentation, the malingerer will sometimes try to produce it.

(5) When feigning illness, many of the usual signs and symptoms associated with the real illness may be missing.

There are two other conditions allied to malingering that must be mentioned as they are both of socio-forensic interest. The first is *pseudo-dementia* and the second is the *Ganser Syndrome*.

Pseudo-dementia, as the name implies, is closely akin to malingering or simulation of insanity. The patient may say for example, that 4 + 4 = 9 or the most simple facts will be incorrectly given or strangely twisted. In such cases, the person examining the patient will always have the impression that the individual under examination really knows the right answers. Differential diagnosis is sometimes very difficult because pseudo-dementia may coexist alongside a genuine organic defect or illness.

The Ganser Syndrome is in many ways very like pseudo-dementia. It takes its name from the physician S.J.M. Ganser, who first discussed the condition in 1897. He described a small number of patients exhibiting a number of common features which he suggested justified their being grouped under one heading.*

* It is of interest that he called his lecture 'A Peculiar Hysterical State'.

'The most obvious sign which they present consists of their inability to answer correctly the simplest questions which are asked of them, even though by many of their answers they indicate that they have grasped, in a large part, the sense of the question, and in their answers they betray at once a baffling ignorance and a surprising lack of knowledge which they most assuredly once possessed, or still possess.'

(Schorer 1965)

The passage just quoted (which is from a translation of Ganser's original paper) provides us with the essentials of the condition, notably the tendency to give approximate answers or to talk at cross purposes (*vorbeirden*). In order to make a substantive diagnosis of a Ganser state it has been suggested that there should also be present hallucinations, defects of memory, and clouding of consciousness (Scott 1965). For practical purposes, it is of course sometimes very difficult to distinguish a Ganser state from behaviour caused by some organic disease or disorder or by conscious simulation. Scott (1965) suggests that its

'manifestly slight relationship with crime is probably dependent, in the case of the symptom, on the vigilance of prison medical officers in discouraging simulation, and in the case of the syndrome, on the similarly light correlation of crime with frank mental illness, *which is all the more reason for treating it with respect when it does appear* [my italics].'

Hysterical amnesia

From time to time, offenders claim an amnesic episode for their crime or for the events leading up to or immediately following it. In Chapter 2, I made mention of the case of Podola and I noted there how his defence of unfitness to plead on the grounds of amnesia was not accepted by the court. For obvious reasons, the more serious the crime charged, the more likely it will be that amnesia for it may be claimed; homicide being a case in point. It is important therefore that courts are able to satisfy themselves as to the genuineness of such a claim and to discern whether it be feigned, genuinely hysterical, or due to organic causes. O'Connell (1960) examined the relationship between homicide and amnesia. He defined the latter for the purpose of his investigation as 'an alleged interruption of consciousness, complete or partial, with alleged inability of the accused to recall his actions during that time.' He concluded on the basis of a fairly extensive review of the literature that the difference between malingered and hysterical amnesia is more likely to be one of *degree* than of kind. Support for this view may be found in Neustatter (1953) and in the statement by Hays (1961) that it is well-nigh impossible to distinguish hysterical amnesia from apparent memory loss due to conscious deception. Both conditions may coexist in the same individual and be serving a common purpose, namely loss of memory for an alleged crime. Power (1977) makes a number of important suggestions concerning the means by which a genuine (hysterical) amnesia may be elicited.

(1) By studying the character of the alleged amnesia itself – an amnesic episode of 'sudden onset and termination is suggestive of feigned memory loss'.
(2) By paying attention to the character of the crime itself. 'A motiveless crime may be committed impulsively, without premeditation or attempt at concealment, with needless violence and even in the presence of witnesses.'
(3) By comparing carefully the story given by the accused with that given originally by the police. If necessary these procedures should be repeated in oprder that inconsistencies may be detected.
(4) By attempting to assess whether the accused seems in general to be an honest person. One does this by reference to past social history and by paying special attention to alleged past amnesic episodes.

From a treatment point of view, true hysterical amnesia can often be remedied by psychotherapeutic methods. One must first gain the confidence of the person concerned and then patiently endeavour to help him to recall the nature of the original conflicts that led to the use of the defence of hysterical amnesia in the first instance. Simple psychotherapy may not be sufficient of course to penetrate deep enough into the origins of these conflicts and some workers find hypnosis and/or hypnotic drugs a useful adjunct to 'talking' therapy. Amnesia due to organic or kindred causes is of course a different matter and is considered later.

Obsessional states

Strictly speaking, it would be more accurate to write about obsessive-compulsive and phobic states, but for brevity I have chosen to use a shorter, but admittedly less accurate umbrella title. These states have little direct association with criminality. In the main they are characterized by feeling compelled to think or do certain things or by being obsessionally fearful. Such feelings are all pervasive, are known by the sufferer to be irrational and yet are out of his or her control. They are so predominant that all normal patterns of work and social life may be severely interrupted or virtually destroyed. Occasionally, one comes across a case of so-called compulsive stealing (kleptomania). It is very doubtful if such stealing is truly compulsive in the sense that it can be classified as a form of true neurosis. It is more likely to be a form of personality disorder in which impulses are poorly controlled. As Neustatter (1953) has aptly pointed out, in true compulsive states, certain rituals are performed over and over and over again, (as for example in ritualistic hand-washing). If such a pattern was to be seen in stealing 'there would need to be an endless repetition of taking the same object by a precisely similar set of acts. What occurs is that periodically the desire to take something appears to be overwhelmingly strong and is then gratified by the theft'. Neustatter goes on to suggest that such behaviour may be 'far more suggestive of a symbolic attempt at sexual gratification'. Certainly, there is evidence to suggest that some apparently non-sexual offences are committed because of underlying sexual conflicts or are a substitute for or are a prerequisite of some sexual activity. Certain cases of arson come into the former category and the latter are seen in the fetishistic activities of those who steal ladies' underwear from clothes-lines. (These matters will be dealt with in more detail in the chapters on arson and sexual offending.) We should also note here that it has been suggested that some people commit offences because of an underlying and unassuaged sense of guilt that can only be purged by this indirect form of punishment. Their offences may well have a highly repetitive quality until the original source of guilt is tracked down, brought into consciousness and dealt with. The case quoted earlier of the youth who stole cars would come within this category.

MENTAL DISORDER AS A RESULT OF INFECTIONS, DISEASE, METABOLIC DISTURBANCES, AND TRAUMA

For the sake of simplicity I propose to consider the above under the broad heading of 'organic' disorders. Physical *handicap* and its relationship to criminality is not considered here; I have dealt with some aspects of this elsewhere (Prins 1973). However, it should be noted in passing that certain handicapping conditions and disfigurements may lead people into criminality by way of their needing to compensate for feelings of inferiority or perhaps because of a need to act out of spite. In examining 'organic' disorders, we are concerned with those that may give rise to mental signs and symptoms and to changes in behaviour. I indicated in Part One of this chapter, that the numbers of offenders appearing to suffer from obvious organic disease and disorder were small, though Woddis (1964) in fact reports ten such instances in his sample of ninety-one cases. However, he does not distinguish different types of organic disorder and includes cases of epilepsy in his sample. Faulk (1976) does not report any organic cases in his sample of prisoners. Despite, or perhaps because of their apparent rarity, such cases are of importance as organic conditions are sometimes overlooked.

Infections

These include meningitis, encephalitis, and a number of viral infections. It is not uncommon for marked changes in behaviour to occur after encephalitis, and in particular these changes may be accompanied by the development of aggressive tendencies. As I indicate in Chapter 5, it has been strongly suggested that some forms of psychopathic personality disorder may be caused by such infections. It is also thought that a type of herpes virus may be responsible for some cases of mild brain damage (which may result in behaviour disorder), though the incidence of such cases is hard to determine. Stott (1963) produced some interesting evidence that mild or minimal brain damage may be of more importance in the causation of criminality than has been supposed hitherto. He suggests that those so minimally damaged may be particularly vulnerable to social stresses.

Huntington's Chorea

This is a comparatively rare, directly transmitted, hereditary condition. The onset of the illness is more likely to occur in the middle years of life and is characterized by a progressive deterioration of mental and emotional functioning. In addition, there is considerable progressive physical disability. Sufferers from this condition may sometimes behave unpredictably and become anti-social, though such instances are uncommon.

General Paralysis of the Insane (GPI)

This disorder develops as a result of syphilitic infection, attacking the central nervous system (CNS). Symptoms may appear very many years after the original infective incident. The patient may suddenly indulge in uncharacteristic acts of impropriety or show extraordinary lack of judgement; some of these may take a delinquent form and the patient may thus come to the attention of the judicial and penal authorities. Any 'outrageous' behaviour on the part of a person of previous impeccable behaviour should alert us to the possibilities of the existence of such a condition. Fortunately GPI is seen rarely these days, due largely to earlier diagnosis of the condition and to the use of antibiotic drugs.

Alcoholic poisoning

The problem of alcoholism and its relationship to crime will be dealt with more fully in Chapter 9, but for the sake of completeness, brief mention should be made here of certain organic states that are produced by the heavy and prolonged ingestion of alcohol. Such conditions are seen in cases of chronic alcoholism and also in the more rare condition of alcoholic psychosis. One of the chief characteristics of these conditions is severe memory impairment. Sometimes such a patient will confabulate (i.e. fill in the gaps in their story with their imagination) in order to make good the deficit. Such a state may give rise to issues concerning criminal responsibility such as those discussed in Chapter 2. In a recent article, Cutting (1978) has emphasized the deleterious effects of alcohol ingestion. He studied a group of patients, *none* of whom had been given a previous diagnosis of alcoholic psychosis, so in some respects these could be regarded as *milder* cases. He found on psychological testing that memory was significantly impaired as were some of those mental functions associated with the temporal lobe areas of the brain. Brewer (1974), in an interesting contribution, has drawn attention to the need to consider carefully the possibilities of alcoholic brain damage in the case of certain offenders.

Other toxic compounds

Very occasionally, an individual will start behaving oddly for no apparent reason and all preliminary exploratory investigations may prove negative. However, later and more detailed enquiries may reveal that the person concerned has been exposed to such toxic substances as carbon monoxide fumes, lead, or industrial chemicals. Such cases will arise rarely, but again, it is the rare and apparently inexplicable case that should be deserving of our attention. Some of these issues are discussed in an article by Blair (1977).

Endocrine disorders

Hypoglycaemia (referred to in Chapter 2) may occur in certain predisposed individuals who have gone without food for a prolonged period. Their judgement may become impaired and they may show extreme irritability. Individuals in such a state may occasionally come into confrontation with the legal authorities. Neustatter (1953) gives two interesting case examples of the possibilities of low blood sugar being responsible for delinquent behaviour. In a more recent case, (that of Quick, in 1973)*, the defence sought to use such a condition in order to support a plea of automatism. The plea itself failed, but the defendant's conviction was quashed by the Court of Appeal in any case on technical rather than medical grounds. Similar recent cases are described by Blair (1977) and Power (1977).

Brain trauma and brain tumour

Most people who have worked with delinquents and their families for any length of time have come across references by parents of delinquent offspring to a 'knock on the head' or some similar incident as a possible explanation of the delinquent family member's subsequent lapses into crime. Thus a blow on the head or kindred injury may be given as a convenient explanation for any impulsive, aggressive, or unpredictable behaviour that, more likely than not, has its origins in a defective social environment rather than in any organic cause. Having said this, it is important to emphasize, that from time to time, genuine cases of brain trauma or tumour are missed – sometimes with tragic consequences. An injury to the brain (however caused) is more than likely to produce a degree of concussion which may sometimes be prolonged. Such injuries may result in a degree of subnormality or may give rise to epileptic seizures (see below). These patients may be amnesic and such amnesia may be different in form from the hysterical forms of amnesia discussed earlier. Thus, following recovery of consciousness (which may have lasted several days or longer) there may be clouding of consciousness or noisy

*[1973] 3 All E.R. (347).

delirium – conditions not seen in hysterical or malingered amnesia. Such organically amnesic patients may sometimes appear to be normally initially, and only gradually, following careful examination, does it emerge that they have been behaving 'automatically' or confabulating (see above). In contrast, in cases of hysterical amnesia, memory may return spontaneously within twenty-four hours or so. The organically amnesic patient is likely to want to do his best to remember and may appear to be annoyed by his defective memory. The hysterical amnesic may show a 'complete and absolute inability to recall any events before a given time. Usually it is for the whole of a patient's life, or alternatively for a considerable period of it, generally one during which the patient [has been] . . . engaged in somewhat dubious activities' (Neustatter 1953). Moreover, unlike the organically amnesic individual, the hysterically amnesic patient may have a perfect command of speech and be well in command of his other faculties. Careful history taking – particularly from relatives – is of prime importance. Some useful suggestions concerning this are to be found in a paper by Kaufman (1978). The degree to which concussion following head injury is related to criminality was examined by Lidberg (1971). He investigated 439 persons seen by the Forensic Psychiatry Department at the Karolinska Institute in Stockholm. Eighteen per cent of his sample had suffered concussion by the age of twenty-one, but having said this, it should be remembered that Lidberg's was a highly selective sample. Moreover, when he came to look at these percentages in relation to the general population, he found these were not significantly different from mentally healthy Swedish military conscripts. But, he did find a statistically significant correlation between crimes of *violence* and concussion in his sample.

Brewer (1976) has stated that 'it is remarkable how rarely the cerebral status of serious offenders is seriously investigated'. He considers it to be essential that anyone charged with serious violence should be offered full X-Ray, EEG (Electroencephalogram), and psychological investigation if there is the slightest possibility of brain disease. In a more recent paper, he refers to the '. . . difficulties in establishing the diagnosis [which] arise when brain disease is not of the more obvious kind or when the fact of earlier convictions for fairly 'ordinary' crimes suggest that the court is dealing with a fairly 'ordinary' criminal' (Brewer 1978). He goes on to suggest that cerebral *tumours* as such are a rare cause of criminal behaviour but he provides interesting case material which indicates that cerebral *atrophy* (degeneration) may well be. Such atrophy is a common sequel to many kinds of brain disease and may also be a sequel to head injury. The use of recently developed radiological scanning devices, which are a considerable improvement on ordinary X-Ray techniques, now offers a more accurate, in-depth, form of investigation.

Epilepsy

Trethowan (1973) points out that, 'Epilepsy is a symptom as much as a disease', and even so-called normal people may be stimulated artificially into epileptic attacks. He indicates that about '5 per cent of all persons have an epileptic attack at some time in their lives'. Gunn (1977) defines epilepsy as follows.

> 'Epilepsy is said to occur in someone who has had 3 or more epileptic seizures, either during the past two years, or if before that time, is still on regular anti-convulsant medication. An epileptic seizure is an intermittent, stereotyped disturbance of behaviour, emotion, motor function, or sensation, which on clinical grounds is judged to be the result of pathological neuronal discharge.'*

Epilepsy may be due to a variety of causes, some of which (as indicated earlier) are already known, or it may be of unknown origin (idiopathic). There are several types of epileptic phenomena; Grand Mal (a major convulsion); Petit Mal (momentary loss of consciousness without convulsions and sometimes imperceptible to the on-looker); Temporal Lobe Epilepsy, often characterized by 'sudden explosive changes of thought mood or behaviour' (Blair 1977); Jacksonian

* Reproduced with permission of the author and publisher – Academic Press Inc. (London) Ltd.

Epilepsy, a localized cerebral convulsion following traumatic brain damage (named after the celebrated nineteenth-century physician Hughlings Jackson, whose pioneering studies on epilepsy were undertaken as a result of the illness in his wife); partial seizures, and more generalized convulsive seizures. The psychiatric aspects of epilepsy have been usefully summarized by Scott (1978). Epileptic automatism (see Chapter 2 also) may be pleaded as an infrequent, but important, defence in cases of serious crime. Murder is a good example and Gunn (1978) has written an account of a most interesting and unusual case. In recent years, he has also carried out extensive and more general investigations into the relationship between epilepsy and criminality in penal populations (Gunn and Bonn 1971; Gunn 1974; Gunn 1977). We can summarize his valuable work (in a simplified way) as follows. He found more epileptic males were taken into custody than would be expected by chance – a ratio of some 7–8:1000. This is considerably higher than the proportion of epileptics found in the general population. One third of the cases examined by Gunn and his colleagues were found to be suffering from temporal lobe epilepsy (see above). In 15 per cent of those diagnosed as epileptic, the current offence was for violence as against 22 per cent in a non-epileptic control group. Temporal lobe cases were found to have a higher previous conviction rate, but it was the group suffering from idiopathic epilepsy who received disproportionately more previous convictions for violence. Gunn (1974) has put forward four very important points in attempting to explain the large number of epileptics in penal populations. In doing so, he sought to determine in what ways organic and social factors could lead to imprisonment over and above the chance findings of epilepsy in prisoners. He suggests four main routes:

'A. Brain dysfunction is responsible for both the ictal phenomena and the antisocial behaviour.

B. The epilepsy generates social and psychological problems (e.g. rejection, feelings of inferiority) which in their turn lead to antisocial reactions.

C. Harmful social factors such as overcrowding, parental neglect and the like lead to an excess prevalence of both epilepsy and antisocial behaviour.

D. Environmental factors, such as parental rejection, subcultural norms etc. lead to behaviour disturbances which not only produce conflict with the law but also accident and illness proneness (because of self neglect and recklessness). Such accidents and illnesses in their turn produce an excess prevalence of epilepsy.'

(Gunn 1974:514)

Senile and pre-senile dementia

These conditions are similar in some respects to a number of those already described – especially those in which memory is impaired and social behaviour is seen to deteriorate markedly. They are characterized chiefly by increasing memory loss for recent events and by confusion. Emotions become very labile and we may observe childish petulance, irritability, rigidity, and impairment of intellectual functions. From time to time, a person suffering in this way may appear in court on a charge such as shoplifting, indecent behaviour, or breach of the peace. As with many of the other organic conditions already described, such behaviour developing in someone of previous good character and of hitherto predictable habits is worthy of careful investigation so that the most humane disposition of the case may be effected.

Personality disorders (abnormal personalities)

These consist of a group of disorders in which the basic personality appears to be noticeably abnormal, either in the balance of its components and their quality and expression, or in its total aspect. There is considerable confusion and disagreement, both as to the use of the terms personality disorder or abnormal personality, and to the extent to which such disorders should be classified and described as mental disorder in the more closely circumscribed sense of that word. In some instances they are so described 'only when they appear at the extreme end of a range of behaviour from 'relatively normal' at one end to 'extremely deviant' at the other' (McCulloch and Prins 1978). The problem was well formulated by a group of experts who produced the much used *Glossary of Mental Disorders*:

> 'This category refers to a group of more or less well defined anomalies or deviations of personality which are not the result of psychosis or any other illness. The differentiation of these personalities is to some extent arbitrary and the reference to a given group will depend initially on the relative predominance of one or other group of character traits . . .'
> (General Register Office 1968)

Some authorities maintain that the term is used not only far too loosely, but also as a 'dustbin' category to which are assigned deviant or uncooperative individuals whose behaviour varies from the norm only in *degree*. Others limit the classification and definition and see such disorders as lesser variants of true illness states.

With this degree of confusion, it is not surprising to find that personality disorder or psychopathy figure more prominently than any other mental disorder in selected samples of criminal populations (see *Table 3(1)* p. 46). The problem is further complicated by the fact that a number of workers do not attempt to distinguish between various types of personality disorder. To add to the confusion they also use the terms personality disorder and psychopathy interchangeably. (I shall suggest in Chapter 5, that there is some justification for maintaining the descriptive term psychopathic disorder as a separate entity.) Causation of personality disorder is obscure: some consider that there are constitutional and genetic factors; others subscribe to the view that environmental (particularly familial) factors have pre-eminence in aetiology. Psychopathy or severe anti-social personality disorder is considered to be at the extreme end of the spectrum and from our point of view is the most important of these disorders. I shall therefore discuss this separately in Chapter 5, not merely because of its importance, but because it exemplifies acutely the dilemmas involved in determining the aetiology and classification of personality disorders in general. Some of these have recently been reviewed usefully by Lion (1974); (the chapter by Penna, in the same volume is particularly helpful). We should also note here that attempts have been made to delineate certain well-defined types of personality disorders, such as the paranoid, the affective, the cyclothymic, the schizoid, the explosive, the hysterical, the obsessive, and the affectionless. Illustrations of some of these may be found in McCulloch and Prins (1978: Chapter 6).

Psycho-sexual Disorders and their Relationship to Criminality are considered separately in Chapter 8.

Alcohol and Other Drug Addictions are considered in Chapter 9.

MENTAL SUBNORMALITY (DEFICIENCY, HANDICAP, RETARDATION)

These terms are frequently used synonymously; however, in recent years the term mental *retardation* seems to be preferred to others.* The layman often, but understandably, confuses mental illness with mental retardation; the two conditions are entirely separate though they may coexist in some patients. In general and oversimplified terms, it can be said that the mentally ill individual starts life with normal intellectual endowments, but for some of the reasons described earlier in this chapter, he may become ill and thus deviate from normality, whereas the subnormal person never had the endowment of intellectual normality, or lost it in infancy or in early life. This point is demonstrated very clearly in the use of the older descriptive term for subnormality – *amentia* – which means literally 'lack of mind'.

Mental subnormality (I shall use this description merely for convenience since it is the term used in the Mental Health Act,

* However, 'Mental *handicap*' is the term which is preferred by the DHSS. The law in Scotland retains the term 'mental deficiency'.

1959) is a relative concept. It is often assumed, quite incorrectly, that the degree of subnormality can be assessed purely in terms of intellectual capacity (IQ). Though this is an important aspect, it is imperative to have regard equally for the social functioning of the individual, in particular family and kindred supports or lack of them. However, it is possible to indicate an approximate range of intellectual functioning that is associated with the four different classifications of mental subnormality customarily described in the literature. It must be stressed that these are generalizations and somewhat imprecise in social terms.* These four groupings are:

(1) *Mild subnormality* (Mental Retardation) IQ is estimated to be between 50–70;

(2) *Moderate mental subnormality* (Mental Retardation) IQ range 35–49;

(3) *Severe mental subnormality* (Mental Retardation) IQ range 20–34;

(4) *Profound mental subnormality* (Mental Retardation) IQ under 20.

The above are social and clinical classifications. The *legal* classification as set out in the Mental Health Act, 1959 recognizes two forms – *severe subnormality* and *subnormality*.

Causal factors

There are some 300 known possible causes of the various forms of mental subnormality, but it is possible to define an exact cause in some 35 per cent of cases only. Some of the chief causes are summarized below:

(1) Infection in the parent – for example Rubella (German Measles) contracted in the early pregnancy of the mother.

(2) Disease in infancy or early childhood – for example

---

* It is particularly important to point out here that IQ figures should not in any event be quoted without qualification. Much will depend upon the type of tests used by psychologists and what particular aspects of intellectual functioning the tests were designed to examine.

meningitis or encephalitis (see earlier discussion).

(3) Brain damage to the infant before, during, or after birth. This may occur as a result of prematurity or as a result of anoxia (lack of oxygen) due to various causes. Brain damage after birth may occur of course as a result of 'battering' (non-accidental injury) by parents or others.

(4) Chromosomal abnormalities. The best known of these is Mongolism (Down's Syndrome). (Chromosomal abnormalities are discussed in a little more detail later.)

(5) Other 'inborn' causes, for example phenylketonuria – a condition in which some children are unable to cope with the phenylalaline content of normal diets. If correct dietary programmes are not observed, severe mental subnormality will ensue.

(6) Exacerbation of an existing mild subnormality (from whatever cause) by lack of social and intellectual stimulation, malnutrition, and poor ante and post-natal care.

(7) Exposure to certain 'prohibited' drugs in pregnancy such as LSD; or exposure to therapeutic drugs and vaccines used in infancy.

(8) Exposure to radiation.

Mental Subnormality and Crime

From a socio-forensic point of view, we are most likely to be concerned with cases of mild or moderate forms of mental subnormality. Reference to *Table 3(1)* (p. 46) shows the wide disparities in the suggested prevalence of mental subnormality in the various studies quoted. We need to remember that any studies carried out on penal populations at the end of the last century and the beginning of this one are likely to reveal a high incidence of subnormal persons due to the lack of hospital provision for such individuals at that time. Because of this, many found their way into the prisons. Another difficulty arises when we wish to interpret the qualitative significance of the statistics. Few of the studies quoted give any indication of gradations of subnormality so that we may have grades of varying severity lumped together without any attempt to discriminate between them.

It is highly unlikely that the profoundly subnormal will come to the attention of the courts for their condition is sadly almost inevitably accompanied by severe physical disability so that they spend most of their lives in hospital care. We are more likely to be concerned with those showing mild or moderate degrees of mental subnormality. In this context we need to remember that in any event most criminological studies show a lack of direct association between intelligence and crime *per se*. Woodward (1955) in what is still probably the most comprehensive study of the subject, concluded that offenders were not more than eight points below the general average; but even this slight depression may be explained in part by the fact that these could well be the offenders who are caught and therefore subjected to study. The offender's capacity to communicate his thoughts and feelings seems to be of cardinal importance. In addition, the problem of alleged low and low-average intelligence is frequently exacerbated by low social class status, lack of education, and other opportunities. Confirmation of this view as it relates to offenders can be found in an important study by Gibson and West (1970). They discovered that on tests of verbal and non-verbal intelligence, boys convicted before the age of fourteen were not only of substantially lower IQ, but had come from the community's more impoverished and deprived families.

In whatever manner we interpret the disparities in the statistics relating to mental subnormality and crime, we are faced with the inevitable fact that the penal and allied services will have to deal from time to time with a number of offenders who suffer from subnormality in varying degrees. Indeed, one of our 'special' hospitals – Rampton in Nottinghamshire – caters specifically for such subnormal offender/patients. We need now to consider more precisely the extent to which mental subnormality may be associated with crime. First, the degree of subnormality may be severe enough to prevent the individual concerned from understanding that his act was legally wrong. In such cases, questions of criminal responsibility may arise. However, one experienced specialist in subnormality suggests that the measurable level of intelligence of itself is not necessarily of fundamental importance in this respect (Shapiro 1969).

Second, the mild or moderately subnormal offender may be more easily caught in the act. Third, such offenders may be very easily used by others in delinquent escapades and find themselves acting as accomplices – sometimes wittingly, sometimes not. Weber, writing twenty-five years ago about such 'borderline defective' delinquents makes a compelling observation. 'His more intelligent contemporaries find him boring and dull, so that he has to find companionship where he may. Often kindly, but with little mind of his own, he too frequently becomes the easy prey and suggestible tool of more intelligent minds with criminal tendencies' (Weber 1953). Fourth, his subnormality may be associated with an organic disorder that makes him particularly impulsive and unpredictable. The following case illustrates this point. A man of twenty-six was charged with causing grievous bodily harm to a young woman by hitting her over the head with an iron bar. She was entirely unknown to him, and although he denied the offence vehemently he was convicted on the clearest possible evidence by the Crown Court. He had suffered brain damage as a child. This had resulted in a moderate degree of subnormality accompanied by impulsive, unpredictable behaviour. He had come before the courts on a number of occasions having been committed eventually to a mental subnormality hospital. Some years later, he was discharged to the care of his mother. During this period, he committed the offence described earlier and was placed on probation. His response was poor. He was impulsive, erratic, and regressed to very childish forms of conduct when under stress. The family background was quite disturbed – mother and father had divorced when the patient was quite small. A brother suffered from a disabling form of epilepsy and various other family members were decidedly 'eccentric' in their behaviour. Shortly before the probation period expired, he committed a particularly vicious assault on a small girl and was sent to prison. The outlook was considered to be very unfavourable.

Fifth, a number of subnormal offenders have quite understandable problems in making understood their often harmless intentions. Thus, a friendly social overture may be misinterpreted by an uninformed or unsympathetic recipient as an attempted assault. The initial overture may be rebuffed therefore. This may lead to surprise and anger on the part of the subnormal patient and he may then retaliate with aggression. Sixth, a few subnormal patients suffer from types of disorder that make them subject to explosive outbursts. However, this can usually be controlled to some extent by medication. Seventh, moderately mentally subnormal persons may be easily goaded by others so that they may be provoked quite readily into an uncharacteristic act of violence; such a case is described in detail elsewhere (McCulloch and Prins 1978: 171–72). Eighth, the attitudes to legitimate expressions of sexuality of some mentally subnormal patients may be naive, primitive, or unrestrained. This may account in part for the significantly high proportion of sexual offences in the background of compulsorily detained mentally subnormal patients. Shapiro (1969) gives a figure as high as 35 per cent. Tutt (1971), examining a sample of forty-four known delinquents admitted to the psychopathic unit of a subnormality hospital found that 15.91 per cent had been convicted of a sex offence immediately prior to admission. These figures are significantly higher than the figures for sex offenders in the general population (something in the order of 3 per cent). Ninth, mentally subnormal persons may be particularly vulnerable to changes in their social environments that would not have the same impact upon their more well-endowed brethren. A moderately subnormal individual may manage perfectly well as long as he has the support of parents or other relatives. Should this be disrupted by death or for any other reason, he may be particularly vulnerable to social pressures and stresses. He may then indulge in delinquency as a means of trying to resolve them.

Unlike some forms of mental illness, there is no cure, as such, for mental subnormality. The worst impact of the condition can be ameliorated, and in some cases alleviated by various forms of training and support – both within institutions and in the community. Those who clamour for the closure of our mental subnormality hospitals probably have little idea of the excellent rehabilitative work that goes on in many of them. In the absence of essential substitute community-based resources, premature closure of these hospitals would probably mean that many of these subnormal patients would find their way once again into penal institutions – as they did at the end of the last century.

Chromosomal abnormalities*

Brief reference has been made already to chromosomal abnormalities as a cause of one form of mental subnormality – namely mongolism (Down's Syndrome). In recent years, considerable interest has been shown in men having been found to carry an extra Y chromosome. (West 1969; Forssman 1970; Scott 1975; Pitcher 1975.) It has been suggested that such men (when found in special hospital or penal populations) are frequently taller than average, come from *essentially non-delinquent backgrounds* and may occasionally have records of violence. However, to date little large-scale work has been done in estimating the presence of such anomalies in normal populations. Until this is done, and the evidence is available, there is little to suggest that we have found a clear genetic causal factor in criminality. More than twenty years ago, the distinguished geneticist Sir Lionel Penrose stated that 'criminality is not a suitable trait for [genetic] studies except where it is associated with a clearly defined pathological condition . . . it is certain that the disposition to crime is not a single gene effect . . .' (Penrose 1955).

However, it could be that as our laboratory and other technical skills become more sophisticated we *may* find evidence that would lead us to suggest a closer link between genetic endowments and crime than exists at the present time. So far, the

* A brief word of explanation of normal chromosomal disposition is necessary. Normal human cells contain 46 chromosomes; these are arranged in 23 pairs of different shapes and sizes. These may be seen and classified under a high power microscope once they have been suitably prepared for examination. Different chromosomes contain different genes. One pair of chromosomes called X and Y determine sex. In the female, these consist of a matched pair XX and in the male a pair XY. The normal patterning may sometimes become altered in a variety of ways. This can result in an extra X or extra Y chromosome or some other variant.

courts have not been quick to accept evidence of chromosomal abnormalities in exculpation from criminal responsibility, though Hall Williams (1969) quotes one or two interesting and isolated instances.

Conclusions

In the first part of this chapter, I endeavoured to outline some of the difficulties involved in attempting to demonstrate clear causal links between mental disorder and criminal conduct. In the second part, I attempted to examine some of these associations in relation to specific disorders. The rationale for this was that although almost all mental disorders are only rarely *directly* associated with crime, it is in these rare instances that we need to be on the alert so that opportunities for effective intervention will not be missed. At a time when global and somewhat 'political' statements are made about the behaviour of individuals and groups it seemed useful to examine exceptional and singular instances in order to correct the balance. In Chapter 4, I shall examine briefly some of the relationships between psychiatry, the courts, and the penal system. In subsequent chapters some further aspects of the mental disorders examined here will be discussed in the context of their association with particular offence behaviour.

References

Ashley, M.C. (1922) Outcome of One Thousand Cases Paroled from the Middletown State Homeopathic Hospital. *State Hospital Quarterly* (New York) **8**: 64–70.

Banay, R.S. (1942) Alcoholism and Crime. *Quart. J. Studs. Alcohol* **2**: 686–716.

Banks, C. (1964) In *Studies in Psychology*. London: University of London Press.

Blair, D. (1977) The Medico-Legal Aspects of Automatism. *Med. Sci. Law* **17**: 167–82.

Bluglass, R.S. (1966) *A Psychiatric Study of Scottish Prisoners* (unpublished M.D. Thesis). Quoted in J. Gunn (1977) Criminal Behaviour and Mental Disorder. *Brit. J. Psychiat.* **130**: 317–29.

Brewer, C. (1974) Alcoholic Brain Damage: Implications for Sentencing Policy. (With a Note on the Air Encephalogram.) *Med. Sci. Law.* **14**: 40–3.

—— (1976) *Psychiatry and the Control of Criminal Behaviour — Two Cheers for the Medical Model.* In J.F.S. King (ed.) *Control Without Custody?* Cambridge: Institute of Criminology. (pp. 141–48).

—— (1978) Bad Brains and Bad Behaviour. *World Medicine* 8 August 1978: 33–6.

Brill, H. and Malzberg, B. (Undated report) *Statistical report based on the arrest record of 5,354 male ex-patients released from New York State Mental Hospitals during the period 1946–1948. Mimeographed.* (Quoted by Guze 1976).

Bromberg, W. and Thompson, C.B. (1937) The Relation of Psychosis, Mental Defect and Personality Type to Crime. *J. Crim. Law and Criminol.* **28**: 70–89.

Brown, G.W. and Harris, T. (1978) *Social Origins of Depression.* London: Tavistock.

Cobb, S. (1948) *Foundations of Neuropsychiatry.* Baltimore: Williams and Wilkins.

Cohen, L.H. and Freeman, H. (1945) How Dangerous to the Community are State Hospital Patients? *Conn. State Med. J.* **9**: 697–700.

Cramer, M.J. and Blacker, E.J. (1963) 'Early' and 'Late' Problem Drinkers Among Female Prisoners. *J. Hlth. and Human Behav.* **4**: 282–90.

Croft, J. (1978) *Research in Criminal Justice. Home Office Research Study. No. 44.* Home Office Research Unit Report. London: HMSO.

Cutting, J. (1978) Specific Psychological Deficits in Alcoholism. *Brit. J. Psychiat.* **133**: 119–22.

Edwards, G., Hensman, C., and Peto, J. (1971) Drinking Problems Amongst Recidivist Prisoners. *Psychol. Med.* **1**: 388–99.

Faulk, M. (1976) A Psychiatric Study of Men Serving Sentences in Winchester Prison. *Med. Sci. Law.* **16**: 244–51.

Feldman, M. (1977) *Criminal Behaviour: A Psychological Analysis.*

London: John Wiley.

Forssman, H. (1970) The Mental Implications of Sex Chromosome Aberrations. *Brit. J. Psychiat.* **117**: 353–63.

Fulcher, G. (1975) *Schizophrenia: A Sociologist's Views of Psychiatrist's Views.* In A.R. Edwards and P.R. Wilson (eds.) *Social Deviance in Australia.* Melbourne: Cheshire.

General Register Office (1968) *Studies on Medical and Population Subjects. (No. 22). A Glossary of Mental Disorders.* London: HMSO.

Gibbens, T.C.N., and Prince, J. (1962) *Shoplifting.* London: ISTD.

Gibbens, T.C.N. (1966) *Aspects of After-Care. Annual Report,* London: Roy. Lond. Prisoners' Aid Soc. (pp. 8 – 11). Quoted by Faulk (1976).

Gibbens, T.C.N., and Silberman, M. (1970) Alcoholism Amongst Prisoners. *Psychol. Med.* **1**: 73–8.

Gibson, H.B. and West, D.J. (1970) Social and Intellectual Handicaps as Precursors of Early Delinquency. *Brit. J. Criminol.* **10**: 21–32.

Gillies, H. (1965) Murder in the West of Scotland. *Brit. J. Psychiat.* **111**: 1087–094.

Glueck, B. (1918) A Study of 608 Admissions to Sing Sing Prison. *Mental Hygiene* **2**: 85–151.

Gunn, J., and Bonn, J. (1971) Criminality and Violence in Epileptic Prisoners. *Brit. J. Psychiat.* **118**: 337–43.

Gunn, J. (1973) *A Psychiatric Study of Offenders in the South-East Region of England.* Quoted in Faulk (1976).

—— (1974) Social Factors and Epileptics in Prison. *Brit. J. Psychiat.* **124**: 509–17.

—— (1977a) Criminal Behaviour and Mental Disorder. *Brit. J. Psychiat.* **130**: 317–29.

—— (1977b) *Epileptics in Prison.* London: Academic Press.

—— (1978) Epileptic Homicide: A Case Report. *Brit. J. Psychiat.* **132**: 510–13.

Gunn, J., Robertson, G., Dell, S., and Way, C. (1978) *Psychiatric Aspects of Imprisonment.* London: Academic Press. (Chapter II).

Guze, S.B. (1976) *Criminality and Psychiatric Disorders.* Oxford:

Oxford University Press.

Hall Williams, J.E. (1969) *Chromosome Abnormalities and Legal Accountability*. In D.J. West (ed.) (1969).

Hays, P. (1961) Hysterical Amnesia and the Podola Trial. *Med. Leg. J.* **29**: 27–32.

Jahoda, M. (1958) *Current Concepts of Positive Mental Health*. New York: Basic Books.

Kaufman, A. (1978) *Medico-Legal Aspects of Head Injuries: Intellectual Impairment and Clinical Psychological Assessment*. *Med. Sci. Law.* **18**: 56–62.

Kloek, J. (1969) *Schizophrenia and Delinquency: The Inadequacy of our Conceptual Framework*. In A.V.S. de Rueck, R. Porter (eds) *The Mentally Abnormal Offender*. London: J. and A. Churchill (for CIBA Foundation).

Laing, R.D. and Esterson, A. (1964) *Sanity, Madness, and the Family*. London: Tavistock.

Lidberg, L. (1971) Frequency of Concussion and Type of Criminality. *Acta. Psychiatrica Scandinavica* **47**: 452–61.

Lion, J.R. (1974) *Personality Disorders. Diagnosis and Management*. Baltimore: Williams and Wilkins.

Maule, H.G. and Cooper, J. (1966) Alcoholism and Crime – a Study of the Drinking Habits of 50 Discharged Prisoners. *Brit. J. Addict.* **61**: 201–12.

McClintock, F.H. and Avison, N.H. (1968) *Crime in England and Wales*. London: Heinemann.

McCulloch, J.W. and Prins, H.A. (1978) *Signs of Stress. The Social Problems of Psychiatric Illness*. London: Woburn Press.

Mechanic, D. (1968) *Medical Sociology*. New York: Free Press.

Mendels, J. (1970) *Concepts of Depression*. London: John Wiley.

Munro, A. and McCulloch, J.W. (1975) *Psychiatry for Social Workers* (2nd edition). Oxford: Pergamon Press.

Neustatter, W.L. (1953) *Psychological Disorder and Crime*. London: Christopher Johnson.

Nicol, A.R., Gunn, J.C., Gristwood, J., Foggitt, R.H., and Watson, J.P. (1973) The Relationship of Alcoholism to Violent Behaviour Resulting in Long-Term Imprisonment. *Brit. J. Psychiat.* **123**: 47–51.

O'Connell, B.A. (1960) Amnesia and Homicide: A Study of 50

Murderers. *Brit. J. Delinq.* **X**: 262–76.

Oltman, J.E. and Friedman, S. (1941) A Psychiatric Study of One Hundred Criminals. *J. Nerv. Ment. Dis.* **93**: 16–41.

Penrose, L.S. (1939) Mental Disease and Crime: Outline of a Comparative Study of European Statistics. *Brit. J. Med. Psychol.* **18**: 1–15.

—— (1955) Genetics and the Criminal. *Brit. J. Delinq.* **VII**: 15–25.

Pitcher, D.R. (1975) *The XYY Syndrome*. In T. Silverstone and B. Barraclough (eds) *Contemporary Psychiatry*. Ashford: Headley Brothers.

Pollock, H.M. (1938) Is the Paroled Patient a Menace to the Community? *Psychiatric Quarterly* **12**: 236–44.

Power, D.J. (1977) Memory, Identification and Crime. *Med. Sci. Law* **17**: 132–39.

Prins H.A. (1973) *Criminal Behaviour*. London: Pitman.

Rappeport, J. and Lassen, G. (1965) Dangerousness – Arrest Rate Comparisons of Discharged Patients and the General Population. *Amer. J. Psychiat.* **121**: 776–83.

—— (1966) The Dangerousness of Female Patients: A Comparison of the Arrest Rate of Discharged Psychiatric Patients and the General Population. *Amer. J. Psychiat.* **123**: 413–19.

Rollin, H. (1969) *The Mentally Abnormal Offender and the Law*. Oxford: Pergamon.

Schipkowensky, N. (1969) Cyclophrenia and Murder. In A.V.S. de Rueck, R. Porter (eds) *The Mentally Abnormal Offender*. London: J. and A. Churchill (for CIBA Foundation).

Schorer, C.E. (1965) The Ganser Syndrome. *Brit. J. Criminol.* **5**: 120–31.

Scott, D.F. (1978) Psychiatric Aspects of Epilepsy. *Brit. J. Psychiat.* **132**: 417–30.

Scott, P.D. (1964) Approved School Success Rates. *Brit. J. Criminol.* **4**: 525–56.

—— (1965) Commentary on Schorer (1965).

—— (1969) Crime and Delinquency. *Brit. Med. J.* **I**: 424–26.

—— (1975) Medical Aspects of Delinquency. In T. Silverstone

and B. Barraclough (eds) *Contemporary Psychiatry*. Ashford: Headley Brothers.

Selling, L.S. (1940) The Psychiatric Findings in the Cases of 500 Traffic Offenders and Accident-Prone Drivers. *American J. Psychiat.* **97**: 68–79. Quoted in Guze (1976).

Shapiro, A. (1969) Delinquent and Disturbed Behaviour Within the Field of Mental Deficiency. In A.V.S. de Rueck, R. Porter (eds) *The Mentally Abnormal Offender*. London: J. and A. Churchill (for CIBA Foundation).

Slater, E. and Roth, M. (1969) *Clinical Psychiatry* (3rd edition). London: Bailliere Tindall and Cassell.

Stott, D.H. (1963) New Possibilities in the Aetiology of Delinquency. *Int. Annals. Criminol.* **2**: 1–11.

Szasz, T. (1962) *The Myth of Mental Illness*. London: Secker and Warburg.

Thompson, C.B. (1937) A Psychiatric Study of Recidivists. *Amer. J. Psychiat.* **94**: 591–604.

Tinklenberg, J. (1972) *Drugs and Crime. A Consultant's Report Prepared for the National Commission on Marihuana and Drug Abuse.* Quoted in Guze (1976).

Topp, D.O. (1973) Fire as a Symbol and as a Weapon of Death. *Med. Sci. Law.* **13**: 79–86.

Trethowan, W.H. (1973) *Psychiatry* (3rd edition). London: Bailliere Tindall.

Tupin, J.P., Mahar, D. and Smith, D. (1973) Two Types of Violent Offenders with Psychosocial Descriptors. *Dis. Nerv. Syst.* **34**: 356–63.

Tutt, N. (1971) The Subnormal Offender. *Brit. J. Mental Subnorm.* **17**: 42–7.

Valentine, M. (1955) *Introduction to Psychiatry* (1st edition). Edinburgh: E. and S. Livingstone.

Walker, N. (1968) *Crime and Insanity in England (Vol. 1)*. Edinburgh: Edinburgh University Press. (p. 4).

Weber, H. (1953) The 'Borderline Defective' Delinquent. *Brit. J. Delinq.* **III**: 173–84.

West, D.J. (1963) *The Habitual Prisoner*. London: Macmillan.

—— (1965) *Murder followed by Suicide*. London: Heinemann.

—— (Ed.) (1969) *Criminological Implications of Chromosome*

Abnormalities. Cambridge: Institute of Criminology.

Wing, J.K. (1978) Diagnosing Schizophrenia. *New Society* **818**: 535–36.

Woddis, G.M. (1957) Depression and Crime. *Brit. J. Delinq.* **VIII**: 85–94.

—— (1964)Clinical Psychiatry and Crime. *Brit. J. Criminol.* **4**: 443–60.

Woodward, M. (1955) The Role of Low Intelligence in Delinquency. *Brit. J. Delinq.* **VI**: 281–303.

FURTHER READING

More detailed coverage of psychiatric material may be found in the following textbooks:

Fish, F.J. (1978) *An Outline of Psychiatry for Students and Practitioners* (3rd edition) (edited by Max Hamilton). Bristol: John Wright.

Forrest, A.D., Affleck, J.W., and Zealley, A.K. (1978) *A Companion to Psychiatric Studies* (2nd edition). Edinburgh: Churchill-Livingstone.

Rees W.L. (1976) *A Short Text-book of Psychiatry* (2nd edition). London: Hodder and Stoughton.

Current issues and dilemmas are well reviewed in:

Clare, A. (1976) *Psychiatry in Dissent. Controversial Issues in Thought and Practice.* London: Tavistock.

Wing, J.K. (1978) *Reasoning About Madness.* Oxford: Oxford University Press.

—— (Ed.) (1978)*Schizophrenia. Towards a New Synthesis.* London: Academic Press.

On epilepsy and allied disorders see:

Lishman, W.A. (1978) *Organic Psychiatry.* Oxford: Blackwell (Chapter 7).

Penfield, W. (1975) *The Mystery of the Mind. A Critical Study of*

Consciousness and the Human Brain. Princeton N.J.: Princeton University Press.
Scott, D.F. (1978) *About Epilepsy* (3rd edition). London: Duckworth.

On mental subnormality see:

Ward-Heaton, W.A. (1967) *Mental Subnormality. Subnormality and Severe Subnormality*. Bristol: John Wright.
—— (1977) *Left Behind: A Study of Mental Handicap.* Plymouth: Macdonald and Evans.

On psychiatry and crime generally see:

MacDonald, J.M. (1969) *Psychiatry and the Criminal*. Illinois: Charles Thomas.
Sadoff, R.L. (1975) *Forensic Psychiatry*. Illinois: Charles Thomas.

CHAPTER FOUR

Psychiatry, the courts, and the penal system*

> Between the bishops who assure us that the
> family is the one and only seedbed of all the
> virtues, and the psychiatrists who warn us
> that it is the hotbed of all the vices, we hardly
> know how to advise any child to enter upon
> the hazard of existence.
>
> DOROTHY L. SAYERS

In the two previous chapters I endeavoured to show some
aspects of the relationship between mental disorder, criminal
responsibility, and criminal behaviour. In this chapter, I propose to discuss some of the ways in which the courts seek
psychiatric help and to consider some of the expectations
shown by sentencers and probation officers concerning
psychiatric services. I shall also comment briefly upon the role
that psychiatry may play within the penal system once the
accused is in custody or has been sentenced. Before dealing
with these matters more specifically it will be useful to detail
briefly some historical background to this topic, since this
history has had (and continues to have) a marked influence
upon the ways in which psychiatry and the law can operate
either as 'warring partners' or coexist as companionable bed-
fellows.

* Some of the statistical and case material in this chapter has appeared in two
journal articles. I am grateful to the *Institute for the Study and Treatment of
Delinquency* for permission to quote from my paper 'Psychiatric Services and
the Magistrates' and Juvenile Courts' which appeared in the *British Journal of
Criminology* 15(4) 1975, and to the Editor of *Medicine, Science and the Law,* to
quote from my paper 'Remands for Psychiatric Reports' which appeared in
Medicine, Science and the Law 16(2) 1976.

Harper (1974) has made the significant point that the influence of the 'mental health professions' is greatly affected by the varying dominance of two differing philosophies. The first she describes as a 'conservative philosophy'. This holds that man is innately evil and that in as much as deviance resides in the individual, then corrective measures should seek to change that person. The second philosophy, she suggests, holds that people are 'essentially good', but, as they are shaped by their environments, any corrective measures to be applied should seek to change that environment; such a philosophy is regarded essentially as liberal or reformist. We would have to admit that such a 'neat' distinction between these two philosophies is somewhat simplistic; nevertheless, it holds the germ of two ideologies that have significantly influenced approaches to the treatment of offenders.

Foucault (1978) has recently surveyed the 'psychiatrization' of delinquency' in the eighteenth, nineteenth, and early twentieth centuries. In doing so he has demonstrated the complex web of circumstances that led to increasing psychiatric intervention in judicial and penal matters. He comes to a number of conclusions, some of which are pertinent to the matters to be discussed in this chapter.

(1) The intervention of 'psychiatric medicine' in the nineteenth century penal system was 'neither the consequence nor the simple development of the traditional theory of the irresponsibility of those suffering from *dementia* or *furor*' (italics in the original). (See also Chapter 2.)

(2) Such intervention arose from the 'functioning of medicine as a [form of] . . . public hygiene' and from the operation of legal punishment as a means of changing the individual.

(3) Foucault also stresses that psychiatric intervention was closely bound up with the development of increasing *state control* over the individual in the nineteenth century.

(4) Psychiatry in the nineteenth century was used to delineate those individuals who were 'dangerous' and the stigmata that accompanied this delineation (e.g. moral and instinctive insanity and degeneration). (See also Chapter 6.)

(5) Developments in psychiatry led to the abandonment of the idea that mental illness was merely an affliction of thought or of consciousness but that it also affected emotions and instincts.

(6) In order to deal with incomprehensible behaviour — whether it took the form of a bizarre killing or some minor peculation, new legal-psychiatric categories were introduced. Foucault quotes the following in illustration; Necrophilia (1840), Kleptomania (around 1860), Exhibitionism (around 1876) and the legal 'annexation of behaviour like pederasty and sadism'.

Foucault reminds us, therefore, in his illuminating sociolegal commentary that the developing relationship between psychiatry and law was not only complex but inextricably bound up with developments in the behavioural sciences, in philosophy, and politics.

During the twentieth century, psychiatrists have become increasingly involved in offering opinions about a wide range of social behaviour that goes far beyond that of formal mental illness. Some people consider that these excursions have gone too far; to be fair, some psychiatrists have tried to resist the pressures upon them to pass opinion upon such matters as personal happiness, immorality, and politics. One such psychiatrist has said:

> 'In deviation from the normal, particularly where behaviour is concerned, there may not necessarily be a medical contribution at all. The treatment may be purely legal or social action. The aim is to bring the behaviour into conformity . . . the psychiatrist comes into the study of some human problems only by invitation, and this invitation may not be wholehearted. *It is as if the psychiatrist is expected to claim authority in every problem of living, only to have that claim challenged even while his help is being sought* . . . [my italics].'
>
> (Kahn 1971)

It is as though society has tried to re-deify the physician in his guise of psychiatrist; an interesting reversion to ancient times when priest and physician were indeed quite often one and the same person (Prins and Whyte 1972). In support of this contention we may note that Zeegers has recently written of 'The Many Headed Psychiatrist', identifying, amongst others, the following hydra-like appendages – Physician, King, Poker Player, Priest, Judge, and Police Officer (Zeegers 1978). Of course, it is not only the psychiatrist who may appear in this hydra-like form; the same ascribed roles can be found in other categories of physicians, however they seem likely to be seen more dramatically and emotively in the psychiatrist (see also Robitscher 1978).

Whatever the reasons for this increasing involvement of psychiatry within the criminal courts and the penal system, we must agree with Grunhut's summary of the position:

'The recognition of medical cases within the orbit of criminal liability bears witness to the growing tendency of modern psychiatry to extend its scope beyond the treatment of mental disease and the care of mental defectives into the field of personal conflicts within the sphere of normal mental life. In the administration of criminal justice, medical psychology is no longer restricted to the negative function of determining the limits of criminal responsibility, but has become part of preventive medicine by contributing a rational classification of offenders and by the design and application of remedial treatment of social deviants . . .'

(Grunhut 1963)

The degree to which psychiatry has 'offered a rational classification of offenders' and the extent to which it has offered significant advances in treatment is perhaps more open to question; some aspects of this will be touched upon later in this chapter.

Legal and administrative procedures

Before proceeding to offer some analysis of the expectations of psychiatric services held by sentencers and others, it seems important to set out very briefly the legal and administrative procedures for obtaining psychiatric reports and to outline the psychiatric 'disposals' that are available to the courts. Some of these were referred to in passing in Chapter 2; it will now be necessary to expand upon that brief exposition at this point.

REMANDS FOR PSYCHIATRIC REPORTS

The power to remand for medical (psychiatric) reports in the magistrates' court derives from Section 26 of the Magistrates' Courts Act, 1952. Under this section a court may remand on bail or in custody for a medical report if satisfied that an offence has been committed but is of the opinion that an enquiry ought to be made into the accused's mental or physical condition.* However, the accused can only be remanded *to prison* under this section if the offence is one for which he could be sent to prison *if convicted*. This provision for remanding for reports *prior to conviction* is valuable since it enables a court, if the accused is found upon examination to be suffering from mental illness or *severe* subnormality (but *not* psychopathy or subnormality), to order detention in hospital without proceeding to conviction.

In addition to their powers under Section 26 of the Magistrates' Courts Act, magistrates have powers under Section 14(3) of the same Act to remand a convicted offender for medical or other reports whether or not the offence is one that carries a sentence of imprisonment. If the defendant is remanded in custody for reports, the remand period is for three weeks at a time; if reports are to be obtained on bail, the court may (under Section 30 of the Criminal Justice Act, 1967) remand for four weeks at a time. There are variations in attitude towards remands on bail or in custody as we shall see later. It is difficult to obtain firm figures for the numbers of persons remanded on bail for psychiatric reports, but it has been calculated that about one third of all remands on bail are

* The terms 'medical report' and 'psychiatric report' tend to be used synonymously. Most remands are in fact for *psychiatric* examination, which may of course include an investigation of the accused person's physical health. Remands for the *specific* investigation of physical health are not common. In this chapter I shall also use the terms *medical* and *psychiatric* synonymously.

for reports of one kind or another (for example, medical or social background reports) (Gibson 1960). With regard to remands in custody for medical reports, there were some 6,000 reports asked for in 1961 and nearly double that number (11,900) in 1975 (Home Office 1961 and 1975). It seems likely that larger numbers of offenders could be examined on bail than is the case at the present time; indeed, it appears that courts are reluctant to use bail facilities even when these are made available specifically. In 1973, the Home Office indicated that bail facilities existed for 'out-patient' examination at four remand prisons, but to date the take up for this provision has been very disappointing.

The procedures outlined above relate to the provision of reports for the magistrates' courts. Higher Courts also obtain psychiatric and other reports; their authority to do this derives generally from the extensive powers of Judges to remand defendants for a variety of purposes. Although, as we shall see later, the number of instances in which psychiatric reports are asked for by all courts is very small, it is of interest to note that the degree to which the court accepts and acts upon a recommendation for psychiatric treatment is usually high. Thus, Sparks (1966), concluded that the 'courts followed definite recommendations for mental treatment in 90 per cent of the cases in which such recommendations were made' and De Berker (1960) reports a 92 per cent agreement rate. Other writers have found slightly lower agreement rates – mainly in relation to juveniles; Clouston and Lightfoot (1953) – 82 per cent; Litauer (1957) – 82.7 per cent; and Kahn and Nursten (1963) – 84 per cent. However, in some of these instances the psychiatrists were exercising a wider brief than a mere recommendation for psychiatric treatment, and were suggesting additional forms of disposal to the court.

The Butler Committee (Home Office and DHSS 1975) examined certain aspects of the facilities available for medical examination. They were concerned that as many offenders as possible should be examined on bail or on similar conditions.*

* It should be noted here that the Bail Act, 1976 introduces a general presumption in favour of bail for all defendants.

(In Scotland, the court can make an order for hospital examination. In England and Wales the requirement to reside in hospital is merely a condition of a defendant's bail.) The Butler Committee identified four situations in which there seemed to be a need for a court to have power to remand a mentally disordered person to hospital as an alternative to a custodial remand.

(1) Where a medical report is required on a convicted defendant.
(2) Where a defendant requires medical care during a custodial remand.
(3) Where a period in hospital is required to determine whether a Hospital Order would be the most suitable form of disposal for a convicted offender.
(4) Where a defendant is found to be 'under disability in relation to the trial' but the medical advice indicates the possibility of recovery within a few months; at least to the point at which he would be fit to stand trial. (See Chapter 2.)

The Committee proposed the creation of a new form of court order for all the situations outlined above. This would be available equally at Special Hospitals or local psychiatric hospitals and would provide for the remand of a defendant to a particular hospital for a specified period of time. It would last a maximum of three months in situations (1) and (2) above and for three months extendable by a month at a time up to a maximum of six months in situations (3) and (4). 'Remand to hospital' would only be considered if remand on bail was not feasible. In general, these proposals have been welcomed though some people have expressed concern that difficulties would arise if all four situations were to be covered by the same form of order; some people have queried whether the resources would be available for such remands and others have considered a three-month period too long.

POWERS OF THE COURTS TO MAKE ORDERS FOR
PSYCHIATRIC TREATMENT

We noted in Chapter 2 that in certain instances the police
might decide not to take prosecutory action in respect of a
person who had committed a criminal offence if he was considered to be clearly mentally disordered. However, if a person
is found guilty of an offence and his mental state is successfully
pleaded in mitigation, the court may proceed to make one of
the orders listed below, or, it may choose to deal with the
defendant in such a way that will facilitate arrangements for
voluntary treatment (for example, by way of a fine, or a condi-
tional discharge). Alternatively, the court may decide, whatever the psychiatric factors in mitigation may be, that a custodial penalty is the only appropriate course of action and
impose a sentence of imprisonment.

The powers of courts to make more formal psychiatric 'disposals' derive from the Mental Health Act, 1959, and the
Powers of Criminal Courts Act, 1973. These are now summarized briefly below.

(A) *Hospital and guardianship orders*
(1)   Section 60 (1) of the Mental Health Act, 1959 enables
      courts to make hospital orders or guardianship orders, *in
      the event of:*
      (a) Conviction for an offence (but, as we have seen
          above, in certain cases they may make an order with-
          out proceeding to conviction).
      (b) *Two* doctors (at least one of whom is approved by a
          local health authority for the purpose under Section
          28 of the Act) stating that the offender is suffering
          from mental illness, psychopathic disorder, subnor-
          mality, severe subnormality of a nature or degree
          *which warrants detention for medical treatment or reception
          into guardianship.*
      (c) *A hospital is willing to accept the person or the local health
          authority is willing to receive him into guardianship.*

(d) The circumstances are such that an order is the most suitable method of dealing with the case.

(2) *Orders for Restriction*. (Section 65 of the Mental Health Act.) These may be made by *Crown Courts*, if the protection of the public seems to require this, having regard to the nature of the offence, the antecedents of the offender, and the possible risk of his committing a further offence if he is set at liberty prematurely. *The patient may not be set at liberty without the consent of the Home Secretary.*

(3) *Power to Transfer*. A person already in custody (either undergoing sentence or awaiting trial), whose mental state becomes such as to require compulsory detention in a hospital, may be transferred under Sections 72 and 73 of the Mental Health Act, 1959.

(B) *Probation and mental treatment*

Section 3 of the Powers of Criminal Courts Act, 1973 enables a court to make a probation order (for a period not exceeding three years) with a requirement that the offender submit to in- or out-patient psychiatric treatment provided that:

(1) The patient consents. (Unlike the case of the hospital order where the consent of the offender is *not* required.)

(2) A hospital (or other establishment) will receive him, and is able to provide treatment. Hospitals have become increasingly reluctant to accept offender/patients in recent years.

(3) The oral or written evidence of *one* doctor (approved under Section 28 of the Mental Health Act) indicates that the offender's condition requires, and may be susceptible to treatment, but is not such to warrant his detention in pursuance of a hospital order.

Numbers of orders made

The Courts do not make extensive use of either Hospital or Psychiatric Probation Orders.* Approximately 1,500 of each

* The use of Hospital Orders has in fact been declining quite sharply in recent years – see Chapter 11.

type of order are made every year. Guardianship Orders under the Mental Health Act (which give the local authority the same rights over the person made subject of the order as those exercised by parents over a child under 14) are used very rarely indeed. The Butler Committee (Home Office and DHSS 1975) suggested that more use should be made of this form of disposal and suggested that local authorities could well view the use of such orders more positively.

(In the final chapter of this book I shall consider some of the problems that face those who would seek to implement the orders outlined above and I shall make some observations concerning their effectiveness.)

Expectations of magistrates and others

Over the years, magistrates and sentencers in the courts of higher jurisdiction have made comment upon the help they consider a psychiatrist might give the court. They have also commented upon what facts his report should contain. Coddington (1950), writing on the criteria for remands for psychiatric reports, suggested that these would include:

'any odd, or disinterested behaviour of the defendant, charges of sexual offences, of petty thefts of useless articles, or repeated thefts of the same article, or from a multiple store; a sudden outbreak of a series of similar offences after a blameless life, offences committed in circumstances where they would certainly be detected, or otherwise involving a risk out of all proportion to the expected gain; and finally a record of ill-health, or of nervous breakdown or of serious family discord . . .'

Coddington's criteria seem somewhat all-embracing and if applied in all cases would involve psychiatrists in examining a very large number of offenders. But, as we shall see shortly, a group of magistrates and probation officers whose opinions were sought by means of a questionnaire, came up with very similar lists. Page (1948), a former Metropolitan magistrate of considerable experience, stressed the need for the psychiatrist to always be an independent witness and to avoid appearing to take sides. Henriques (1951), a London juvenile court magistrate of many years standing, expected the psychiatrist to take 'the trouble to find out exactly the powers of the court and the kind of information required . . .' At the time that Henriques was writing, there were probably fewer psychiatrists involved generally or more specifically in court work than there are today; postgraduate training in psychiatry now includes a fair degree of emphasis on forensic matters, information concerning the composition and powers of courts, and the resources available for dealing with offenders. The penologist Fox (1952) – a former Chairman of the Prison Commission – in an overview of the examination of offenders by the courts, stated the general aim of such examination to be as follows:

'. . . to provide the judge with data that will help him (i) determine responsibility [see Chapters 2 and 3] (ii) to give full weight both to the more obvious motives behind the crime and to those hidden in the mind of the offender; (iii) to determine the most appropriate sentence and to appreciate the medical, social and psychological issues affecting all therapeutic measures influenced by his decision . . .'

A similar view was put forward in the report of the Steatfeild Committee in 1961 (Home Office 1961). Sparks (1966), in his study of the use of psychiatric remands by three London Metropolitan magistrates' courts, concluded that the proportion of offenders remanded for psychiatric reports varied according to the policies and views of individual magistrates; this is confirmed to some extent by my more recent survey – to be reported upon later. Clearly, the degree to which magistrates are made aware of the importance of psychological and psychiatric factors during their training will have an important bearing upon the ways in which they see the value of psychiatric services. Some courses for magistrates in training place considerable emphasis upon these factors and psychiatrists make a useful contribution to the training programme. Although little work has been done to assess the effects of such training on magistrates, a start has been made by Lemon (1974). He found that the recently introduced compulsory initial training programmes for magistrates had a 'demonstrable effect upon . . . attitudes and on their sentencing practice.'

Psychiatrists and their co-workers have also made known their views upon what a court may expect of a psychiatrist and how he views his own role. As long ago as 1927 Norwood East was stressing the need for psychiatrists to be impartial in their reporting (East 1927). In 1948 Kennedy stressed the need for the psychiatrist's view to be easily understood by the court: 'Any view that cannot be put into plain English is quite likely not to be a sound one . . .' Some years later, Neustatter (1967) found himself in agreement with the judicial view already quoted that independence was of primary importance. Scott (1953) tried to sum up the needs of both sides: 'The psychiatrist's report to the court should be clearly understandable, accurate, logical, modest, and appearing to be made by a physician, and therefore by one who is impartial and genuinely concerned with the welfare of the offender . . .' In a later paper, he made the interesting and somewhat controversial suggestion that the psychiatrist may not necessarily be the best man for the job in making this kind of investigation, since in 'not more than 17 per cent of cases can a classical psychiatric diagnosis be given . . .' (Scott 1960). This somewhat unusual statement may be explained in part by the fact that Scott was accustomed to working with a closely knit socio-psychiatric team; he was possessed of a very happy aptitude for eliciting the best efforts from his colleagues and for enabling them to feel fully and equally involved in the compilation of the final report to the court. Scott's suggestion concerning accuracy, modesty, and logicality, are echoed in a more recent paper by another forensic psychiatrist, Gibbens (1974). Examples of the views of a number of other workers may be found in West (1971), Dell and Gibbens (1971), Kolvin and Ounsted (1968 a and b), Tennent (1971), Woodside (1971, 1976), and Bluglass (1979).

FREQUENCY OF REMANDS FOR REPORTS

Reference has been made already to the procedure for remanding for reports. Although, from the small number of studies that have been undertaken, there is found to be some variation in the frequency of requests for reports from one part of the country to the next, it seems safe to conclude from these surveys (Sparks 1966; Prins 1976; Soothill and Pope 1974; Gibbens, Soothill, and Pope 1977) that reports are asked for overall in about 2 per cent of cases. However, there is considerable variation in relation to the *type of crime* committed. For more serious (indictable) offences, the proportion may rise to something over 8 per cent and for less serious (summary) offences it is likely to be as low as about 1 per cent. There is also variation in remanding practice as between different parts of the country. Gibbens, Soothill, and Pope (1977) found that there were considerable differences between the Wessex region and the London Metropolitan Court area. This cannot be accounted for entirely by the different types of criminals in these two areas (though London may certainly attract more psychotic vagrant types). The differences are more likely to arise as a result of the varying attitudes on the part of sentencers in different parts of the country. Much will also depend upon the outlook and skills of those advising the magistrates in the first instance – namely the probation officers. The Butler Committee suggested that probation officers should play a more prominent role in the initial screening of defendants for signs of possible mental disorder. 'We propose that greater use should be made of social enquiry reports as a screening process for mental disorder and to indicate the need for a full psychiatric report' (Home Office and DHSS 1975). This recommendation has implications for the future training of probation officers. It is my experience that not all probation officers (and other social workers for that matter) are as good at spotting the signs of likely mental disorder as they might be. I shall return to this important topic in Chapter 6. Clearly, as Gibbens, Soothill, and Pope (1977) point out, the *reasons* for requesting reports are of fundamental importance. Sometimes, one suspects if the person remanded for a report has been in custody there may have been an implicit punitive element involved. The magistrates may hope that three weeks in custody to savour something of imprisonment will help the offender to consider the 'error of his ways'. That this is a quite improper use of remand for enquiries was established in a High Court case as long ago as 1939, but one suspects that it still occurs from time to time. In a recent paper, Faulk and Trafford (1975) have shown that in at least one court area remands for reports in custody were only made when this was imperative. One wishes that this state of affairs existed over the country as a whole.

Because of these doubts and difficulties I was anxious to investigate the attitudes of magistrates and probation officers towards psychiatric services. The detailed findings are reported upon elsewhere (Prins 1975, 1976) but it will be helpful to summarize here the main results. The study was mounted in a large Northern town. Both magistrates and probation officers were issued with largely similar questionnaires eliciting their views on a number of matters concerning psychiatric services.

Magistrates

Some 39 per cent of the magistrates replied (105 circulated: 41 replies received). *Table 4(1)* indicates the types of offence in which the magistrates would seek a psychiatric opinion.

Table 4(2) indicates the factors *other than the offence* which would lead magistrates to seek a psychiatric opinion.

Probation Officers

All twenty-six members of the probation service in question were circulated with the questionnaire. Twenty responded – a response rate of 78 per cent.

Table 4(3) indicates the types of offence in which the probation officer would suggest that the court seek a psychiatric opinion.

Table 4(4) indicates the factors *other than the offence* which

Table 4(1)   *Types of offence in which the magistrates would seek a psychiatric opinion*

Sexual*	28
Drugs	14
Wanton damage to property **	6
Shoplifting***	13
Offences out of keeping with previous conduct	2
Violence	6
Habitual drunkenness	2
First-time theft	1
Offences against relatives or family	1
Obvious police haters	1
Persistent (habitual) offenders	13
Stealing or pilfering	3
Breach of probation	1
Gambling****	1
Taking and driving away	4
Infanticide	1
Cruelty to children	3
Respondents N = 38*****	

* This description included indecent exposure, incestuous behaviour, assaults on young children, gross indecency, indecent assault, rape, 'Peeping Tom'.
** Including two references to arson.
*** Several magistrates stressed the importance of frequent apparently irrational offences.
**** Two magistrates suggested the 'compulsive' nature of this kind of offence.
***** In a number of sections, the total number of answers considerably exceeds the number of respondents since multiple answers were given in most replies. There were three non-respondents to this part of the questionnaire.

would lead the probation officers to seek psychiatric opinion.

Comparison of views of magistrates and probation officers

From the statistical material gathered, a limited attempt was

Table 4(2) *Factors other than the nature of the offence which would lead the magistrates to ask for a psychiatric opinion*

Appearance, demeanour, and attitude in court	13
Previous offences of the same type	7
Offences out of character with previous conduct*	15
Contemplation of removal from home or concern about apparent ineffectiveness of previous treatment ordered by the court	6
Previous medical/mental history	23
Age of offender	3
Stressful circumstances at the time	1
Views of defending counsel**	1
Unable to generalize	1
Respondents N = 38***	

* One or two magistrates referred to such indicators as inexplicable behaviour or possible 'pleas for help'.
** 'Where one can trust to the good sense of counsel', as one magistrate put it.
*** Three non-respondents to this part of the questionnaire. Two magistrates did not answer the questionnaire; they indicated lack of knowledge, due to recent appointment to the bench. The other stated that a magistrate could recognize a mental disorder without the help of a psychiatrist!

made to compare and contrast the views of magistrates and probation officers both in relation to the types of offence for which a psychiatric report should be obtained and in relation to factors other than the nature of the offence. No detailed comparison is possible, but some general trends emerge. Proportionately *fewer* magistrates considered that sexual offences should be referred for psychiatric examination, and *fewer* felt that drug offences also required this attention. Many *more* magistrates than probation officers considered that shoplifting deserved the attentions of psychiatric inquiry, and one wondered whether 'middle-class' attitudes were influential here. Conversely, there was a slightly larger proportion of magistrates who considered that cruelty to children, and taking and driving away, warranted further inquiry. There is

Table 4(3)   *Types of offences in which officers would suggest that the court seek a psychiatric opinion*

Sexual*	19
Drugs	9
Wanton damage to property**	5
Arson	8
Shoplifting	2
Repeated or single offences with no clear motivation	7
Violence***	8
Theft of unusual items	2
Persistent drinking (alcoholism)	3
Neglect of and cruelty to children	1
Breaches of the peace ('peeping Tom', obscene phone calls)	1
Taking and driving away (under-25 age group)	1
Respondents N= 19	

* Various types specified (e.g. offences with children, indecent exposure, indecency with adolescents, incest). In their replies to this section, two officers referred to the circumstances of the offence as indicators for psychiatric opinion rather than the offence itself. One of these was a very experienced senior officer, and the other was young, university trained, and in his first year of service.
** One respondent referred specifically to wilful damage to windows.
*** Serious or persistent violence towards family members, or apparently motiveless violence.

some slight evidence to suggest that the magistrates, compared with the probation officers, were probably more concerned to seek psychiatric help in cases where the protection of the public was involved, e.g. cases of 'persistent offending' (*not mentioned by the probation officers*), 'obvious police haters', and 'breach of probation'. Against this feeling, however, must be set the fact that a small number of magistrates saw the significance of 'compulsiveness' in certain types of offenders.

Proportionally, a slightly larger number of magistrates regarded the demeanour of the offender in court as important, which probably reflects the way in which they are able to

Table 4(4) *Factors other than the nature of the offence that would lead officers to suggest a psychiatric opinion*

Strange behaviour in court or at interview	5
Evidence of tensions within the home, faulty family relations	5
Erratic conduct, or conduct out of keeping with previous behaviour (e.g. at school or at work)	10
Physical abnormality or illness	3
History of mental illness in defendant, or in family background*	17
Intangible factors	2
Second opinion	1
Respondents N = 19	

* Including low intelligence, autism, alcoholism.

see the case 'as a whole' and to observe rather more objectively the demeanour of the offender as the case is 'unfolded' before them. The probation officers are probably more likely to see the importance of early history and the personal and dynamic aspects of the offender's past and present behaviour. This last supposition seems supported by the fact that *fewer* magistrates saw the previous history of the offender as important (though the number is still high), and *fewer* considered that offences out of keeping with previous behaviour were of significance. Whereas *no* probation officers indicated that psychiatric advice might be advantageous at a point when a decision to remove from home might have to be made, six magistrates did so. Although the number is small, it is an interesting indication of the manner in which magistrates may have difficulties in making these important decisions in the lives of offenders. As with the comparisons made concerning types of offence, the comparisons in relation to factors other than the offence reflect differences in perceived roles and the training afforded to the two groups involved. (See also Gibbens, Soothill, and Pope 1977.)

To what extent did the actual practice of the court reflect the views expressed by the magistrates and probation officers?

In order to test the extent to which the views expressed by the magistrates and probation officers were reflected in the actual practice of the courts, figures relating to the number of cases actually remanded for reports, and the total number of offences in these categories, were obtained for the year of the survey. These, and a summary of the expressed views of magistrates and probation officers, are summarized in *Table 4(5)*.

Table 4(5) *Comparison of magistrates' and probation officers' opinions about psychiatric services and the actual practice of the juvenile and adult courts in a selected group of offences (one year period)*

	no. respondents who would ask for report		cases actually remanded for reports		total number of offenders before court	
	magi-strates (N=38)	pro-bation officers (N=19)	adult	juven-ile	adult	juven-ile
Sexual	28	19	3	1	32	13
Drugs	14	9	4	–	31	–
Violence (assault)	6	8	–	3	–	12
Shop-lifting	13	2	2	–	330	–

(For a more detailed breakdown, see Prins (1975).)

It will be seen that although both groups considered that sex offenders and those involved in drug abuse should be investigated psychiatrically, these views were not reflected in the actual remand practice of the court. However, it could be that decisions *not* to remand for psychiatric enquiries were made by the magistrates who did *not* answer the questionnaire, and I had no means of ascertaining whether or not this was case. (See Prins (1975) for fuller discussion of this issue.)

Other matters studied

I was also interested in a number of other matters, including preferences for reports being obtained on bail or in custody. (It will be recalled that earlier in this chapter I indicated that bail facilities seem to be under-used.) Some of these other findings are summarized below.

(1) Whereas the probation officers tended to suggest that the court seek a psychiatric opinion in cases where the defendant had a known psychiatric history, the magistrates appeared to regard appearance and demeanour in court as being important as criteria for remands.

(2) Both groups considered that sex offenders and those involved in drug abuse should be investigated psychiatrically, *but these views were not reflected in the actual practice of the courts.*

(3) A higher percentage of magistrates considered that shoplifting offences merited psychiatric enquiry and it was thought that class attitudes might be relevant in this context. Although the magistrates as a group did not appear to pay as much attention to psychiatric history as did the probation officers, one or two of them considered that apparent compulsive behaviour in offenders merited further investigation.

(4) Overall the magistrates' answers indicated a greater (but perhaps understandable) degree of concern for public safety than did those of the probation officers.

(5) A considerable number of magistrates indicated that they welcomed psychiatric help in difficult decisions concerning removal from home. (See also Gibbens, Soothill, and Pope 1977.)

(6) A larger number of magistrates than anticipated appeared to welcome a firm recommendation by the psychiatrist; this again supports the point made in (5) above, that they

appear to require help with the problem of decision-making. This supposition is further attested to by Soothill (1974), who examined the extent to which certain offenders were subjected to repeated medical remands.

(7) A larger number of the magistrates than anticipated appeared dissatisfied with facilities for remand for reports in custody *to the prison*; of the two provisions for reports to be obtained on bail – *out-patient* and *in-patient*, they much preferred the latter.

(8) The probation officers were understandably more concerned with the degree of cooperation they could anticipate from the offender during proposed treatment than were the magistrates. Bowden (1978) has recently shown that when a psychiatrist offers clinical facilities within a probation office, although the 'take up' may be small, the opportunities for consultation are welcomed.

(9) Rather surprisingly, a larger percentage (86 per cent) of the probation officers were satisfied with the service provided than the magistrates (73 per cent). However, both groups suggested that more *special and secure units* were required, and that a speeding-up of the examination process was also necessary.

The importance of attitudes has already been stressed. Gibbens, Soothill, and Pope (1977) also comment on this matter. They refer to:

'complex relationships between probation officer, magistrates, solicitors, and psychiatrists – the probation officer who adjusts to the demands of his magistrates in deciding what is or is not possible, the magistrates whose scepticism about psychiatry is mirrored in the local area by the attitudes of offenders themselves and society around them . . .'

Bowden (1978) suggests that 'existing cooperation between probation officers and psychiatrists is ineffective and is in need of review'. He suggests that 'inadequate liaison between the professions could be remedied if psychiatrists provided a consultancy service to probation officers . . .' Unhappily, his own offer does not seem to have been taken up with any great enthusiasm. (See (8) above.) In my view, the problem has deeper roots. Until doctors and social workers are made more aware of the differences and similarities in their roles at an *early stage of their respective trainings,* we shall not achieve much progress by merely trying to develop good working relationships at the post-basic-qualification level. Some of the newer medical schools (for example, at Leicester) are trying to remedy this deficiency by not only exposing medical students to the behavioural and social sciences at a very early stage in their training, but are also trying to provide opportunities for shared learning experiences between medical undergraduates and social work students. This is not to deny the relevance or importance of similar opportunities at postgraduate level, but contact at an early stage in the careers of both professional groups could do much to remove the understandable apprehensions and misconceptions that each may hold of the other.

What kind of cases are remanded for reports? — some case illustrations

I have already provided some statistical information concerning the types of offences considered worthy of further investigation. By way of bringing this part of the chapter to a conclusion, it may be helpful to provide some case illustrations to put flesh as it were upon the statistical 'bare bones'.

(A) *Juveniles*
(1) Y, aged thirteen years, came before the court for stealing £1.75 in cash. She had three previous offences: breaking and entering and stealing; simple larceny; and stealing a letter from a house. For the first offence she had been discharged conditionally, and for the last two offences placed under supervision on each occasion. The probation officer had suggested a psychiatric report because of the *frequency* of the offences. The child had been ascertained as ESN, was a poor attender at school and suffered from diurnal enuresis. Family background was considered to be poor. She was the eldest of six children. Father and a sister both had convictions, and at

one time the family had been evicted for rent arrears. The father had been married and divorced. The woman he was living with currently was not, however, his legal wife. The psychiatrist thought that further exploration of the family situation was necessary and showed some optimism with regard to prognosis despite the poor family history. He recommended attendance at the child guidance clinic. This recommendation was accepted and a supervision order made with a requirement for treatment.

(2) V, aged fourteen years, came before the court for non-attendance at school. Remand for psychiatric report was recommended by the probation officer. She had no previous record of offences, court appearances, or treatment at a child guidance clinic, etc. However, she had a previous history of non-prosecuted dishonesty, and had been known to the police juvenile liaison officer two years earlier. She stayed out at night and on admission to the assessment centre was found to be verminous. Her history was one of disturbance in early rela-tionships. She came from a family of six children; one brother was away at residential ESN school. Her home was described by the probation officer as 'untidy and dingy'. Her father had left home some years earlier, and her mother had remarried, but had then separated from her second husband. The psychiatrist stated that this child should 'receive sympathetic care and consistent discipline away from home'. The court accepted this recommendation and made a care order.

(3) W, aged twelve years, came before the court for assault occasioning actual bodily harm to a girl. He had no previous court record. The probation officer had discovered a history of aggressiveness during the previous three years and had suggested a psychiatric report. W was the fifth of seven chil-dren. The eldest child was ESN. The family was well known to the social services department. The boy was a poor attender at school and was often dirty and unkempt. He was below aver-age intelligence. There were poor standards in the family and both parents were felt to be inadequate and lacking in control. The psychiatrist did not find any abnormality and recom-mended attendance at the child guidance clinic to improve

self-esteem and to try to ease the family tensions. The court accepted this recommendation and made a supervision order with a requirement that the boy attend the child guidance clinic.

(4) J, aged fifteen years, came before the court for stealing, having with others entered a building as a trespasser. He had a previous court appearance in the same year for housebreaking and larceny and taking and driving away (plus two offences taken into consideration). For these offences he was ordered to attend an attendance centre for twenty-four hours and to make restitution of £11.00. No previous history of other problems was recorded. He attended a high school, but gave a recent history of 'opting out' and of truancy. This boy was the middle of three children (sisters aged sixteen and two years). There were good material standards at home, but the father was away working and there seemed to be a feeling of loss of interest on his part, accompanied by growing insolence on the part of this boy. There was some jealousy of the youngest child and an awareness of the competence of the older one in comparison with himself. The psychiatrist found nothing abnormal and thought that the boy was self-centred and in need of strong supervision. The court made a supervision order.

(5) P, aged eleven years, was before the court for breaking and entering and stealing. He was already in the care of the council having appeared before the juvenile court about two years earlier. He had been seen earlier at the child guidance clinic because of behaviour difficulties whilst in care. Of late he had been particularly unsettled. He was attending an ESN school and was regarded as 'unhappy'. He was one of a family of six. His mother was unable to cope and his father was in prison with a record of previous offences. The psychiatrist recommended placement in either a community home or maladjusted school. The court made a care order.

(B) *Adults*

(1) S, aged thirty-three, came before the court for wilfully ill treating a child in a manner likely to cause injury to health. The

child was her illegitimate daughter aged five years. Both were found in a gas-filled room. The *defending solicitor** asked for a psychiatric report. S had no previous criminal record. She had been separated from her mother in infancy, was with foster parents until the age of twelve years and then the foster mother was taken into hospital. S was a life-long lesbian, with apparently no wish to change. She had served without blemish in the Women's Royal Naval Service and showed a varied, though reasonable, work record. Her family history can be said to be 'weighted' from a psychiatric point of view – her father was admitted to a mental hospital, a brother hanged himself when aged twenty-one years and a sister aged twenty-three years was a mental hospital patient. S had been taken into care after alleged sexual assaults by her father. The psychiatrist found no psychiatric illness apart from the personality deviation of lesbianism and he did not make a specific psychiatric recommendation. The court made a probation order for three years and ordered that the child be brought before the juvenile court.

(2) A, aged sixty years, came before the court charged with two cases of indecent assault on a small boy. The magistrates asked for a psychiatric report. A had three previous offences, including an indecent assault on a girl twenty-three years earlier. The other offences were of receiving. This man had been

---

* Defending counsel (solicitors or barristers) may themselves ask for reports. They may also on occasion have had the defendant medically examined *before* the case comes to court. In my own study (Prins 1976) I found that about a third of the requests for reports in the magistrates' court had emanated from the defence. Gibbens, Soothill, and Pope (1977) report that only a small number of reports emanated from the defence and an even smaller number of unsolicited or voluntary reports were proferred by the prison medical service. As the authors rightly point out, the degree to which 'defence' reports are supplied will be influenced largely by the availability and cooperation of psychiatrists in any given area. In some parts of the country a small number of joint Home Office and NHS consultant forensic psychiatric appointments have been made. It appears that these have not been entirely successful, due no doubt to the problems of conflicting loyalties inherent in such joint arrangements. It seems likely that these appointments upon which so much faith was pinned originally, are likely to be reduced or possibly phased out in the not too distant future. (See also Chapter 11.)

deaf and dumb from birth, and had four siblings who were also deaf. He did well at a school for the deaf and was said to have come from an upper working-class home background where relationships were satisfactory. For most of his working life he had been in the same employment in the meat trade, but latterly had lived on social security benefit. He had married in the 1930s but his wife left him after about five years. The psychiatrist made no specific recommendation, suggesting that he was neither amenable to treatment nor mentally ill. The magistrates fined him for one offence and gave him a suspended prison sentence of six months for the other.

Psychiatric services within the penal system

So far I have discussed mainly the role of psychiatric services in relation to the courts and how such services are proffered. It now remains for us to consider the role of this service within the penal system – that is, once sentence has been passed, or, in more limited circumstances, when the defendant is in custody for any other reason. The role of psychiatry within the penal system is closely bound up with the development of prison medical services in general. The history of the latter has been fully outlined by Prewer (in Blom-Cooper 1974), Topp (1977), and Gunn *et al*. (1978) so that only a very brief outline need be given here. No medical appointments as such seem to have been made within the prisons before the late seventeenth century. Prewer (1974) refers specifically to the year 1692, when one of the surgeons from St Bartholomew's Hospital was appointed to visit the inmates of Newgate. However, it was not until the middle of the eighteenth century that Parliament passed legislation requiring that 'a reputable surgeon or apothecary should be appointed to every prison . . .' Central government oversight of the health of the prison population was recognized in the appointment in 1877 of the first full-time Medical Inspector within the newly established Prison Commission (Topp 1977). We saw earlier in this chapter that towards the end of the nineteenth century and in the early part of the twentieth, as a result of developments in the social and behavioural sciences and in the growing recognition of psychiatry as a respectable speciality in medicine, greater emphasis came to be placed upon the importance of psychological factors in criminality. One of the pioneers in this field was the prison medical officer at Birmingham prison, Hamblin-Smith. In a series of publications in the 1920s and early 1930s he drew attention to the psychological needs of prisoners and to the possibilities of using psychotherapeutic methods. He also urged the need for the closest cooperation between all staff who were concerned with the treatment of the prisoner (Gunn *et al.* 1978: Chapter 1.) However, it was not until just before the outbreak of the Second World War that East and Hubert (1939) produced their now classic report upon the psychological treatment of crime (East and Hubert 1939). One of the most important recommendations of this report was for the creation of a special kind of penal-psychiatric institution. This was to serve three main functions. First, the specialist investigation of specific cases and as a locus for socio-forensic research. Second, as an establishment in which offenders would be subjected to specialized forms of treatment not available in ordinary penal establishments. Third, as an institution in which some attempt could be made to treat the less adequate offender even though the prognosis was considered to be poor. Some twenty-five years were to elapse before the East-Hubert proposals were to be put into effect in the form of Grendon Underwood Psychiatric prison. This is a specialized prison-hospital and the governor is a doctor. The aims and objectives of Grendon and its effectiveness are described by Tollinton (1966), Gray (1973), and more recently in considerable detail by Gunn *et al.* (1978). Suffice it to say at this stage that, not unexpectedly, Grendon has its staunch advocates on the one hand and its more cynical detractors on the other. To maintain a balanced view it is important to remember that Grendon (by prison and psychiatric hospital standards) is still in its infancy and can still be said to be feeling its way. Moreover, as Gunn *et al.* (1978) point out, simple and crude re-conviction rates cannot really be regarded as a satisfactory test of the effectiveness of such establishments.

Much depends upon how one views the function of imprisonment. To suggest that it is merely concerned with crude reconviction rates is to seriously oversimplify a very complex issue. Gunn *et al.* also make the important point that the particular kind of management approaches in use at Grendon – namely an emphasis on the development of self-responsibility within a largely self-governing atmosphere – can be applied elsewhere. There is evidence that this is happening at certain other penal establishments – for example, on selected wings at Wormwood Scrubs and at Parkhurst.

Understandable preoccupation with what has been happening at Grendon has probably detracted publicity from important approaches being pioneered in other establishments. Considerable work has been carried out with sexual offenders at Wormwood Scrubs and work on alcohol addiction has been carried out for some years at Wakefield. Feltham Borstal has pioneered work with the more seriously disturbed young adult offender and psychiatry has played a significant part in the work of that institution.

Psychiatric treatment and management is of course only one part of the work of the prison medical service. The latter serves to provide treatment similar to that available in the National Health Service. As evidence of this, some of our larger prisons have fully equipped hospitals with supporting staffs (nurses, pharmacists, physiotherapists, radiographers) and the aim is to treat all but the most serious or complex cases. However, there are many people who question the advisability (and indeed the viability) of trying to maintain a separate prison medical service with its inevitable isolation from main-stream developments in the National Health Service. Moreover, if, as Topp (1977) suggests, the main *raison d'etre* for the medical officer's presence is 'to ensure that every consideration is given to caring for people who are sick, in fear or are suffering . . .' might not this be better achieved if the doctors carrying out this role were located in the National Health Service? Additionally, it would also be another means of breaking down the barrier the offender so often feels to exist between himself as an inmate and the outside community.

One also wonders to what extent prison medical personnel tend to feel alienated, not only from other prison staff, but more particularly from their colleagues outside. This issue came into prominence recently when certain prison medical officers were accused (wrongly) of drugging large numbers of prisoners for non-therapeutic purposes. For myself, I have no reason to doubt that most, if not all prison medical officers, adopt the same varying ethical positions as do their colleagues outside. Moreover, when the public and the media become hypercritical it is as well to remember that these prison medical staffs are more often than not ministering to a group of people that the rest of us have rejected and stigmatized. It does not make their task any the more easy when the public rush to make what are for the most part ill-founded accusations of malpractice.

Such special vulnerability would confirm me in my view that prison medical staff might have more protection and a lesser degree of alienation if they were part of the National Health Service and not a separate medical service within the penal system.

In the final chapter of this book I shall be examining some of the difficulties that arise in reaching a decision as to whether prison or hospital is the most appropriate place for treatment and custody. There is little doubt at the present time that senior prison medical staff are concerned about the numbers of mentally disordered persons found within the prisons. Indeed, the Director of the Prison Medical Service has recently stated that 'prisons can offer little more than custody to the mentally disordered [and] that a significant number of offenders become mentally disturbed in some way as a result of their containment in prison . . .' (Orr 1978). This concern is understandable, but it would be a pity if prisons were merely to become repositories for the intractable cases and because of this, possibilities for therapeutic intervention were removed from penal staffs. Grendon attests to the possibilities of psychiatric-prison type institutions. It also serves as a reminder that those who pioneered the idea (East and Hubert) themselves rejected the idea that the psychiatrically disturbed should always be removed from the prison environment. They had grounds for believing that penal staffs (and especially the prison medical service) could develop special competency in this area of work. What we need is surely a degree of flexibility of movement between prisons and hospitals; a flexibility that is currently difficult to achieve within the somewhat restricted formulae for transfers under the relevant sections of the Mental Health Act. This greater degree of flexibility might be facilitated further if the prison medical staff (psychiatrists and others)* were part of the National Health Service. Boundaries could thus be crossed more easily and as already stated, alienation might be lessened and resources deployed more profitably.

Bartholomew (1970) has summarized the different roles a psychiatrist can play in the penal situation. First, a role in diagnosis and classification – either for the courts, for release (parole) purposes, or for purposes of decision-making in relation to further modes of treatment. Second, staff support and consultation. It is unfortunate that due to pressures of other work, all too few prison psychiatrists – either full- or part-time, find enough opportunities for this very vital work. It also has to be said that this role is not an easy one to assume; not all psychiatrists can carry it easily, and there is little adequate training for it. Third, acting as the head of a psychiatric-penal establishment, as Bartholomew does at Pentridge in Melbourne, Australia, and as the Medical Superintendent does at our own Grendon Prison.

Psychiatrists working in the prison system, like prison probation officers, have their own external affiliations and can thus

* In this chapter I have not included specific reference to the important work of the prison psychological service. Prison psychologists play an important role in offering diagnostic and classificatory facilities. In more recent years they have also become involved in personal and group counselling activities. Ideally, they, the prison medical officers and the social work staffs could work as a treatment team. However, staffing ratios, differences in tenure of appointment, and the differences in perceived roles militate against this to some extent. (For a very useful account of the work of the prison psychological service, see Trasler (1974).)

afford good links with the 'world outside'. Indeed, for the psychiatrist, this may be one of his most important roles. As Topp (1977) suggests, 'The population [they] have to cope with is about the most troublesome, demanding, difficult and disturbed from amongst the population at large. Although they do not endear sympathy, they nevertheless need to be shown it by our caring society, and doctors have an important role to perform in fulfilling this task . . .' Gunn *et al.* emphasize this important link with the community. 'In the future we shall undoubtedly continue to use the prison service for punishment, for containment of the persistently dangerous, for the first stages of treatment of some mentally abnormal offenders . . .' However, they go on to state: 'It will be our decision as a community, whether we also concern ourselves with crime prevention in the community; institutions cannot take that responsibility away from us . . .' Gunn *et al.* (1978).

Conclusion

An historical perspective reveals that over the last two hundred years, psychiatry has played an increasingly influential role in penal affairs. Early on, it was involved primarily with issues concerned with the determination of responsibility, but increasingly it has been expected to offer guidance and advice on numerous other matters, particularly those involving the disposition of a wide range of cases coming before the courts. Within penal institutions psychiatric treatment and management interventions have developed out of the provision of more general prison medical services. Court reporting has claimed pre-eminence over other work such as inmate treatment, staff counselling and support. The use to which psychiatric services are put by the courts and the penal system is significantly determined by prevailing public and professional attitudes towards crime and its causes. The small body of research in this area reveals an understandable ambivalence and uncertainty, on the part of sentencers and social workers on the one hand, and on the part of psychiatrists themselves on the other. It seems likely that improvements could be brought about if all parties concerned could be exposed to the roles and views of the others at an early stage in their respective training programmes. The nature of the likely conflicts in this area demonstrates the inter-disciplinary and 'boundary' nature of this field and has been one of the main justifications for writing not only this particular chapter, but the book. Some of these inter-disciplinary and 'boundary' problems will be commented upon further in the final chapter.

References

Bartholomew, A.A. (1970) The Forensic Psychiatrist's Place in Correction. *Aust. and N.Z. J. of Criminol.* **3**: 83–91.

Bluglass, R. (1979) The Psychiatric Court Report. *Med. Sci. Law* **19**: 121–29.

Bowden, P. (1978) A Psychiatric Clinic in a Probation Office. *Brit. J. Psychiat.* **133**: 448–51.

Clouston, G.S. and Lightfoot, W. (1953) The Child Guidance Clinic and the Juvenile Court. *Brit. J. Delinq.* **4**: 269–80.

Coddington, F.J. (1950) The Probation System Under the Criminal Justice Act. *J. Crim. Sci.* **2**: 31.

De Berker, P. (1960) State of Mind Reports. *Brit. J. Criminol.* **1**: 6–20.

Dell, S. and Gibbens, T.C.N. (1971) Remands of Women Offenders for Medical Reports. *Med. Sci. Law* **11**: 117–27.

East, W.N. (1927) *An Introduction to Forensic Psychiatry in the Criminal Courts.* London: Churchill.

East, W.N. and de B. Hubert, W.H. (1939) *Report on the Psychological Treatment of Crime.* London: HMSO.

Faulk, M. and Trafford, P.A. (1975) The Efficacy of Medical Remands. *Med. Sci. Law* **15**: 276–79.

Foucault, M. (1978) About the Concept of the 'Dangerous Individual' in 19th-Century Legal Psychiatry. *Int. J. Law. and Psychiat.* **1**: 1–18.

Fox. L.W. (1952) Psychological and Social Examination of Delinquents. *Brit. J. Delinq.* **3**: 85–103.

Gibbens, T.C.N. (1974) Preparing Psychiatric Court Reports. *Brit. J. Hosp. Med.* September: 278–84.

Gibbens, T.C.N., Soothill, K.L., and Pope, P.J. (1977) *Medical Remands in the Criminal Court. Maudsley Monographs. No. 25.* Oxford: Oxford University Press.

Gibson, E. (1960) *Time Spent Awaiting Trial. Studies in the Causes of Delinquency and the Treatment of Offenders. No. 2.* London: HMSO.

Gray, W.J. (1973) The English Prison Medical Service; Its Historical Background and More Recent Developments. In *The Medical Care of Prisoners and Detainees.* CIBA Foundation Symposium No. *16.* Amsterdam: Elsevier Excerpta Medica.

Grunhut, M. (1963) *Probation and Mental Treatment.* London: Tavistock.

Gunn, J., Robertson, G., Dell, S., and Way, C. (1978) *Psychiatric Aspects of Imprisonment.* London: Academic Press.

Harper, M.J.R. (1974) Courts, Doctors and Delinquents: An Enquiry into the Uses of Psychiatry in Youth Corrections. *Smith College Studies in Social Work:* **XLIV**: 158–78.

Henriques, B.L.Q. (1951) *Indiscretions of a Magistrate.* London: Harrap.

Home Office (1961) *Report of the Interdepartmental Committee on the Business of the Criminal Courts (Streatfeild Committee)* Cmnd. 1289. London: HMSO.

—— (1961) *Report on the Work of the Prison Department.* London: HMSO.

—— (1975) *Report on the Work of the Prison Department.* London: HMSO.

—— (1977) *Report on the Work of the Prison Department.* London: HMSO.

Home Office and DHSS (1975) *Report of the Committee on Mentally Abnormal Offenders (Butler Committee).* Cmnd. 6244. London: HMSO.

Kahn, J.H. and Nursten, J. (1963) Child Guidance Procedure in Relation to the Juvenile Court. *Brit. J. Criminol.* **3**: 294–301.

Kahn, J.H. (1971) Uses and Abuses of Child Psychiatry: Problems of Diagnosis and Treatment of Psychiatric Disorder. *Brit. J. Med. Psychol.* **44**: 229–38.

Kennedy, A. (1948) Juvenile Delinquency with Special Reference to Remand Homes. *Proc. Royal Soc. Med.* **41**: 197–208.

Kolvin, I. and Ounsted, C. (1968a and b) Survey of Boys on Psychiatric Remand, and Remand Delinquents, the Court and the Psychiatrist. *Med. Sci. Law.* **8**: 88–95 and 109–18.

Lemon, N. (1974) Training, Personality and Attitude as Determinants of Magistrates' Sentencing. *Brit. J. Criminol.* **14**: 34–48.

Litauer, W. (1957) *Juvenile Delinquents in a Psychiatric Clinic.* London: ISTD.

Neustatter, W.L. (1967) The Psychiatrist in the Witness Box. *Jnl. Roy. Soc. Hlth.* **87**: 325–29.

Orr, J.H. (1978) The Imprisonment of Mentally Disordered Offenders. *Brit. J. Psychiat.* **133**: 194–99.

Page, L. (1948) *The Sentence of the Court.* London: Faber and Faber.

Prewer, R.R. (1974) Prison Medicine. In L. Blom-Cooper *Progress in Penal Reform.* Oxford: Oxford University Press.

Prins, H.A. and Whyte, M.B.H. (1972) *Social Work and Medical Practice.* Oxford: Pergamon Press. (Chapter 2).

Prins, H.A. (1975) Psychiatric Services and the Magistrates' and Juvenile Courts. *Brit. J. Criminol.* **15**: 315–32.

—— (1976) Remands for Psychiatric Reports. *Med. Sci. Law* **16**: 129–38.

Robitscher, J. (1978) The Limits of Psychiatric Authority. *Int. J. Law. and Psychiat.* **1**. 183–204.

Scott, P.D. (1953) Reports for Magistrates' Courts. *Brit. J. Delinq.* **4**: 82–98.

—— (1960) Assessing the Offender for the Courts. *Brit. J. Criminol.* **1**: 116–29.

Soothill, K. and Pope, P. (1974) *Medical Remands in Magistrates' Courts.* London: ISTD.

Soothill, K.L. (1974) Repeated Medical Remands. *Med. Sci. Law* **14**: 189–99.

Sparks, R.F. (1966) The Decision to Remand for Mental Examination. *Brit. J. Criminol.* **6**: 6–26.

Tennent, G. (1971) The Use of Remand on Bail or in Custody by the London Juvenile Courts. *Brit. J. Criminol.* **11**: 80–5.

Tollinton, H.P. (1966) Grendon Prison. *Brit. J. Criminol.* **6**: 39–48.

136 *Offenders, Deviants, or Patients?*

Topp, D.O. (1977) The Doctor in Prison. *Med. Sci. Law.* **17**: 261–64.

Trasler, G. (1974) The Role of Psychologists in the Penal System. In Blom-Cooper (ed.) *Progress in Penal Reform.* Oxford: Oxford University Press.

West, A.C. (1971) Medical Treatment as a Condition of Probation. *Brit. J. Criminol.* **11**: 371–81.

Woodside, M. (1971) Probation and Psychiatric Treatment in Edinburgh. *Brit. J. Psychiat.* **118**: 561–70.

—— (1976) Psychiatric Referrals from Edinburgh Courts. *Brit. J. Criminol.* **16**: 20–37.

Zeegers, M. (1978) The Many-Headed Psychiatrist. *Int. J. Law. and Psychiat.* **1**: 167–81.

FURTHER READING

Association for the Psychiatric Treatment of Offenders (1971) *The Court and the Expert: Writing Reports Vol. 1.* APTO Monographs No. 3. London.

Bearcroft, J.S. and Donovan, M.D. (1965) Psychiatric Referrals from Courts and Prisons. *Brit. Med. J.* **2**: 1519–523.

Binns, J.K., Carlisle, D.H., Nimmo, D.H., Park, R.H., and Todd, N.A. (1969a and b) Remanded in Custody for Psychiatric Examination. *and* Remanded in Hospital for Psychiatric Examination. *Brit. J. Psychiat.* **115**: 1125–132 and 1133–139.

Bluglass, R. (1979) The Psychiatric Court Report. *Med. Sci. Law* **19**: 121–29.

Essex-Cater, A. (1961) Boys in Remand – A Study of 367 cases. *Brit. J. Criminol.* **2**: 132–48.

King's Fund Centre and Howard League for Penal Reform (1978) *Medical Services for Prisoners.* London.

Pope, P.J. and Gibbens, T.C.N. (1979) Medical Aspects of Management Problems in Maximum Security Prisons. *Med. Sci. Law* **19**: 111–17.

Prins, H.A. (1969) Survey of the Agencies Dealing with Offenders in a North of England Town. *Int. J. Off. Ther.* **13**: 35–41.

Ratcliffe, T.A. (1951) Co-operation Between Juvenile Courts and Child Guidance Clinics. *Brit. J. Delinq.* **2**: 155–56.

Wardrop, K. (1967) Disturbed Delinquents and the Work of the Forensic Psychiatric Clinic. *Howard J. of Penol. and Crime Prev.* **12**: 93–102.

West, D.J., Bearcroft, J.S., and Smith, A. (1960) The Choice of Bail or Custody for Offenders Remanded for a Psychiatric Report. *Int. J. Soc. Psych.* **6**: 34–50.

CHAPTER FIVE

Psychopathy — concept or chimera? *

'And, therefore, since I cannot prove a lover,
I am determined to prove a villain . . .'

RICHARD III

I have already used the descriptive term psychopathy in Chapters 2 and 3. In this chapter, I wish to examine the concept of psychopathy as a form of personality disorder in more detail and in particular, to trace something of the way in which it was evolved. I shall also comment on the special characteristics of so-called psychopaths, the possible explanations of the causes of this disorder (if this is what indeed it is), and make some suggestions concerning the management of those so described.

'A rose by any other name . . .'

For more than a hundred and fifty years, the condition we have come to describe as psychopathy has proved a fascinating (and sometimes heated) arena for debate within the disciplines of psychiatry, psychology, philosophy, law, and with perhaps a degree of importance not always sufficiently recognized by the

* Parts of this chapter are expanded and modified versions of material that I have published elsewhere. I am grateful to the Institute for the Study and Treatment of Delinquency for permission to reproduce sections of my pamphlet: *Psychopathy Reviewed*, 1977, and also to the Editorial Board of the *Prison Service Journal* for permission to reproduce certain parts of my paper, 'I think they call them psychopaths . . .' which appeared in Vol. 28, 1977 of that journal.

foregoing disciplines, of semantics. The dilemma involved in trying to adequately describe the Psychopath was aptly stated many years ago by Curran and Mallinson with the statement: 'I can't define an elephant, but I know one when I see one' (East 1949). And, whilst on the subject of elephants, there is also the story – 'The Disagreement as to the Description and Shape of the Elephant' in which, those who handle one in the darkness only understand it in respect of the part they touch. As East also suggested, such a story has implications for those who try to understand the psychopath.

Although the history of the development of the concept of psychopathy has been very well documented (Maughs 1941; Gurvitz 1951; McCord and McCord 1956; Craft 1956; Walker and McCabe 1973; Lewis 1974; Bleechmore 1975; Pichot 1978), it would seem useful to sketch in at this point, even if only briefly, some of the essential developmental steps. As I indicated in Chapter 2, attempts had been made from very early times to distinguish, however ineffectively, those 'mental disorders' due to psychological causes and those due to medical disease. I also showed how these attempts received impetus in the nineteenth century when efforts were made to discern which mental disorders were due to defects in emotion, intellect, or in volition. The great humanitarian psychiatrist – Pinel – is usually given the credit for first describing what we regard as psychopathic disorder; the term he used was *'manie sans délire'*. However, close inspection of Pinel's work suggests that he probably included many people in this description that we would not now define as psychopaths. But, as we shall see later in considering the work of Henderson (1939) and Cleckley (1976), his concept of *'manie sans délire'* may have had more significance than he perhaps realized at the time.[*] In the 1830s, the English psychiatrist and anthropologist Prichard formulated the concept of 'moral insanity'. He described it as a 'madness, consisting of a morbid perversion of the natural feelings, affections, inclinations, temper, habits, moral dispositions and natural impulses, without any remarkable disorder

---

[*] The intervention of psychiatry in the system of criminal justice in the nineteenth century is discussed in detail by Foucault (1978).

or defect of the interest or knowing and reasoning faculties' (Prichard 1835). In the context of this quotation we should note that 'moral' meant emotional and psychological and was not intended to denote the opposite of immoral as used in modern parlance. This view of 'moral insanity' rested on the then, fairly widely held, but also controversial, belief that there could be a separate moral sense which could be diseased. To understand such beliefs, they need to be seen against the background of the very rudimentary state of psychological knowledge at that time – psychology was still very much at the 'philosophy of mind' stage. (See also Chapter 2.) In the 1880s, Koch formulated the concept of *constitutional psychopathy*, implying that there was a considerable constitutional (innate) predisposition; a line of thinking much in keeping with the contemporary interest in hereditary factors in the causation of delinquency and deviation. In 1917, Mercier laid claim to have been the originator of the terms 'moral defective' and 'moral imbecile' – these eventually finding their way into the Mental Deficiency Act of 1913.

Certain trends in the 1930s were of importance. Findings from the fields of neurology and physiology were being applied to such disorders as encephalitis, epilepsy, and chorea, and questions were being asked about the relevance of these disorders to the aetiology and treatment of psychopathic states. Psychoanalysts and psychoanalytically oriented psychiatrists in the 1930s and 1940s were also active in this field. For example, Alexander described the 'neurotic character' as a form of personality deviation and attempted to fit this into a Freudian perspective. Perhaps of more importance for present purposes, was the work of Partridge who 'rejected the clinical concept of psychopathy, substituting the term 'sociopathy' to designate a deviation in social relations whether it be with individuals or groups' (Gurvitz 1951). This should be compared with the view of the eminent authority, Henderson, who considered that the psychopath's 'failure to adjust to ordinary social life is not a mere wilfulness or badness which can be threatened or thrashed out . . . but constitues a true illness' (Henderson 1939). As we shall see shortly, this is a view shared to a great extent by Cleckley in his book *The Mask of Sanity* (1976). Further work on the intra-psychic life of the psychopath was carried forward by the psychoanalysts Lindner (1944) and Karpman (1948). In more recent years, the work of Craft (1968), Maxwell Jones (1963), and Whiteley (1968) in this country – particularly in the area of institutional treatment – has been of considerable significance. However, any examination of the historical development of the concept reveals, as one might expect, that it is 'strongly affected by current cultural notions of responsibility and decency' (Treves-Brown 1977).

More recently, the two Government reports referred to in Chapter 2 have highlighted once again the problematic nature of the concept. First, the Butler Committee (1975), with the suggestion that when the Mental Health Act is reviewed, consideration might be given to the deletion of psychopathy from the definition of mental disorder, with a consequent substitution of the much broader term personality disorder. (See Chapter 3.) As Wootton (1977, 1978) states:

'The Committee obviously hankered after the idea of dispensing with psychopathy as a legal category altogether, but, as their terms of reference related only to *offenders*, they could not make a recommendation to this effect, since it would necessarily have also been applicable to other persons classified as psychopaths who were not criminals: to have used different definitions in different parts of the Act would have been manifestly absurd . . .'

The Committee, in following up their line of argument, suggest that in future 'dangerous anti-social psychopaths' who have shown no previous mental or organic illness or identifiable psychological or physical defect should be dealt with through the prison rather than the hospital system. Such a recommendation has important social policy implications and I shall examine some of these elsewhere in this book.

Second, the DHSS report – *A Review of the Mental Health Act, 1959* (DHSS 1976) – also indicates dissatisfaction with the current definition. The authors of this report suggest inter alia, a modification, namely the substitution of the term 'severe personality disorder', which they go on to define as 'a persistent abnormality of mind of such a kind and degree as seriously to affect the person's life and adjustment to society and which is so marked as to render him a serious risk to himself or to others'. Readers of this book who are familiar with the definition of psychopathy in the Mental Health Act, 1959, will note the similarity, though the suggested definition in the DHSS report is a somewhat ambivalent attempt to be more specific. (The relevant section of the 1959 Act reads: 'A persistent disorder or disability of the mind (whether or not including subnormality of intelligence) which results in abnormally aggressive or seriously irresponsible conduct on the part of the patient and requires or is susceptible to medical treatment'.) In addition, the authors of the report suggest a new descriptive term for conditions that are less serious than 'severe personality disorder' – namely, 'severe behaviour reaction'. This current dissatisfaction with the term and the search for a more useful substitute merely serve to remind us of the statement of one eminent psychiatrist over thirty years ago. 'If we were to drop the term altogether, we should be obliged to invent an equivalent or to overlook a whole series of clinically very important phenomena . . .' (Slater 1948).

It may be helpful to summarize the historical development of these terms (see *Figure 5(1)*).

Figure 5(1)

manie sans délire ——▶ moral insanity ——▶ moral imbecility
(defectiveness)——▶ (constitutional) psychopathic inferiority
——▶ 'neurotic character'——▶ psychopathy and sociopathy ——▶
severe (antisocial) personality disorder

Figure 5(1) requires an explanatory comment. The term 'neurotic character', already referred to, has not, apparently, found much approval as a classification and strictly speaking, did not antedate the formulation of the term psychopath. It is inserted here because it represents one important psychoanalytic contribution of the early 1930s. The term 'antisocial' is frequently employed as a prefix for the particular type.

of personality disorder we are discussing here.

Causal factors

It would be foolhardy in a comparatively short chapter to attempt to summarize the vast amount of literature concerning the suggested causation of psychopathy. It seems to me to be more productive to concentrate on one or two aspects that seem to merit further consideration and then to formulate a fairly simple classification, though I suspect it is one which will not find favour with a number of less clinically minded readers.

As with many other aspects of mental disorder, the 'nature' versus 'nurture' debate has raged for many years in relation to psychopathy. Evidence has been adduced from twin, neurological, chromosomal, and other studies to suggest the importance of innate factors. Equally convincing evidence has been provided by the environmentalists to suggest that family background and social milieu are all important, particularly in relation to the psychopath's singular lack of capacity for 'role taking' (Gough 1956). In considering causal factors and their implications for management, it seems useful to see psychopathy as part of a spectrum of personality (behaviour) disorder.* I have attempted to do this in *Figures 5(2)* and *5(3)* below.

Figure 5(2)

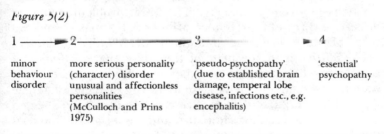

1	2	3	4
minor behaviour disorder	more serious personality (character) disorder unusual and affectionless personalities (McCulloch and Prins 1975)	'pseudo-psychopathy' (due to established brain damage, temperal lobe disease, infections etc., e.g. encephalitis)	'essential' psychopathy

---

* I have used the terms personality and behaviour disorder synonymously. Some authorities reserve the term behaviour disorder for use in childhood conditions. Since we are concerned with the behavioural problems shown by those adjudged to be exhibiting disorders of personality I have exercised some semantic licence.

I have introduced two *new* terms in *Figure 5(2)* – *'pseudo-psychopathy'* and *'essential' psychopathy*. Groups 3 and 4 are, of course, very closely linked. The term 'pseudo-psychopathy' is meant to denote an 'as if' situation. That is, the disorder has the appearance of 'essential psychopathy', but it is one in which it seems possible to ascribe some fairly clear cause. There is, for example, a good deal of evidence to suggest a clear link between the development of seriously antisocial behaviour (linked particularly with aggression) following exposure to infections of various kinds (Cleobury *et. al.* 1971), encephalitis, meningitis, or to brain injury. Some supporting evidence for these links can be found for example in cases where psycho-surgery has been used inappropriately in the treatment of certain cases of neurosis. This may produce side effects which can consist of bouts of aggression and antisocial conduct. The classification I have suggested in column 2 would have consigned to it the swindlers, cheats etc., who appear to act without remorse (the affectionless personalities) and the unusual personalities, such as Lawrence of Arabia (described by Henderson as the 'creative psychopath'). Gunn and Robertson have indicated in a recent paper that those persons I have suggested should be consigned to column 2 could best be given 'a diagnostic category of "neurosis (antisocial behaviour)" ' (Gunn and Robertson 1976). It is important to note that those labelled as psychopaths are almost invariably male. Few females seem to carry the psychopathic label. The whole problem of how we discern and respond to female offenders is a matter for considerable current debate and will be dealt with later in this book. Suffice it to speculate at this point that a number of female psychopaths may well be diagnosed as hysterics or hysterical personalities. In support of this speculation, Guze (1976) in a very careful piece of research found an unexpected association between psychopathy and hysteria. He suggests that if this finding is confirmed by further studies, it would help to account for the 'striking sex differences in the two disorders'. He suggests also that 'these differences are limited to overt manifestations and that underlying etiologic and pathogenetic processes are similar'. He raises some important questions that could follow from further research. For example, what are the biological and cultural factors which contribute to the sex differences and to what extent will changes in the status of women affect these sex differences? (See also Chapter 10.) The causal factors in relation to 'essential psychopathy' can be hotly disputed but I suggest that its possible causation can be shown in the following fashion:

Figure 5(3)

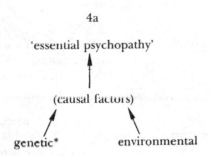

The classification of 'essential psychopath' in *Figure 5(3)* would include the 'true' psychopath as described by Cleckley (see later) and perhaps such personalities as Patrick Mackay (Clark and Penycate 1976).

Need for differential diagnosis

Having suggested that there is some merit in delineating 'essential psychopathy', I am now obliged to offer some basis for this delineation and for trying to distinguish it from ordinary recidivist criminality. Blair (1975), a psychiatrist of considerable forensic experience, makes the very important point that psychopathic disorder must be differentiated from:

'1   Personality Disorders

* Operating singly or in combination but of unknown origin.

2 Severe Psychoneurosis
3 Ordinary Adolescents
4 Hardened Criminals.'

He goes on to emphasize that in order to make an adequate diagnosis, it is essential to have a detailed life history since in almost all cases, the 'essential' psychopath has exhibited severe disturbance in all areas of behaviour from a very early age. How can the 'essential' psychopath be distinguished from the ordinary recidivist offender? Cleckley (1976) comes to our aid. The following is a summarized account of some of the distinctions he makes.

(1) The ordinary criminal often seems to work to his own advantage through his crimes; that is, he seems to be more purposive. But, the psychopath on the other hand appears so much more likely to be found out that his criminality has almost an 'insane' quality to it.

(2) The career of the psychopath seems to begin earlier (see above) and spreads into many areas of his social and personal behaviour. He seems to be more unmoved than the ordinary recidivist offender by overtures of help or by punishment and his criminal career is more rapidly continuous. *His words seem to bear no relation to his feelings.* (I will say more about this important feature later.)

(3) The psychopath's antisocial acts are often quite incomprehensible and he seems to indulge in them for quite obscure reasons. He also seems to be injuring himself; in fact, the greatest degree of harm he often does to others is brought about largely through their concern for him and his rejection of them. Thus, he often leaves a chain of chaos in his wake.

(4) In the area of sexual behaviour his not infrequent perverse activities seem to be fleeting only and are indulged in at whim.

(5) The ordinary recidivist criminal seems, in some instances, to have a certain loyalty to family and to his fellow criminals. The 'essential' psychopath almost always appears to have none and is essentially a 'loner'.

The above criteria go some way to suggesting the possibility of a differential diagnosis. There will, of course, be areas of overlap and ambiguity and some well-known authorities (for example Scott) have questioned the need to differentiate between psychopaths and recidivists. 'In practice nothing is gained by trying to draw a distinction between psychopathic and chronic offenders' (Scott 1960). I would suggest, however, that something *is* to be gained by trying to make the distinction and that despite ambiguities and overlap such distinction is possible.

SOME KEY CHARACTERISTICS

Having tried to provide some clue as to the difference between the 'essential' psychopath and the recidivist criminal, it is now appropriate to outline some further key characteristics of the former. Cleckley, in the fifth edition of his book, sums up some of these very well. He states:

'We find the typical psychopath not consistently seeking to inflict major disaster on anyone. More characteristic is the psychopath's pettiness and transiency of affect (both positive and negative) and his failure to follow a long range plan, either for good or evil. The emotional damage he may (and often does) inflict on his mate, parents, children etc., is not, it seems, inflicted for any major voluntary purpose or from a well focused motive but from what weighs in at little more than whim or caprice . . . in the disaster he brings about he cannot estimate the affective reactions of others which are the substance of the disaster. A race of men congenitally without pain sense would not find it easy to estimate the effects of physical torture on others. A man who has never understood visual experience would lack appreciation of what is sustained when the ordinary person loses his eye.'

(Cleckley 1976: 322)*

* Reproduced by permission of the author, Professor Harvey Cleckley, and the publishers, The C.V. Mosby Company.

He states elsewhere that the psychopath 'is invincibly ignorant of what life means to others' (Cleckley 1976: 386). In these brief extracts, we can discern three essential components of the condition – namely, lack of affect, an inability to relate real feelings to the words with which they are expressed, and the chain of destruction and chaos that the psychopath characteristically leaves behind him. The lack of affect and chaos has been well described by numerous authorities, but less attention has been given to the singular disparity between speech and feelings. In this connection, it has been well stated that the psychopath 'knows the words but not the music' (Johns and Quay 1962). I can think of one clear example from my own experience, of this singular disparity. I once interviewed an offender/patient who admittedly had been already labelled as a psychopath. He told me a highly complicated tale which was so obviously untrue from start to finish that his story had a quality of complete irrationality and a feeling akin to 'madness' about it. This offender knew that the facts could have been checked with the minimum of difficulty and that they were so glaringly untrue that any normal individual would have known that they could not possibly deceive. In addition, the statements he was presenting as 'truth' were clearly lies of such a grandiose nature that again, this curious quality of 'madness' came across even more forcefully. However, he was *not* regarded as clinically deluded in the sense that he might have been suffering from 'delusions of grandeur' due to psychotic illness. His lying was, in my view, the clearest possible example of that demonstrated by Cleckley's 'true' psychopath. It was no doubt this disparity between speech and feelings that led Cleckley to formulate his interesting concept of *semantic disorder* or *dementia*. In developing this idea, Cleckley drew upon work that had been done by Henry Head in relation to a condition known as semantic aphasia. This concept of Cleckley's has received relatively little attention, perhaps because of its complexity; it is admittedly difficult to prove, though clearly it is deserving of further exploration. Crudely put, and at the risk of distortion through compression, Cleckley suggests that just as damage to certain higher nerve centres in the brain may produce a physical inability to comprehend or produce language, so with the psychopath, some form of neural damage (unspecified, but likely to be within that part of the brain dealing with the higher functions of speech and meaning), might produce this strange inability to 'gear in' to the needs and wants of others.* Cleckley indicates that the psychopath is able to present to the outside world a façade of normality, which in fact conceals a seriously disabled and often irresponsible individual. This connection (or rather lack of it) between words and emotion is of interest from another angle. In his book, *The Murdering Mind*, Abrahamson (1973) illustrates how an unusually large proportion of murderers and others charged with acts of serious personal violence seemed to share two common characteristics – serious errors in verbal usage and curious, but strangely consistent, spelling mistakes. Such mis-spellings he describes as *onomatopoiesis* – the making of a word or a name from a sound. Abrahamson suggests that 'these people who make spelling errors are not really anxious to communicate. Rather their verbal communication is a means of exhibiting themselves.' He goes on to suggest that such phenomena may offer diagnostic and predictive clues. Clearly, one cannot make too much use of such findings; they would require careful experimental validation and they are no more than peripherally linked with Cleckley's formulation. Nevertheless, they do provide food for further serious thought. Cleckley's concept of semantic aphasia is perhaps exemplified to some extent by what Patrick Mackay had to say about the senseless and horrific crimes he committed. One small passage will suffice. 'I feel terrible about what happened all the more because I do not know why or what made me do it. I find it all a confusing matter. You see I'm scared of myself' Clark and Penycate 1976).

Finally, it is of interest to note that some empirical research

* The relationship between the activity of the brain (neurophysiological processes) and states of mind is an exceedingly intriguing and complicated one. A most lucid and well-written account is that by the neuro-surgeon Wilder Penfield (1975). The author does not presuppose any prior knowledge of anatomy or physiology in his readers.

work undertaken by Blackburn (1975) at Broadmoor shows, by use of the statistical device of cluster analysis, that it is possible to identify four profile types for the psychopath. The first of these is essentially similar to the clinical characteristics shown by Cleckley's psychopath, and is directly comparable with my suggested classification of 'essential' psychopathy (above).

RECENT CONTRIBUTIONS TO AETIOLOGY

Hare (1970) has made a substantial contribution to the study of psychopathy. In his book *Psychopathy: Theory and Research*, he presents an experimental psychologist's approach to the problem. He summarizes and brings together studies from the fields of abnormal psychology, neuro- and psycho-physiology, learning theory, and socialization. Some of these findings are discussed in more detail by Hare and Schalling in *Psychopathic Behaviour* (1978). Much of the experimental evidence he produces seems to support the day-to-day experience of clinicians and other workers in the socio-forensic field. What follows is a somewhat bald and compressed summary of some of Hare's conclusions and due acknowledgement is made to that author for the use of these. Hare classifies them under four headings: Cortical Studies; Psychopathy and the Autonomic Nervous System; Psychopathy and the Concept of Arousal; Psychopathy and Learning.

Cortical studies

Over the years, studies by use of the EEG (Electro-Encephalogram) have tended to show that the slow wave activity in the cortex found in some psychopaths bears some resemblance to the EEG patterns usually found in children. These findings (which I have oversimplified here) have led to the formulation of a hypothesis of cortical immaturity. Two further views derived from work in this field should be noted. First, that psychopathy may be associated with a defect or malfunction of certain brain mechanisms concerned with emotional activity and the regulation of behaviour. Second, it has been suggested that psychopathy may be related to a lowered state of cortical excitability and to the attenuation of sensory input; particularly input that would, in ordinary circumstances, have disturbing consequences. (It is interesting to link these observations with those made earlier concerning the relevance of brain damage or injury.)

Psychopathy and the autonomic nervous system

Clinical and other experience has always tended to demonstrate the psychopath's general lack of anxiety, guilt, and emotional tension. More recently, experiments carried out under laboratory conditions have tended to give confirmation to these clinical impressions. Thus, it has been shown that during periods of relative quiescence, psychopathic subjects tend to be *hypoactive* on several indices of autonomic activity, including resting level of skin conductance, and cardiac activity. However, it must be pointed out that lack of anxiety, guilt, and emotional tension are not characteristics perculiar to psychopathic subjects. Rather that they seem to show this lack in a more extreme form than in the general population.

Psychopathy and the concept of arousal

There is also some evidence to suggest that psychopathy is related to cortical under arousal. Because of this, the psychopath may actively seek stimulation with arousing or exciting qualities. However, in the process, he may be unaware of, or unattentive to many of the more subtle cues required for the maintenance of socially acceptable behaviour and for adequate socialization. Readers wishing to pursue this interesting aspect further should consult the work of Anthony (1973) and the more recent contribution by Mawson and Mawson (1977). They claim that psychopaths are 'characterized by a greater degree of variability in autonomic functioning than normals'. They suggest that a biochemical disturbance may manifest itself in abnormal oscillations in neurotransmitter functioning and that research could usefully be directed towards exploring this hypothesis further. They also suggest that such research might elucidate possible links in disturbances in neurotransmitter functioning in such conditions as schizophrenia, Parkinson's Disease, and hyperactivity in children.

Psychopathy and learning

It also seems possible to conclude – albeit tentatively – that psychopaths do not develop conditioned fear responses readily. Because of this, they find it difficult to learn responses that are motivated by fear and reinforced by fear reduction. There is also evidence (again confirmed in clinical and allied practice) that psychopaths are less influenced than are normal persons by their capacity to make connections between past events and the consequences of their present behaviour.

The findings summarized by Hare are attractive in that they seem to afford some 'scientific' (i.e. laboratory) confirmation of clinical experience. However, we should note that some of Hare's work has been criticized recently, and in particular by Feldman (1977). Feldman suggests that too many of Hare's conclusions are based solely upon the results of laboratory tests and that too few comparative studies have been undertaken of 'control' populations derived from non-penal or non-specialist hospital sources. Feldman also criticizes Hare on the grounds that few people are consistently 'psychopathic' and that there is not enough evidence to suggest that criminality and psychopathy are distinct entities. He suggests that the term 'psychopathic behaviour' is a more accurate and useful one than the more general label 'psychopath'. Some of Feldman's criticisms are valid, but overall I do not consider that he has made out a strong-enough case against the attempt to identify the small and distinctive group of individuals that I have described here as 'essential' psychopaths.

Management

There is little doubt from both research and clinical evidence that personality disorders in general and psychopathy in particular are very difficult conditions to treat. For example, in child guidance practice, it is well established that it is easier to treat anxieties and phobic conditions in children than it is to treat behaviour disorders; though some such disorders, particularly those involving hyperactivity, seem to be amenable to behaviour modification techniques. (See, for example, Herbert (1978), especially Chapter 11.) As for the more serious cases, we have to confess that in the present state of our knowledge and skills, these are most intractable. This is the more tragic since we know also from careful research studies such as those carried out by Lee Robins (1969) that such behaviour disordered children of today, often become the 'psychopaths' of tomorrow. Such failure, in the light of what was indicated earlier in this chapter about the lack of knowledge concerning explanations of psychopathy is hardly surprising; it is, therefore, very tempting to write off such offenders as untreatable.

One of the arguments often advanced for finding a new term for psychopathy is that it has become a word of abuse and a 'dustbin' category to which we have assigned all those clients, charges, or patients who seem unwilling to be helped, who are unpredictable, unresponsive, and who, in addition, show socially unacceptable behaviour to a severe degree. There is, of course, much truth in this but it is only a partial explanation. It seems that whatever label we are going to use – be it psychopath, sociopath, psychopathic personality, or severe personality disorder – we are *still* going to have to face problems of engagement, acceptance, and communication. A number of writers have drawn attention to the reluctance of professionals in the penal and allied services to deal with psychopaths. Admittedly, the label we use *can* be used pejoratively and as a defence against involvement; as in the statement 'oh, he's just a psychopath, there's nothing that can be done'. The basic issue is that which psychotherapists describe as 'counter-transference' – that is, developing an especial awareness not only of the rejecting feelings that such clients arouse in us but an awareness also of the way in which we can rationalize our negative responses by use of the 'label'. Somehow, we have to rise above the rejecting behaviour of these clients, to 'hang on' to them, sometimes over many years, and hope that gradually there may be some modification of their attitudes. I shall return to this theme shortly. By adopting the type of classification I have suggested it may be possible to make our attempts at management more discriminating and realistic. For example, those persons I have assigned to Categories 1 and 2 may well respond to comparatively simple methods of management, though some should be left to go their own way, provided always that they do not come into serious conflict with the law and are not 'a danger to themselves or to others'. Kittrie has some very trenchant things to say about the extent to which people have, as he puts it, *The Right to be Different* (1971). Offenders in my third category may well respond to certain forms of medication or other methods aimed at improving, modifying, or curing the underlying physical condition that has given rise to what I have described as 'pseudo-psychopathy'. These offenders may also need the application of additional measures, for example, containment for a time, or exposure to one of the varieties of behaviour modification or retraining. (See for example the chapter by Suedfeld and London in Hare and Schalling 1978.) Offenders in Category 4 – the 'essential' psychopaths – present the gravest problems in management. We have to admit that as yet, we have no known cure; for some, containment under conditions of strict security within penal establishments for very long periods of time *may be* the only answer. But, I consider the emphasis should be on the *may be*, for there is clinical evidence to suggest that even the 'essential' psychopath may be enabled to modify attitudes over time. Schmideberg, (1949, 1954, 1958, 1965), who gave up using traditional insight-promoting, psychoanalytical approaches in therapy with 'major criminals' (many of whom were psychopaths) suggests that a much more reality-based confronting approach is necessary. Psychopaths need, time and time again, to be brought up against the consequences of their behaviour. This means that the therapist (be he psychiatrist, field social worker, or institution staff member) needs to bear in mind the realities of the condition I have described as 'essential psychopathy' on the one hand and not to allow himself on the other to be *personally* affronted at being misled, lied to, evaded, and made to feel helpless. Schmideberg reminds us also that it is very necessary for those who are trying to help the psychopath to try to divest themselves of society's less rational punishing attitudes.

'We must see things from the patient's point of view, realising not only that he has wronged society but that society has also wronged him and owes him something . . . a great deal of patience is required in dealing with them . . . More important still, the . . . (therapist) . . . must have some knowledge and feelings for *their* world which differs so radically from our safe and respectable one . . .'

(Schmideberg 1949)

Patience has also been one of the keynotes of Stürup's treatment regime as psychiatrist in charge of Denmark's famous institution for 'chronic criminals' (psychopaths) at Herstedvester. He stressed the importance of continuity of staff contact with such offenders; many of his institutional staff were also responsible for the long-term follow up and after-care of such offender/patients when they left the institution. Such continuity of contact would be very difficult to achieve in this country because prisons and the special hospitals receive inmates from country-wide catchment areas. Until fairly recently it has been also a comparatively rare occurrence for many local authority social workers and probation officers to stay in one area for any significant length of time before moving on. Thus, they are unable to gain sufficient first-hand experience of working with such difficult people over any reasonable period of time. They are also unable to provide the 'follow-up' and continuity of contact which seems so vital in trying to help these particular clients learn or 'relearn' socially acceptable modes of behaviour. Stürup also reminds us very wisely that we should not set our goals too high. 'Treatment in the field of clinical criminology has limited goals, the chief one being a crime-free future for the offender. Our program has always been directed toward this practical objective and we have been eclectic, intuitively using whatever approach we thought most valuable in any given situation . . .' (Stürup 1968). The use of an eclectic approach has much to commend it. Social workers who have tried to work within too narrowly defined a conceptual framework and, who, like some psychiatrists, have clung too rigidly to a psychoanalytical model have not met with as much success as those who are prepared to encourage a sense of reality, and who are not afraid to exercise authority and control in a firm but kindly fashion (Grossbard 1962; Prins 1968, 1969). The development of this sense of reality seems to be vital for all workers in this field. Stürup suggests that 'the key to all our work is a sense of reality'. He says that 'we call for unbiased rationality, both in our workers and in the inmates . . .' He also suggests that 'deep prejudices may complicate the realistic integration of the inmate as a principal collaborator in the treatment . . .' And, much nearer home, Scott once reminded us that:

> 'wherever possible . . . psychopaths should be kept out of custody, for detention carries risks of its own. As soon as offenders or the anti-socially inclined are segregated there is the tendency for staff and inmates to consolidate at opposite poles; a hierarchy tends to develop among the offenders; a threat is thus offered to the staff which calls out a repressive authoritarian regime and the possibility of a vicious circle of resentment and counter-resentment . . .'
>
> (Scott 1960)

Some institutions have sought to offset the dangers described by Scott through the introduction of more open approaches and by using group work techniques. In these, group pressures are used to confront the offender with his behaviour and to help him develop some awareness of it. (See Craft 1968; Miles 1969; Hare 1970.)

In a fairly recent contribution, an American lay author, Harrington (1972) collected information on the characteristics of psychopaths from a variety of expert sources. Most of these characteristics have already been outlined in this chapter. One additional factor that emerged and which does not seem to have been commented upon by other writers to quite the same degree, is that concerned with the psychopath's lack of sense of time. Now this is important, if for no other reason than the very practical one that the therapist must take it into account when making arrangements for contact and in not feeling *personally* rejected when the psychopath does not turn up for pre-arranged meetings. As one of Harrington's expert witnesses pointed out: 'They never see their behaviour in the context of tomorrow . . . if I'm a psychopath and I have an appointment to meet you but – all at once, unexpectedly – I run into an old friend on the street I might spend my afternoon with him and simply not show up for our meeting . . .' (Harrington 1972: 215). In summing up their characteristics from the point of view of those who have to try to manage them, it would probably not be an exaggeration to state that their behaviour and attitudes in their most extreme forms are the opposites of those one expects to find in most other client/patient groups. Thus a capacity for making contact, for some show of empathic warmth, for carrying out suggested courses of action, for truthfulness and for reliability will almost invariably all be lacking. If, as I suggested earlier, we can rise above these negative responses and remain 'dispasssionately compassionate', then there is the possibility that over time, the psychopath may be helped towards not only more law abiding behaviour but perhaps towards a more satisfactory life style for himself as well.

Conclusion

Whatever descriptive term one chooses to use, there seems little doubt that there is a group of individuals whose behaviour is such that it is markedly different from that of the ordinary recidivist criminal. It may be that the term 'psychopath' can lead to unproductive labelling, but this seems to be a fault that may lie within the user of the label rather than with the intrinsic quality of the label itself. The most persistent and damaging forms of psychopathic behaviour described in the literature would seem to fit into my classification of 'essential psychopathy'. It is on these grounds that I would argue for retention of the word rather than for the substitution of the more all embracing term 'personality disorder'. Moreover, in adopting the type of classification I have outlined, I would hope that management would be more discriminatory and thus more effective. However, it remains a sad truth that few well-designed research studies using control groups have been made to test the efficacy of treatment for psychopathic subjects. A few exceptions may be found, notably in the work of Craft (1968) and Miles (1969) to which I have already referred; and more recently Watts and Bennett have shown that quite seriously socially deviant patients can be coped with satisfactorily in a day hospital setting: 'There is no basis for excluding such patients from day hospitals on the assumption that they are less likely to be helped than other non-psychotic patients' (Watts and Bennett 1978).

References

Abrahamson. D. (1973) *The Murdering Mind.* London: Harper. Colophon Books. (pp. 27 ff)

Anthony, H.S. (1973) *Depression, Psychopathic Personality and Attempted Suicide in a Borstal Sample.* London: Home Office Research Unit HMSO.

Blackburn, R. (1975) An Empirical Classification of Psychopathic Personality. *Brit. J. Psychiat.* **127**: 456–60.

Blair, D. (1975) The Medico-Legal Implications of the Terms 'Psychopath', 'Psychopathic Personality' and 'Psychopathic Disorder'. *Med. Sci. Law* **15**: 51–61 and 110–23.

Bleechmore, J.F. (1975) Towards a Rational Theory of Criminal Responsibility: The Psychopathic Offender. *Melbourne University Law Review. Parts I and II.* May and September 19–46 and 207–24.

Clark, T. and Penycate, J. (1976) *Psychopath. The Case of Patrick Mackay.* London: Routledge and Kegan Paul.

Cleckley, H. (1976) *The Mask of Sanity* (5th edition). St Louis: The C.V. Mosby Co.

Cleobury J.R., Skinner, G.R.B., Thouless, M.E., and Wildy, P. (1971) Association Between Psychopathic Disorder and Serum Antibody to Herpes Simplex Virus (Type I). *Brit. Med. J.* **1**: 438–39.

Craft, M. (ed.) (1966) *Psychopathic Disorders.* Oxford: Pergamon.

—— (1968) Psychopathic Disorder: A Second Trial of Treatment. *Brit. J. Psychiat.* **114**: 813–20.

DHSS, Home Office, Welsh Office, Lord Chancellor's Department (1976) *A Review of the Mental Health Act, 1959.* London: HMSO.

East, N. (1949) *Society and the Criminal.* London: HMSO.

Feldman, M.P. (1977) *Criminal Behaviour. A Psychological Analysis.* London: John Wiley.

Foucault, M. (1978) About the Concept of the 'Dangerous Individual' in 19th-Century Legal Psychiatry. *Int. J. of Law and Psychiat.* **I**: 1–18.

Gough, H.G. (1956) A Sociological Study of Psychopathy. In A.M. Rose (ed.) *Mental Health and Mental Disorder.* London: Routledge and Kegan Paul.

Grossbard, H. (1962) Ego Deficiency in Delinquents. *Social Casework* **43**: 171–78.

Gunn, J. and Robertson, G. (1976) Psychopathic Personality: A Conceptual Problem. *Psychol. Med.* **6**: 631–34.

Gurvitz, M. (1951) Developments in the Concept of Psychopathic Personality. *Brit. J. Delinq.* **II**: 88–102.

Guze, S.B. (1976) *Criminality and Psychiatric Disorders.* Oxford: Oxford University Press.

Hare, R.D. (1970) *Psychopathy: Theory and Research.* London: John Wiley.

Hare, R.D. and Schalling, D. (1978) *Psychopathic Behaviour: Approaches to Research.* London: John Wiley.

Harrington, A. (1972) *Psychopaths.* London: If Books.

Henderson, D. (1939) *Psychopathic States.* New York: Norton and Co.

Herbert, M. (1978) *Conduct Disorders of Childhood and Adolescence.* London: John Wiley.

Home Office and DHSS (1975) *Report of the Committee on Men-*

tally Abnormal Offenders (Butler Committee). Cmnd. 6244. London: HMSO.

Johns, J.H. and Quay, H.C. (1962) The Effect of Social Reward on Verbal Conditioning in Psychopathic and Neurotic Military Offenders. *J. of Consulting Psychol.* **26**: 217–20.

Jones, M. (1963) The Treatment of Character Disorders. *Brit. J. Criminol.* **3**: 276–82.

Karpman, B. (1948) Conscience in the Psychopath. *American J. of Orthopsychiatry* **18**: 455–91.

Kittrie, N.M. (1971) *The Right to be Different. Deviance and Enforced Therapy.* Baltimore: Johns Hopkins. (pp. 169–209).

Lewis, A. (1974) Psychopathic Personality: A Most Elusive Category. *Psychol. Med.* **4**: 133–40.

Lindner, R.M. (1944) *Rebel Without a Cause.* New York: Grune and Stratton.

Maughs, S.B. (1941) Concept of Psychopathic Personality: Its Evolution and Historical Development. *J. of Criminal Psychopathology* **2**: 329–56 and 365–99.

Mawson, A.R. and Mawson, C.D. (1977) Psychopathy and Arousal: A New Interpretation of the Psychophysiological Literature. *Biological Psychiatry* **12** (1): 49–74.

McCord, W. and McCord, J. (1956) *Psychopathy and Delinquency.* New York: Grune and Stratton.

McCulloch, J.W. and Prins, H.A. (1975) *Signs of Stress. The Social Problems Associated with Psychiatric Illness.* Plymouth: McDonald and Evans. (pp. 115–16).

Miles, A.E. (1969) The Effects of a Therapeutic Community on the Interpersonal Relationships of a Group of Psychopaths. *Brit. J. Criminol.* **9**: 22–38.

Penfield, W. (1975) *The Mystery of the Mind.* New Jersey: Princeton University Press.

Pichot, P. (1978) Psychopathic Behaviour: A Historical Overview. In R.D. Hare, and D. Schalling (1978). London: John Wiley.

Prichard, J.C. (1835) *A Treatise on Insanity and Other Disorders Affecting the Mind.* Philadelphia: Haswell, Barrington and

Haswell. (Quoted in McCord and McCord.)

Prins, H.A. (1968) The Social Casework Treatment of the Seriously Delinquent Offender. *Case Conference* 15: 145–50.

—— (1969) Casework and the Treatment of Offenders. *J. Applied Social Studies* 1: 181–87.

Robins, L.N. (1969) *Deviant Children Grown Up: A Sociological and Psychiatric Study of Sociopathic Personality.* Baltimore: Williams and Wilkins.

Schmideberg, M. (1949) The Analytic Treatment of Major Criminals: Therapeutic Results and Technical Problems. In K.R. Eissler (ed.) *Searchlights on Delinquency.* New Psychoanalytic Studies. London: Imago. (pp 186–89).

—— (1954) Is the Criminal Amoral? *Brit. J. Delinq.* IV: 272–81.

—— (1958) Treating the Unwilling Patient. *Brit. J. Delinq.* IX: 117–22.

—— (1965) Reality Therapy with Offenders. *Brit. J. Criminol.* 5: 168–82.

Scott, P.D. (1960) The Treatment of Psychopaths. *Brit. Med. J.* 2: 1641–646.

Slater, E.T.O. (1948) Psychopathic Personality as a Genetical Concept. *J. of Mental Science* 94: 277.

Stürup, G. (1968) *Treating the Untreatable. Chronic Criminals at Herstedvester.* Baltimore: Johns Hopkins.

Treves-Brown, C. (1977) Who is the Psychopath? *Med. Sci. Law* 17: 56–63.

Walker, N. and McCabe, S. (1973) *Crime and Insanity in England.Vol. 2.* Edinburgh: Edinburgh University Press. (Chapters 9 and 10).

Watts, F.N. and Bennett, D.H. (1978) Social Deviance in a Day Hospital. *Brit. J. Psychiat.* 132: 455–62.

Whiteley, S. (1968) *Factors in the Treatment and Management of Psychopaths.* In D.J. West (ed.) *Psychopath Offenders.* Cambridge: Institute of Criminology.

Wootton, B. (1977) Aubrey Lewis 'Paper on Health as a Social Concept Reviewed' in the Light of Today. *Brit. J. Psychiat.* 131: 243–48.

—— (1978) *Crime and Penal Policy. Reflections on Fifty Year's Experience.* London: George Allen and Unwin. (Chapter 12.)

FURTHER READING

CIBA Foundation (1968) *The Mentally Abnormal Offender* (ed. A.V.S. de Rueck and R. Porter). London: J. and A. Churchill. (Especially contributions by Craft, Gibbens *et al.*)

Craft, M. (1965) *Ten Studies into Psychopathic Personality.* Bristol: John Wright.

Hare, R.D. and Schalling, D. (1978) *Psychopathic Behaviour: Approaches to Research.* London: John Wiley. (Offers a very comprehensive and up-to-date review of theories of causation and approaches to management.)

Lion, J.R. (1974) *Personality Disorders. Diagnosis and Management.* Baltimore: Williams and Wilkins.

West, D.J. (ed.) (1969) *Criminological Implications of Chromosome Abnormalities.* Cambridge: Institute of Criminology.

CHAPTER SIX

Are such men dangerous? *

All tragedy is the failure of communication.
                    JOHN WILSON

I hope it will have become apparent from the preceding chapters that some offender/patients may have behaved or have been considered likely to behave in a manner that might cause serious harm to others; in other words, they have been considered to be 'dangerous'. The case of the psychopath, Patrick Mackay, quoted in Chapter 5 is a good illustration. As we shall see shortly, the concept of dangerousness has received much attention in recent years. Before we consider this in detail an introductory and important point needs to be made by way of clarification. Not all mentally disordered offenders are dangerous and not all dangerous offenders are necessarily mentally disordered. Tennent (1975) suggests that, theoretically, there are three types of relationship that can exist between 'aberrant or dangerous behaviour and mental disorder'. First, dangerous behaviour can occur as a result of mental illness (as illustrated in Chapter 3). Second, some aberrant and dangerous behaviour may occur in those offenders with mental illness, but for whom, treatment of the mental illness will not necessarily affect the aberrant or dangerous behaviour. Third, dangerous behaviour may be found in individuals without any evidence of mental disorder.

Because dangerous and potentially dangerous behaviour often comes to the attention of the psychiatric, penal, and

*Some of the case illustrations in this chapter appeared in my paper 'A Danger to Themselves and Others'. *British Journal of Social Work* 5(3): 1975. I am grateful to the Editor of that journal for permission to reproduce them here.

allied professions, whether or not it is connected specifically with mental disorder, it seems useful to deal with dangerousness as a generic concept rather than divide it into 'normal' on the one hand and 'abnormal' on the other. In most instances, the diagnostic and management procedures will be the same though the services involved may be different. The development of current interest in the problem of dangerousness has recently been well documented by Bottoms (1977). Such interest has developed very largely out of widespread community concern regarding the behaviour of one or two mentally disordered offenders, who, having been discharged into the community, have re-offended, sometimes with disastrous consequences. It was the conduct of one such offender, Francis Graham Young, that led to a committee of enquiry, the Aarvold Committee (Home Office 1973) being set up to examine specifically the procedures for the discharge and supervision of offender/patients subject to special restriction and then more generally to the establishment of the Butler Committee. However, it is important to point out here that quite apart from the case of Young and one or two others that had attracted notoriety (and to be described in more detail shortly), a number of reform groups had been deeply concerned about more general matters touching upon the treatment of the mentally disordered offender, particularly those sections of the Mental Health Act, 1959 that applied to this group. It is thus of 'more than passing interest to note as a phenomenon of social history, how frequently, the general and the particular combine to give rise to inquiries into matters of social concern and amelioration' (Prins 1976). The cases of Graham Young, Terence Iliffe, and some others will now be discussed as they illustrate vividly some of the problems in this field.

In 1962, Graham Young was convicted of administering poison to his father, his sister, and a schoolfriend. Fortunately, they all recovered. At his trial it was suggested that his behaviour was highly deliberate and dangerous; he was made subject of a Hospital Order with restrictions on his discharge (Section 65). During his nine years' detention in Broadmoor, Young apparently made good progress and he was able to be conditionally released in 1971. Young found work on his discharge; hindsight now indicates that his employment as a storekeeper where he had access to noxious chemicals, might have given premonition of the danger that could ensue. Very shortly after he started work, some of Young's workmates began to suffer from severe stomach pains, sickness, and other indications that they had been poisoned. Young was arrested. Following police investigation, his room at his lodgings was found to contain some very strange items – a variety of bottles, crude drawings of graveyards, swastikas, and syringes. It transpired subsequently that Young had administered the highly noxious chemical thallium to his workmates. Hindsight also revealed that Young had successfully concealed his interest in, and potential access to, various highly poisonous substances from those responsible for his supervision. As a result of the Aarvold enquiry, it appeared that effective communication between the personnel concerned with his after-care had been lacking and tighter measures have now been introduced to monitor and report upon the behaviour of such patients. Young was subsequently sentenced to imprisonment for life. His tragic story is reported in detail by Holden (1974). Although as we shall see later, it is impossible to make predictions of such behaviour with any absolute certainty in such cases, it should be possible to develop and improve our powers of observation and assessment to the extent that we may make the best attempts possible to avert tragedy.

Another *cause célèbre* was the case of Terence John Iliffe. Iliffe, who like Young, had been conditionally discharged from Broadmoor, was sentenced to life imprisonment in 1974 for the murder of his *fourth* wife. In fairness it must be stated that Iliffe was conditionally discharged from Broadmoor because, as the Butler Committee point out:

'the assessments made of him gave no reason to believe that he would present any general risk to the public . . . it was appreciated however that if Iliffe *were to remarry* [my italics] there might be a specific risk to his wife, and it was recognised by the supervising social workers as well as by the hospital that if he indicated any such intention his prospective wife must be fully informed of his background. It was not forseen that he would actually remarry without the knowledge of his supervising officer. When this fact was discovered appropriate action was taken to inform Mrs Iliffe about her husband, but tragically to no avail.'

(Home Office and DHSS 1975)

It is apparent from both these cases that once a carefully considered decision has been made to discharge such persons into the community there are limitations as to the degree of control that can be exercised. Short of the supervising officer monitoring his client/patient day and night it is well nigh impossible to prevent such behaviour occurring. However, it is vital for all those responsible for the supervision of such offenders to be in possession of as full a picture of the total situation as possible. It is equally important for them to be in regular and full communication with each other. If this occurs there can be less valid cause for criticism after the event. This is a matter that will be referred to again later.

In addition to these two *causes célèbres*, there have been a number of other cases reported in the press, all of which demonstrate similar problems. Some of these are now quoted as supporting evidence. As they all received full press coverage, the usual precautions preserving anonymity have not been taken.

(1) The case of Kenneth Johnson, reported in *The Guardian* on 15 March 1974. This man was able to get out of an unlocked ward in a psychiatric hospital; he went home and killed his five-year-old son by stamping on his head. Mr Justice McKenna was reported as saying: 'One of the matters that has disturbed me is that, after making threats with a knife serious enough for the police to take him to hospital he was kept during the day time in an unlocked ward.' Johnson pleaded guilty to manslaughter on the grounds of diminished responsibility and was committed to Broadmoor.

(2) The case of Mrs. Wiggins, reported in *The Guardian* on 9 May 1974. This lady of fifty-seven who had been released from Broadmoor ten years earlier was sent back there for the mur-

der of her ten-month-old granddaughter. Her earlier detention had been ordered after she had been convicted of murdering her seven-year-old son. In the present instance, she had
killed her granddaughter in a way exactly similar to that in
which she had killed her son seventeen years earlier. Mr Justice
Waller, in passing sentence, stated that no criticism could be
made of the authorities at Broadmoor for releasing her initially or of the doctors and social workers who had followed her
medical progress at that time.

It is relevant to note here that on the day the defendant
killed her granddaughter she is reported to have told the
police officers: 'while I was on the bus the baby was crying and I
had no milk or nappies for it. Something just keeps coming
into my head to do something to the baby.' Such comments are
not unlike those made by some 'battering parents' in the way
they denote their unbearable tension, anxiety, and confusion.

(3) The case of Lyndon Nott, reported in *The Guardian* on 9
August 1974. Nott had been sent to Broadmoor for murdering
a woman. Subsequently, as part of normal pre-discharge policy
he had been allowed out and had attacked a young girl. The
newspaper accounts at the time stressed that ordinary psychiatric hospitals felt under considerable pressure from the
DHSS to take cases the special hospitals considered to have
recovered sufficiently to allow out on trial.

(4) The case of Barry Jones, reported in *The Guardian* on 19
March 1975. Jones had assaulted and tried to strangle a
fourteen-year-old girl within only two months of being
released from hospital by a Mental Health Review Tribunal.
The Court was told that Mr Jones had spent thirteen of his
thirty-two years under detention in mental and special hospitals. Following his release, his parents had become very disturbed by his behaviour. They had sought advice, but 'with no
satisfaction'. The court sent him back to a special hospital for
an indefinite period. (Section 65 of the Mental Health Act.)

(5) The case of Barry Robinson, reported in *The Guardian* on
15 October 1974. Robinson, a former Broadmoor patient,
kidnapped a policeman and two other men. He was sentenced
to life imprisonment for the second time in twelve years. His

previous life sentence had been for hitting an old man with a brick and robbing him. He had had a drink problem for many years and had also been imprisoned for an axe attack on a garage attendant in the course of a robbery. It is interesting to note that he was said to be a talented artist and that his work had attracted the attention of experts. Significantly, perhaps, his last job before his court appearance was to 'paint lurid murals on the side of the Count Dracula's Castle Ride'. The significance of painting and phantasy as possible indicators of potentially dangerous behaviour will be the subject of later comment.

(6) The case of Pauline Tidy reported in *The Guardian* on 29 July 1976. Miss Tidy (aged eighteen) was convicted of suffocating a nineteen-month-old baby boy, wrapping him in a sheet and placing the body in a deep freeze. She was found guilty on manslaughter on the grounds of diminished responsibility and was ordered to be detained in Broadmoor without limit of time. Miss Tidy had been employed as a child-minder by the infant's parents. It had not been disclosed to them that she had been receiving psychiatric treatment. It was also alleged that on more than one occasion she had told those treating her that she 'wanted to do something terrible' and had said 'I was going to do it. I said I was going to do something to somebody, but I wasn't believed.' It also transpired at her trial that whilst at school she had dropped a breeze-block on another pupil. In a *Guardian* leader of 30 July 1976 it was suggested that Miss Tidy was a 'potential murderer in search of a victim'.

(7) The case of Michael William Parrott, reported in *The Guardian* on 6 November 1976. In 1972, Parrott had been convicted of indecently assaulting a nine-year-old boy. An order had been made that he should be detained in hospital for an unspecified period of time, but he had been released twelve months later. In August 1976, he took an eleven-year-old boy into his home and strangled him. Parrott, who was said to be suffering from a psychopathic disorder, pleaded guilty to manslaughter. He was ordered to be detained in Broadmoor for an unlimited period. The Judge commented that he hoped the authorities would hesitate before releasing him again. At

his first court appearance in 1972, the psychiatrists who examined him had suggested that he go to Broadmoor, but he was admitted to an ordinary psychiatric hospital where he had received hormone treatment to help reduce his sexual urges. When questioned by the police about the current offence, Parrott is alleged to have said: 'There was this laughing and voices in my head. I have had this before, but not as bad as today. I had this sudden urge and placed my hands round (his) neck and applied pressure.' Parrott had then 'phoned a psychiatrist saying that he was trying to commit suicide and that there was a boy in the house. Upon arrival at the house the police found the boy's body.

(8) The case of Christopher Simcox, which has been very fully reported upon by Blom-Cooper (1965). This man's first marriage ended in divorce, but not before he had been convicted for assault upon his wife, and also upon his mother-in-law. His second marriage ended more violently – he was convicted of murdering his wife with a knife wound to the throat. He was sentenced to death, but reprieved, and ten years later released from prison on licence. In 1961 he married for the third time, but after a short while, he was again in court, having been 'caught in the preparatory stages of violent action'. The charge he was actually convicted of was one of carrying an offensive weapon. Evidence was given that a calculated risk might be taken and the Judge made a probation order, with a condition that Simcox never saw his wife again. Within less than two weeks, that order had been breached, and Simcox had killed his sister-in-law and wounded another of his wife's relatives. At his second trial for murder, evidence was given that Simcox was a paranoid personality. Blom-Cooper (1965) in discussing this and comparable cases, makes the important point that:

'a paranoid personality is not acquired overnight, nor is it a temporary condition. Hindsight tells us that Simcox telegraphed his future homicidal behaviour, both by telling people that he intended to kill both his wife and himself, and by actually being convicted, only 11 days before killing his sister-in-law, of prowling around his wife's house with a dangerous weapon . . .'

Fortunately, the kind of events quoted above occur rarely. On the whole, offender/patients discharged from the special hospitals and similar institutions do not re-offend with any degree of seriousness. Following the implementation of the Aarvold Committee's recommendations in respect of restricted patients, the procedures for their review have now been tightened up; under these new procedures very few patients have re-offended whilst in the community. However, one cannot gainsay the fact that difficult predictive decisions have to be made all the time and that there will be occasions when human judgement will be in error. These problems were stated clearly by the members of the Aarvold Committee.

> 'The making of recommendations and decisions about the discharge and continuing care of mentally disordered offenders entails, fundamentally, the assessment and pred-iction, by one group of human beings, of the probable future behaviour of another. Prescribed procedures can offer real safeguards against the chance of human error going undetected, but we do not believe that in this sort of situation there can be an absolute guarantee of infallibility. Indeed, there might be a risk that the adoption of over-elaborate proceedings could reduce the quality of judge-ments made, by *weakening the sense of personal responsibility* which those who care for these unfortunate individuals bring to their tasks [my italics]. The complete elimination of any risk to the public could only be achieved by continuing to detain these patients perhaps indefinitely, long after many of them recovered from their mental disorder and for periods in excess of any term of imprisonment they might have served as sentence for their offences. We are sure that in our society this would be seen as an inhumane avoidance of the responsibility for making a proper judgement in each case.'

(Home Office 1973).

The cases I quoted do throw up a number of issues for examination. First of all we shall have to consider what we mean when we use the term 'dangerous' and the extent to which the law recognizes explicitly the concept of dangerousness. Second, we shall need to consider some of the ethical issues that may flow from any concepts of dangerousness that we adopt. Third, we shall need to examine a number of issues concerning the assessment, prediction, and management of the so-called dangerous offender. In this latter connection, we shall return to some of the cases already cited since they afford a number of useful illustrations of the possibilities or otherwise of effective intervention.

What do we mean by the term dangerousness?

Dangerousness is a relative concept and can mean many things to many people. As Tennent (1975) suggests there are 'many forms of danger, both of people and of objects, concrete or abstract. We speak of social danger, political danger, moral danger, as well as physical danger.' I have suggested elsewhere that we may have to ask ourselves who is the more dangerous, the murderer, the rapist, the arsonist, the bank-robber, the drunken driver, the embezzler, the spy, the revolutionary, or the zealot? (Prins 1975). Most people would agree with Walker (1978) when he states that we are primarily concerned with 'dangerous people'. As he rightly goes on to point out 'dangerousness is not an objective quality, but an ascribed quality like trustworthiness. We feel justified in talking about a person as dangerous if he has indicated by word or deed that he is more likely than most people to do serious harm, or act in a way that is likely to result in serious harm . . .' Walker goes on to suggest that most people would interpret harm in this context to mean such acts as homicide, rape, mutilation, or the promotion of destitution. The propensity to cause personal harm weighed very heavily in the considerations of the Butler Committee when they examined the question of dangerousness. 'We have come to equate dangerousness with a tendency to cause serious physical injury or lasting psychological harm. Physical violence is, we think, what the public are most worried about, but the psychological damage which may be suffered by some victims of other crime is not to be underrated.' Elsewhere, I have equated dangerousness with impulsive, uncensored, personal violence towards others, and, indeed, sometimes towards self (Prins 1975). Scott (1977), in a seminal paper on this subject, reminds us that the social context is all important and that it is 'easier to say what dangerousness is not than what it is. It is not simply that which is noxious or evil, and it is not necessarily a violent or explosive trait of an individual.' As Scott says, the man who smokes on an oil tanker is potentially dangerous by reason of the explosive material around him; if he refuses repeatedly to 'douse that glim' it is likely to be assumed that he has dangerous intentions rather than that he is merely feckless. We shall see when we consider issues concerning management, that the social context of the offender will be of paramount importance in considering his potential for dangerous behaviour.

It is worth noting here the relationship between *violence* (which, as Scott says, is aggression concentrated into brief time) and dangerousness. In general the nature of the behaviour which society is likely to describe as dangerous is that which is violent. But, as Sarbin (1967) suggests, the concepts of danger and the concepts of violence are not necessarily coterminous. As he says 'violence denotes action; danger denotes a relationship'. This latter observation is of crucial importance and we shall need to consider it in more detail when we discuss problems of management.* In summary, we may concur with Scott (1977) when he says that 'Dangerousness then is an unpredictable and untreatable tendency to inflict or risk serious, irreversible injury or destruction, or to induce others to do so. Dangerousness can, of course be directed against the self.' (See also Prins 1975.)

---

* Sarbin makes an interesting comment concerning the etymology of the word 'danger'. Contrary to popular belief it is derived from the Latin *dominiarium* – meaning Lordship or Sovereignty and not to 'physicalist' conceptions. Sarbin goes on to suggest that this derivation has meaning in terms of the positions held by individuals in the social structure based on relative power and esteem. He argues that this meaning has important implications in relation to a man's concept of his social identity and to the actions he (or others) may take, as a social animal, to confirm or deny it (Sarbin 1967).

Dangerousness and the law

Unlike some other countries we do not define dangerous individuals specifically by statute (Levine 1975). It is true that the law recognizes offences such as dangerous driving, endangering the lives of passengers, having vehicles in a dangerous condition, or being in possession of dangerous drugs, and dangerous behaviour may of course be implied in prosecutions for negligence. Offenders who persist in crime, but not always in dangerous, physical, assaultive crime, may be liable to periods of extended imprisonment if the court is satisfied that they are eligible for such a sentence on the basis of previous criminal record and present offence. (The criteria for imposition of such a penalty are quite strict.) It is also true that the dangerous proclivities of some offender/patients are recognized in the relevant statutes setting up and maintaining our special hospitals in that they exist, *inter alia* for those offender/patients who exhibit 'dangerous, violent or criminal propensities' (Mental Health Act, 1959; restated in the National Health Service Act, 1977). In considering the legal and administrative provisions required for those offenders considered to be dangerous, the Butler Committee (Home Office and DHSS) made a number of recommendations. First, that a *new form of sentence* should be introduced from which release would be dependent entirely on the issue of dangerousness. Such a sentence would be for offenders who are dangerous, who present a history of mental disorder which could not be dealt with under the Mental Health Act, and for whom the life sentence is not considered to be appropriate. The sentence would be reviewable at two-yearly intervals. Upon release the offender would be under compulsory supervision and subject to statutory review. Second, the imposition of such a sentence would be restricted to conviction for those offences which caused or might have caused grave harm to others. The Committee provided two schedules indicating what would constitute such offences. Amongst others they included murder, manslaughter, rape, arson and criminal damage endangering life, firearms and explosives offences,

Hi-jacking, infliction of grievous bodily harm with intent, sexual offences, robbery, aggravated burglary, ill-treatment of children, and carrying an offensive weapon in a public place. (See Appendix 4 of the report for further details and also 'The Dangerous Offender: A Consultative Document' (1977) for discussion of some of the difficulties evisaged in interpreting the law on this matter.) Third, the Home Secretary should have the power to transfer a prisoner serving a reviewable sentence from prison to hospital under Section 72 of the Mental Health Act, 1959. In such instances, a restriction order would be placed upon the discharge of the prisoner from hospital. Fourth, the two-yearly review would be carried out by the Parole Board and release would be on licence of unlimited duration; however, the conditions would be subject to a two-yearly review, with the possibility of their eventual removal.

It seems clear that the Butler Committee were anxious to give legal and administrative recognition to classes of person who can be considered to be dangerous. Such recognition introduces a new legal category and raises a number of ethical issues. We must now consider some of these.

Ethical issues

In assessing dangerousness in individuals we are concerned with degrees of harm, particularly grave harm. These are hard to define, particularly if we accept the view of Scott and the Butler Committee that harm can include psychological harm. The degree of such harm is of course well-nigh impossible to measure with any degree of accuracy, but some attempt must be made to do so. As we have seen, once such persons have been identified and labelled they may be liable to be detained for very long periods of time and may only be released on the exercise of executive and not judicial discretion. The nature of the offence itself, or to be more precise, its legal classification, does not necessarily give an accurate indication of the degree of harm caused, either actual or potential. I know of an offender who was convicted and given a comparatively light sentence for quite a serious indecent assault on a youth. Careful inspection of the case revealed considerable force was used in the perpetration of the offence and the young man was put in considerable fear. The offence classification and the sentence imposed gave no indication of the real severity of the offence or of the offender's likelihood of committing a further (and perhaps more serious) offence in the future. Walker (1978) is concerned to limit as far as is possible the infliction of measures that would deprive the offender of his liberty for very long periods of time. He suggests that such measures of detention should be used only to 'prevent serious and lasting hardship to other individuals, of a kind, which, once caused, cannot be remedied.' He suggests a set of five useful rules that might go some way towards resolving many of the ethical dilemmas involved. First, he suggests that we might exclude property offences from our consideration since most loss or damage to property can be remedied by compensation. He would also exclude from considerations of grave harm cases of temporary alarm (for example, threats with imitation or unloaded weapons) and minor threats to decency, for example, indecent exposure. (I find this latter exclusion somewhat questionable since the amount of psychological harm caused may well depend upon the circumstances in which the offence took place; some children, and even a few adults, find the confrontation of indecent exposure very frightening.) However, he *includes* the offences of rape, blackmail, kidnapping, and by implication, all serious assaults. Walker does not state that the harm must actually have been done. If the offender *intended* the harm or must have appreciated that harm was a highly likely result of what he did or attempted he should come within Walker's first rule. It is likely that this question of intent would be a difficult matter to establish in this context. Second, he suggests a further safeguard against unjustified detention; the actions or behaviours to which his first rule would apply should not be isolated, out-of-character episodes. Previous similar conduct would help to establish whether or not a pattern existed, as would, for example, declared intentions of future vengeance. Third, Walker suggests that a further rule would operate in the offender's favour if the incentives for his initial offending had ceased to exist, or, through incapacity, he was considered to be unlikely to repeat his behaviour. The former criterion might be less easy to substantiate than the latter since it has not been unknown for those who have murdered to find surrogate victims. Fourth, Walker argues that if there is any possibility of the use of measures other than detention they should be used. He also suggests a greater use of supervision and control in the community. I have much sympathy with this point of view. One must acknowledge, however, that probation officers and other social workers have declared their disquiet about acquiring any greater powers of control over offenders than they have available at present. I suggest that what they may fail to recognize is that unless they are prepared to move increasingly into the 'control business', many dangerous and potentially dangerous offenders may be detained in prisons and hospitals for longer periods of time than necessary. Walker also makes the suggestion (with which I have much sympathy) that it should be possible to disqualify people from undertaking certain jobs, such as responsibility for the care of children. As he rightly points out we are not normally reluctant to disqualify those adjudged to be dangerous motorists from holding driving licences. Fifth, he suggests that if we do have to impose measures of 'preventive' detention, then the conditions of this detention should be as humane and tolerable as possible.

As we shall see, there have been indications in recent years that social workers and others have been more than a little reluctant to initiate active interventions that might well have averted a tragedy. The kind of limitations and safeguards suggested by Walker have a general applicability; within such a clearly delineated framework those who have to deal with the dangerous and potentially dangerous offender might feel a little less self-conscious about imposing their authority and power to enforce sanctions.

Prediction, assessment, and management

Sadly, there are no statistical or actuarial measures available that offer the prediction of dangerousness with certainty, although a useful beginning in this field has been made by workers such as Payne, Walker, and McCabe (1974), by Nichol *et al.* (1972), by Megargee (1976), and Greenland (1978). Despite the fact that much research has been carried out into the prediction of criminal behaviour more generally (see, for example, Simon 1971) this merely seems to suggest that although actuarial techniques can discriminate between high-risk and low-risk groups, there will always be a residual majority in the middle-risk groups, whose re-offending rates are too near 'fifty-fifty' to be of much use.

An interesting study is one undertaken by Kozol and his colleagues (1972). They obtained follow-up information on a sample of offender/patients who had been discharged despite the fact that the psychiatrists responsible for their care had classified them as being dangerous. Only about a third of the group actually became involved in violence on discharge. As Kozol and his colleagues aptly state: 'If three people are released, one of them will attack someone, but we do not know which one of the three will do so.' Not unnaturally, we find that psychiatrists and their colleagues tend to err on the side of caution when asked to make predictions about future behaviour. In what has now become a classic study, Steadman and Cocozza (1974) examined a group of allegedly dangerous mentally abnormal offenders who had been freed from detention as a result of an important American high court decision. This was that a patient – one Johnnie Baxstrom – had been incarcerated unconstitutionally. One effect of the 'Baxstrom decision', as it is now called, was that a large number of other patients also had to be discharged into the community. Steadman and Cocozza were therefore afforded a unique opportunity to test out the validity or otherwise of prolonged detention for so-called criminally insane and dangerous offenders. As a result of their large-scale and careful survey the authors concluded that psychiatrists were too cautious in their predictions and that prolonged incarceration was not required for the majority of such patients. However, it should be pointed out here that a large number of these offender/patients were over fifty years of age when released. Had this research involved a younger and potentially more aggressive age group the findings might have been different.

In the absence of any fool-proof actuarial devices, and the tendency for those concerned to come up with what statisticians describe as 'false positives', are we left with any indicators of the *probability* of dangerous behaviour? It has been said, no doubt somewhat cynically, that nothing predicts behaviour like behaviour. We know for example that some groups of offenders will *tend* to repeat their behaviour. Exhibitionists (see Chapter 8) tend to repeat their offences, but only occasionally do they go on to indulge in more serious sexual criminality. Men with several convictions for violence are considerably more likely than their fellows to be convicted of violence in the future. The Butler Committee, in recognizing the limitations of objective assessment, wondered whether it was better to rely upon a 'continuing process of treatment and subjective assessment in which checks on adjustment are constantly made in the light of the developing pattern of behaviour evinced by the individual concerned' (Home Office and DHSS). In the absence of any firm statistical measures we are forced to rely upon human judgement and the degree of error implicit in it. Whilst recognizing that our judgement *may* sometimes be wrong, I suggest that there have been occasions when the professionals concerned have not taken as many opportunities as they might have done to confront, analyse, and work with potentially dangerous situations. With this in mind I can now return to some of the examples from the press already cited. From a consideration of these cases it emerges that although some of the individuals concerned gave premonition of their intended behaviour, this was either not recognized, or ignored. Before examining these matters in any detail, there are some general observations to be made. Social workers are often in a pre-eminent position to become involved in the social backgrounds of offender/patients and thereby to observe and monitor changes in behaviour. In the past, social workers were taught the value of taking a full 'social history'. They were also encouraged to see how this history taking would add to the picture of the patient derived from other sources. In this way, a full assessment could be made of the patient's present situation, the stresses within it, and in the light of this, potential for recovery. Unfortunately, the reorganization of social services departments, of local government areas, and of the NHS, has brought with it rapid movements of staff with a consequential dilution of specialist skills. This has been nowhere more apparent than in the field of mental health social work. From the point of view of some psychiatrists, much of the expertise of the old mental welfare officer has been dissipated. I know from my experience as a social work teacher that there is also a considerable degree of reluctance to deal with the mentally ill, particularly the potentially violent and more severely disturbed, on the part of social work students and the newly qualified. Many writers on socioforensic matters have attested to the need for a full investigation of the social history and current situation in cases where dangerous behaviour has been shown or was thought to be likely. This need is very well attested to by Blair (1971) in his discussion of the case of Richard Holmes. Holmes, aged twenty-two, was sentenced to life imprisonment for wounding with intent to murder. Shortly after sentence, he committed suicide. Blair, in a very sensitive and detailed account of this sad case, draws attention to the fact that the prison medical officer did not feel it necessary to interview Holmes's parents, nor, apparently, were reports called for from 'any psychiatric social worker or probation officer.' He suggests that had full and detailed information been available, not only would a much clearer understanding of this young man's history and mental state have been possible, but a tragedy might also have been averted. The need for careful elicitation of all the facts, and the ways in which these might be obtained, is also referred to by Scott (1977). 'It is patience, thoroughness and persistence in this process, rather than any diagnostic or interviewing brilliance that produces results. In this sense the telephone, the written request for past records and the checking of information against *other informants*, are the important diagnostic devices [my italics].' Would that all psychiatrists and social workers always followed such good advice.

In recent years, social workers (perhaps with some justification) have become somewhat preoccupied with the rights of individuals to privacy. This and the encouragement of the idea of equal or reciprocal relationships between client/patient and worker both in residential and field social work has led to reluctance on the part of some social workers to ask direct questions and to follow them up. It is more than likely that a large proportion of these clients/patients not only expect to be asked quite searching questions but are often relieved when they have been. They often say that they have been pleased to have been given the chance to unburden themselves. Success will be achieved if such questions are put in a non-threatening, sympathetic, and non-accusatory fashion. The following is an example of the type of omission I have in mind. A student had taken a social history from the relatives of a schizophrenic patient; he had obtained useful information about the habits of the patient, including the fact that he shut himself away for a good deal of time in his room. The student omitted to take the questioning one stage further and enquire how the patient occupied himself during the time he was on his own. Had he done so, he would have found, as subsequent enquiry revealed, that he spent his time filling numerous notebooks with writings that revealed morbidly aggressive and bizarre phantasies.

One final point now needs to be made. It concerns the unfortunate 'anti-psychiatry' attitudes shown by some social workers. (See Chapter 3.) Though not as prevalent as in the 1960s they are still not uncommon and have important implications for the development or otherwise of a harmonious team approach which is so vital to the total treatment of the dangerous or potentially dangerous offender. Some social workers have been stridently over-critical of psychiatrists, often on the basis of very flimsy evidence. Lest social workers consider that they are the only people concerned about the possible abuses of patient's rights we should note what Doctor McGrath of Broadmoor Hospital has to say:

'It is enormously important for the hospital to keep in touch with the after-care agencies who often feel out of their depth in caring for homicides in the community, and who have to be supported to cope with the repugnance at their own feeling that they may be instruments in the readmission of a patient who has not yet offended again. This potential guilt is not the sole prerogative of the . . . caseworker, but is shared by doctors, who do not delight in incarcerating the legally defenceless . . .'

(McGrath 1968)

In concluding this brief exploration of the general climate of opinion and attitudes affecting work in this field, we should not underestimate the enormous turnover of social workers particularly in social services departments. This precludes not only the opportunity for experience of *long-term follow up* of offender/patients, but also the opportunity to gain regular first-hand experience in this specialist area of work.

I have already stressed the need for a careful review of the total social situation of the dangerous or potentially dangerous offender/patient and I referred to the reluctance of some workers to ask the questions that might give important prognostic clues. Further aspects of this reluctance are now considered. One important and additional reason for this hesitance may be the tendency for workers in this field, be they social workers, psychiatrists, or institutional staff, to over-identify with the offender/patient. Because of this, they may not take into account important aspects of the individual's less desirable behaviour as reported by family members and others. Johnston (1967) has stated that 'many psychiatrists identify too closely with the patient and become too sympathetic with his problem, and as a result, come up with a judgement which is not based on the stark reality of the situation.'

Usdin (1967) has stated that we may often miss the clues given us by our clients. He suggests that we do not like to hear some of the things that these people are saying; as he puts it, 'we might get alarmed or insulted . . .' He goes on to argue that the mechanism of denial is not one reserved for patients: '. . . quite often our antennae did not pick up what they were saying and that they were relating important material. As numerous studies have reported, the suicidal patient nearly always gives warnings that he is contemplating suicide. There is no reason to believe that the homicidal patient does not do likewise . . .' Some recent studies have shown a high incidence of mental illness *coupled with premonitory signs* in cases where serious violence has been demonstrated. Faulk (1974), in a study of twenty-five men remanded in prison on charges of seriously assaulting their wives or co-habitees, found in almost 70 per cent of cases that there were premonitory signs of violence. Seven of the wives had received a warning but had not acted upon this. Cuthbert (1970) has also drawn attention to these and allied phenomena. He suggests that sometimes 'the writing was on the wall for all to see'. He gives three illustrations of this. First, the case of a murderer of an adolescent homosexual. 'The probability of the assailant becoming a murderer had been recorded in the prison case records some years before, *and* while he was serving one of his numerous offences for sadistic offences.' Second, the case of a murderer who had given 'many indications that he would ultimately kill someone while intoxicated and sexually stimulated; medical advice had twice been sought but not followed up . . .' Third, the case of a fifteen-year-old boy, delinquent and solitary, indicted for killing his mother by shooting. Shortly before the killing he had strangled two cats and left them, as Cuthbert says 'on a doorstep for all to see'. Reference to the cases cited at the beginning of this chapter also confirms that the premonitory signs are frequently there, yet nobody takes action. It may be as Macdonald (1969) suggests, that the 'non directive psychiatric interview facilitates avoidance of violence when this is the wish of the patient, his relatives and the physician'. Many of us are likely to be uncertain in our reactions to threats of violence, particularly if these are homicidal. These threats can too easily be met with a bland reassurance such as 'You wouldn't do anything like that would you?' When a person with a background of violent behaviour threatens extreme violence, for example, towards a spouse, our traditional psychotherapeutic response might be to say something like 'This must upset you a lot, would you like to tell me a bit more about your marriage

. . .?' We might do better by asking, 'What plans have you made . . .?'

In trying to assess an offender/patient's potential for dangerous behaviour we need to have in mind a number of areas for examination. I now enumerate these with some comment on each.

(1) What seems to have been the nature of the precipitating stress factors in the offender's social environment in the past? Have these been removed? If not, to what extent can they perhaps be moderated if the offender is allowed to go free in the community? (I have already referred to Walker's rule on this matter.) Sadly, as already suggested, an offender who has caused serious harm to a relative may still need to destroy a surrogate. The earlier quoted cases of Simcox and Iliffe are good examples of this. To what extent was the original offence caused by provocation, conscious or unconscious? In this context, Macdonald (1967) reminds us of the 'female hysterical character who continues to wear dresses that are several inches too short and to behave in a flirtatious manner despite the angry response of a jealous husband . . .' He quotes the further example of a youth who had been hospitalized for threatening to kill his father. The boy rang his father to ask him if he would take him home for the day. The father indicated that he would be down 'right away'. The boy asked when that would be. The father, who only lived twenty minutes away, said 'two hours'. We need to remind ourselves constantly of the need to be on the look out for victim-precipitated encounters in which the probable victim is continually provoking the potentially dangerous person. These people may of course be drawn into such encounters to satisfy sado-masochistic needs. At a more practical level, should not social workers and others be on the alert for ways in which we might prevent the means of destruction being available too readily? One remembers here the ease with which Graham Young secured a form of employment which gave him easy access to the means of destroying others. A more recent example is the case of the

sixteen-year-old American girl quoted in *The Guardian* of 31 January 1979. She is alleged to have killed two men, and wounded eight children aged between six and fourteen and a policeman in a sniping attack before finally surrendering to the police. She was said to like television violence and setting fire to cats by pouring petrol on their tails. More ominous perhaps, is the statement by a school classmate. 'Her father bought her a rifle for Christmas and she was always boasting about the guns her father had.' I have already referred to the suggestion made by Walker (1978) that certain individuals might well be disqualified from placing themselves in situations in which they may be especially vulnerable. Macdonald has a very apt quotation from Shakespeare's *King John*: 'How oft the sight of means to do ill deeds makes ill deeds done.'

(2) What is the offender/patient's capacity for sympathetic identification with others? In what way may the previous history given by both the patient and those near to him confirm or refute this? Has he still some capacity left for learning by experience?

(3) Does he seem to derive satisfaction from the infliction of pain or suffering on others? Can we ascertain whether his violence was directed against a particular individual for specific reasons or was it directed against the world in general? Is he the sort of person who continually feels threatened and persecuted? We should note here the remarks made about the paranoid and mobidly jealous in Chapter 3.

(4) In addition to personal behaviour and expressions of attitude, are there other clues we might use? Sometimes, the eliciting of violent or sadistic phantasies or preoccupations may give us useful clues. However, too much importance should not be attached to this because we do not know the extent to which such preoccupations are indulged in by those who never actually behave dangerously. Having said this, some clues do seem to have ominous prognostications. It will be remembered that Barry Robinson seemed to derive satisfaction from painting lurid mur-

als on Count Dracula's Castle Ride. Brittain (1970), in a paper on the sadistic murderer, has provided us with a detailed account of the manner in which some people develop *but at the same time* attempt to conceal their sadistic and murderous phantasies. One wonders whether the course of events might have been different if those responsible for Young's supervision had gained access to his room and taken note of the ominous array of articles it contained. Finally, a combination of sadistic phantasy with *actual violence* can be regarded as a very ominous finding.

(5) Can we gain any clues from choice of previous employments or occupations? Scott (1977) suggests that very occasionally these may provide us with useful hints. Butchering and work in abattoirs is sometimes found in the employment records of those convicted of particularly sadistic offences; sadistic children sometimes show a preference for work as veterinary surgeons, showing an unusual interest in sick and damaged animals. It is noted that these quickly die in their care, as do their own pets.

(6) Can we learn anything from the way in which the offender talks about his offence and his behaviour? Occasionally, it is difficult to distinguish between a near hysterical threat of murderous intent and one that is made quietly, calmly, but with absolute conviction. It is sometimes an ominous sign if the offence is discussed in a dispassionate guilt-free manner. However, we should remember that after the perpetration of a particularly serious offence, such as homicide, many protective mechanisms come into play. These can present as callous indifference. Time is needed for these mechanisms to be dissipated and the underlying attitudes revealed. It is equally easy to be misled initially by expressions of guilt and contrition. Russell and Russell (1961) state that a 'person who expresses guilt [in this context] is to be regarded with vigilance. His next move . . . may be . . . to engineer a situation in which he can repeat the activities (about which he expresses guilt), but this time with rationalisations and hence without guilt. He will therefore try to manipulate his victim into giving him a pretext . . .'

So far I have concentrated specifically upon techniques of investigation and assessment and said less about the more personal attributes the worker should bring to his dealings with dangerous or potentially dangerous clients. It is maybe no 'accident' that I have left this important subject to be considered last, because most of us are reluctant to admit that these types of clients may frighten us. Sometimes we may find it very difficult to put this fear into words. We say that we have a 'hunch', or, I have heard some people say 'it is something in his eyes'. This may sound absurd and indeed I have been criticized by one colleague (Webb 1976) for explaining dangerous behaviour *post hoc* and for suggesting that we should rely on hunches. But sometimes we *may* have to act upon informed hunches rather than upon proven facts and try to apply what we have learned the hard way from one case to the next. We may well ask ourselves, what is it we are afraid of? We can certainly be afraid of physical violence. Lion (1972) has drawn attention to some aspects of this including the fact that some violent persons may not only wish to be controlled, but are in fact afraid of their own violent urges. Cox (1974), in a paper on the psychotherapist's anxiety in dealing with offender/patients, reminds us of the importance of our own anxieties in this area. He also suggests that some offender/patients may be frightened to talk about their feelings and phantasies because they feel the therapist is himself too frightened to want to listen to them. There is a close link here with the comments I made earlier about the operation of the denial defence mechanism. Of what then are we afraid, if it is not the threat of physical violence? Is it the fear that we may *unwittingly provoke* a violent and unpredictable assault, or are we more afraid that our own ego may be overwelmed by that of the dangerous offender/patient and that somehow we may be engulfed by his violent phantasy system? As already indicated, it is only after an intensive study of the individual, his past history and his life style that we may be afforded clues as to the likelihood of violent and unpredictable outbursts. A useful illustration of this would be an assault committed in circumstances that amounted to homosexual 'panic'. The so-called normal person who violently attacks another because of an alleged homosexual overture, may well need to have his actions understood more in terms of his own possible repressed homosexuality than solely as the reactions of an outraged male responding to an unwelcome overture. As a general rule, I would suggest that the greater degree of violence shown, the more precarious the so-called normal person's defences may be. These phenomena have been discussed very helpfully by Woods (1975).

In order for us to operate effectively and humanely in work with dangerous and potentially dangerous clients, it is necessary for us to have tried to come to terms with our own potential for violent or dangerous behaviour. It is also helpful if we can learn to behave calmly when explosive behaviour threatens. If we can 'keep the scream out of our voice' this may help. In certain circumstances we may have to attempt quietly and firmly to remove a dangerous weapon from a person using it. A quiet voice and calm movements will probably help; with some violent offender/patients it is probably best to avoid eyeball-to-eyeball confrontation by looking obliquely at them. As Jordan and Packman (1978) point out, there is no particularly good reason why social workers (or psychiatrists for that matter) should be naturally good at dealing with violent situations. They suggest that the kind of person who wishes to be a social worker may frequently be of a personality type not suited to engagement in violent confrontations. They are unlike policemen, who they suggest, might reasonably be expected to be 'rather extraverted, confident, physically large and physically brave'; there are no good reasons for suggesting that social workers should be any of these things. In fact, the opposite may be nearer the truth, for by and large social workers are likely to be recruited from the ranks of the introverted and possibly less physically robust. It may be that social workers and others are sometimes particularly effective in these explosive situations, because, unlike officers of the law, they are in no position to enforce or carry through any kind of physical submission. They have only themselves and their personal skills to rely upon. They may, therefore, be the best people to open up lines of communication. In this connection one is mindful of the work of Sarbin (1967) quoted earlier in this chapter. As Sarbin suggests, danger is not to be construed solely as the expression of a personality trait, but rather as a relationship of relative power in a role-system. If this be so, then a social worker may find communication easier in a danger-laden situation than may a police officer or other easily identified law enforcement officer. As Sarbin says: 'The experience of potential danger alters the perceptual accuracy of guards, policemen and others in reciprocal positions to . . . those . . . defined as non-persons. Misperceptions may lead to premature power displays which in turn exacerbate the degredation process . . .'

We can now summarize some of the essential attributes needed by those who have to work with dangerous clients or in situations where danger threatens.

(1) To be honest with oneself and to acknowledge one's own violent potential. This can only come about through effective support and supervision from more experienced colleagues. These colleagues can also alert us to our 'blind-spots' and to the dangers of over-identification and denial already referred to.

(2) We should remember also that a 'panic reaction' on our part in a moment of particular stress may prevent us from hearing significant words or messages from the client or it may blind us to the importance of certain things that are left unsaid.

(3) The development of a capacity to take a rounded and objective view of the person adjudged to be dangerous or potentially dangerous. This will include all the points made earlier about the need for a careful in-depth examination of the person's social situation and the forces operating for stress – both past and present.

(4) Trying to present as a 'still centre' in dangerous or potentially dangerous situations. This will often convey calm to the client.

(5) If, after careful consideration, we judge the situation to be right, we may have to take our courage in our hands and intervene quite directly, for example, by removing a

weapon from someone who is threatening to use it. This is always a finely poised issue, there may be little time for reflection, and one can only judge the situation as it appears at that particular point in time. A calm voice, an averted gaze, and slow calm movements augur for a better response than a panic-stricken grab or strident command. In general, it is better to sit than to stand. If we stand in a confronting position in relation to a potentially dangerous client, he may feel overwhelmed and panic-stricken. A position taken at the rear of such a client may be particularly threatening.

(6) Being prepared to respond speedily to a developing crisis situation. From time to time, offender/patients feel that things are beginning to 'blow up'. The opportunity for temporary readmission, compulsorily or (preferably) otherwise, should not be missed. George Stürup, who was for many years medical superintendent of Denmark's famous psychopathic institution at Herstedvester, relates how a former inmate appeared at their gates and asked how many offences he had to commit before he could be readmitted! Fortunately, Stürup and his colleagues acted upon such a *cri de cveur* and arranged for the man's readmission (Stürup 1968). McGrath has described a somewhat similar provision at Broadmoor (1958). It could well be that some of the disasters that have occurred might have been avoided if our social, penal, and psychiatric services were able to provide temporary 'asylum' or, as is now happening in some areas, a crisis intervention service staffed by psychiatrists and social workers. Support for the introduction of such schemes can be found in a paper by Craft (1974). He suggests that staff knew offenders so well 'that they could swiftly locate and treat the dangerous mood that almost always prefaced mayhem danger and absconsion.' The question of provision in the community will be discussed further in Chapter II.

(7) By attempting to mobilize the offender/patient's 'cognitive resources to discuss what he fears may happen' (Ball 1977). Such work may include asking questions about intent as

already discussed. It will also include discussion of the use of alcohol and other drugs which, as is well known, may precipitate or facilitate violent and unpredictable behaviour. Sometimes it may be possible to 'talk through' a potentially dangerous episode. In addition, one can attempt to point out the likely consequences of further dangerous behaviour in some cases. This is unlikely to be successful with severely paranoid or delusionally jealous clients; with others who are more in touch with reality it may well appeal to the rational part of their being, to their ego and to their self respect.

(8) Finally, be aware of the fact that, as already stated, some dangerous offenders try to give premonition of the harm they feel they may do and others seem to respond positively to attempts to contain them.

Conclusions

Although there are difficulties in defining dangerous individuals and predicting dangerous behaviour, those who work with offender/patients have to find ways of combating the worst effects of dangerous conduct. Sometimes they will have to rely more on hunches than anything more substantial. To offer the most effective service, they must examine carefully the total situation of the offender under review, must be responsive to the direct and indirect pleas for help that are made, and be on the lookout for other premonitory signs. Equally important is the capacity of the worker to come to terms with his own potential for violent and dangerous behaviour. This is best enhanced by supervision from more experienced workers, be they lay or medically qualified. Good communication between all involved is vital in this work. Greenland (1978) summarizes what needs to be achieved when he says: 'We need to be better informed, more skilled, and certainly more sophisticated in our efforts to provide community care for dangerous offenders. Hopefully this will enable us to avoid the extremes of prolonged confinement in a special security institution or a return to the streets with supervision of the kind received by Graham Young.'

References

Ball, M. (1977) Issues of Violence in Family Casework. *Social Casework* **58**: 3–12.

Blair, D. (1971) Life Sentence Then Suicide. The Sad Case of Richard Holmes. *Med. Sci. Law* **11**: 162–79.

Blom-Cooper, L. (1965) Preventable Homicide. *Howard J. of Penol.* **XI**: 297–308.

Bottoms, A.E. (1977) *Reflections on the Renaissance of Dangerousness. Inaugural Lecture,* University of Sheffield. 12 January 1977. Also in *Howard J. of Penol. and Crime Prev.* **16**: 70–96.

Brittain, R.P. (1970) The Sadistic Murderer. *Med. Sci. Law* **10**: 198–208.

Cox, M. (1974) The Psychotherapist's Anxiety: Liability or Asset? (With special reference to Offender/Patients.) *Brit. J. Criminol.* **14**: 1–17.

Craft, M. (1974) A Description of a New Community Forensic Psychiatric Service. *Med. Sci. Law* **14**: 268–72.

Cuthbert, T.M. (1970) A Portfolio of Murderers. *Brit. J. Psychiat.* **116**: 1–10.

Faulk, M. (1974) Men who Assault their Wives. *Med. Sci. Law* **14**: 180–83.

Greenland, C. (1978) The Prediction and Management of Dangerous Behaviour: Social Policy Issues. *Int. J. Law and Psychiat.* **1**: 205–22.

—— *Comments on Walker's 'Dangerous People'.* In D. Weisstub (ed.) *Law and Psychiatry.* New York: Pergamon.

Holden, A. (1974) *The Life and Crime of Graham Young.* London: Hodder and Stoughton.

Home Office (1973) *Report on the review of procedures for the discharge and supervision of psychiatric patients subject to special restrictions. (Aarvold Committee).* Cmnd. 5191. London: HMSO.

Home Office and DHSS (1975) *Report of the Committee on Mentally Abnormal Offenders (Butler Committee).* Cmnd. 6244. London: HMSO.

Institute of Criminology (1977) *The Dangerous Offender. A Consultative Document.* Cambridge: (Mimeo).

Johnston, W.C. (1967) Releasing the Dangerous Offender. In

J.R. Rappeport (ed.) *The Clinical Evaluation of the Dangerousness of the Mentally Ill.* Illinois: Charles C. Thomas.

Jordan, B. and Packman, J. (1978) Training for Social Work with Violent Families. In J.P. Martin (ed.) *Violence and the Family.* London: John Wiley.

Kozol, H.L., Boucher, A.M., and Garofalo, R.F. (1972) The Diagnosis and Treatment of Dangerousness. *Crime and Delinquency* **18**: 371–92.

Levine, D. (1975) *The Concept of Dangerousness: Criticism and Compromise.* (Paper presented to National Criminology Conference, Cambridge, 9–11 July 1975.) Cambridge Institute of Criminology: (Mimeo).

Lion, J.R. (1972) *Evaluation and Management of the Violent Patient.* Illinois: Charles C. Thomas.

Macdonald, J.M. (1967) In J.R. Rappeport (ed.) *The Clinical Evaluation of the Dangerousness of the Mentally Ill.* Illinois: Charles C. Thomas.

—— (1969) *Psychiatry and the Criminal.* Illinois: Charles C. Thomas.

McGrath, P.G. (1958) The Treatment of the Psychotic Offender. *Howard J.* **X**: 38–44.

—— (1968) Custody and Release of Dangerous Offenders. In A.V.S. de Rueck and R. Porter (eds.) *The Mentally Abnormal Offender.* London: J. and A. Churchill (for the CIBA Foundation).

Megargee, E.I. (1976) The Prediction of Dangerous Behaviour. *Criminal Justice and Behaviour* **3**: 3–22.

Nicol, A.R., Gunn, J.G., Foggitt, R.H., and Gristwood, J. (1972) The Quantitive Assessment of Violence in Adult and Young Offenders. *Med. Sci. Law* **12**: 275–82.

Payne, C., McCabe, S., and Walker, N. (1974) Predicting Offender/Patients' Reconvictions. *Brit. J. Psychiat.* **125**: 60–4.

Prins, H.A. (1975) A Danger to Themselves and to Others. (Social Workers and Potentially Dangerous Clients.) *Brit. J. Soc. Wk.* **5**: 297–309.

—— (1976) The Butler Committee's Report. Community Care Aspects. *Brit. J. Criminol.* **16**: 181–83.

Russell, C. and Russell, W.M.S. (1961) *Human Behaviour*. Boston: Little Brown.

Sarbin, T.R. (1967) The Dangerous Individual: An Outline of Social Identity Transformations. *Brit. J. Criminol.* **7**: 285–95.

Scott, P.D. (1977) Assessing Dangerousness in Criminals. *Brit. J. Psychiat.* **131**: 127–42.

Simon, F.H. (1971) *Prediction Methods in Criminology. Home Office Research Studies, No. 7*. London: HMSO.

Steadman, H.J. and Cocozza, J.J. (1974) *Careers of the Criminally Insane*. Lexington. Mass: D.C. Heath.

Stürup, G. (1968) *Treating the Untreatable*. Baltimore: Johns Hopkins.

Tennent, T.G. (1975) The Dangerous Offender. In T. Silverstone and B. Barraclough (eds.) *Contemporary Psychiatry*. Ashford, Kent: Headley Brothers. (pp. 308–15).

Usdin, G.L. (1967) Broader Aspects of Dangerousness. In J.R. Rappeport (ed.) *The Clinical Evaluation of the Dangerousness of the Mentally Ill*. Illinois: Charles C. Thomas.

Walker, N. (1978) Dangerous People. *Int. J. Law and Psychiat.* **I**: 37–50.

Webb, D. (1976) Wise After the Event: Some Comments on 'A Danger to Themselves and to Others'. *Brit. J. Soc. Wk.* **6**: 91–6.

Woods, S. (1975) *Violence: Psychotherapy of Pseudohomosexual Panic*. In S.A. Pasternack (ed.) *Violence and Victims*. New York: Spectrum Publications.

FURTHER READING

Gostin, L.O. (1977) *A Human Condition. Vol. 2*. London: MIND (NAMH).

Halleck, S.L. and Bromberg, W. (1968) *Psychiatric Aspects of Criminology*. Illinois: Charles C. Thomas.

Hankoff, L.D. (1969) *Emergency Psychiatric Treatment*. Illinois: Charles C. Thomas.

Johnson, R.N. (1972) *Aggression in Man and Animals*. Philadelphia: W.B. Saunders.

Macdonald, J.M. (1968) *Homicidal Threats*. Illinois: Charles C. Thomas.

Mark, V.H. and Ervin, F.R. (1970) *Violence and the Brain*. Maryland: Harper and Row.

Scott, P.D. (1973) Violence in Prisoners and Patients. In: CIBA Foundation Symposium. *Medical Care of Prisoners and Detainees*. Amsterdam: Excerpta Medica.

Toch, H. (1969) *Violent Men*. Harmondsworth: Penguin Books.

Tutt, N. (1976) *Violence*. London: HMSO (DHSS).

CHAPTER SEVEN

Fire-raising and fire-raisers *

Fire is a good servant but a bad master.
SEVENTEENTH-CENTURY PROVERB

In previous chapters I made brief reference to offences of
arson and alluded to the serious harm that can be caused by
persons committing such crimes. I now propose to consider
arson (or fire-raising) in more detail and to discuss some of the
characteristics of those who set fires. Before discussing these
matters, some general introductory remarks about the place of
fire in history will perhaps be helpful.

The universal phenomenon of fire, both past and present, is
well attested to. The late doctor Jacob Bronowski, in his literary and scientific epic entitled *The Ascent of Man*, reminds us
that 'Fire has been known to early man for about 400,000 years
. . .' (Bronowski 1976). The legends of mankind are replete
with references to fire and its fascination. The folklore of
ancient Egypt contains the story of the legendary Phoenix.
This remarkable mythical bird was said to live for hundreds of
years, burn itself to death and then rise again out of an egg
from the ashes of its funeral pyre. Greek mythology contains
the story of Prometheus, who, having stolen fire from Olym
pus, was condemned by Zeus to the everlasting torment of
having his liver torn out by vultures. It may be over the genera-

* Some of the statistical material in this Chapter appeared in my paper 'Their
Candles are All Out . . . Or Are They?' published in the *Journal of the Royal
Society of Health* **98** (4), 1978. I am grateful to the Society for permission to
reproduce the relevant extracts here.

tions that this myth has strengthened the force of our injunctions to be mindful of the harm that can be caused by the illicit uses of fire.

There are numerous references to fire and its uses in the Bible. The Almighty revealed Himself to Moses in the burning bush; fire guided the Israelites by night through the wilderness and it served too as a means of making sacrifice to the Lord. Fire was also associated with notions of punishment: 'The Lord thy God is a consuming fire, even a jealous God' (Book of Deuteronomy). Its use in the Christian era as a purifier of souls considered to be corrupt is exemplified in the burning of heretics and witches (Topp 1973). In the Hindu religion its use in less overt punishing form can be seen in the practice of *Suttee* – the symbolic ritual of self-immolation performed by widows on the funeral pyres of their husbands. I shall return to this phenomenon of self-immolation later. Its magical qualities have been attested to throughout the history of mankind. They probably found their zenith in the middle ages as the means through which the 'Alchemist's Gold' might be obtained. From very early times, physicians sought the use of fire for purposes of healing, though its widespread use for major cauterization was not without its critics. Its use was possibly influenced by the religious belief that true 'believers' were protected and sanctified by fire as exemplified in the fire confronting activities of the Fakirs and other Eastern mendicants. These early beliefs and rituals were probably responsible also for the subsequent use of the 'ordeal by fire' as a means of establishing truth or falsehood in the stories put forward by those accused of criminal acts.

Today, the significance of fire in its many forms can be found in the references to it that abound in common parlance. A few of these are cited: 'to burn ones boats'; 'to burn the candle at both ends'; 'burning curiosity'; 'burning desire'; 'burning passion'; 'to go through fire'. (See also Scott 1974, and Topp 1973.) The socio-cultural and historical aspects of fire have been summarized very well by Topp (1973). Fire, he says 'offers a form of Almighty-like power within the reach of the individual, though the majority carefully respect this violent potential. However, as a symbol it plays an active and varied part in different cultural rituals though in all there is some degree of opposing association between punishment, re-incarnation and procreation in its interpretation.'

In the middle of the nineteenth century, medical men began to turn their attention and interest to what were considered to be pathological forms of fire setting. Topp (1973) notes that it was the Frenchman Marc, who, in 1833, first described the condition of 'pyromania'. Later on, German medical men were to take up this interest suggesting that such forms of fire-raising were most likely to be seen in sexually frustrated teen-age country girls and also in older men, where it was associated with the achievement of orgastic satisfaction. This association between fire and sexuality was developed further through the work of Freud and his followers, particularly Jung, who saw it as a symbolic and archetypical outlet for sexual impulses. An interesting illustration of the classical psychoanalytical approach can be found in Simmel (1949). Today, less extreme interpretations of its sexual connotations prevail, but, as we shall see when we consider a classification of fire-raisers, there are probably a few cases in which a more specific association between fire and sexual activity is of importance. In more recent years, forensic psychiatrists, clinical psychologists, and sociologists have all made significant contributions to both aetiology and treatment. Some of these will be the subject of comment later in the chapter.

The legal definition

Until the implementation of the Criminal Damage Act of 1971, arson was a common law offence. The new statutory definition is broader than that under the old common law; the latter confined the offence largely to its commission in dwelling houses. Section I (1) of the Criminal Damage Act, 1971 states that a person who without lawful excuse destroys or damages any property belonging to another, intending to destroy or damage such property, or being reckless as to whether any such property would be destroyed or damaged, is guilty of an offence punishable with imprisonment for a maximum of ten years. If the destruction or damage *is by fire*, the offence is that of arson, and is punishable with a maximum sentence of imprisonment for life. Furthermore, if a person endangers the life of another through such activity, the Act also provides a maximum penalty of life imprisonment (Jones and Card 1976). The offence of criminal damage endangering life is now separately recorded in the criminal statistics, as can be seen from the figures in *Table 7(2)*.

The size of the problem

Examination of the Criminal Statistics (Home Office 1976) reveals a steady rise in the number of cases of fire-raising (customarily described as arson) as known to the police during the years 1971–75. It can be seen from *Table 7(1)* that the number of reported cases has almost doubled between 1971 and 1975; apart from a slight decrease in 1974, this increase has been steady year by year. Inspection of *Table 7(2)* reveals a somewhat similar picture for the offence of criminal damage endangering life, except that there was a sharp decrease in 1975.

Table 7(1)   *Cases of arson recorded as known to the police*

1971	1972	1973	1974	1975
3,562	5,706	7,181	7,094	7,468

When considering these figures as indicators of an overall increase, we need to recall that the Criminal Damage Act, 1971 broadened the definition of arson.

Table 7(2)   *Cases of criminal damage endangering life recorded as known to the police*

1971	1972	1973	1974	1975
*	99	102	144	85

*The figures for 1971 are not recorded separately; the Criminal Damage Act came into being that year.

The number of cases of arson and criminal damage endangering life dealt with by the Crown Courts and the Magistrates Courts in 1975 are shown in *Tables 7(3)* and *7(4)*. It can be seen from these that only about a third of the cases of arson and about half of the cases of criminal damage endangering life reached the courts. To complete the picture we must also note the number of cautions given by the police for both offences. These are shown in *Table 7(5)*.

Table 7(3) *Arson — Magistrates' Courts (numbers tried and sentenced)*

	1975
males	1,916
females	194
total	2,110

Table 7(4) *Arson and criminal damage endangering life — Crown Courts (numbers tried and sentenced)*

1975			
arson		*criminal damage endangering life*	
males	604	males	41
females	70	females	2
total	674	*total*	43

Table 7(5) *Cautioning*

1975		
arson		*criminal damage endangering life*
males	659 (508 of these were under 14)	6 (all were juveniles)
females	83 (44 of these were under 14)	
total	742	

The cases that are actually prosecuted or cautioned are comparatively few in number, even if we make allowance for these additional numbers. The reasons for this are not hard to find. Experienced fire officials and police officials emphasize that it is not only enormously difficult to distinguish accidental from deliberate fire-setting, but even if there is good evidence that the crime of arson has been committeed, it is often impossible to find the culprit. However, some small progress has been made in tackling this problem. The Nottinghamshire Fire Service has been able to reduce the number of instances in which a finding of 'due to unknown causes' has had to be recorded by the introduction of a special highly skilled 'on the spot' investigation unit (Boggis 1978). In addition to the increase in the number of arson cases recorded as known to the police, we should note that the number of fires of 'malicious or doubtful origin' as known to the fire services has also increased. The figures for the years 1971–74 are given in *Table 7(6)*.* Moreover, it is generally agreed that there are probably many more fires started deliberately than are shown in the fire statistics. This is due no doubt to the problems involved in ascribing cause already referred to and to the difficulties which flow from being able to make rough classifications only (Fry and le Couteur 1966; Chambers 1967).

Table 7(6) *Fires of malicious or doubtful origin*

1971	1972	1973	1974
5,288	6,985	8,074	8,300

Source: UK Fire Statistics (Home Office 1974: 13). It is interesting to compare these figures with those for arson recorded as known to the Police for the same years. See *Table 7(1)*.

*It is worth emphasizing that although the problem of damage to persons and property through fire is one of some magnitude, the criminal offences of arson and criminal damage endangering life constitute only about one per cent of all offences against property as recorded in the annual Criminal Statistics.

I have referred to the caution expressed by fire service officials in interpreting fire statistics. In addition, they are reluctant to use legal terms such as arson, preferring the description 'malicious fire-raising' (Scott 1974) or 'malicious ignition' (Fry and le Couteur 1966). As we shall see later, some fire-raisers are motivated by the prospect of obtaining financial gain from their illegal behaviour. During the period of the fireman's strike, from 14 November 1977 to 16 January 1978, it was alleged that the cost of damage to property more than doubled compared with the figures for the previous year – from £52.2 millions to £117.5 millions (*The Guardian* 17 August 1978.) With the help of the fire and police forces in Leicestershire, I carried out a small survey of the incidence of fire-raising in the county during the period of the strike. This also revealed that there had been a marked increase during the period in question, and adds confirmation to the national picture. (See Prins 1978.) It is not difficult to speculate about some of the reasons for this apparent increase in fire-setting of all kinds. First, it has been shown that some buildings have not been protected adequately against the ravages of fire; one is mindful here of some of the tragedies that have recently occurred in homes for the elderly infirm and for the disabled. Modern building and furnishing materials seem to lend themselves easily to what can best be described as insidious conflagration, with the result that disaster point may be reached before the appropriate service can be called in to deal with it. In former times, the use of wood, though full of its own hazards, ignited in a way that was more immediately apparent. Second, there has been an increase in the number of flammable materials available for use in incendiary devices; some of these are described by Macdonald (1977). Third, it has been stressed that we may all be less fire conscious than in the past. Increasing use of indirect (central) heating prevents the exposure of children to the old open fire and consequential parental injunctions as to its hazards. One of my students has also suggested it is possible that the less frequent presence of the open fire means that there are fewer legitimate opportunities to explore its properties. Fourth, it seems likely that

people are very careless with electrical equipment. One wonders how many people obey the sensible instruction to unplug
the television set when they retire for the night, or see that
electric blankets are installed correctly? There are also still
tragic instances of the use of defective paraffin heaters. Fifth,
the increase in fires of doubtful origin and in malicious fire-
setting must be seen against the background of a more general
increase in crime – notably offences of violence and vandalism.
Finally, in an age in which the media confronts us with visions
of bombing, killing, and Hijacking almost every day, it would
not be surprising if we became inclined to take these and
similar hazardous events for granted and, of necessity, insensi-
tive to their effects.

Classification

Scott (1974) has pointed out that it is very important to attempt
some classification of fire-raisers so that appropriate modes of
management may be applied. Before doing this, it is necessary
to make one or two observations about the terms currently
employed to describe those who set fires. Pyromania, a term
popular at the end of the nineteenth century, is not used
frequently today. When first introduced, it was used to
describe motiveless, irrational behaviour and was held to
denote a form of insanity. Today, we tend to reserve the term
solely for compulsive acts of fire-raising in which rising tension
seems to be one of the keynotes and in which the behaviour is
associated with the achievement of vicarious sexual satisfaction. Some use the term incendiarism as an alternative for
arson or fire-raising. They imply that its use denotes a degree
of recidivism. It is not always easy to distinguish the recidivistic
pattern of these 'fire-bugs' as some call them from true compulsive fire-setting (pyromania). For most purposes, 'malicious
fire-raising' seems to be the most useful term to use because it
places the emphasis upon *intention*. In the classification I shall
put forward I shall include some acts that would not necessarily be regarded as fire-raising in the more usual sense. I have
included them here in order to discuss the problem as fully as

possible. Numerous attempts at classification have been made (see for example, Fry and le Couteur 1966; Inciardi 1970; Scott 1974; Macdonald 1977; Mather 1978). I would suggest that the following groupings may help to distinguish the various motivations involved.

(1) *'Professional' fire-raising*. This is fire-raising for financial reward and/or to cover up another crime such as murder. (For illustrations of such cases see Scott (1974) and Macdonald (1977).)

(2) *Fire-raising for political purposes*. This would include setting fires to synagogues by members of fascist organisations, acts of anarchy (such as the activities of the 'Angry Brigade' in England, and terrorist bombings in Northern Ireland).

(3) *Self-immolation as a political gesture*. Admittedly, this is not fire-raising in the conventional sense but I have included it here to complete the picture. A spate of such activities occurred in the late 1960s and early 1970s. However, it appears that some of these political self-immolators may have been mentally disturbed; they could, therefore, also be placed within the group to be considered next.

(4) *Fire-raising committed for pathological reasons and for mixed motives*. Cases falling within this heading will be those most likely to come to the attention of workers in the socio-forensic field. This classification can be subdivided as follows.

(i) *The dull and subnormal fire-raiser*. McKerracher and Dacre (1966) made a study of such persons detained in Rampton – which as already mentioned is the Special Hospital for (mainly) subnormal offender/patients. They suggested that these abnormal fire-raisers were more emotionally labile than other Rampton patients. They were found also to display a wider variety of psychiatric symptoms than are found in other subnormal special hospital residents. Two such patients are known to me. One set fire to her own home as a means of drawing attention to herself. The other had a very long history of setting fires to property which had begun at a very early age. This behaviour had been associated with various acts of aggression towards his family and others. His difficulties were exacerbated by the fact that he also suffered from severe epileptic seizures. (See below also.) Such complications are not altogether uncommon. Woolf (1977) has reported an interesting and unusual case of fire-raising in a patient suffering from the rare Moebius syndrome, a condition known also as congenital facial diplegia and which may sometimes be associated with a degree of mental subnormality.

(ii) *The pathological self-immolator*. I have already suggested that amongst the so-called political self-immolators there may be some whose motivations are not clear-cut or in which there may be pathological elements. Topp (1973) has drawn attention to the extent to which self-destruction by fire has been occurring infrequently but with some regularity in penal establishments in recent years. He suggests that such individuals, who choose a particularly painful method of death are likely to be those who have some capacity for splitting off feeling from consciousness. It seems likely that some of these offenders may be schizoid or schizophrenic individuals; more rarely they may be epileptics in a state of disturbed consciousness. People vary of course in their pain thresholds. Some of us would probably succumb very quickly to such a painful method of self-destruction. Asphyxiation and shock would probably occur within a short space of time so that the severe pain caused by the burning of vital tissues might not have to be endured for long. Newton (1976) has described an unusual case of suicide by fire; this seems to cross the pathological/political boundaries and is therefore particularly interesting.

(iii) *The psychotic fire-raiser*. I made brief references to the association between mental illness and fire-raising in Chapter 3. Some individuals may set fire to buildings as a result of hallucinatory experiences – as in some forms of schizophrenia. One said: 'I set fire to the room to get rid of the evil in it.' Some will allege that they have seen the image of God and heard Him directing them to set fires. Fry and le Couteur (1966) report a considerable number of such offender/patients in a Broadmoor group; (Broadmoor caters in the main for offender/patients suffering from psychosis). Occasionally, the schizoid or overtly schizophrenic tramp may set fire to premises in the course of his confused wanderings. Some offenders may set fires whilst suffering from manic-depressive illness. Scott (1974) describes the well known case of Jonathan Martin, the nineteenth-century incendiarist who fired York Minster, as one example. For the person suffering from severe depression, it is possible that the fire may satisfy the need not only for the purgation of guilt through 'the fiery furnace', but also for purification. Sometimes, the depressive fire-raiser may indulge in his acts of fire-raising as a means of getting back indirectly at the real objects of his depression. I know of one man being severely depressed because his wife had left him who set fire to a large warehouse under such stress. More rarely, a hypomanic individual may engage in fire-raising. In such persons there may be marked irrationality of thought associated with delusional systems – perhaps of persecution; there may even be hallucinatory experiences. (See Chapter 3 also.) Fire-raising by persons suffering from alcoholic psychosis is not unknown; such persons may also occasionally set fire to themselves as a result of the voices they hear. They may of course set fire to themselves and their dwelling by accident, and Scott (1974) has reported one such case. More generally, it seems to be quite well established that a history of alcoholism or indulgence in heavy drinking is not infrequently associated with fire-raising (Inciardi 1970). Epilepsy does not of itself seem to play a large part in the aetiology of fire-raising though it is as well to be on the lookout for the rare but nonetheless important case. In such cases the act may be committed following an epileptic attack when the person is not in a state of clear consciousness. Other rare instances may occur in persons suffering from early or senile dementia or who are suffering from GPI (General Paralysis of the Insane).

(iv) *The revenge motive in fire-raising*. Frequently, fire-raising will be indulged in by those motivated by revenge. This motivation can be classified in the following way: (a) A general revenge against the social order. Some political fire-raising activities could well come within this category. (b) Revenge against employers and others. This is not uncommon. Considerable damage to property is sometimes caused by those seeking to redress what they regard as an unjust dismissal from work. Schoolchildren engage in this kind of activity from time to time and may cause damage worth thousands of pounds to school buildings. I know of a number of such cases. Sometimes, the offence seems to come 'out of the blue' though past animosity towards teachers can often be elicited. In some cases, the fire-raising is associated with demonstrations of aggression and other anti-social conduct. (c) A more generally jealous group. This group may well include those who have a fairly well encapsulated delusional system and the classification will overlap with those who are said to fall within the category of the psychotically motivated. Such people may be particularly dangerous; as we saw in Chapter 6 they present serious problems for those who have to make decisions as to fitness for their discharge into the community.

(v) *The 'hero' group*. In this group, we find those who need to be at the centre of things and who demand attention. They set fires in order to derive satisfaction from the arrival of the fire brigade and the excitement and commotion that may accompany this. These are the people who, having set the fire, will often inform the brigade of the conflagration, busy themselves at the scene, and offer their unsolicited services to the firemen. The volunteer or auxiliary fireman may perhaps be one of these fire-setters. One such 'aide' was thought to be responsible for a series of fires in the New Forest following the serious droughts of 1976. Lewis and Yarnell (1951) found fifty-one cases of volunteer firemen who had set fires on their own and a further forty-one instances where groups of men belonging to a volunteer fire department had been arrested for deliberately setting fires. It has been suggested that where volunteer firemen are paid for each occasion on which they have to turn out there may be an inducement to set fires deliberately in order to reap the financial rewards.

(vi) *Fire-raising as a disguised cry for help*. People will sometimes engage in fire-raising as a means of drawing attention to themselves. Macdonald (1977) quotes the case of a young woman who engaged in two episodes of fire-setting in this way. She was described as a lonely unhappy young woman who derived much satisfaction from the attention she received as a result of fire-setting activities. Women may occasionally engage in apparently motiveless fire-raising as a means of drawing attention to their plight following a sudden separation or unanticipated bereavement.

(vii) *Sexually motivated fire-raising*. I have referred briefly to the possible relationship between sexuality and fire-raising. It would appear from the small number of empirical studies that have been undertaken (Lewis and Yarnell 1951; Tennent *et al.* 1971) that arsonists seem to show a disproportionate degree of psychosexual maladjustment when compared with other offenders in penal establishments and special hospitals, though the association between the two phenomena is by no means as clear cut as has been suggested by psychoanalysts in the past. One must treat such postulated relationships with much caution, but it has been found that a number of such offenders are often very infantile in their behaviour and responses. A large proportion of males are unmarried, and, interestingly, there is often a long-standing history of enuresis. This is regarded as significant by the psychoanalytically minded, for as Freud and his followers suggested, there may be some phantasied connection between the penis and the fireman's hose, between urination and the extinction of fires with water. On a broader level of conceptualization, it is possible to speculate that for the inadequate and under-achieving male, fire may be a means whereby compensation for feelings of inferior masculinity may be obtained. Certainly the almost mystical association between fire, virility, and procreation gives some support to the psychoanalytical point of view. Finally, Stekel (1924) observed that the histories of some male fire-raisers revealed them to be suffering from impotence of varying degrees of severity and I know of one or two cases where this has seemed to be an important element in the offender's background.

(viii) *Fire-raising by children*. Studies of fire-raising by children have been carried out by Lewis and Yarnell (1951), Bender (1953), Macht and Mack (1968), and Vandersall and Wiener (1970). It seems that fire-setting in children can be seen either as a developmental experimental phase or as part of a more serious disturbed behaviour pattern. In the latter cases, the home backgrounds were often characterized by a degree of severe parental stress and psychopathology. In the children, behaviour disturbances of one kind or another had been observed from an early age. Vandersall and Wiener state: 'A sense of exclusion, loneliness, and unfulfilled dependency needs were prominent.' The backgrounds of children showing serious fire-raising propensities often include the demonstration of a wide range of other behaviour disorders such as aggressiveness, persistent truancy and running away from home, enuresis, acute fears, anxieties, and nightmares. In some cases these difficulties and the propensity to set fires may be associated with a degree of minimal brain damage. However, it is often difficult to establish with any degree of certainty the presence of such damage.

In concluding this section on motivation it is important to stress that there will be a significant degree of overlap in all the above classifications. I have pointed out that the political self-immolator may well be suffering from a psychotic disorder as indeed may the fire-raiser who operates from a feeling of revenge. Despite this overlapping, it seems important to attempt some classification, however crude, for only by so doing can we begin to be more discriminating and hopefully more effective in our management.

FURTHER CHARACTERISTICS OF FIRE-RAISERS

Some of the characteristics of fire-raisers have already been alluded to, albeit somewhat indirectly. In this concluding section of the chapter an attempt will be made to describe some of the characteristics of fire-raisers in a prison population. It will have become apparent from the statistics already quoted, that convicted arsonists, in common with most other offenders, are predominantly male. Concerning female arsonists, Tennent *et al.* (1971) report on a study they undertook of such women in a special hospital. They report that these women offender/patients differed significantly from a non-arsonist control group in respect of more adverse early environments, greater sexual difficulties, and more overt aggressive behaviour. One of the most detailed studies of male imprisoned arsonists is probably that published by Hurly and Monahan (1969). They studied fifty cases of men sentenced for arson and detained in Grendon Underwood psychiatric prison. They were able to compare their sample with 100 controls. Some of their findings are of interest and they confirm some of my earlier statements concerning classification. 10 per cent had previous convictions for arson; revenge was a fairly common motive (in thirteen out of the fifty). For the remainder, motivation was seen as 'pathological, irrational and neurotic'. 46 per cent had been drinking prior to the offence (as compared with 31 per cent of the control group). In twenty-two cases, that is in nearly half, there had been a history of alcoholism. 80 per cent had a history of psychiatric symptoms in adolescence or in adulthood prior to the offence and 40 per cent had symptoms of psychoneurosis and/or a behaviour disorder before the age of twelve. 26 per cent had attempted suicide on more than one occasion. 20 per cent had a history of head injury with loss of consciousness but without other neurological sequelae. (It is of interest to compare this finding with the observations made earlier concerning the possible relationship between epilepsy and fire-raising.) 36 per cent had previously received psychiatric treatment. In view of what was said earlier about the importance of parental background their finding that in *only ten out of the fifty cases* were there 'complete parental homes without recorded pathology . . . [my italics]' is significant. Bad relationships with fathers or their complete absence predominated; 37 per cent described 'affectionless' mothers. 54 per cent had clear psycho-sexual and marital problems and 60 per cent described difficulties in social relationships with women. The overall conclusion to be drawn from this careful study is that compared with other offenders these fire-raisers' social dysfunctioning was very severe. They seemed to be more socially inept than other offenders, more isolated and more psycho-sexually disturbed. Finally, 46 per cent of the group had a history of repeated arson offences. For these men 'arson had become a preferred habitual act . . .' This high rate of recidivism is noteworthy, but Grendon is a psychiatric prison and probably has a higher proportion of psychiatrically disturbed offenders overall than other penal establishments. In contrast to the high rate of recidivism in this study, Soothill and Pope (1973), found in their twenty-year cohort survey of arsonists convicted in 1951 that the vast majority were not reconvicted for this type of offence. The few people who were reconvicted tended to be those who did it for revenge or as a response to conflict with authority.

More recently, Sapsford, Banks, and Smith (1978) studied a group of prisoners serving *life sentences* for arson. They compared them with a group who were serving or had served determinate sentences of *eighteen months or less*. They found that the 'lifers' had little in common with the short-sentence men, but were very much like the men serving sentences of five years or more, the exception being that their medical records showed a greater preponderance of diagnosis of sexual disorder and psychopathy. They also found that the life sentence group included some men who had a compulsive element in their offending. This was considered to be predominantly sexually motivated and is of interest bearing in mind the earlier discussion of pyromania. Such men were found less commonly in the determinate sentence population.

Conclusions

Fire is a ubiquitous and fascinating phenomenon. The increase in its destructive potential and its use for unlawful purposes should give us much cause for concern. The motivations of fire-raisers are many and complex and we are ignorant of the nature of most of them. Much more research is needed in this somewhat neglected area. From a treatment and preventive point of view we need to isolate more clearly those who are vengeful, those who are seriously psychiatrically disturbed and those for whom fire-raising is only one aspect of a multifaceted handicap. Failure to do this will result not only in material destruction but in continuing the profound distress encountered by both offenders and their victims.

References

Bender, L. (1953) Firesetting in Children. In: *Aggression, Hostility and Anxiety in Children*. Illinois: Charles C. Thomas.

Boggis, J.J. (1978) Fire Brigade's Investigation Team. *Fire* January: 389.

Bronowski, J. (1976) *The Ascent of Man*. London: B.B.C. Associates (p.124).

Chambers, E.D. (1967) Incendiarism: An Underrated Danger. *Security Gazette* **9**: 107–12.

Fry, J.F. and le Couteur, N.B. (1966) Arson. *Medico-Legal Journal* **XXXIV**: 108 21.

Home Office (1974) *U.K. Fire Statistics*. London: HMSO.

—— (1976) *Criminal Statistics 1975*. Cmnd. 6566. London: HMSO.

Hurly, W. and Monahan, T.M. (1969) Arson: The Criminal and the Crime. *Brit. J. Criminol.* **9**: 4–21.

Inciardi, J. (1970) The Adult Firesetter. A Typology. *Criminology* **8**: 145–55.

Jones, P.A. and Card, R.I.E. (1976) *Cross and Jones' Introduction to Criminal Law*. (8th edition). London: Butterworths.

Lewis, N.D.C. and Yarnell, H. (1951) *Pathological Firesetting. Nervous and Mental Disease Monograph*. No. 82. New York.

MacDonald, J.M. (1977) *Bombers and Firesetters*. Illinois: Charles C. Thomas.

Macht, L.B. and Mack, J.E. (1968) The Firesetter Syndrome. *Psychiatry* **31**: 277–88.

Mather, J. de V. (1978) Arson. *The Police Surgeon* **13**: 20–5.

McKerracher, D.W. and Dacre, A.J.I. (1966) A Study of Arsonists in a Special Security Hospital. *Brit. J. Psychiat.* **112**: 1151–154.

Newton, J. (1976) Suicide by Fire. *Med. Sci. Law* 16: 177–79.

Prins, H.A. (1978) Their Candles are all Out . . . Or are They?: Some Reflections on Arson and Arsonists. *J. Royal Soc. Hlth.* **98**: 191–95.

Sapsford, R.J., Banks, C., and Smith, D.D. (1978) Arsonists in Prison. *Med. Sci. Law* **18**: 247–54.

Scott, D. (1974) *Fire and Fire-Raisers*. London: Duckworth.

Scott, P.D. (1977) Assessing Dangerousness in Criminals. *Brit. J. Psychiat.* **131**: 127–42.

Simmel, G. (1949) *Incendiarism*. In K.R. Eissler (ed.) *Searchlights on Delinquency*. London: Imago.

Soothill, K.L. and Pope, P.J. (1973) Arson: A Twenty-Year Cohort Study. *Med. Sci. Law* **13**: 127–38.

Stekel, W. (1924) *Peculiarities of Behaviour*. New York: Liveright.

Tennent, T.G., McQuaid, A., Loughnane, T., and Hands, N.J. (1971) Female Arsonists. *Brit. J. Psychiat.* **119**: 497–502.

Topp, D.O. (1973) Fire as a Symbol and as a Weapon of Death. *Med. Sci. Law* **13**: 79–86.

Vandersall, T.A. and Wiener, J.M. (1970) Children Who Set Fires. *Arch. Gen. Psychiat.* **22**: 63–71.

Woolf, P.G. (1977) Arson and Moebius' Syndrome – A Case Study of Stigmatization. *Med. Sci. Law* **17**: 68–70.

CHAPTER EIGHT

Sexual behaviour and sexual offending

No man shall approach a blood relation for
intercourse.
You shall not lie with a man as with a woman:
that is an abomination.
You shall not have sexual intercourse with
any beast to make yourself unclean with it.
  BOOK OF LEVITICUS (NEW ENGLISH BIBLE)

An explanation is needed for my choice of title for this chapter.
It is simply this; sexual offending and sex offenders cannot be
seen in isolation from sexual behaviour in general and from
contemporary views about this. Some might even consider that
sexual offenders should not be seen as a special group and
would find it difficult to justify my decision to devote a chapter
to them in their own right. My reasons for doing so are
twofold. First, despite some superficial appearances to the
contrary, there is still a good deal of ignorance about normal
sexual practices and even more about those held to be deviant:
the subject of sex is an emotive one and I shall attempt in this
chapter to give as cool and as balanced an account as I can.
Second, because the subject is so emotive, much that may
militate against successful management and treatment may lie
within the person offering it; it is therefore not only necessary
to be as well informed as possible, but more particularly to be
aware of one's own sexual 'blind-spots'. The biblical injunctions quoted at the heading of this chapter are still reflected in
many of our attitudes to sexuality. Our contemporary confusion can be seen in the well-intentioned, but in my view, somewhat misguided polemical statements of the 'supressors' on the

one hand (such as Mrs Whitehouse) and of those who wish to see more licence on the other (for example those who want to increase the opportunities for acts of paedophilia). The material in this chapter will be divided as follows. First, I shall attempt to clarify some of the terms commonly used, such as sexual deviation, perversion, sexual variation, and sexual dysfunction. Second, I shall offer two forms of classification – clinical and legal – with comment on some disadvantages in each of them. Third, I shall provide statistics of the volume of sexual crime. Fourth, I shall deal with certain sexual offences in more detail and make some observations concerning treatment.

Terminology

Examination of the literature reveals that the early sexologists used terms such as perversion, abnormality, anomaly, and inversion almost synonymously. Some of these terms have somewhat pejorative overtones and even as dispassionate a clinician as the late Sir Norwood East preferred the term perversion which he defined in the following way:

> 'A true sexual perversion may be regarded as sexual activity, in which complete satisfaction is obtained without the necessity of heterosexual intercourse. It must be persistently indulged in, preferably in reality, at any rate in phantasy, and not merely as a substitute for a preferred heterosexual activity which is unobtainable for some reason.'

(East 1949)

Today, although we would probably agree with most of the content of East's definition, we would probably prefer to use the terms deviation or variation for such behaviour; this is because the word perversion, being derived from *perverse,* tends to have connotations of sin and wickedness (Oxford English Dictionary). The term sexual disorder is used occasionally to cover both sexual deviation and sexual dysfunction. This is erroneous. Sexual dysfunction should be used only to cover conditions such as impotence, frigidity, and premature ejaculation. As such, they will not be the subject of further comment in this chapter, though we should acknowledge that there are occasions when these dysfunctions may be associated with deviant sexual conduct. The work of the early sexologists (such as Havelock Ellis) and cultural anthropologists (such as Malinowski and Margaret Mead) alerted us to the wide variations in sexual practice and to the fact that although there are biological determinants of sexual behaviour, its form and shape is heavily determined by culture. In more recent years, the sexual inclinations and activities of Westerners have been scrutinized in the USA by Kinsey and his co-workers, by Ford and Beach, and by Masters and Johnson, and in this country by Schofield. These workers have shed much light on the infinite variety of human sexual response. As a result, it *may* be that people feel less guilty about acknowledging not only their own sexuality, but that of others. One unfortunate side effect of these findings has been a preoccupation with sexual prowess and skill. It is not surprising therefore that we have seen a rapid growth of sex-aid shops, parlours, and text books devoted to improvements in sex techniques. Again, this may be helpful in some respects, but it tends to put an over-emphasis on 'performance' and tends also to establish a dichotomy between physical sex and human relationships in their wider context. This development is also paralleled by the way in which the media and advertising place considerable emphasis on the need to appear physically attractive to the opposite sex. Travellers on London's Underground will be well aware of the almost salacious impact of such advertising. We need not be altogether surprised if some of our young people are confused about the place of sex in their lives. Overall, there is therefore much more open presentation of sex – verbal, literary, and visual. Whether this has really led to people being any better informed is more questionable. Those who work with young people find some astonishing areas of ignorance despite the pseudo-sophistication that abounds. But, at least we have rid ourselves of some of our more quaint euphemisms. No longer does a certain Sunday newspaper describe buggery as 'a serious offence' or as 'an unnatural act', though it is probably true to say few people realize the real implications of calling someone a 'bugger'.

Because of the information explosion already referred to, and because we have tended to take a more liberal view of some forms of sexual activity (such as consenting homosexuality between adults in private) (Sexual Offences Act, 1967 – Section 1(1),* it has become increasingly difficult to make sharp distinctions between so-called normal and deviant sexual behaviour. In addition, people use the word sexuality in a fairly imprecise fashion. They tend to forget that sexuality and its expression encompasses contributions from chromosome sex, gonadal sex, internal and external morphological (structural) characteristics, and gender. The concept of gender is important and we must briefly mention two aspects. Gender *identity* is what the individual feels about his or her maleness or femaleness; gender *role* is concerned with an individual's manifest behaviour of masculinity or femininity. Concepts of gender become of importance in understanding problems of transexualism and, to a lesser extent, transvestism. Both conditions are outside the scope of this chapter. The reader interested in pursuing them should consult Crown (1976), particularly the chapter by Hertoft, and the recent work by Jehu (1979). It is a mistake to see maleness and femaleness as separate and distinct attributes. There is enough evidence from work done in the field of bisexuality to validate the assertion that all of us have components of the opposite sex within us and that the balance of these components will vary within individuals. Indeed, as Charlotte Wolff points out in her fascinating study of bisexuality, mythology is full of references to the bisexual nature of men and women (Wolff 1977). This is for many people a very uncomfortable notion, but it is one that has to be faced by those who would work successfully with people requiring help with sexual problems.**

* The changes in this law do not apply to Northern Ireland.
** Perhaps it is important to emphasize that an individual's basic sexual orientation, unless he or she is very young, rarely alters, and all one can hope to achieve in treatment is to suppress the activity, and replace it with more socially acceptable behaviour. This is what makes 'treatment' so difficult and 'cure' an inappropriate word. (Mather 1979 – personal communication.)

In the light of all these difficulties referred to above, can we make any useful distinctions between so-called normality and deviation? I think we can, but we must remember that they will be culture-bound, that they may change over time, and can only be treated as broad generalizations. They will also be dependent upon differences in individual aesthetic beliefs. We may say that *normal* sexual behaviour encompasses those forms of sexual activity between two adults which are acceptable to both parties, do not involve coercion, exploitation, or degradation, and, if performed in public, do not cause outrage. Thus some couples will derive mutual satisfaction from some forms of sexual behaviour that others would find quite unacceptable on aesthetic and other grounds. Examples are oral sexuality (fellatio and cunnilingus), anal intercourse and its variations. Deviant sexuality can be defined much as it was in the second part of East's statement some thirty years ago. More simply and perhaps a little less pejoratively, we may describe it as that form of sexual expression in which the exclusive practice of the particular behaviour is preferred or regarded as an essential concomitant to normal sexual activity. Some people prefer to use the term variation for deviation, thus hoping to reduce the pejorative element still further. It will be obvious that our main concern in this chapter will be with behaviour that the law holds to be coercive, exploitive, degrading, or an affront to public decency. With this in mind we can now attempt to make some classifications – clinically and legally. In doing so we must bear in mind that the law does not hold illegal all forms of sexual deviation or variation.

Classification

CLINICAL CLASSIFICATION

The following is a very simple classification of sexual deviations:

(1) Reduction of intensity of sex drive (leading to sexual dysfunction);
(2) Over intensity of sex drive (leading to nymphomania in

the female and satyriasis in the male);
(3) Misdirection of the aim of sex drive (for example in exclusive homosexual activity or bestio-sexuality);
(4) Misdirection of the manner in which sexual satisfaction is obtained (for example in seeking unusual methods of sexual gratification).

The above classification, however, is too general; we need something a little more elaborate to denote the variety of forms that sexual deviations may take. A number of more refined classifications have been suggested in the past, for example, East (1949), Allen (1949), Scott (1964), Prins (1973), and Brandon (1977). The following derives from these, but has been modified to suit present needs.

Sexual deviations (variations)

Only some of the following will come within the purview of the criminal law.

(1) *Sexual activity not requiring a human partner.* For example the use of animals (bestio-sexuality, zoophilia), objects, or materials (fetishism).
(2) *Sexual activity not requiring a willing partner.* Rape, (both heterosexual and homosexual), Peeping Tom, troilism (involvement of three individuals in simultaneous sexual activity), voyeurism, rubbing (frotteurism), exhibitionism, necrophilia (use of a dead or insensible partner).
(3) *Requiring a willing partner*
   (a) Masturbatory activities of various kinds without proceeding to copulation. (Mutual masturbation, fellatio, cunnilingus, anal sex).
   (b) Requiring unusual conditions, for example, a partner of the same sex, a child (paedophilia), old person (gerontophilia), forbidden partner (incest), requiring punishment or suffering (masochism and sadism).
(4) *Others*
   (a) Kleptomania (we have already noted the tenuous relationship between sexuality and stealing in Chapter 3).

(b) Pyromania (this is dealt with in Chapter 7).

(c) Coprophagia, coprophilia, saliromania (these are terms used to indicate the derivation of sexual pleasure from contact with, or sight of, body wastes or other secretions).

LEGAL CLASSIFICATION* (SEXUAL OFFENCES)

There are a number of ways in which these may be classified. The following has been modified from the suggestion of James (1964).

(1) *Offences in which the sex drive seems normal in its aim, but may be distorted*

    (a) Rape and attempt to rape.

    (b) Indecent assault on females.

    (c) Some forms of sex murder.

    (d) Molestation of children of the opposite sex.

    (e) Female prostitution.+

+The act of prostitution itself is not illegal. Soliciting in public for prostitution constitutes the offence and the law is being reviewed at the present time. Prostitution as such will not be dealt with here, but in Chapter 10.

(2) *Offences in which the sexual drive seems to be more clearly deviant*

    (a) Punishable male homosexuality (buggery and attempts, gross indecency, soliciting males, and indecent assault).

    (b) 'Peeping Tom' activities (this is a form of voyeurism)

    (c) Indecent exposure.

    (d) Buggery with animals (bestiality).

    (e) Buggery with a female.

    (f) Necrophilia.**

* To avoid repetition, the relevant legislation is noted here: The Vagrancy Act, 1824; The Sexual Offences Act, 1956; The Indecency with Children Act, 1960; The Sexual Offences Act, 1967; The Sexual Offences (Amendment) Act, 1976.

** Punishable under common law. Not a statutory offence.

With regard to male homosexuality, we should note that although the Sexual Offences Act, 1967 removed consenting male homosexual acts in private from the statute book, this only applies when (i) both parties are over twenty-one; (ii) if two people only are involved (an offence is committed if more than two people take part or are present); (iii) the act is in private. It is left to the courts to decide what constitutes a public place, but a public lavatory would be so regarded. Nothing in the act prevents homosexual acts from still being held to be offences when committed by members of Her Majesty's Armed Services or the Merchant Service. We should also note that Section 128 of the Mental Health Act, 1959 makes special provision in respect of sexual offences committed against mental hospital patients.

The crimes listed above would be regarded by most people as being fairly obvious sexual offences. However, we must add to this list some others that are perhaps less obvious, but whose inclusion is necessary in order to complete our survey. These could well include the following.

(1) Offences of pornography, particularly those involving children as participants. This is an issue that has caused much concern recently.

(2) Making obscene telephone calls.

(3) Conspiracy to corrupt public morals. The case most usually cited is that of Shaw in 1962. This arose out of Shaw's complicity with others in the publication of a 'Ladies Directory' giving the names, addresses, and sexual practices of certain prostitutes. A later case is that of Knuller in 1973. This concerned an agreement to publish advertisements soliciting homosexual acts in private. This was held to be conspiracy even though the conduct itself is no longer a criminal offence in England and Wales.

(4) Bigamy. This might best be considered an offence against family life and not as a sexual offence.

(5) Adultery. We should note that this is still a criminal offence in some countries.

(6) Abduction of females.

(7) Procuration of others for the commission of sexual offences.
(8) Certain 'masked' offences. In this category I would include certain forms of stealing to satisfy fetishistic desires (for example, larceny of ladies' underwear from clothes lines), and some murders or violent assaults that arise out of sexual activities (see later). It has also been suggested that there are some offences of a 'proving' variety that arise out of displaced sexual desires. (One example is stealing motor cycles by youths in order to prove their virility. Some have suggested they can be seen as a substitute for 'riding a woman'.) It is perhaps significant that the 'Hell's Angels' are noted for their motor cycle addiction *and* for their violent and predatory sexual activities.

The size of the problem

We may now proceed to consider the size of the problem as shown in the criminal statistics. In examining the tables which follow it should be remembered that sexual offences constitute less than 3 per cent of all offences. There is also a wide discrepancy between the numbers of such offences *known* to the police and the numbers *dealt with or prosecuted*. We should also note that the police exercise a considerable degree of discretion concerning prosecution. In certain cases, prosecution may only be launched with the approval of the Director of Public Prosecutions. Most sexual offences are dealt with by non-custodial penalties, but rape, buggery, incest, and indecent assaults are dealt with most frequently by way of imprisonment.

Table 8(1) *Indictable sexual offences known to the police, 1971–1975**

1971	1972	1973	1974	1975
23,621	23,505	25,736	24,698	23,731

*Source for all statistical material, Criminal Statistics, England and Wales (Home Office 1976).

Table 8(2)   *Selection of the more serious indictable sexual offences known to the police, 1971–1975**

	1971	1972	1973	1974	1975
rape	784	893	948	1,052	1,040
buggery	593	532	667	587	720
attempted buggery	2,887	2,985	3,052	3,096	2,885
incest	307	322	288	337	349
indecent assault on female	12,400	11,977	13,294	12,417	11,809
unlawful sexual intercourse with girl *under 13*	22	256	323	304	327
unlawful sexual intercourse with girl *under 16*	5,060	5,129	5,180	4,746	4,533

Table 8(3)   *Number of males found guilty and cautioned for sexual offences in 1975**

found guilty	6,809
cautioned	3,497
total	10,288

Note to Table 8(3)
In 1975, there were also 2,495 males found guilty of indecent exposure, 3,292 convictions for prostitution, 591 for male importuning, and 126 for living on immoral earnings. (With the exception of living on immoral earnings, all these are *non-indictable* offences and almost all are dealt with in the Magistrates' Courts. The more serious indictable offences are dealt with in the Crown Courts).

*Source for all statistical material, Criminal Statistics, England and Wales (Home Office 1976).

From an examination of *Table 8(1)* we can see that the number of offences remain much the same from year to year, but that there was a slight decrease in 1974 and 1975. In *Table 8(2)*, I have given statistics for what are regarded as some of the most serious sexual offences. However, as was pointed out in Chapter 6, the statutory description of an offence may not accurately represent its real seriousness. An indecent assault may constitute anything from an unsolicited pinch on the bottom to a serious attack akin to attempted rape. The physical trauma caused by some sexual assaults is frequently underestimated and this aspect will be referred to again later. In *Table 8(3)* I have given the figures for the number of males found guilty and cautioned for indictable sexual offences in 1975. We can see that this represents under half of all those known to the police. The reasons for this are not hard to find. Witnesses are often reluctant to come forward or corroboration may be hard to find. There may be a reluctance to acknowledge the commission of some offences which have been between consenting parties. We know also that many more sexual offences are committed than are even recorded as known to the police. Again, there may be reluctance to admit involvement, or some form of blackmail may be involved so that the victim prefers to remain silent. The parties concerned may not realize that an offence has been committed, particularly in youthful consanguinous offences. In other cases, the victim may not wish to suffer the embarrassment of a public appearance in court (as in rape cases), or parents may wish to spare a child a similar ordeal. Men who have been the subject of male importuning may be reluctant to report the matter in case they too are thought to be guilty of making sexual advances. We can conclude then that the number of sexual offences reported and prosecuted are probably but a very small fraction of those that actually take place. Small though the actual numbers may be, some of these offenders cause considerable distress to their victims, some are the hapless victims of their own misfortunes, and a small minority cause grave physical and psychological harm to their victims and pose a serious threat to the general public. I shall now give detailed consideration to some of these offenders and their offences.

Consideration of some specific sexual offences

There are dangers in discussing sexual offences under separate headings for an offender may well commit more than one type of sexual offence during his criminal career. Thus, an indecent exposer may go on to commit sexual assault or a man having convictions for minor sexual assaults may become a rapist, but there are certain characteristics which can be held to be fairly specific to particular offences. For the sake of clarity it seems sensible to consider them as separate entities. Having said this, I must emphasize again that there will always be areas of overlap and that each case has to be examined in the context of its highly individual features.

INDECENT EXPOSURE (SOMETIMES ALSO DESCRIBED AS EXHIBITIONISM)

This is the commonest of all the sexual offences, accounting for about half of all sex offences recorded each year. It appears that although the rates of offending for adults remain more or less static, there has been an increase in the number of prosecutions for those aged twenty-one and under (Rooth 1972). The relevant statute is the Vagrancy Act, 1824. This provides that it is an offence for a man wilfully and indecently to expose his person with intent to insult a female. In a fairly recent case it has been held that 'person' means the penis.* Such behaviour may also be dealt with under the Town Police Clauses Act of 1847 and by various by-laws. (The penalties under the latter Act are somewhat less severe.) Most prosecutions, however, are taken under the Vagrancy Act. It is interesting to note that this is a specifically male offence. There is no provision for the prosecution of females for public exposure of the genitals, but presumably a woman who did so could be prosecuted for

*In *Evans* v. *Ewels* [1972] 2 All ER 22.

breach of the peace or for some public order offence. It might be said that women now have more legitimate outlets for exposure – for example, appearing 'topless' in certain establishments. Biologically, indecent exposure can be seen against the background of the male's need for sexual display; this is well attested to, not only in the lower animal kingdom, but in the extent to which, at various times in history, men have used devices to draw attention to their sex organs; the 'cod-piece' is a good example. The law and public opinion seem to have been quite happy for males to draw attention to themselves in this way in the past; more recently, tight jeans and to a lesser extent 'stripping' and 'streaking' have become fashionable amongst young males. It is only when we publicly divest ourselves of our coverings that the law seeks to step in and take action. It seems likely for the reasons given above that exhibitionism has been common throughout history. Those familiar with the *Canterbury Tales* will recall that in the *Miller's Tale*, Nicholas exposes his 'ers' out of the window: 'This Nicholas was risen for to pisse . . . And up the windowe did he hastily, and out his erse he putteth privately, over the buttok to the haunche-bon . . .' As a young man, Rousseau is said to have indulged in exposing his buttocks. However, exhibitionism in the male usually refers to exposure of the penis. James (1964) cites no case earlier than that of Sir Charles Sedley in the reign of Charles II. Rooth (1975) suggests that the legislation of 1824 was introduced as a result of a spate of exposing in the London parks. Both Rooth (1975) and Macdonald (1973) have reviewed legal and clinical aspects of the condition at some length. It is important to remember that the terms indecent exposure and exhibitionism are sometimes used synonymously, but Rooth (1975) makes the important point that it is helpful to make a distinction between the two phenomena. He distinguishes between indecent exposure (the offence) and exhibitionism (which is a clinical pattern of behaviour).

'Thus the term exposer will apply to anyone convicted, or liable to conviction, of indecent exposure. The term exhibitionist is confined to those exposers for whom genital display to a member of the opposite sex is an end in itself;

they are thus distinguished from those other exposers in whom the behaviour simply expresses a wish for intercourse or masturbation; or is the preliminary to an intended sexual assault.'

Most victims are adult females or children of either sex. The prognosis for the offender is generally considered to be worse in those cases where children are exposed to. Exposers will return frequently to the same place such as a park to indulge in their deviant behaviour. Sometimes the offender will merely expose himself; sometimes he will masturbate at the same time; he may make some verbal suggestion to the victim – such as, 'what do you think of this then?' – the intention being to shock. He may solicit the victim to touch him, or he may, exceptionally, touch the victim. Few studies have been made of the victims of indecent exposers; an interesting exception is that carried out by Gittleson, Eacott, and Mehta (1978). Gittleson and his colleagues interviewed one hundred female nurses at a psychiatric hospital in order to assess the frequency of their having been the victims of indecent exposure and to describe the experience. Forty-four of the subjects had been victims of exposure and one third of these had been on two or more occasions. They found that the attitudes of those who had been victims were no different from those who had not; one third of all the incidents had not been disclosed to anyone. In over one fifth of the episodes the reaction of family and friends had been more distressing to the victim than the episode itself.

Numerous attempts have been made to classify exhibitionists – most of them not very successful. But, on the basis of an extensive review of the literature, Rooth (1973) suggests that two broad types can be discerned. The first type is usually an inhibited young man, who struggles against his impulses to expose himself and feels guilty and anxious about his behaviour. He exposes with a flaccid penis, does not indulge in masturbation after the event, and seems to derive very little pleasure from his behaviour. The second type is described in the literature as less inhibited, he exposes with an erect penis, may masturbate at the time of exposure, seems to obtain great pleasure from the act and seems to feel little guilt. It has also been noted that exposers of this type may show other types of sexual disorder and may have sadistic tendencies. It is this minority who may go on to commit more serious sexual crimes. The great majority of indecent exposers have a good prognosis, with convictions falling off in the forties as part of the maturation process. However, as Rooth (1975) points out, the chances of reconviction 'increase dramatically with a second conviction'. More recently Jacoby (1978) found that out of 100 cases sixty-three had no further convictions, sixteen had further convictions for indecent exposure, fourteen were convicted for non-sex crimes, and seven for other sex offences – two of these for rape.

We can now carry Rooth's classification a little further and subdivide the categories in the following way.

(1) Simple or regressive types of exhibitionism. This may occur as a feature of adolescence (notably as a result of dawning adolescent sexuality in a home where sex is a taboo subject or fraught with various spoken and unspoken prohibitions). It may also occur as a result of ageing and be a feature of organic disease or of a dementing process. (See also Chapter 3.)

(2) Compensatory types of indecent exposure. These have been described by Maclay (1952). He suggests that the individual is relatively normal but his exposing is in the nature of anomalous form of sexual advance. Such individuals he considered to be shy and sexually repressed. (These would fit into Rooth's first typology.) It can be regarded perhaps as a form of love-making at a safe distance.

(3) Exposure precipitated by over-indulgence in alcohol. Some cases in this category are probably prosecuted for urinating in the street under local by-laws, but there may also have been an accompanying intention to indecently expose.

(4) Exposure committed by dull and subnormal individuals. (See Chapter 3.)

(5) Exposure committed by a chronically psychotic individual (for example a schizophrenic). This is not likely to be done with the deliberate intention to insult by exposing the penis, but is more likely to take the form of a show of total nakedness accompanied by bizarre behaviour.

(6) Cases in which the exposure is closely associated with some kind of marital stress. The offending behaviour may cease when the marital situation has been investigated and treated.

(7) Cases in which the sex drive is very strong and in which the exposure is part of a broader pattern of deviant and aggressive sexuality. These are likely to be individuals who also have convictions for non-sexual offences. They may proceed to more serious sexual crime and are potentially a dangerous group.

(8) Exposure in persons suffering from some form of physical disorder. From time to time cases are reported of men exposing themselves who are found to be suffering from enlargement of the prostate gland. Others may engage in this behaviour as a result of hypoglycemia or other metabolic disorder. (See Chapter 3.)

(9) A group regarded by Maclay as 'true exhibitionists' who practice exposure as the sole means of sexual relief.

(10) The 'neurotic' exhibitionist. Pollock (1960) has described one such case. This man, a first offender, had been sentenced to imprisonment for his minor part in a big fraud. He had never been charged with a sex offence and his exhibitionistic practices only came to light by chance. From the history as given by Pollock (a prison doctor) this man had fought for many years to combat his impulses. These seemed to have their origins in a complex and fraught relationship with his mother.

Causal explanations

Some of the explanations for this type of offending can be discerned from the classification listed above and therefore require no further elaboration. One or two additional comments are in order. The behaviour may be an extension of early childhood exhibitionism and be a way of emphasizing masculinity. It may be a form of behaviour carried out because of feelings of unattractiveness to females and thus may be the only way that a sexual overture can be made. Psychoanalytic theory postulates that the behaviour may seek to reassure against a fear of castration. Such motivation may operate in the man who exposes to little girls rather than to adult women since the latter are seen as having the power to castrate. There may also be, as we have seen earlier, an aggressive element and the exposure, with its aim to insult and shock, may be a suppressed expression of a wish to commit rape. In these cases, women may be regarded as dangerous creatures. It is therefore not suprising that impotence and homosexuality may be found in the backgrounds of these type of exposers. A sensitive account of a persistent exposer is that given by Harry Mills in Parker's book *The Twisting Lane* (Parker 1970).

Treatment

It is vital to obtain as broad a picture of the background and circumstances in each case as is possible. This is an essential prerequisite, for any treatment plan must depend on a full knowledge of the offender. For some exposers, the court appearance and its attendant publicity will suffice. For the youthful and inhibited exposer, some counselling about sex matters, coupled with help with the development of social skills may be all that is required. An interesting account of successful treatment along these lines may be found in Barnett (1972). For the exposer whose offence is associated with a complex marital situation, the involvement of the spouse is of paramount importance. Sometimes a good deal of work will be required to enable the husband to become a more dominant partner without this having an adverse effect on his wife. Some workers have experimented with the use of groups for exhibitionists with some degree of success; the members seem to derive a good deal of support from each other and begin to feel that they do not carry their burden alone (Mathis and

Cullens 1971; Milo 1976). The use of feminizing hormones and similar compounds has been tried in some cases, particularly the use of cyproterone acetate. (I shall refer in more detail to the use of this preparation in the discussion of rape.) Behaviour therapy has also been tried and some success reported, particularly in cases where the offender has been encouraged to try to develop more normal masturbation phantasies (see Rooth 1973). More recently, Jones and Frei (1977) report success with fifteen offenders by the use of provoked anxiety as the choice of treatment. The somewhat Draconian procedure involved the subject undressing before a mixed sex audience, video-taping, and subsequent replay to the patient. During the period of nakedness, the offender describes in detail the events, his expectations and attitudes, and those attributed to his victim during his exposure. The success of the treatment, in the authors' words 'appears to depend on the profound anxiety induced'. They comment upon the powerful and unpleasant form of technique used and suggest that it is only suitable for chronic cases who are aware of what they are going to let themselves in for. The authors report that in ten out of fifteen cases the persistent exposing was eliminated and in the remainder, a marked reduction in frequency was noted.

Overall, it would seem that treatment aimed at helping the offender to control his offending behaviour quickly holds out the best hope. Thus, behavioural methods, and the development of social skills are probably to be preferred to long-term psychotherapy. However, in those cases where the exhibitionism seems to be closely related to deep-rooted inter-personal conflicts and stresses, it may be that group or individual psychotherapy would be the treatment of choice. As with all forms of deviant social conduct, the best results are probably obtained from a multi-method approach and an open mind on the part of the therapist. For all sex offenders, the communicated genuineness and warmth of the therapist is more important than the particular school of thought he espouses or the model of practice he adopts.

SEXUAL ASSAULTS ON CHILDREN (PAEDOPHILIA, CHILD MOLESTATION)

Sexual offences against children and young persons vary considerably in their form and in their intensity. For example, incest can be regarded as one kind of sexual offence against a child, but, as such, we will consider it in the section dealing with incestuous behaviour rather than here. In similar fashion, acts of buggery and attempted buggery are often committed against children, but the criminal statistics do not distinguish these acts from those committed against adults. Those who commit sexual offences against children (almost always men) are usually referred to as paedophiles, though pederasty is the term sometimes employed for those who commit sexual offences against male children or youths. Child molesters span the age spectrum and they come from diverse educational and social groups. Law (1979) studied a group of child molesters in Hong Kong, comparing his findings with those available for Western countries. He found many common characteristics, one notable exception being that, in Hong Kong, offences tended to occur more frequently in places to which the public had access. The use of the term paedophilia (or pedophilia) has some inherent difficulties. Gordon (1976) points out that the term has tended to be used solely for the expression of love for children or youth that is pathological in its intensity and form. But we need to remember that a love of children is a fairly universal phenomenon and that there are probably many people who may be physically attracted towards children but who manage either to keep their inclinations in check, or not be wholly aware of the true nature of their feelings. Thus, we may find that the horror with which paedophiliac activities are regarded is an over-reaction in many people and a means of keeping dangerous and unbearable impulses at bay. Lambert (1976) adds confirmation to this in his analysis of the etymology of the work paedophilia. He points out that the Greek words involved are *paidos* and *philia*. *Paidos*, meaning a child, finds expression in words such as paediatrics, pedagogy, and pederasty. He points out that in common usage today only the work paediatrics 'carries an undertone of commendation'. The other two carry 'pejorative undertones'. *Philia* is associated with a group of words which all connote love; *eros, philia, agape*; in Greek literature all were used interchangeably and were present in all types of interpersonal relationships. *Philia* gradually came to be associated with love between 'master and slave, gods and men', but gradually, 'something of a darker, more instinctual . . . undercurrent . . . became . . . involved'. Lambert concludes that 'what is involved is a warm, loving affection towards a child in relation to whom responsibility is felt and undertaken'. We can readily see that harmful consequences may flow from such love in at least two ways. First this love may become over-possessive and selfish.* The result may be that the child never grows towards independent adulthood. He or she may in fact always remain a child, indulging in childish pursuits which may include the carrying over of childish sexual games into adulthood. Second, this love may go beyond the limits of normal care and protection and become inappropriate in situations that are both physically and emotionally traumatic to the child concerned. This etymological digression will have served an important purpose if it reminds us of the ever present 'darker side' of ourselves. It also supports the statement I made earlier that in order to work with sexual deviant behaviour we have to acknowledge our own blindspots. It also reminds us of the particular vulnerability of those who find employment in professions or occupations involving direct contact with children. It comes as no surprise, therefore, to find that a large number of sexual offences against children are committed by those who have ready access to them and who are in positions of tutelage or trust. Many such people give accounts of disordered family relationships or of their own corruption in youth, though the extent to which the latter is rationalization of their offence behaviour is not always easy to determine. The accounts offered by Russell George and Wilfred Johnson in Tony Parker's *The Twisting*

---

* Two literary accounts that illustrate some of these phenomena are Nabokovov's *Lolita* and Mann's *Death in Venice*. The former is of course particularly illuminating concerning the role of the so-called 'victim'.

Lane are sad and, for me, convincing personal narratives of the forces that can shape behaviour that society has to condemn as harmful. We are forced to acknowledge that some of these offenders have been victims themselves and certainly the role played by the victim in any sexual offence is most important. Some children, because of their particular social or family situation, crave for affection; it is all too easy for them to behave in a seductive fashion towards those who may be tempted to behave indecently with them. Sometimes this behaviour is quite unintentional or subconscious. Others are quite unscrupulous in their behaviour, are prepared to offer sexual favours for financial reward, and are not averse to indulging in a little blackmail. In acknowledging this seductive and manipulative behaviour we must not blind ourselves to the fact that adults put in a position of tutelage or trust should try to control their sexual predilections, even though some children make it well nigh impossible for them to do so. Virkkunen (1975) in a study of sixty-four cases of paedophilia found that the victim's 'precipitating behaviour' was important in 48.4 per cent of cases, involving visits made to the offender 'on the victim's own initiative and in taking some kind of initiative in the offence itself'. In a more recent study, Ingram (1979) finds seductive behaviour on the part of the child to be important. He also states: 'I do not think (that) there is any evidence from my study that any of the children were worse off for the activity . . . I can see how a lot of harm can come from a violent reaction to the act, and suggest that counselling should replace legal procedures wherever possible . . .' However, we should note that in Ingram's ninety-two cases, most of the incidents were more in the nature of sexual 'horse-play' than serious attempts at sexual connection or assault.

It is difficult to be precise as to the harm that may be caused to children and young people as a result of sexual molestation. Much will depend upon constitutional factors, the social situation, and the reactions of parents and other close adults. Homosexual experiences between children and young people (as in boarding schools) are probably not particularly harmful. It is accepted that most adolescents go through a 'normal' homosexual phase and then grow out of it. There is, however, a danger if, for any reason (such as an unhealthy family situation) the youngster is predisposed to the development of some form of deviant sexuality; an active homosexual experience may fixate him at this point. Regarding assaults by *adults* upon children, the evidence is less clear cut. Some children, superficially at least, seem to be markedly resilient. One boy alleged to have been the subject of attempted buggery said he 'just went on eating his apple as though nothing had happened'. Where the assault is violent *and unexpected* (either in respect of the place or in respect of the person concerned) the experience is more likely to be traumatic. Those paedophiles who have been arguing for a lowering of the age at which children may be legally involved in such behaviour underestimate not only the delicate balance of the psyche in early adolescence, but the need also to preserve distance between child and adult. (See also Power 1976.) They also underestimate the physical trauma that may be caused. Paul (1975, 1977) an experienced medical examiner of such cases of sexual assault, provides ample evidence of the damage that may be caused to both the genitalia in the female and the rectum in the male. This is particularly likely to be the case if virginity was previously intact in both cases.

From what has been said already, it will be apparent that the offence behaviour may take many forms. It may include exhibitionism, attempts to put the hand up the knickers of a young girl, feeling the breasts or genitalia, touching the penis, or masturbatory activities in which the child may be asked to masturbate the adult, orally or manually. It may also involve direct attempts at sexual intercourse – both heterosexual and homosexual. (See also Law 1979.)

It is difficult to classify such offenders, but the following rudimentary classification may be helpful. The injunction I gave earlier that classification is always arbitrary is relevant and overlapping should still be borne in mind.

(1) Bisexual (rather than homosexual) inadequate adolescents who are able to bribe children. They may have been placed

by adults in positions of trust towards the victims.

(2) A more dangerous adolescent offender, who makes serious assaults; he often has a history of having been assaulted in his own childhood (see above).

(3) The middle-aged paedophile who is almost always lonely and isolated. He may seek out the company of little girls in order to find solace. These offenders seem quite unable to assume an adult sexual role.

(4) The senile pederast, whose inclinations have not been dulled by age even if his ability has. Their continuation in this form of behaviour may be part of a dementing process. (See Chapter 3.)

(5) The paedophile of low or subnormal intelligence who may not always be aware of the significance of his behaviour. The assaults may be due in part to lack of social skills.

(6) Those whose sexual offences against children seem to be part and parcel of a more generalized inability to achieve social conformity. These are likely to be the offenders who also may have convictions for non-sexual offences.

(7) Those whose offending seems to be a reaction against sexual or emotional frustration at an adult level. (Some indecent exposers would of course fit into this category.) (See Fitch 1962.)

(8) The exclusively homosexual paedophile (the pederast). He often regards himself as the 'protector' of disadvantaged young boys, cannot see that his behaviour is wrong or unusual, and is quite impervious to treatment.

Treatment considerations

Experience within the penal, probation, and psychiatric services suggests that paedophilia is a very difficult condition to treat. This is partly because the sexual predilection may have become fixed at a very early age; techniques based on insight therapy (such as traditional psychoanalysis) do not seem to be very successful. In cases where the paedophile is an adolescent it may be possible to attempt sex counselling to try to redirect energies into more constructive channels and to develop social skills. In those cases where the behaviour seems to be temporary or situational, efforts to locate and treat the particular stresses offer some hope of success. Successful treatment depends entirely upon a desire on the part of the offender to change. It is unfortunate that a great number of adult paedophiles seem reluctant to change their life-styles or are so lacking in a capacity for the development of insight that therapy cannot make any impact. For these offenders, particularly the exclusively homosexual paedophiles, the only treatment likely to be effective will be that which may serve to 'damp down' their sexual desires. Feminizing treatments have already been referred to. In recent years a number of approaches have been introduced that make use of female hormones and anti-hormones in the treatment of paedophilia. Unfortunately, many of these have unfortunate side effects, such as breast enlargement and changed fat distribution. One drug that seems to have less serious side effects is cyproterone acetate (already referred to). Readers wishing to examine some of the work on the use of female hormones, anti-hormones, and other drugs should consult the work of Field and Williams (1970), Davies (1970), Field and Williams (1971), Field (1973), Tennent, Bancroft, and Cass (1974). Aversive techniques have been advocated by some workers; descriptions of the techniques used and their effectiveness may be found in McGuire and Vallance (1964), McGuire, Carlisle, and Young (1965), Mather (1966), and Bancroft (1969). In some cases castration and surgical interference with parts of the hypothalamus (stereotactic procedures) have been tried (Roeder, Orthner, and Muller 1972). The irreversible nature of these procedures presents ethical problems of some magnitude, even though the informed consent of the offender/patient may be sought. There are also ethical implications concerning the use of reversible procedures such as hormone implants or injections. For the pederast serving a long term of imprisonment it may be tempting for him to accelerate his chances of parole by agreeing to subject himself to such treatment even though his real motivation for change may be slight. There are arguments against this of course. *If* his informed consent has been given, *if* he is fully aware of the implications, and *if* he is prepared to subject himself to follow up after discharge, not only is he likely to be less of a menace to children but he may be able to make a useful contribution to society and enjoy the benefit of his freedom.

INCEST

Incest is one of the sexual crimes that provokes the most emotive reactions. Taboos against its practice have existed from time immemorial. There have been exceptions, however, notably in the ancient cultures of Egypt, Japan, and Greece where it seems to have been permitted amongst those of Royal blood. In the middle ages it also seems to have been practised amongst certain noble families. Mythology and literature are replete with allusions to incestuous conduct or incestuous themes. We find references to it in the Old Testament, in the myths concerning the God Zeus, in the behaviour of Salome, and of course in the legend of Oedipus. Incestuous themes appear in *Hamlet,* in *The Duchess of Malfi,* in *Wuthering Heights*, in Poe's *Fall of the House of Usher,* and more contemporarily in Murdoch's *A Severed Head.* There is little doubt that the crime of incest arouses feelings of revulsion in many people and it is likely that religious influences have contributed to this. This is illustrated perhaps by the fact that until 1908 it was regarded solely as an ecclesiastical offence.

Many reasons have been advanced for the strict prohibitions against incestuous behaviour. First, as already mentioned, there are the religious injunctions. Second, there appears to be a deeply held and primaeval horror of consanguinous sexual relationships between parents and their offspring. Third, there is the Freudian belief (based upon Darwin's theory of the 'primal horde') which suggests that in primitive societies, the younger menfolk would have banded together in order to destroy the paternal 'tyrant', who had kept the females of the tribe for his own sexual use. Competition and rivalry would have followed such banding together amongst the younger brethren. This would have resulted in very severe interference with the social order. It is therefore suggested that the incest taboo was erected to prevent such destruction taking place. As is well known, Freud built further upon this theory in his development of the Oedipus and Electra conflicts in which small children are said to wish to possess the parent of the opposite sex. Small wonder then that incest taboos are so strong. Fourth, it has been suggested that taboos are also strong because of the confusions in role that can occur when close kin have had sexual relationships. Fifth, there has been evidence put forward in recent years to suggest that incestuous relationships produce a higher incidence of genetic weaknesses than that found in normal sexual unions. 'Studies clearly demonstrate that the children of incest suffer from higher infant mortality, severe congenital malformations and lowered intelligence levels' (Nakashima and Zakus (1977). See also Roberts (1967) and Browning and Boatman (1977).) But, as we shall see later, incestuous relationships often take place in very socially disordered families and it is more likely that it is the *combination* of poor ante-natal care, poor nurturing environment, *and* incestuous relationships that produce such a severely disadvantaged group.

As already indicated, incest in England and Wales did not come within the purview of the criminal law until 1908 (in Scotland, it was punishable by death until the late 1880s). The present law (as incorporated into the Sexual Offences Act, 1956) now states that a man who has sexual intercourse with a woman whom he knows to be his grand-daughter, daughter, sister, or mother is guilty of incest, as is a woman of or above the age of sixteen, who, with consent, permits her grandfather, father, brother, or son to have sexual intercourse with her. The offence is punishable with a maximum sentence of imprisonment for seven years; in the case of the offence being committed against a girl under thirteen, it is punishable with imprisonment for life. Comparatively few cases come to the attention of the police, and even fewer are actually prosecuted. The comments made earlier about the difficulties involved in prosecuting sexual offences apply very strongly to cases of incest. Frequently, it comes to light because of pregnancy, because of an attempt at blackmail, through the investigation of some non-related offence behaviour, or as a result of a 'confession' by one of the parties. Nearly all those prosecuted are men and very few women are brought to the attention of the police or of the courts. Lukianowicz (1972) in one of the very few surveys of incest carried out in recent years reports a 4 per cent incidence of incest amongst an unselected group of female psychiatric patients in Northern Ireland. Hall-Williams (1974) has contributed a useful survey of a selected group of imprisoned incest offenders. He examined the records of sixty-eight men eligible for parole in the period 1970–71. These would of course be the more serious cases, including those sentenced to imprisonment for eighteen months or more and would not include those dealt with by means of non-custodial penalties. Most of these offenders had been sentenced to imprisonment for three to four years or more. 25 per cent were regarded as being of low or subnormal intelligence and 25 per cent of the sample had previous convictions for sex offences. Although the primary charge was that of incest, 22 per cent had also been charged with buggery, 27 per cent with unlawful sexual intercourse, and 4 per cent with rape. In 16 per cent of the cases, the wife was dead or the partners had been separated or divorced. In a number of other cases the marriages were under strain. Alcohol was found to be closely associated with the offence, a feature found also in a series of cases examined by Virkkunen (1974). In 53 per cent of cases, the victim was the man's own child and in 15 per cent a step-child was involved. In 60 per cent of cases the ages of the children were between ten and sixteen and in about 20 per cent the partner was sixteen and over. Hall-Williams' findings seem consonant with those reported upon by Maisch in his German study (Maisch 1973). In a more recent paper, Gibbens, Way, and Soothill (1978) examined the careers and criminal records of *sibling* and *parent-child* incest offenders. They took as their sample all incest cases appearing in the higher courts in 1951 (102) and in 1961 (177). This allowed for a long follow-up period. They were particularly interested in any differences that might be found between sibling offences and parent-child offences. They discovered that a large majority of the fathers (61 per cent) were first offenders, 12 per cent had subsequent convictions, and some 13 per cent of the fathers had prior sexual offences. (This is a smaller proportion than that found by Hall-Williams, but he was dealing with a group who had all been sentenced to imprisonment, whereas Gibbens and his colleagues were examining *all* cases before the higher courts.) 72 per cent of their cases were over forty at the time of the offence and 90 per cent of them went to prison. Gibbens, Way, and Soothill found that some 60 per cent of the sibling offenders were aged twenty or less and 74 per cent of them received non-custodial sentences. 54 per cent of them had previous convictions or findings of guilt, but few were for sex offences. However, over the next twelve years they continued to be heavily convicted; 49 per cent for property offences and 14 per cent for violence. The authors cannot give any firm explanation for these differences, but suggest three possible reasons. First, incest behaviour may have come to light more often in cases where the family was already under surveillance by social workers. Second, sibling incest may well be more common in large overcrowded families where a high rate of ordinary criminal behaviour is common. Third, this may have been a group of young recidivists who continued offending wholly or partly because of sexual maladjustment which may not always be revealed in actual convictions for sexual offences. (This would be in keeping with my earlier remarks concerning 'masked' sexual offences.) These findings also alert us to the importance of the family dynamics in all incest cases. Maisch (1973) (quoted in Hall-Williams 1974) makes a pertinent comment: '. . . The development of the victim's personality [is not] fully comprehensible nor can a measured judgement be passed on the incest situation unless one considers the wife and mother and her role in the management of the family . . .'

It is not hard to see that incest will arise from a variety of causes and that the family composition and life-style are highly significant. With this in mind it is possible to make a somewhat rudimentary classification of those conditions that may promote incestuous behaviour. By so doing, we can then apply the most appropriate mode of management.

(1) Incest occurring in large, overcrowded families, where the participants almost slip into an incestuous pattern of behaviour. In some cases, this tendency may be exacerbated by alcohol abuse and by the use of threats and violence by the father.

(2) Incestuous relations developing because of intellectual impairment or psychotic illness in either or both of the parties.

(3) Where the wife is either absent through death or separation and where the daughter(s) may take over the wife's role. It will also occur in cases where the wife is still present but where she has abrogated her sexual role. In such instances it appears that she is quite cognisant of what has been going on, and is, in fact, quite prepared to collude in the practice.

(4) Cases in which the father is a dominant individual, apparently of normal intelligence and personality and who seduces the children in the full knowledge that such behaviour is wrong.

(5) Occasional instances, where the parties do not know that they are in a consanguinous relationship. For example, a brother and sister separated from each other very early in life, may then meet much later and unknowingly enter into a sexual relationship.

(6) Cases described by Bagley (1969) which he describes as 'object fixation incest'. He suggests that incest may occur in those instances where the dominant partner was sexually fixated on an earlier object of sexual gratification, a child or an adolescent, with whom he had his first sexual experience when he was a child himself.

Treatment considerations

Those who work with incest cases have to face the force of the taboos that exist and possibly their own incest anxieties and fears. The Courts seem to deal severely with adult males convicted of incest with their children. In some cases one wonders whether more harm than good is done by the additional stress that is created for the family by sentencing the father to a long term of imprisonment. Against this, we have to see that the welfare of children is protected, but there are now elaborate precautions taken by both the probation service and social services departments in all cases where children have been, or are likely to be, the subject of attack or injury from whatever cause. (See DHSS Circulars LAC/78(22) and 107/78.) Some have argued quite strongly, Morris and Hawkins (1970) for example, for the removal of the crime of incest from the statute book because it would be quite easy to take the necessary prosecutory and precautionary steps under existing sex offence legislation. In this way, the special abhorrence with which the offence is viewed might be diminished to some extent. It could then be viewed for what it really is, an offence connected with adverse family living conditions, calling for socio-psychiatric intervention rather than irrational feelings and punitive wrath. The use of the global term incest also means that we link together all its varieties and treat them all alike. As we have seen, we need to try to be more discriminating in order to offer more effective treatment. Perhaps the law should only come down most heavily in those situations I have listed under category (4) above. In other instances, arrangements would have to be made for the father's withdrawal from the family (perhaps by means of a probation order with a requirement of residence) while the complexities of the situation are clarified. The local authorities have adequate powers already for the supervision of the children and to undertake their removal should the situation 'blow up'. The aim overall should be to restore family functioning rather than to disrupt it further by the use of inflexible and punitive sanctions.

RAPE

Rape is another sexual offence that arouses strong emotions. It must be emphasized again that it is not always easy to distinguish between rape and indecent assault; to rely solely on the statistics of such offences as indicators of their severity is misleading. Reference to the Criminal Statistics *(Table 8(2))* shows that indecent assaults on females not only constitute a large proportion of known sexual offences, but that their frequency seems to remain fairly constant. This may be due to changing attitudes towards rapists and rape victims; some of these will be discussed later. Stereotypes of the rapist and his victim abound and attempts to shake firmly held prejudices are beset by difficulties. The act of rape, like some other serious sexual offences, has its place in myth, art, and literature. Mythical accounts and paintings seem to present rape in a singularly bland and almost impersonal fashion; they depict none of the horror and distress that so often accompanies it. Mistaken interpretations of anthropology and history have also added to this tendency. Many men seem to subscribe to the belief that manhood and virility can only be demonstrated by 'caveman' behaviour. Primitive cave paintings of early man carrying off his 'chosen' woman by the hair merely support these notions. Another popular myth is that women somehow welcome being 'taken by force' and that they may encourage such behaviour, becoming disappointed and frustrated when it is not forthcoming. In some cases such disappointment is said to be the motivation behind the complaint of having been raped. It is true of course that aggression and physical sexuality are closely linked. A woman may well enjoy 'giving' of herself in full orgasm with a *chosen* partner. I can find no evidence that women enjoy such behaviour when it is forced upon them in terrifying circumstances which are not of their choosing. I fear, however, that not a few males pretend they do. Many of these notions will affect how we attempt to classify the behaviour of rapists and will have implications for their treatment.

Some statistics

The statistics of rape have been alluded to briefly already, but some elaboration is necessary. In 1975, just over a thousand cases of rape were reported as known to the Police (*Table 8(2)*). Of these, about one third (328) were convicted and 241 of these were sent to prison. The sentences ranged from approximately two to seven years. Soothill and Gibbens (1978) examined the records of a large number of rapists and followed their criminal careers over a twenty-year period. They also found that about one third had been acquitted and that those acquitted were just as likely to commit further sexual offences as those convicted. They also made another interesting discovery, namely, that a sizeable proportion of serious sex offenders (and there were many rapists amongst them) are re-convicted *a long time after their first conviction*. This finding emerged because of the long-term nature of this follow-up. They suggest as a result of this, that, as many research studies of serious offenders concern themselves only with short-term follow-up, outcomes can therefore be misleading. (See also Soothill, Jack, and Gibbens 1976.) They also found that some 25 per cent of their sample had further quite serious convictions for sex violence. In considering these findings it is also interesting to note a recent study by Howells and Wright (1978). They found when sexual offenders and non-sexual offenders were given a test designed to discern sexual attitudes, that the sex offenders were found to score significantly higher on scales measuring sexual maladjustment. Of more importance was the finding that they scored significantly higher on scales designed to measure *loss of control*. A number of studies have been made of what we might loosely describe as the epidemiology of rape. Of these, that by Amir (1971) is probably one of the most comprehensive. He studied not only the characteristics of rapists, but such matters as location, time of day, seasonal variation, and relationship of victim to assailant. He found that about one third of the victims had been in previous contact with their assailants (a finding supported by other studies). Alcohol was an important factor in two thirds of his cases; in 75 per cent of cases the rape had been planned. 50 per cent of the victims failed to resist their attackers. He also found a very high proportion of multiple rape cases (43 per cent). In contrast to the views of some other authorities, he suggests that the significance of the victim as a precipitator of the event was frequently underestimated. The accompanying brutality had been less severe than anticipated. I have only presented a fraction of Amir's interesting findings and his work is well worth careful study. Two other major texts deserve mention. The first is by Schultz (1975), in which the focus is very much on the victims. The second is by Macdonald (1971). This is a thoughtful overview of the whole area. The most recent major contribution is that by West, Roy, and Nichols (1978); this work will be referred to again later.

Legal aspects

Barbara Toner, in Chapters 5 and 6 of her book *The Facts of Rape* (1977) provides a very useful summary of the history of the law concerning rape and of the current position. As we shall see, it is only very recently that the ingredients of the offence of rape have been defined statutorily. Before this time, rape had always been a crime at common law, the only statutory reference to it being in Section I of the Sexual Offences Act, 1956. This stated merely that it was a felony for a man to rape a woman, and that a man who induced a woman to have sexual intercourse with him whilst impersonating her husband was guilty of rape. It is worth noting here, that it is not a criminal offence for a man to rape his wife (unless a separation order is in force). There have been moves recently, particularly by the feminist movement, to correct what appears to be an anomaly in the law. In 1978, a case in the USA attracted a good deal of publicity. In that instance the wife lost her case against her husband. However, a husband who uses force in exercising his 'rights' against his wife may be found guilty of assault. The weakness in the law, until very recently, was that rape was not defined adequately. Before stating the new provisions (as contained in the Sexual Offences (Amendment) Act, 1976) it will help to give a little of the background to this legislation. The first element influencing reform can be seen in the work of the feminist movement who viewed the legal approach to the crime of rape as an example of discrimination by men against women. (See for example Brownmiller (1975).) In 1975, the Law Lords in the case of *DPP* v. *Morgan*, ruled that belief in a woman's consent, *even if unreasonable*, must exonerate the accused. The case in question involved an RAF sergeant who invited three of his friends to his home to have sexual intercourse with his wife. It was alleged that he told them she would welcome such activity but that she would struggle a bit as she was 'kinky'. The men pleaded their belief that she had consented and that therefore there was no intention to rape. This ruling resulted in the setting up of a Government committee of enquiry into the law of rape. This committee reported in December, 1975. (It is noteworthy that the Chairman was a woman judge, Mrs Justice Heilbron.) It did not disagree with the Law Lords' decision, but it made certain recommendations concerning anonymity, sexual history, and on jury membership in rape cases. (Namely that both sexes should be represented, with not fewer than four members of either sex.) The main provisions of the Sexual Offences (Amendment) Act, 1976, which was enacted following acceptance of most of the committee's findings, concern definition of the offence and the question of consent. The law now holds that a man commits rape if (a) he has unlawful sexual intercourse with a woman who at the time of the intercourse does not consent to it; and (b) at that time knows that she does not consent to the intercourse or is reckless as to whether she consents to it. Concerning the matter of consent the law now states that if at a trial for a rape offence the jury has to consider whether a man believed that a woman was consenting to sexual intercourse, the presence or absence of reasonable grounds for such a belief is a matter to which the jury should have regard, in conjunction with any other relevant matters, in considering whether he so believed. Further sections of the act are designed to protect the anonymity of the victim (and of the defendant until found guilty), and to prevent questioning the victim about her past sexual experience or reputation unless the court gives leave to do so.

Now that questions of definition and consent have been clarified to some extent, interest has centred on sentencing in rape cases. Public opinion was aroused recently by the case of an army serviceman, Holdsworth, who was released on a suspended sentence after having sexually assaulted with extreme brutality a girl of seventeen. The judge awarded the sentence in the hope that his Army career would not be terminated. Jack Ashley, Labour Member of Parliament for Stoke on Trent, sought to introduce a Bill that would have allowed the prosecution to appeal against sentences considered to be too light in rape and other sexual offences. His Bill was overwhelmingly defeated. In concluding this section, we should note that sentencing and the law of rape are currently being reviewed by the Criminal Law Revision Committee. In general, the recent changes in the law seem helpful and they may well lead to more frequent reporting of rape cases, though for reasons which will be given shortly, women are still very reluctant to do so.

Victims

As stated earlier, literature, both classical and popular, tends to underemphasize the physical and emotional trauma caused to rape victims. Some of the more recent literature on rape victimology helps to redress the balance as does the work of the feminist movement. Concerning the latter it is unfortunate that their otherwise excellent work is sometimes vitiated by the more strident utterances of some of their members. Much is often made in rape cases of a woman's complicity or acquiescence and of the trouble she may have created for herself by making herself vulnerable. Examples given are hitch-hiking alone, wearing provocative clothes,* or leaving bedroom windows or doors open. I am prepared to accept that some women (sometimes for unconscious reasons) may take unnecessary risks and by doing so expose themselves to potential harm, but I do not see that this really excuses the conduct of the offender. Carrying the 'asking for trouble' argument to its logical conclusion, one might as well say that we *deserve* to lose our cars if we leave them unlocked or have our houses burgled if we leave doors insecurely fastened. Prudent behaviour in sexual mat-

* Those familiar with court proceedings will have noticed how the provocatively dressed adolescent schoolgirl may impress quite differently when clad in school gym slip in court.

ters is obviously to be encouraged, but Power (1976) makes an important observation when he says that 'what the victim actually did is held as less significant than how the assailant interpreted her actions'.

We have already noted that rape is an under-reported offence. This is hardly surprising, when we consider that women may be very reluctant to go through the ordeal of a searching medical examination and a public exploration of the circumstances of the alleged assault. Some women are not unnaturally reluctant to report the offence to their husbands or other family members. They may suffer considerable torment and unrelieved feelings of guilt as a result. The physical sequelae, apart from vaginal and other injury that may have been caused, are important. The victim may have become pregnant, have contracted venereal disease, or one of the increasingly common genital herpes (HSV–2) infections (Burt 1979), and this just compounds their misery. A sympathetic attitude on the part of all those concerned in investigating the complaint is essential. It is good to note that police officers are now being encouraged to have more regard for the emotional state of the victim. Counselling in respect of all areas mentioned above is vital. Many women feel defiled and damaged at the time of the offence, sometimes feeling compelled to scrub their genitalia with disinfectants repeatedly. The long-term effects can also be severe. The work of the recently established rape crisis centres in some of our major cities is an encouraging development, but all who may come into contact with rape victims and their families require to develop knowledge and skills in this area. Some helpful accounts of the help that can be offered are now available. See for example, Abarbanel (1976), Hardgrove (1976), and Hall (1977).

Far less attention is given to cases of male rape. These acts would be covered in the statistics as acts of buggery or attempted buggery. Sometimes such acts are committed with great force and the person concerned (frequently a minor) may be put in great fear. Moreover, the reluctance to talk about it or to report it is probably just as great as it is for women. The physical and emotional trauma (apart from pregnancy) and its sequelae is just as severe. Apart from accounts of rape in prison and allied institutions in the USA (for example, Scacco 1975) we have very few documented accounts of the incidence and effects of anal rape. A report in *The Guardian* of 31 May 1977 suggested that in San Francisco over 300 men were raped in 1976. This is a subject worthy of further investigation since as we have said, the sequelae can be most harmful.

Attempts at classification

The arbitrary nature of attempts at classification (as with other sex offences) must again be acknowledged, as must the degree of overlap between the groups. Two simplified classifications are now described. The first is by Gibbens, Way, and Soothill (1977). They discerned three groups:

(1) Paedophiliac rapists – involving girls aged 14 or under (see previous discussion of paedophilia).
(2) Aggressive rapists (these offenders will often have committed other aggressive offences).
(3) Isolated rape offences. This group would include a wide range of offences, from those of mistaken consent to the highly pathological rape 'allied to the once-for-all rape murderer'

A second simple classification is that provided by Hall-Williams (1977). He examined the records of a series of seventy-eight men eligible for parole and discerned four types.

(1) The extensively aggressive (fourteen in sample);
(2) A mixed aggressive group (thirty-seven in sample);
(3) Serious sexual offences used as a means of resolving personal problems or as reactions to stress (fourteen in sample);
(4) Essentially paedophiliac types (thirteen in sample).

A difficulty in classification arises because we are sometimes describing the offence by the nature of the behaviour displayed (for example, aggressive or over-inhibited), sometimes by the choice of victim (for example, children or old people), and sometimes by the presence of other features such as mental disorder. In trying to get the best of all worlds I put forward the following classification, thought I recognize that if you try to get the best of all worlds you probably end up with none!

Types

(1) The well-adjusted sexually virile young man out for what he can get, whose hedonism is not counterbalanced by finer scruples or caution.

(2) The inhibited shy younger man who is trying to overcome his feelings of sexual inferiority. He may mistake the responses of his victim as a 'come on'. In this category we could place some rapists who are latently homosexual and whose behaviour may be a defence against their homosexuality.

(3) The sexually violent and aggressive. These offenders may have records of other forms of violence and alcohol will play a large part in the commission of their crimes. Most researches show that alcohol plays a significant part in aggressive sexual criminality. It may be that some rapists hold the mistaken belief that alcohol will heighten sexual capacity. The fact of the matter is that, as the Porter says in Macbeth, 'it provokes the desire, but it takes away the performance'. Some may take it of course to summon up courage.

(4) A group who are severely sexually maladjusted; they need to gain reassurance for their masculinity by a show of force. In West's intensive study of a group of men undergoing psychotherapy for serious rape offences one of the cardinal characteristics emerging was that these men suffered from severe feelings of inferiority concerning their masculinity (West, Roy, and Nichols 1978). This group includes those who set out to defile and denigrate their victims. Such men may force their victims to participate in perverse activities such as buggery or fellatio or subject them to repeated acts of intercourse. They are the women haters, who may move on to become the sadistic sexual

murderers described later in this chapter.

(5) A sub-group of (4) above. These are men who have psychopathic tendencies and whose sexual appetites are insatiable. They may in fact need the resistance of the victims to arouse their potency. They may also indulge in homosexual rape.

(6) Those who are suffering from some form of mental disorder, such as an organic psychosis, brain tumour, hypomania, or from subnormality. (The relevance of these disorders has already been discussed in Chapter 3.)

(7) Those who rape in groups or packs. These rapists tend to be younger, and may belong to groups such as the notorious 'Hell's Angels'. They are likely to have previous convictions for violence and sexual offences. They are also inclined to indulge in perverse activities and like the rapists in group (4), frequently seek to defile their victims. Their offences are often associated with prior ingestion of alcohol.

Treatment considerations

Much of what was said earlier about other serious sexual assaults will apply with equal force here. Classification will give some clues to the kind of treatment mode that may be successful. It will also help us to discriminate between the transient, fairly inoccuous offender and the offender who is highly dangerous or potentially highly dangerous. West, Roy, and Nichols (1978) demonstrate that prolonged psychotherapy within a secure institution seems to be successful with some of the rapists I have assigned to group (4). Some forms of brief counselling or psychotherapy may be useful in groups (1) and (2). Those in group (7) may outgrow their proclivities as they mature, but they may also have to be put out of circulation for a period, both for the protection of society and for the reinforcement of their own consciences. Those in group (6) may respond to treatment of management for their underlying mental disorder. Those in group (3) are less likely to be amenable to treatment, but attempts that recognize the multifaceted nature of their disturbance are more likely to offer some chance of success. The combination of chemo-therapy and counselling (either individual or group) has much to commend it. Shaw (1978a and 1978b) describes a limited attempt. This concerned a group of serious sex offenders who were receiving monitored injections of the anti-androgen drug cyproterone acetate. They were also being treated simultaneously in a group. The success of the scheme depended upon a number of factors. First, the cooperation of a local general practitioner, who supplied and monitored the medication. Second, the willingness of probation staff (both professional and voluntary) to give a good deal of time to the group. Third, the cooperation of the local courts in placing a group of men on probation who would otherwise have been sent to prison for very long periods of time. Unfortunately, for various reasons, the experiment had to be abandoned after a comparatively short time, so that no extensive follow-up was possible, nor was a control group available. Despite these shortcomings, the indications were that such combined forms of treatment are viable and probably offer the best approach to carefully selected groups of offenders convicted of rape or other serious sexual attack.

SEXUAL OFFENDING AND DEATH

In order to complete our picture of sex offenders it is necessary to say something about the ways in which deviant or delinquent sexual behaviour may result in, or be associated with, death.

Sadistic sexual murder

Crimes of extreme violence in which the underlying motivation is sexual, as for example, in the 'crime passionel', or murder committed because of pathological sexual jealousy. In other cases, the motivation may not be so clear cut and at first sight it may be very difficult to discern the meaning of the sexual killing. Hyatt-Williams (1964) has written a highly interesting account of such sexual killers, revealing at one and the same time the complexities of their life situations and of their motives. Although his interpretation is fairly strongly psychoanalytical, it is none the less compelling and affords many insights into the minds of such killers. He stresses how different parts of the murderer's personality seem to be out of touch with each other. 'Kindness and compassion existing closely side by side with cruelty and savage destructiveness'. This capacity for 'splitting' seems to be a particularly important characteristic in the sadistic sexual murderer. In Chapter 3 I referred to sadistic sexual killers and cited Neville Heath as an example. We can now develop our observations on this matter further in an attempt to fill in the picture. The following description draws heavily upon a very illuminating contribution from the late doctor Robert Brittain who possessed an almost unique combination of skills and qualifications in that he was a pathologist and a forensic psychiatrist. His contribution derives from many years' experience, not only of interviewing and assessing such offenders, but also from an examination of the locations of their crimes and the physical circumstances surrounding them. A word of caution is necessary before we proceed. In giving what he called a profile, Brittain emphasized that this was in fact in the nature of a composite picture. The characteristics should not be viewed in isolation, neither should they be viewed as needing to be present in every case. His intention was merely to alert those who had to deal with such offenders to their possible attributes (Brittain 1970).

He suggested that such a person was more likely than not to be of an introverted, over-controlled, even timid nature. He might even appear to be prim and prudish and be offended by 'dirty jokes'. He was most likely to be thirty-five or over, come from any occupational status, but interestingly, a number of them had been employed in abattoirs. He may have had previous convictions for minor sexual offences. In a number of cases such persons might reveal markedly ambivalent feelings towards their mothers – the devoted son on the one hand, and the mother-hater on the other. The mothers of such men tend to be gentle and overindulgent, whilst the fathers were often rigidly strict or absent. Careful examination and assessment often revealed an active and bizarre phantasy life, preoccupied with literature depicting violence and pornography. They are likely to show morbid interest in atrocities, the Nazi regime, Black Magic, and horror films. They might harbour collections of knives and other paraphernalia of violence. They tend to be very preoccupied with what they regard (often quite erroneously) as their own inadequate or poorly developed genitalia. Their actual sex performance is often poor. They may plan the murder over a period of several weeks or months. They seem to show no remorse or guilt for the appalling cruelty they inflict. In fact, the sight of the helpless victim may well serve to add to their sex frenzy. Asphyxia is said to be the commonest method of killing, since by this means the victim's suffering may be regulated or prolonged. Sexual intercourse may not take place and orgasm may not occur; masturbation may be indulged in at the side of the body. Sometimes the offender will insert articles (such as a torch) with great force into victim's vagina or rectum. Such offenders are highly dangerous and may need to be detained for life. The prognosis by most authorities is said to be poor; those in charge of such persons have to guard against being misled by *appearances* of good behaviour and protestations of reform. To be fair, some do desire to be contained because they are frightened of their sadistic impulses and are grateful for the containment that prison or special hospital provides. Brittain sounds a warning note: 'Given the opportunity, the sadistic murderer is likely to murder again and he knows this . . .'

Other situations which may result in death

Sexual deviants and offenders may commit suicide. This may occur either as a result of guilt feelings or fear of exposure. It may also occur amongst adult male homosexuals as a result of a broken 'love affair' or when an ageing male homosexual feels he is no longer attractive to youthful male partners. Rupp (1970), writing from experience in the USA, suggests that those investigating sudden death in the 'Gay World' find indiscriminate homosexuals more prone to sudden death than the average citizen. There are other ways in which sexual deviance or offending may result in death. A man who makes his homosexual inclinations too obvious may be at the prey of 'queer bashers' and although not intended, such overtures may end in sudden death. Sometimes an overture towards the wrong person may result in violent retaliation of the type referred to in Chapter 6. Finally, death may occur accidentally in the course of the sexually deviant act itself. Cases have been reported where death has occurred in the course of fellatio due to aspiration of ejaculate or from impaction of the penis in the hypopharynx. Strangulation may occur as a result of pressure applied to the neck during anal intercourse. Such incidents are rare of course, and some may view the discussion of them as prurient or unhealthy sensationalism. They have been referred to merely to show that serious harm *may* occur as a result of certain sexual practices. This is particularly important at a time when pseudo-liberalism has become popular and where liberty is sometimes confused with licence in the absence of a full acknowledgement of all its implications.

Necrophilia

This form of behaviour rarely comes to light. The reason is fairly obvious as it is unlikely there will be witnesses. The literature on this subject is somewhat sparse, but some of it has been reviewed usefully by Bartholomew, Milte, and Galbally (1978). Three forms of necrophilia have been suggested in the past: (a) lust murder; (b) necrostuprum – corpse stealing; (c) necrophagy – corpse mutilation and/or eating. In some cases, it is difficult to ascertain whether a murder has been committed purely for the purposes of sexual molestation after death.*
Bartholomew, Milte, and Galbally (1978) cite a case in which the offender lived out his necrophiliac phantasies by first killing and then sexually assaulting a young man. He then disposed of the body down a mine shaft. They describe a second case in which it was strongly *suspected*, but not proved, that

* Mather (1979) personal communication.

necrophiliac activity had been committed after the murder of a nine-year-old boy. Such offenders will be grossly disordered of course and their behaviour can be seen in the context of the discussion of the sadistic sexual murder above. Occasionally, patients will admit to necrophiliac activities in the course of investigations for other offences. It has been suggested that occupations such as that of mortuary attendant may well lend themselves to such activities in those already inclined to behave in this fashion. Kennedy (1961) suggests that Christie may have been a necrophiliac, but his account does not enable one to draw firm conclusions. More recently, Lancaster (1978) has described the case of a man indicted for murder. In the course of the investigation he admitted breaking into a mortuary and attempting sexual relations with female corpses.

Concluding comments

I hope that the information in this chapter will have demon-strated some of the difficulties involved in describing, classify-ing, and treating sexual offenders. I would wish to emphasize once again that in work with such persons we need to try to be aware of our blind-spots, to examine our feelings and to try to respond as dispassionately as possible to what is sometimes bizarre and sickening behaviour. The capacity to listen and to respond non-judgmentally in these situations is crucial for success. Despite some appearance to the contrary, a number of sexual offenders are distressed and disturbed by their behaviour and its effects upon others. Only when they discern a dispassionate and compassionate recipient for these feelings can they begin to unburden themselves; by so doing, this may help to ease some of the tensions that may have contributed to their offending. Others are of course quite unmotivated for change and are therefore untreatable. Treatment takes time, as West, Roy, and Nichols (1978) have shown. A detailed his-tory of the total situation is vital for diagnosis. Only by such means can all the facts be appraised. Workers in this field owe it to their professional disciplines to make themselves as well informed as possible; only by doing so can they hope to begin to discriminate between those sex offenders who have a social nuisance value and those who are, or who may move on to be, a serious danger to the community. Finally, a multi-method approach to treatment is likely to be the most successful. This is why collaboration between general practitioners, psychiatrists, psychologists, and social workers is so necessary in this area of work. Let the last word come from an eminent psychiatrist – Professor Sir Denis Hill (who was a member of the Aarvold Committee). In his paper on 'The Qualities of a Good Psychiatrist' he says: 'Personal and emotional maturity, . . . means freedom from personal neurotic nostalgia with one's own past' Hill (1978). There are lessons to be learned here by all of us.

References

Abarbanel, G. (1976) Helping Victims of Rape. *Social Work* November: 478–82.

Allen, C. (1949) *The Sexual Perversions and Abnormalities*. Oxford: Oxford University Press.

Amir, M. (1971) *Patterns in Forcible Rape*. Chicago: Chicago University Press.

Bagley, C. (1969) The Varieties of Incest. *New Society* 21 August 1969: 280–82.

Bancroft, J. (1969) Aversion Therapy of Homosexuality. *Brit. J. Psychiat.* **115**: 1417–431.

Barnett, I. (1972) The Successful Treatment of an Exhibitionist. *Int. J. Off. Ther.* **16**: 125–29.

Bartholomew, A.A., Milte, K.L., and Galbally, F. (1978) Homosexual Necrophilia. *Med. Sci. Law* **18**: 29–35.

Brandon, S. (1975) Management of Sexual Deviation. *Brit. M.J.* 19 July 1975: 149–51.

Brittain, R.P. (1970) The Sadistic Murderer. *Med. Sci. Law* **10**: 198–207.

Browning, D.H. and Boatman, B. (1977) Incest: Children at Risk. *Am. J. Psychiat.* **134**: 69–72.

Brownmiller, S. (1975) *Against Our Will: Men, Women and Rape*. London: Secker and Warburg.

Burt, J.L. (1979) The Epidemiology of Genital Herpes

(HSV–2) Infections. *J. Roy. Soc. Hlth.* **99**: 31.

Davies, T.S. (1970) Cyproterone Acetate in Sexual Misbehaviour. *Med. Sci. Law* **10**: 237.

East, N. (1949) *Society and the Criminal.* London: HMSO.

Field, L.H. and Williams, M. (1970) The Hormonal Treatment of Sexual Offenders. *Med. Sci. Law* **10**: 27–34.

—— (1971) A Note on the Scientific Assessment and Treatment of the Sexual Offender. *Med. Sci. Law* **11**: 180–81.

Field, L.H. (1973) Beniperidol in the Treatment of Sexual Offenders. *Med. Sci. Law* **13**: 195–96.

Fitch, J.H. (1962) Men Convicted of Sexual Offences Against Children. *Brit. J. Criminol.* **3**: 18–37.

Gibbens, T.C.N., Way, C., and Soothill, K.L. (1977) Behavioural Types of Rape. *Brit. J. Psychiat.* **130**: 32–42.

—— (1978) Sibling and Parent-Child Incest Offenders. *Brit. J. Criminol.* **18**: 40–52.

Gittleson, N.L., Eacott, S.E., and Mehta, B.M. (1978) Victims of Indecent Exposure. *Brit. J. Psychiat.* **132**: 61–6.

Gordon, R. (1976) In W. Kraemer (ed.) *The Forbidden Love.* London: Sheldon Press.

Hall, J. (1977) Rape and Some of its Effects. *Midwife, Health Visitor and Community Nurse.* **13**: 96–100.

Hall Williams, J.E. (1974) The Neglect of Incest: A Criminologist's View. *Med. Sci. Law* **14**: 64–7.

—— (1977) Serious Heterosexual Attack. *Med. Sci. Law* **17**: 140–46.

Hardgrove, G. (1976) An Inter-agency Service Network to Meet the Needs of Rape Victims. *Social Casework* April: 245–53.

Hertoft, P. (1976) Sexual Minorities. In S. Crown (ed.) *Psychosexual Problems.* London: Academic Press.

Hill, D. (1978) The Qualities of a Good Psychiatrist. *Brit. J. Psychiat.* **133**: 97–105.

Home Office (1976) *Criminal Statistics. England and Wales. 1975.* Cmnd. 6566. London: HMSO.

Howells, K., and Wright E. (1978) The Sexual Attitudes of Aggressive Sexual Offenders. *Brit. J. Criminol.* **18**: 170–74.

Hyatt Williams, A. (1964) The Psychopathology and Treatment of Sexual Murderers. In I. Rosen (ed.) *The Pathology and Treatment of Sexual Deviation.* Oxford: Oxford University Press.

Ingram, Fr M. (1979) The Participating Victim. Parts I and II. *Brit. J. Sexual Medicine* Jan: 22–6 and Feb: 24–6.

Jacoby, B. (1978) Exhibitionists Exposed. *Justice of the Peace* **142**: 624–27.

James, T.E. (1964) Law and the Sexual Offender. In I. Rosen (ed.) *Pathology and Treatment of Sexual Deviation.* Oxford: Oxford University Press.

Jehu, D. (1979) *Sexual Dysfunction.* Chichester: John Wiley.

Jones, I.H. and Frei, D. (1977) Provoked Anxiety as a Treatment of Exhibitionism. *Brit. J. Psychiat.* **131**: 295–300.

Kennedy, L. (1961) *Ten Rillington Place.* London: Gollancz.

Lambert, K. (1976) In W. Kraemer (ed.) *The Forbidden Love.* London: Sheldon Press.

Lancaster, N.P. (1978) Necrophilia, Murder and High Intelligence. *Brit. J. Psychiat.* **132**: 605–08.

Law, S.K. (1979) Child Molestation: A Comparison of Hong Kong and Western Findings. *Med. Sci. Law* **19**: 55–60.

Lukianowicz, N. (1972) Incest, 1-Paternal Incest. 11–Other Types of Incest. *Brit. J. Psychiat.* **120**: 301–13.

Macdonald, J.M. (1971) *Rape: Offenders and Their Victims.* Illinois: Charles C. Thomas.

—— (1973) *Indecent Exposure.* Illinois: Charles C. Thomas.

Maclay, D.T. (1952) The diagnosis and treatment of compensatory types of indecent exposure. *Brit. J. Delinq.* **III**: 34–45.

McGuire, R.J. and Vallance, M. (1964) Aversion Therapy by Electric Shock. *Brit. M.J.* **1**: 151–53.

McGuire, R.J., Carlisle, J.M., and Young, B.G. (1965) Sexual Deviations as Conditioned Behaviour. *Behav. Res. Ther.* **2**: 185–90.

Maisch, H. (1973) *Incest* (trans. C. Bearne). London: Deutsch.

Mather, N.J. de V. (1966) The Treatment of Homosexuality by Aversion Therapy. *Med. Sci. Law* **6**: 200–05.

Mathis, J.C. and Cullens, M. (1971) Enforced Group Therapy in the Treatment of Exhibitionism. *Current Psych. Ther.* **11**: 139–45.

Milo, B. (1976) Cui Bono – For Whose Benefit? *Prison Ser. J.* October: 11–13.

Morris, N. and Hawkins, G. (1970) *The Honest Politician's Guide to Crime Control.* Chicago: Chicago University Press.

Nakashima, I.I. and Zakus, G.E. Incest, Review and Clinical Experience. *Pediatrics for the Clinician.* **60**: 696–701.

Parker, T. (1970) *The Twisting Lane. Some Sex Offenders.* London: Panther Books.

Paul, D.M. (1975) The Medical Examination in Sexual Offences. *Med. Sci. Law* **15**: 154–62.

—— (1977) The Medical Examination in Sexual Offences Against Children. *Med. Sci. Law* **17**: 251–58.

Power, D.J. (1976) Sexual Deviation and Crime. *Med. Sci. Law* **16**: 111–28.

Pollock, C.B.R. (1960) A Case of Neurotic Exhibitionism. *Brit. J. Criminol.* **1**: 37–49.

Prins. H.A. (1973) *Criminal Behaviour.* London: Pitman.

Roberts, D.F. (1967) Incest: Inbreeding and Mental Abilities. *Brit. M.J.* **4**: 336.

Roeder, F., Orthner, H., and Muller, D. (1972) In A. Hitchcock, L. Leitinen, and K. Vaernet (eds.) *Psychosurgery.* Illinois: Charles C. Thomas.

Rooth, F.G. (1972) Changes in the Conviction Rate for Indecent Exposure. *Brit. J. Psychiat.* **121**: 89–94.

Rooth, F.G. (1975) *Indecent Exposure and Exhibitionism.* In T. Silverstone and B. Barraclough *Contemporary Psychiatry.* Ashford: Headly Bros.

Rupp, J.C. (1970) Sudden Death in the Gay World. *Med. Sci. Law* **10**: 189–91.

Scacco, A.M. (1975) *Rape in Prison.* Illinois: Charles C. Thomas.

Schultz, L.G. (ed.) (1975) *Rape Victimology.* Illinois: Charles C. Thomas.

Scott, P.D. (1964) Definition, Classification, Prognosis and Treatment. In I. Rosen (ed.) *The Pathology and Treatment of Sexual Deviation.* Oxford: Oxford University Press.

Shaw, R. (1978a) The Persistent Sexual Offender – Control and Rehabilitation. *Probation J.* **25**: 9–13.

—— (1978b) The Persistent Sexual Offender – Control and Rehabilitation (a Follow Up.) *Probation J.* **25**: 61–3.

Soothill, K.L., Jack, A. and Gibbens, T.C.N. (1976) Rape: A 22 Year Cohort Study. *Med. Sci. Law* **16**: 62–9.

Soothill, K.L., and Gibbens, T.C.N. (1978) Recidivism of Sexual Offenders: A Reappraisal. *Brit. J. Criminol.* **18**: 267–76

Tennent, G., Bancroft, J., and Cass, J. (1974) The Control of Deviant Sexual Behaviour by Drugs: A Double-Blind Study of Benperidol, Chlorpromazine and Placebo. *Arch. Sex. Behav.* **3**: 261–71.

Toner, B. (1977) *The Facts of Rape*. London: Arrow Books.

Virkkunen, M. (1974) Incest Offences and Alcoholism. *Med. Sci. Law* **14**: 124–28.

—— (1975) Victim-Precipitated Pedophilia Offences. *Brit. J. Criminol.* **15**: 175–80.

West, D.J., Roy, C., and Nichols, F.L. (1978) *Understanding Sexual Attacks*. London: Heinemann.

Wolff, C. (1977) *Bisexuality. A Study*. London: Quartet Books.

FURTHER READING

Anthropological and related aspects of sexuality.

Ellis, H. (1939) *The Psychology of Sex*. London: Heinemann.

Ford, C. S. and Beach, F.A. (1965) *Patterns of Sexual Behaviour*. London: Methuen.

Malinowski, B. (1929) *The Sexual Life of Savages*. London: Kegan Paul.

Mead, M. (1949) *Male and Female*. London: Gollancz.

Varieties of sexual response

Kinsey, A.C., Pomeroy, W.B., and Martin, C.E. (1948) *Sexual Behaviour in the Human Male*. London: W.B. Saunders.

Kinsey, A.C., Pomeroy, W.B., Martin, C.E., and Gebhard, P.M. (1953) *Sexual Behaviour in the Human Female*. London: W.B. Saunders.

Masters, W.H. and Johnson, V. (1966) *Human Sexual Response*. New York: Little Brown.

—— (1970) *Human Sexual Inadequacy*. New York: Little Brown.
Schofield, M. (1965) *The Sexual Behaviour of Young People*. London: Longmans.
Storr, A. (1964) *Sexual Deviation*. Harmondsworth: Penguin.

Homosexuality

Rosen, D.H. (1974) *Lesbianism. A Study of Female Homosexuality*. Illinois: Charles C. Thomas.
West, D.J. (1960) *Homosexuality*. Harmondsworth: Penguin.

Sexual offending

Cox, M. (1979) Dynamic Psychotherapy with Sex-Offenders. In I. Rosen (ed.) *Sexual Deviation* (2nd edition). Oxford: Oxford University Press.
DHSS (1977) *Selected References on Paedophilia and Sexual Offences Against Children. Bibliography Series. B.91.* London: HMSO.
Gebhard, P.H., Gagnon, J.H., Pomeroy, W.B., and Christenson, C.V. (1965) *Sex Offenders. An Analysis of Types*. New York: Harper and Row.
Meiselman, K.C. (1978) *Incest*. San Francisco: Jossey-Bass.
Walker, M.J. and Brodsky, S.L. (eds.) (1976) *Sexual Assault: The Victim and the Rapist*. Lexington: D.C. Heath.

CHAPTER NINE

Alcohol, other drugs, and crime

Wine is a mocker,
Strong drink is raging:
And whosoever is deceived thereby is not
wise.

BOOK OF PROVERBS

Alcohol merely facilitates expression by nar-
cotising inhibitory processes.

PROFESSOR HARVEY CLECKLEY

'How use doth breed a habit in a man!'

TWO GENTLEMEN OF VERONA

In several of the chapters in this book I have made reference to
the possible relationships between alcohol, other drugs, and
criminal behaviour. We can now examine these in a little more
detail. But before doing so it will be helpful to offer some
general introductory comments on alcohol and other drugs.
This is a vast and complex area of study and has been the
subject of a massive literature in recent years. No attempt will
be made to summarize this literature and my introductory
comments are merely intended to provide a context. Those
who wish to pursue the subject in more depth or to revise it
should consult the recommended reading at the end of this
chapter. There is a danger of course in discussing alcohol and
other drugs as separate entities, but it seems logical to do so for
the following reasons. First, it is legitimate to describe alcohol
as just one of a number of drugs, hence the choice of title for

this chapter. Second, it makes easier presentation if the material is subdivided. Third, there are important differences in the sequence of events and processes involved in the abuse of, or addiction to, alcohol and those in relation to other drugs. A notable difference is that whereas in the case of drugs, dependence is accompanied by a need for increased dosage, in the case of alcohol, this is a transient feature, since the person heavily addicted to alcohol, in the latter stages of his addiction, tends to have diminished tolerance. Fourth, there are a number of differences in the personal characteristics, behaviours, and social backgrounds of those involved in the abuse of alcohol and of other drugs. Finally, and by no means of least significance, is the fact that apart from certain limited exceptions, it is not unlawful to imbibe or be in possession of alcohol. However, the controls on possession, consumption, and availability of many other drugs are very strict and infringement of these controls can incur heavy penalties. This is not to say that there will never be characteristics in common and areas of overlap. Indeed, some people abuse both alcohol and other drugs.

Alcohol

In order to place the problem of alcohol abuse, and alcohol addiction in context, one has to study it from the perspectives of many interrelated disciplines. In additon to psychiatry, psychology and pharmacology, social history, social policy, economics, and social ethics add much to our knowledge of the subject; and of course each discipline has its own particular standpoint. Two major conflicts stand out above all others. On the one hand, there are those who hold the largely religiously based view that alcohol abuse is a weakness and a sign of moral turpitude; on the other, there are those who wish to see it understood and treated as an illness. This dichotomy is probably responsible for the unquestionable fact that services for those who abuse alcohol or who suffer from alcoholism are woefully inadequate. As a society we are remarkably ambivalent about indulgence in alcohol; on the one hand we regard indulgence as bad, but on the other, we somewhat indiscriminately advertise its benefits as a boost to self-esteem or personal attractiveness. And of course, the sale of alcohol contributes much to government revenues through taxation (in the region of £900 million each year). It is therefore not surprising that attitudes towards its ingestion appear confused and conflicting. Views differ as to the best means of limiting alcohol consumption and preventing excessive drinking. Some consider that legislation controlling alcohol consumption provides the most useful means (de Lint, 1974), whilst others argue for programmes of education and the development of acceptable patterns of social drinking (Rix 1974; Rix and Buyers 1976; Wilkinson 1970). It is also worth remembering that:

> 'excessive use of chemicals is not unique to any particular society, though it is true that the type of chemicals used may vary from community to community, and within the same community from time to time. For example, alcohol, hypnotics and amphetamines are more widely misused in materially affluent communities like those in the West, than are opiates and cannabis, which find favour among the materially not so developed countries of South East Asia and the Middle East.'
>
> (Rathod undated essay)

I have already used the words addiction and abuse somewhat loosely. There are good grounds for suggesting that addiction is a rather overused and emotive word and that its use may perhaps obscure issues rather than clarify them. Increasingly the term 'dependence' is being used and this is a more accurate descriptive term. It is hard to be precise as to the quantity of any drug required, or the time that it takes, to produce a state of dependence. In the case of some narcotic drugs, constant usage over a few weeks might create dependence, whereas it might take months in the case of barbiturates and sometimes years in the case of alcohol. (The subject of dependence will be discussed in more detail when we examine drugs other than alcohol.)

Although it has been suggested that alcoholic beverages were consumed in larger quantities in the eighteenth and nineteenth centuries than in the twentieth, the annual consumption of alcohol in this country is still considerable and is rising (Spring and Buss 1977). Moreover, in the last decade, there has been an increase in drinking by those under the age of eighteen. In this context it should be remembered that excessive indulgence in alcohol can commonly cause death by cirrhosis of the liver, malnutrition, road accidents, and by suicide. Indeed, in respect of the latter, Kessel and Grossman (1961) described alcoholism itself as 'chronic suicide'. More recently, Sunter, Heath, and Ranasinghe (1978) examined over 3,000 cases brought to autopsy over a five-year period. They found that in 3.27 per cent of all cases alcohol contributed materially to death. The average age at death was ten years *lower* in the alcohol-associated group than in the autopsy population as a whole. In males of young middle age, a particularly high proportion of deaths was associated with alcohol abuse. Estimates of the number of alcoholics or those excessively dependent upon alcohol vary, but if we average out a number of estimations that have been made it is fair to suggest that there are upwards of 350,000 alcoholics* in Britain, about a quarter of whom show signs of mental and physical deterioration.** Numerous attempts have been made to describe and define the phases through which drinkers may pass, one of the most notable being that by Jellinek (1960). Suffice it to say at this point that we may delineate five groups of people in any community:

(1) those people who never drink at all;

---

* Definitions of 'alcoholism' and 'alcoholic' vary and this problem cannot be discussed at length here. I choose to use the World Health Organisation definition which defines alcoholics as 'those excessive drinkers whose dependence upon alcohol has attained such a degree that they show a noticeable mental disturbance or an interference with their mental and bodily health, their inter-personal relations and their smooth social and economic functioning; or who show the prodromal signs of such developments. They therefore require treatment' (World Health Organisation 1952).

** The problem of obtaining accurate figures is highlighted by the fact that many so-called alcoholics manage to hide their symptoms for long periods – see later discussion.

(2) social drinkers;
(3) excessive social drinkers – such folk drink in company and become intoxicated frequently;
(4) alcoholics;
(5) chronic alcoholics – this group differs from those in (4) in that *physical damage* has now resulted from their drinking.

It must be emphasized that not everyone accepts the phases I have outlined and naturally there will be areas of overlap. Within the five groupings mentioned above various stages of development can be identified. In the stage of *pre-alcoholic, excessive drinking*, the drinker tends to spend more and more time in social drinking, 'sneaking' an extra drink whenever possible. In this phase he tends to become very preoccupied with drinking and with his prowess as a drinker. Frequently, he drinks in response to tension, guilt may follow a spate of heavy indulgence, but his resolve is short-lived. Drink in fact becomes a necessity, with an accompanying rise in feelings of guilt. In *the addictive phase*, amnestic episodes become common and there is an increasing loss of control with regard to drinking which now becomes compulsive. Efficiency at work drops off and absenteeism is frequent. Drinking now occurs at all times of the day and the indulgence brings criticism from both family and employers. This in its train brings about a lowering of self-regard (and incidentally, increases the post-drinking guilt). The sufferer tries to compensate for this whilst amongst his drinking friends by gestures of bravado, and by ill-placed financial generosity.

In the *alcoholic phase*, the addictive element is stepped up and, increasingly, deception is practised in order to prevent disvovery. There is increasing social isolation, there may be violent outbursts, and family relationships deteriorate markedly. These adverse family relationships may be interpreted by the alcoholic in a somewhat paranoid manner and elements of self-pity often manifest themselves. Other signs of deterioration include reduction in libido, loss of appetite, neglect of eating, morning hand tremors, loss of employment, the hiding of supplies of alcohol, and suicidal impulses and attempts. In the *chronic-alcoholism* phase, physical and mental symptoms predominate. Eating becomes virtually non-existent and alcohol tolerance diminishes. Cheap wines and even crude spirits may now be the beverages of choice and there is a rapid deterioration in personal pride and habits. Physical illness and bouts of 'delirium tremens' are not uncommon. In the latter, there will be marked perspiring, a reddening of the face, severe tremors of the hands and upper part of the body, and slurring of speech. Visual hallucinations may be present and these are often accompanied by severe anxiety or even intense terror.

It must be emphasized that the above is much abbreviated and that there is frequently no clear-cut distinction between the development of the phases. I have made minimal comment about the epidemiological and aetiological aspects of alcohol abuse and dependency. These are dealt with at length in the more specialist literature and nothing would be gained by dealing with them in summary fashion here. As stated earlier, the object of the foregoing introductory remarks was merely to provide a context for what follows.

Alcohol and crime

We noted in Chapter 3 that a history of alcoholism or heavy drinking is common in criminals – particularly recidivists. To what extent this relationship is causal has never been established satisfactorily, though as we shall see, a number of studies have been carried out in an attempt to find an answer to this problem. Glatt (1965), in discussing the common factors in criminal and alcoholic behaviour suggested that 'in both forms of behaviour disorder, conduct deviates from the social norm; criminals as well as alcoholics violate the usually accepted social code of behaviour. Both conditions have a multi-factorial aetiology of such things as broken homes and parental disharmony.' In an earlier paper (Glatt 1958) he gave an important reminder of the extent to which alcoholism is present in the parents of a number of juvenile offenders. He emphasized the insecurity that such parents could generate for their children.

In a much later study, Guze (1976) also comments upon this aspect. He discovered a high prevalence of alcoholism amongst first-degree relatives of convicted criminals.

The evidence as to the extent of alcoholism or excessive drinking among populations of offenders is conflicting. (See also *Table 3(1)* in Chapter 3.) Glatt (1958) reviewed a number of studies where the incidence ranged from 10 to 20 per cent. The variations were caused by the differences in the populations from which the samples were drawn. West (1963) found in his sample of recidivist prisoners that 34 per cent were excessive drinkers. In a later study, Gibbens and Silberman (1970) found in a sample of 404 prisoners and *ex-prisoners* from three London prisons, that 40 per cent were excessive drinkers. (They excluded prisoners received on very short sentences for drunkenness – see discussion below.) Hensman (1969) and Edwards *et al.* (1971, 1972) also found, that when the men whose current offence was for drunkenness were excluded, about a fifth of those serving sentences of over three months (presumably for more serious offences), and about a third serving very short sentences, described themselves as drunk at the time of the current offence. Guze (1976) found in his American sample that 43 per cent of his male criminals and 47 per cent of the women satisfied the criteria for a diagnosis of alcoholism. He noted a higher rate of recidivism for alcoholic as distinct from non-alcoholic offenders. This would give some support to West's earlier findings. A similar figure for male recidivists is reported by Bartholomew in an Australian survey (Bartholomew 1968). Bartholomew also took the trouble to check the inmates' accounts by means of interviews with family members. Most other studies rely upon the offender's own account and thus may not be entirely reliable.

Smith-Moorhouse (1966) estimated that between 30 to 40 per cent of the inmates of a central training prison were alcoholic and that 47 per cent of inmates aged between seventeen and twenty in a detention centre had some drink problem. In America, Rubington (1969) gives an overall estimate of 24 to 40 per cent. He suggested that alcoholics were more likely to be involved in crimes against individuals than against property and not surprisingly that the crime was more likely to be impulsive than planned. Washbrook (1977) examined a sample of 5,000 prisoners in a large local prison and found that about half stated that they had consumed alcohol within a period of twenty-four hours prior to the commission of the crime. He suggested that less than 5 per cent in his sample were true alcoholics. In Canada, Haines (1978) reports that 60 to 80 per cent of crimes are alcohol related. It should be noted that this was a highly selected population in that his statistics were derived from a regional psychiatric centre within the Federal Prison system. In a survey of naval offenders, Measey (1973) found 36.7 per cent of all offences were linked with alcohol consumption prior to the offence.

In a recent small-scale study Coope (1979) examined a sample of eighty-two men, received into Norwich Prison, by means of a questionnaire. 68 per cent of them saw themselves as social drinkers, 24 per cent saw themselves as having a problem with drink, and 8 per cent admitted to being 'alcoholic'. Coope – a seconded probation officer working in the prison – carried out his survey in order to ascertain to what extent probation officers had enquired about drink problems when making their Social Enquiry Reports. He says: 'It is disturbing to note that in the sample there was very little attention paid to a man's drinking habits by the probation officer preparing the social enquiry report. Even in cases where large amounts of alcohol had been consumed prior to the commission of the offence no mention was made in the report.'

The degree to which alcohol ingestion is associated with violent crimes seems to have been clearly demonstrated. (See for example the discussion of rape offences in Chapter 8.) Nicol *et al.* (1973) indicated that use of alcohol, particularly in response to stress, facilitates violent behaviour in men with *already severe difficulties in interpersonal relationships* [my italics].

All the studies quoted above have concerned themselves with the extent of excessive drinking or alcoholism amongst prison inmates. Very few studies have been made of the incidence of criminality amongst alcoholic patients. Bartholomew and Kelley (1965) examined a consecutive series of 1,000 alcoholics referred to a psychiatric clinic. They attempted to assess the incidence of criminality. They found that 35 per cent of the male referrals and 10 per cent of the females had a criminal record. This study is much in accord with an earlier one made by Glatt (1958) who found that about one third of 120 male in-patients treated in an alcoholic unit had been before the courts for various offences. Much more recently, Edwards, Kyle, and Nicholls (1977) examined the records of 935 hospitalized alcoholic patients. 32 per cent of the men and 17 per cent of the women had a criminal record.

In summary, we have clear indications of close *associations* between excessive drinking, alcoholism, and criminality; direct causal connections are less obvious. Edwards, Hensman, and Peto (1971), in summing up their examination of 500 recidivist prisoners, concluded with a point of general application, namely that heavy drinking 'sometimes leads rather directly to crime (but) is more usually one among several factors of causal importance, (and) is sometimes coincidental.'

Having examined some of these aspects more generally, it follows that we should attempt to make some more specific classification of the manner in which alcoholism or excessive drinking may be associated with crime, paying particular attention to the problem of the habitual drunken offender.

CLASSIFICATION

We can attempt to classify the relationship between alcohol and offending in the following fashion.

(1) Serious offences against the person or property due directly to the disinhibiting effects of alcohol ingestion. (For example, murder, other serious assaults, criminal damage (arson).)

(2) Other less serious forms of assault against persons or against property.

(3) Offences against the Road Safety and Road Traffic Acts, notably driving whilst unfit through drink or drugs. There

were over 50,000 such cases in 1975. It seems very likely that a number of these offenders will have a serious drinking problem. It may well be that it will first come to light as a result of the offence. Camps (1970) suggests that we miss opportunities to apply some form of supervision to these offenders during the time that their licences have been suspended. He says: 'If such treatment was properly carried out and supervised, then not only would they be less likely to repeat the offence when the licence was renewed, but some restriction on renewal subject to medical certificate, might be considered.' (See also Havard 1975.) This seems a sound suggestion in theory, but it has always been a sad fact that as a community we are reluctant to regard driving offences in a criminal light; it is comparatively rare for example, for such offenders to be remanded for social enquiry or medical reports. In spite of the implementation of the Road Safety Act, 1967 and the Road Traffic Act, 1972 we still seem to regard even serious motoring offences as civil matters rather than as forms of criminal behaviour. Very few studies have been made of the criminal and social backgrounds of serious motoring offenders, but that made by Willett (1964) is a notable exception. He examined 653 cases and found that 104 of these (15 per cent) had been charged with driving under the influence of drink or drugs. He also found that alcohol was a contributing factor in about 8 per cent of all the other serious motoring offences. He also thought this might be an underestimate.

(4) Offences committed in order to obtain supplies of alcohol, for example, acts of stealing or deception.

(5) Those who commit specific offences of drunkenness. (Habitual drunken offenders.)

Glatt (1965) makes a twofold distinction between 'alcoholic criminals' (those who are criminals and who also drink to excess) and 'criminal alcoholics' (those alcoholics who are driven after many years of drinking to behave in a criminal manner as a result of their alcoholism). In practice, it is sometimes very difficult to make such a clear-cut distinction.

We can now move on to consider the specific problems of the habitual drunken offender (Category 5 above).

The habitual drunken offender

Drunkenness itself is not an offence in law. It becomes unlawful when exhibited in 'any highway or other public place, whether a building or not, or any licensed premises' (Licensing Act, 1872, Section 12 as amended by the Penalties for Drunkenness Act, 1962). If found to be drunk and incapable of taking care of himself, the offender may be apprehended and dealt with (Section 1, Licensing Act, 1902). In addition to simple drunkenness in a public place, the law penalizes a variety of offences which exacerbate the act itself; for example, being drunk and disorderly, drunk and indecent, or drunk in charge of a child under the age of seven years (Licensing Acts, 1872 and 1902, and Penalties for Drunkenness Act, 1962). As can be seen from *Table 9(1)* overleaf, the number of convictions for drunkenness, albeit with some fluctuation, has risen steadily in recent years.

However, the figures given in *Table 9(1)* only give a very rough guide to the size of the problem. This is because the statistics merely account for the number of convictions and do not represent the number of *individuals* dealt with during the year. There is evidence that a few individuals, particularly in the older age range, make frequent *reappearances* before the courts in any one year. Parr (1962) examined the records relating to 935 drunkenness offenders who had appeared in five courts in or near London. He found that roughly 20 per cent of the offences were committed by 'habitual offenders'. Gath *et al.* (1968) studied drunkenness offenders appearing in two London courts and found that in the preceding twelve months 51 per cent of the 151 men interviewed had been arrested for drunkenness on at least one other occasion and 30 per cent had been arrested three times or more. In a more recent study, Hershon, Cook, and Foldes (1974) interviewed a group of 132 drunkenness offenders prior to their appearances in court. They found that fifty-two of their sample had between one and ten previous convictions for drunkenness offences and sixty-four had eleven or more.

It is clear that these offenders present the courts with a problem of magnitude. Fining and imprisonment seem quite ineffective; the latter merely serves to provide a very short drying-out period in prisons that are already grossly over-crowded and quite unsuited to this task. (It is interesting to note that alternative measures such as detoxification centres have now been in use for some years in South Africa, Eastern Europe, Scandinavia, and North America.)

It is not perhaps generally known that we still have on our statute books nineteenth-century legislation designed to keep the habitual drunkenness offender out of the penal system.

Table 9(1)   *Men and women found guilty of drunkenness offences England and Wales*

1938	54,518
1946	20,545
1962	83,992
1971	81,000
1975	99,639

Sources: Prins (1973) and Home Office (1976).

Note to Table 9(1)

Between the years 1967 and 1973 there was a steady annual increase of about 5 per cent in the number of drunkenness offences, though there was a slight drop in 1974. It is difficult to interpret the reasons for these fluctuations. They may represent changes in police prosecution practice, public drinking behaviour, or both. The number of younger people of both sexes coming before the courts for offences of drunkenness is increasing considerably. In 1973, as compared with 1964, the rate per 10,000 of the population for males aged between fifteen and seventeen increased about three times, while for males aged between eighteen and twenty there was a twofold increase. For females aged fifteen to seventeen the rates were five times greater in 1973 than in 1964 and for those aged eighteen to twenty there was a threefold increase. (Sources: Zacune and Hensman (1971) and Home Office (1976).)

The Habitual Drunkard's Act, 1879 authorized justices to licence 'retreats' to which habitual drunkards might be admitted on their own application. The Inebriates Act, 1898 made provision for habitual drunken offenders to be sentenced to detention in a State or certified Inebriate Reformatory for up to three years. For reasons that are not altogether clear the retreats were never established and the courts continued to deal with habitual drunken offenders through the usual (and unsuitable) channels.* Concern continued to be expressed about these unsuitable forms of disposal. The Criminal Justice Act, 1967 contained provision for the removal of the penalty of imprisonment for being drunk and disorderly provided the Home Secretary was satisfied that there was suitable alternative accommodation available for the care and treatment of persons convicted of such offences. Section 34 of the Criminal Justice Act, 1972 now empowers a police constable to take such persons to medical treatment centres, in lieu of arresting and charging them, as and when they become available. The Home Office Working Party (Home Office 1971) carried out an extensive review of the facilities needed for these offenders and recommended provision of special detoxification centres and hostels. The Working Party estimated that in order to deal with those offenders who would previously have been sentenced for being drunk and disorderly, facilities such as hostels and other community provisions providing for about 2,000 men and 200 women would need to be made available. As the new form of care got under way, they considered that the maximum number of potential users might be nearer 5,000. To date, our record of provision has been very poor. Three or four Detoxification Centres have been established. The centre at Edinburgh has, alas, been prematurely closed, Reports on the work of this centre were promising and the team there had begun to come to grips with the problems. They were very

* Fifteen reformatories were established under the Act, but by 1921 all had been closed. The Report of the *Working Party on Habitual Drunken Offenders* (1971) suggests that there were four main reasons for this: (1) they were underused; (2) courts were reluctant to use compulsion; (3) the financial sections of the Act were permissive and not mandatory; (4) some courts considered it would be difficult to define a 'habitual drunkard'.

conscious of the limited objectives that should be set for this group of offender/patients. As they put it: 'Alcoholics and drunken offenders are not popular patients with many in the medical profession and some doctors and nurses have strong moral views on alcoholism and drunkenness' (Hamilton *et al.* 1977). They go on to make the important point that detoxification alone will not suffice; there must be adequate social work and allied follow-up. In addition, the relapsing nature of the condition has to be recognized by all those who work in this field. The need for such centres is also attested to in another paper from Scotland by Rix, Buyers, and Finchman (1976). South of the border a similar situation obtains. Plans for an experimental detoxification centre in South London based upon St Thomas's Hospital have now been abandoned. This is due, according to the DHSS, to its prohibitive estimated cost (£1.3 millions) (*The Guardian* 25 January 1979.) The centre in Leeds, run by a voluntary organization with DHSS subvention, is also threatened with closure because the DHSS are withdrawing their funding when the three-year experimental period ends in May 1979. According to the director, the centre 'has been evaluated by two research teams on behalf of the DHSS – both have presented independent interim reports which indicate that the centre is an effective positive way of helping alcoholics, particularly homeless alcoholics' (*The Guardian* 28 February 1979). The DHSS have indicated that the funding for the centre must now be taken over locally and there is considerable ambivalence about this. These difficulties seem to be reminiscent of those that led to the non-implementation of the use of Retreats for Inebriates in the earlier part of this century. They are also a very poignant reminder of the ambivalence towards alcoholics and excessive drinkers I referred to at the beginning of this chapter.

General treatment considerations

For the person found drunk habitually in public places treatment can best be afforded by detoxification, but only if it is followed by intensive after-care and community follow-up.

However, it must be acknowledged that such persons will frequently defy the best therapeutic endeavours of those who seek to help them. The relapsing nature of the condition needs to be stressed yet again as does the ambivalence most people feel toward these unlikeable offender/patients. Hamilton *et al.* (1977) put it well when they say:

'Undoubtedly more hostel accommodation for such patients is necessary. Detoxification alone will be of extremely limited effectiveness . . . but detoxification units should have an essential role in the provision of a comprehensive medico-social spectrum of resources. In this project, early signs of benefit to the individual were observed, but long-term effectiveness can only be assessed when better rehabilitative facilities are available . . .'

The offender who is alcoholic or drinks to excess, or who commits crime because he drinks, presents rather different problems. My earlier comments about the high relapse rate apply here with equal force. The various modes of treatment all have their enthusiastic proponents, be they behavioural, pharmacological, or psychoanalytic. All are probably agreed that treatment can only be effective if there is a real desire on the part of the offender to change his life-style. Those who are both alcoholic and criminal and who are sentenced to longish periods of imprisonment gain at least one advantage, namely a defined period of enforced abstinence from alcohol. Their psychological and physical systems are thus given an opportunity to recover from its effects. However, unless there is a concurrent attempt through group or individual counselling to help the individual to examine why he needs to offend and drink, enforced abstinence will only serve to prepare the individual for early relapse upon discharge. Counselling within the institution must go hand in hand with effective intervention with the family and in the social situation in the community. Many prisons now offer opportunity for inmates to participate in AA (Alcoholics Anonymous) and similar groups. The sharing of common problems has much to commend it, but again there must be a real desire to give up the habit.

Bebbington (1976) has shown some of the difficulties inherent in trying to assess the effectiveness of organizations such as AA. He suggests that its idiosyncratic structure and organization, and its anonymity, make scientific evaluation almost impossible. It is also notoriously difficult to assess the effectiveness of 'after-care'. Davidson (1976) carried out a follow-up study of a hundred alcoholic patients discharged from Warlingham Park Alcoholic Unit during the period 1968–1970. She endeavoured to take account of the role of out-patient groups, AA, Re-union meetings and other informal contacts. She found that just over 50 per cent of the sample available for study (eighty-two) seemed to have benefited. Half-way houses (hostels) for alcoholics have been evaluated by Baker *et al.* (1976). Their findings suggest that 'Little empirical evidence is available . . . to substantiate claims of efficacy for halfway houses.' However, as we shall see when we come to examine the facilities for opiate and other addicts, there are indications that some hostels do seem to be effective provided care is supported with firm but benign sanctions. Evidence from various sources suggests that when alcoholic offenders are imprisoned for periods of eighteen months or more and are released with active statutory supervision they do better than when released without such control. Zacune and Hensman (1971) have summarized many of the findings on the effectiveness of treatment in this area. They state that overall, 'The studies have emphasized that prognosis is determined to a great extent by the previous personality and social stability of the alcoholic and that this may be more relevant to prognosis than the particular treatment given'. (See also Edwards and Grant 1977, Section III.) In relation to alcoholic offenders, this statement seems to be very important. This is because the offender who *also* has a drink problem has two hurdles to surmount, his alcohol problem and the fact that he has been labelled and processed as an offender. Thus the opprobrium that he draws upon his head is doubly compounded and his life-style, and social and interpersonal relationships are that much more difficult to clarify and resolve.

Other drugs

We must now turn to a consideration of other drugs and their relationship to criminality. In introducing the subject of alcohol I made reference to dependence, and it must be emphasized here that occasional use of drugs does not necessarily lead to dependence – a fact that is sometimes forgotten by those who tend to become emotive concerning the use of drugs of one kind or another. In 1952, the World Health Organisation defined drug dependence as a 'state arising from repeated administration of a drug on a periodic or continuing basis' (WHO 1952).* The characteristics of dependence (as they relate to drugs other than alcohol) were further defined by the World Health Organisation (1964) as follows:

(1) Whether or not there is a strong desire or need for the drug.
(2) Whether or not the user acquires 'tolerance' to the drug and therefore needs to increase the dose. (My earlier comments about the differences between alcohol and other drugs should be noted here.)
(3) Whether or not there is a psychic dependence on the drug, so that its presence is required for the maintenance of homeostasis, and an abstinence syndrome develops.

(McCulloch and Prins 1978)

In this book we are most likely to be concerned with two aspects of the problem. First, with what can best be regarded as a compulsive need to continue to take the drug and to obtain supplies by any means – particularly unlawful means. Second, the serious physical and social repercussions for the individual and for society (see Power 1974). The compulsive element is common of course to both alcohol and other drug taking.

---

* Two aspects of dependence require elaboration. First, *psychological* dependence – a condition in which a drug produces 'a feeling of satisfaction and a psychic drive that require periodic or continuous administration of the drug to produce pleasure or to avoid discomfort.' Second, *physical* dependence – 'an adaptive state that manifests itself by intense physical disturbance when the administration of the drug is suspended' (WHO 1974).

Some workers in the socio-forensic field have linked recidivism, alcoholism, and drug taking by means of this compulsive element; in the light of what was said earlier about the strong relationship between recidivism and alcoholism, such a linking theory has indeed much to commend it (Dawtry 1968).

Drug taking in its various forms has been a feature of all cultures from time immemorial, but only in the last fifty years or so, and especially when it reached proportions of escalation in the 1960s, have we been particularly preoccupied with it as a developing problem in this country.

> 'The complexity [of this problem] is related to the great scientific advances in the field of pharmacology in the last fifty years. Today we have at our disposal drugs that literally cover the whole spectrum of human behaviour. Besides the 'Pill' we have pills to sedate us when we are nervous, excite us when we are dull, slim us when we are fat, fatten us when we are thin, waken us when we are sleepy, put us to sleep when we are awake, cure us when we are sick and make us sick when we are well! Drugs can enhance our ability to function, and they can carry our minds out of the realm of reality into loneliness.'
>
> (Glatt *et al.* 1967)

As this quotation shows, drugs of various sorts have now become part of our everyday lives and over-prescribing for example has been a topic of great public concern and limited professional condemnation. Indeed, as a community, we seem as ambivalent about other drugs as we are about alcohol – and tobacco for that matter. Concern with hard-drug addiction dates from the late 1950s when the numbers of those addicted to hard drugs appeared to rise sharply. It is not necessary to detail here the various social policy and other implications of these developments as they have recently been well summarized by Edwards (1979). There has been a levelling off in hard-drug abuse and addiction amongst younger people in recent years and alcohol seems to have taken over to some extent. Wright (1976) conducted a survey of young people during the years, 1969, 1974, and 1978; he found a general decreasing interest in drugs, but an increasing *minority* in contact with drugs. Parties and public houses had become more important as sources of supply than the coffee bars of the sixties. Sedative drugs were more available than LSD and amphetamines.

Despite these indications of a general diminution in interest and use, there seems to have been an increase in the intravenous use of certain drugs and in the potentially lethal ingestion of mixtures. In addition, abuse of other compounds such as glues, solvents, lighter fuels, and nail polishes have been noted (see Voegele and Dietze 1963; Watson 1978). Before proceeding to examine the relationship between drug use and crime in any detail, it will be helpful to remind ourselves of the main categories of drugs which are misused.*

(1) *Amphetamines.* It has been calculated that some 20 per cent of people who use these euphoriant drugs will become habituated. Happily their medical useage is now declining.

(2) *Barbiturates.* The effects of these sedative drugs range from mild sedation to complete coma. The early effects of a large dose can be mistaken for drunkenness – for example in slurring of speech, dilation of the pupils, and poor judgement. Barbiturates cause dependence because there is a craving to continue with them, and a need to increase the dosage which results in both psychic and physical dependence. In respect of the latter there may be withdrawal problems when the drug is withheld. The main source of supply tends to be within the National Health Service. It has been estimated that about 1,200 people in every 100,000 who use these sedative drugs abuse them. The medical profession has been alerted in recent months to the need to be more circumspect in prescribing these drugs.

(3) *LSD (Lysergic acid diethylamide).* This is a potentially lethal hallucinogenic drug. It can be produced comparatively easily by those who have a mind to do so and the necessary

* By misuse, I mean drugs that have been acquired illegally, or those which have been acquired legally, but where the dosage is beyond that of normal requirements.

crude facilities available. There are variations in its effects and this is one of its chief dangers. (Its alleged use in the Lipman manslaughter case was referred to in Chapter 2.) Usually a 'trip' produces bizarre mental reactions and a distortion of the physical senses. One of its less known and more ominous effects is that hallucinations may occur some weeks after the drug has been ingested; this may cause the user to feel he is going insane. It is not physically addicting, though repeated use tends to diminish its effects.

(4) *Opiates*. Heroin is the main drug in this group, and like its companion, morphine, is characterized by very speedy onset of psychological and physical dependence. Estimates as to its illegal use in the United Kingdom vary, but it has been calculated that there may be more than 4,000 illegal users at any point in time. Its potential for harm is extremely high, those who become 'hooked' have a very short life expectation, and the suicide rate for these addicts is very high. Recent investigations into the incidence of deaths amongst opiate users both in Denmark and in this country confirm that the incidence for these users is considerably higher than for deaths in the general population (Voigt, Dalgaard, and Simonsen 1975; Stevens 1978). (See later discussion.)

(5) *Cannabis*. This is another hallucinogenic drug. Generally, the use of cannabis tends to reduce inhibition and it may also slightly impair memory, judgement, and perception. Mood changes are common and the cannabis taker may move from incongruous hilariousness or loquaciousness on the one hand to depression, apprehension, or panic on the other. Sometimes, the constant use of cannabis produces lethargy and self-neglect. A frequently forgotten point is that the user is often deluded by false feelings of increased capabilities and, equally frequently, may become depressed by the consequent disappointments caused by the gap between what he thinks he can do and what he actually achieves (McCulloch and Prins 1978). Cannabis

produces psychological but not physical dependence. Reactions to the prohibitions on, and penalties for, possession of this drug tend to be highly emotive, mainly because the evidence as to its harmful properties seems somewhat inconclusive. However, its active constituents are not often referred to or debated in these discussions so that it is worth emphasizing here that there are a number of pharmacological and allied factors that will determine its degree of harmfulness or otherwise. First, the nature of the smoking process used and the temperature of combustion will influence its effects. Second, the quality of its essential ingredient – tetra-hydrocannabinol (which acts on the brain and the CNS) – varies in the types of plants that are used to produce the substance. For example, it has been demonstrated that the action of the tetra-hydrocannabinol seems to be more potent in cannabis grown and consumed in the United States than here (see Phillips 1973 and Coutsclinis 1974).

TYPES OF DRUG USERS, ABUSERS, AND ADDICTS

At the risk of oversimplification, we may say that the largest group of users and abusers are young, and that males tend to predominate. In the main, drug abusers tend to be solitary people, to be somewhat immature and uncertain in their social relationships. They are often sadly lacking in confidence and turn to drugs to boost their low self-regard. Occasionally, drugs are resorted to in times of personal crisis. Three other more specific groups can be discerned. First, the 'therapeutic' addicts who have become addicted in the course of medical treatment. Second, 'professional' addicts, for example those members of the medical, nursing, and allied professions who have easy access to drugs. Third, a group of people who have marked problems with their interpersonal and social relationships; these are the personality-disordered group whose drug abusing or addictive behaviour may be associated with criminality. It is to this group that we must now turn.

DRUG TAKING AND CRIMINALITY – CLASSIFICATION

It seems likely that the relationship between criminality and drug abuse or addiction has some features in common with that existing between alcoholism, excessive drinking, and crime. We may make a somewhat arbitrary classification of this relationship in the following way. In this connection readers should refer back to the earlier classification concerning alcohol and crime.

(1) Offences against the various Acts established to control the possession, distribution, and consumption of drugs. These are mainly the Pharmacy Act of 1933, the Medicines Act, 1968 (which controls therapeutic substances) and the Misuse of Drugs Act, 1971.* Offences under this Act include unlawful possession, possession with intent to supply ('pushing'), procuration, and use of premises for drug misuse. In 1975, 10,181 males and 1,676 females were proceeded against for specific drug offences. Of these, 7,827 males and 1,240 females were found guilty. In addition, 1,116 offences of forging prescriptions were recorded as known to the police and some 329 persons were found guilty. The cautioning rate for these specific drug offences is very low. Ten males and seventeen females were cautioned in 1975 for forging and uttering prescriptions. (It is interesting to note the higher rate of cautioning for females – this matter will be discussed in Chapter 10.)

(2) Offences committed in order to obtain drugs. These will consist largely of breaking and entering and stealing from premises where drugs are to be found (for example, chemists' shops, other pharmacies, doctors' premises, drug warehouses). The real rate of drug offending is therefore hard to determine, because the *purposes* for which breaking and entering and stealing is carried out is not recorded in the criminal statistics.

* This Act consolidated, drew together, and made certain amendments to previous legislation. Three classes of drugs were introduced: *Class A* – heroin, morphine, cocaine, and LSD; *Class B* – amphetamines and cannabis; *Class C* – non-barbiturate sedative drugs (for example, Mandrax). (Barbiturates are controlled by the Medicines Act, 1968.)

(3) Offences due to the ingestion of drugs. These will include motoring offences, public order crimes, assault, and cases of serious violence or damage to property. (See also Chapter 2 and 3.)

ADDICTION AND CRIME

One needs to recognize a certain danger in drawing too fine a distinction between *addiction* and crime and drug *abuse* and crime in the following discussion since the literature does not always indicate that the researchers have always made these distinctions clear. In addition, writers are sometimes referring to opiates and sometimes to other drugs. Also, the evidence as to association appears to be conflicting, but some attempt will now be made to summarize what is known. Hawks (1970) suggested that about half the known addicts in Great Britain committed offences *before* receiving opiates on prescription.

James (1969) studies fifty heroin addicts in London prisons. He found that 44 per cent had appeared before a juvenile court and 76 per cent had been convicted by a court *before* addiction. Half of the group had been charged with drug offences and just under half with non-drug offences. Four offenders had been charged with both. When he compared this group with a group of unselected first sentence short-term prisoners, he found no greater incidence in the addicted group of childhood deprivation, nervous illness, or history of addiction in the family background. However, compared with 50 per cent of the control group, only 20 per cent had been married, and about half of the wives of the addicts were also addicted. He goes on to make the important point that, 'psychiatric studies have failed to confirm the notion that narcotic drugs turn normal individuals into degenerate dope fiends liable to commit crimes of violence indiscriminately'. In 1973, Gordon published a study of sixty male multiple drug users who had started their drug taking before the age of twenty-one. 92 per cent had court convictions and 48 per cent had been convicted before drug use. Following drug use, particularly heroin, the incidence of violence in his sample increased. He came to the conclusion that criminality and drug dependence emerged as a combined expression of deviancy in the population studied (Gordon 1973). Comparable findings are reported by Cushman (1974) in an American study of 269 narcotics addicts. In 1974, Mott and Taylor published a detailed study of 273 male and 66 female opiate users and the extent to which their opiate was associated with delinquency. They found 'that a considerably greater proportion of both sexes had, by the age of 21 and before definition as addicts, been convicted at least once compared with the proportion expected to have been convicted in the general population'. Theft offences declined after formal notification as addicts to the Home Office and in the two years following notification. There was, however, an increase in specifically drug-related offences (for example for unlawful possession and procuration of opiates). Mott and Taylor rightly question why these specifically drug-related offences should have occurred *after* notification and when supplies would have been legitimately available. They suggest that it may have been because opiate users tend to get into the habit of buying, selling, borrowing, or lending small quantities of drugs to each other, so that they were therefore at greater risk of being apprehended for specific offences concerning drugs. In addition, they suggest that some of these opiate users considered that the legitimate supplies made available were insufficient for their needs. These findings held good for males over a five-year follow-up period (Mott 1978). Mott and Rathod (1976) studied eighty misusers of heroin. More of the heroin users had been convicted of criminal offences *before* they began to misuse drugs than would be expected by chance. The reduction or cessation of use of heroin during a four-year follow-up period was accompanied by a reduction in convictions.

Grimes (1977) reported that 23 per cent of addicts attending clinics during the years 1968 to 1973 were on probation. For males, in the year 1973, this figure had climbed to 29 per cent. Gordon (1978) made a four-year follow-up study of the offender/patients he had reported on in 1973. 43 per cent had become abstinent, 23 per cent had remained dependent, and 15 per cent had died. 97 per cent had been convicted and 73 per cent were convicted during follow-up. Poor outcome related to, amongst other things, earlier first conviction, regular opiate use on arrival at the clinic, irregular clinic attendance beyond one year, and drug conviction. Good outcome was related to an absence of parental loss and later first conviction. During follow-up it was associated with discharge within one year without hospital admission. More recently, Wiepert, D'Orbán, and Bewley (1979) have reported upon 455 male and 120 female opiate addicts treated at drug dependency clinics. They analysed the delinquency patterns of 117 female and 119 male addicts in relation to stages of their addiction, career, and outcome. Treatment had no effect on the overall crime rate, but, as in the study reported upon by Mott and Taylor, there was a significant increase in the proportion of drug offences during the treatment stage. The outcome of treatment was worse for the female addicts.

A number of workers have commented upon the hostility shown by hard-drug addicts. In an Australian study, Rosenberg (1971) concluded that: 'the heightened degree of personality disturbance shown by [the] addicts appeared to be related to the more intense hostility towards their fathers, with whom they could not identify in a positive way ...' In a later Australian study, Bell and Champion (1979) compared two groups – a general cross-section of young people and a cross-section of antisocial deviants. They established that illicit drug use was more extensive amongst those who had suffered parental deprivation and whose parents were separated and/or divorced. The degree of antisocial deviancy correlated highly with the extent of illicit drug use. They also produced another interesting finding, namely that there was also a high correlation of *licit* drug use (for example analgesics and similar compounds) with antisocial conduct. In another recent study, Gossop and Roy (1977) found that convicted addicts tended to score more highly on scales measuring hostility than non-convicted subjects. These differences were observed more clearly on the violent crime variable. They suggest that hostility acts as a personality factor which predisposes the individual towards criminal behaviour and that the more hostile subjects may also be more likely to be apprehended and convicted.

The main conclusion to be drawn from these studies is that the web of interaction between opiate addiction and criminality is part of the addict's complex life style. The compulsive element referred to earlier in this chapter propels the addict towards obtaining drugs by any means at his disposal. In addition, his gravitation towards social and personal deterioration makes him especially vulnerable to the attentions of the medical, judicial, and penal authorities.

THE ABUSE OF 'SOFT' DRUGS AND DELINQUENT BEHAVIOUR

In the late 1960s and early 1970s, interest was being shown in the relationship between amphetamine taking and youthful delinquency. Scott and Willcox (1965) in a study of a sample of 612 young people in two London Remand Homes, found an overall incidence of amphetamine taking of 16 to 18 per cent of the sample. (18 per cent of the 558 boys and 16 per cent of the 54 girls.) They compared the amphetamine takers with a group in which there was no evidence of drug taking. They found no major differences in type of crime committed or in social and family background. They concluded that the taking of amphetamines appeared to be incidental to delinquency, 'probably having similar roots in opportunity and predisposition'. (A finding not dissimilar to that described earlier in respect of opiate addiction.) In a follow-up study of boys and girls in the same remand home five years later, Scott and Buckle (1971) found that overall, there was a reduction in drug taking, but that there was a smaller group of malignant 'drug' takers. This trend of a modest decrease in desire for drug taking is supported by the evidence referred to earlier by Wright (1976). There has been a good deal of speculation and dispute concerning the progression from 'soft' to 'hard' drugs amongst young, delinquent drug abusers. In neither of the studies by Scott and his colleagues did there appear to be any evidence of this. In an attempt to find the differences, if any, between 'soft' and 'hard' drug users, Noble examined a group of boys detained in London's remand home in the years 1965 to 1967. Of forty-seven boys in the 'soft' drugs group he found that forty-three had been charged with a drugs offence. The twenty in the 'hard' drugs group had all taken hard drugs intravenously, but only nine had been charged with a drugs offence. By 1969, 19 per cent of the 'soft' drugs group had progressed to 'hard' drugs. (See also Ball (1967).) It is important to note his finding that those in the 'hard' drug group showed a significantly greater incidence of abnormal personality, family history of psychiatric illness, and disturbed relationships within the family. Noble suggested that:

> 'boys convicted of soft-drug offences should be looked on as at risk for the future progression to hard drugs . . . the majority of adolescent drug takers probably take drugs on only a few occasions and are unlikely to appear before the courts [however] a conviction for drug offence usually provided the first opportunity for medical and social assessment of the treatment needed . . .'

General treatment considerations and concluding comments

As with the alcoholic or excessive drinker, treatment for the drug abuser or addict must have regard to the individual's total life-style and not just his drug taking. As already suggested, those who more than transiently abuse drugs or become addicts have a high degree of personal vulnerability and low self-regard and frequently have unsatisfactory family and social environments. A group of probation officers came near to the truth of the matter when they suggested that:

> 'the person we have called an addict is as he is basically because he is afraid of making relationships. It seems to us that the part of his treatment, which consists in the formation and maintenance of a relationship, is likely in the long run to be the most important part . . . for the addict, his re-integration into society must always depend to a great extent on someone treating him as a *whole person,* not just as an addict [my italics].' (Dawtry 1968)

The problems of those who are actually addicted are of course much greater than those of transient or occasional drug abusers. The addict needs to be offered medical treatment which has now become increasingly available since the setting up of specialist addiction centres and clinics in the late 1960s (see Edwards 1979). However, the prognosis for the confirmed opiate addict is not good and as we have already noted the mortality rate is high. This is not necessarily due to the effects of the drugs themselves, but is more likely to be brought about by physical deterioration and damage from infection as a result of repeatedly injecting with dirty equipment and of course from suicide.

There are three major problems in the field of treatment. First, a large number of drug addicts (like alcoholics) claim that they are not ill and therefore do not need treatment. Second, many of those who start treatment discharge themselves before the treatment has really got under way. Third, the success rate of current treatment methods – be they pharmacological, behavioural, or psychoanalytically orientated – is very low. The fostering of a relationship which combines firmness with genuine concern is an essential prerequisite. This must be combined with a realization that relapses are likely to be frequent and that the addict's attitudes will be provocative, prevaricative, deceitful, and rejecting. Despite this, it is essential to try to 'hang on' to those who present as the most unlikeable and uncooperative of offender/patients. As with the alcoholic, the fact that the drug addict has also been labelled as a delinquent or criminal adds to the difficulty. Somehow, one has to reach down and tap those attributes and feelings that can be harnessed for change. A number of studies have confirmed the need for insistence and persistence. Wilson and Mandelbrote (1978a, 1978b) studied a sample of sixty-one admissions to a therapeutic community for drug dependents. They found an association between increased length of stay in the community and a lack of subsequent reconviction. This confirms a much earlier study by Vaillant and Rasor (1966) in which those who remained in the centre for the maximum period did better when discharged. These studies also indicated that when a stay of reasonable length (most workers would suggest that eighteen months is about the optimum period) is combined with firm after-care and supervision, this is more likely to be successful than an unsupervised return to the community. Melotte (1975) found that those residents in a hostel for drug users who were there on a condition of probation were less likely to abscond. However, in a later study, the same author and a colleague found that although about a third of admissions to a therapeutic centre remained abstinent, those with criminal convictions did worse (Ogborne and Melotte 1977). This experience seems to confirm the elements of exacerbation in the combination of addiction *and* offending.

References

Baker, T.B., Sobell, M.B., Sobell, L.C., and Cannon, D.S. (1976) Halfway Houses for Alcoholics: A Review, Analysis and Comparison with Other Halfway House Facilities. *Int. J. Soc. Psychiat.* **22**: 130–39.

Ball, J.C. (1967) Marijuana Smoking and the Onset of Heroin Use. *Brit. J. Criminol.* **7**: 408–13.

Bartholomew, A.A. and Kelley, M.F. (1965) The Incidence of Criminal Record in 1,000 Consecutive Alcoholics. *Brit. J. Criminol.* **5**: 143–49.

Bartholomew, A.A. (1968) Alcoholism and Crime. *Aust. and N.Z. J. of Criminol.* **1**: 70–99.

Bebbington, P.E. (1976) The Efficacy of Alcoholics Anonymous: The Elusiveness of Hard Data. *Brit. J. Psychiat.* **128**: 572–80.

Bell, D.S. and Champion, R.A, (1979) Deviancy, Delinquency and Drug Use. *Brit. J. Psychiat.* **134**: 269–76.

Camps, F.E. (1970) The Forensic Aspects of Addiction. In R.V. Philipson (ed) *Modern Trends in Drug Dependence and Alcoholism*. London: Butterworths.

Coope, G. (1979) *The Probation Service and the Drink Related Offender in Prison*. (Unpublished ms. Extracts quoted by permission of the author.)

Coutselinis, A. (1974) Some Observations on the Action of Δ^9–

THC on the Human Organism. *Med. Sci. Law* **14**: 117–19.

Cushman, P. (1974) Relationship Between Narcotic Addiction and Crime. *Fed. Pbn.* **XXVIII**: 38–43.

Davidson, A.F. (1976) An Evaluation of the Treatment and After-Care of a Hundred Alcoholics. *Brit. J. Addict.* **71**: 217–24.

Dawtry, F. (ed.) (1968) *Social Problems of Drug Abuse.* London: Butterworths.

de Lint. J. (1974) The Epidemiology of Alcoholism. In N. Kessel, A. Hawker, H. Chalke (eds.) *Alcoholism – A Medical Profile.* London: Epsall.

Edwards, G., Hensman, C., and Peto, J. (1971) Drinking Problems Among Recidivist Prisoners. *Psychol. Med.* **5**: 388–99.

Edwards, G., Gattoni, F., and Hensman, C. (1972) Correlates of Dependence Scores in a Prison Population. *Quart. J. Stud. Alcohol.* **33**: 417–29.

Edwards, G., Kyle, E., and Nicholls, P. (1977) Alcoholics Admitted to Four Hospitals in England: III – Criminal Records. *J. of Studs. on Alcohol.* **38**: 1648–664.

Edwards, G. and Grant, M. (1977) *Alcoholism. New Knowledge and New Responses.* London: Croom Helm.

Edwards. G; (1979) British Policies on Opiate Addiction: Ten Years Working of the Revised Response, and Options for the Future. *Brit. J. Psychiat.* **134**: 1–13.

Gath, D., Hensman, C., Hawker, A., Kelly, M., and Edwards, G. (1968) The Drunk in Court: A Survey of Drunkenness Offenders from Two London Courts. *Brit. Med. J.* **4**: 808–11.

Gibbens, T.C.N. and Silberman, M. (1970) Alcoholism among Prisoners. *Psychol. Med.* **1**: 73–8.

Glatt. M. (1958) Alcoholism, Crime and Juvenile Delinquency. *Brit. J. Delinq.* **IX**: 84–93.

—— (1965) Crime, Alcohol and Alcoholism. *Howard J. of Penol. and Crime Prev.* **IX**: 274–84.

Glatt, M.M., Pitman, D.J., Gillespie, D.G., and Hills, D.R. (1967) *The Drug Scene in Great Britain.* London: Edward Arnold.

Gordon, A.M. (1973) Patterns of Delinquency in Drug Addiction. *Brit. J. Psychiat.* **122**: 205–10.

—— (1978) Drugs and Delinquency: A Four Year Follow-up of Drug Clinic Patients. *Brit. J. Psychiat.* **132**: 21–6.

Gossop, M. and Roy, A. (1977) Hostility, Crime and Drug Dependence. *Brit. J. Psychiat.* **130**: 272–80.

Grimes, J.A. (1977) *Drug Dependency Study: A Survey of Drug Addicts Attending for Treatment.* London: HMSO. Quoted in Edwards (1979).

Guze, S.B. (1976) *Criminality and Psychiatric Disorders.* Oxford: Oxford University Press.

Haines, D. (1978) Alcoholism in Prisons. *Int. J. Off. Ther.* **22**: 127–32.

Hamilton, J.R., Griffith, A., Ritson, E.B., and Aitken, R.C.B. (1977) A Detoxification Unit for Habitual Drunken Offenders. *Health Bulletin* May: 146–54.

Havard, J.D.J. (1975) The Drinking Driver and the Law. In R.G. Smart *et al.* (eds.) *Research Advances in Alcohol and Drug Problems Vol. 2.* New York: John Wiley.

Hawks, D.V. (1970) The Epidemiology of Drug Dependence in the United Kingdom. *Bull. Narcot.* **22**: 15.

Hensman, C. (1969) Problems of Drunkenness Among Male Recidivists. In T. Cook, D. Gath, and C. Hensman (eds.) *The Drunkenness Offence.* Oxford: Pergamon.

Hershon, H.I., Cook, T., and Foldes, P.A. (1974) What shall we do with the Drunkenness Offender? *Brit. J. Psychiat.* **124**: 327–35.

Home Office (1971) *Habitual Drunken Offenders. Report of the Working Party.* London. HMSO.

—— (1976) *Home Office Research Unit Bulletin.* London: HMSO.

—— (1976) *Criminal Statistics for England and Wales, 1975.* Cmnd. 6566. London: HMSO.

Jellinck, E.M. (1960) *The Disease Concept of Alcoholism.* Connecticut: Millhouse Press.

Kessel, W.I.N. and Grossman, G. (1961) Suicide in Alcoholics. *Brit. J. Med.* **2**: 773–74.

McCulloch, J.W. and Prins, H.A. (1978) *Signs of Stress.* London: Woburn Press.

Measey, L.G. (1973) Alcohol and the Royal Naval Offender.

Brit. J. Criminol. **13**: 280–83.

Melotte, C. (1975) A Rehabilitation Hostel for Drug Users: One Year's Admissions. *Brit. J. Criminol.* **15**: 376–84.

Mott, J. and Taylor, M. (1974) *Delinquency Amongst Opiate Users. Home Office Research Studies. No. 23.* London: HMSO.

Mott, J. and Rathod, N.H. (1976) Heroin Misuse and Delinquency in a New Town. *Brit. J. Psychiat.* **128**: 428–35.

Mott, J. (1978) A Long Term Follow-up of Male Non-Therapeutic Opiate Users and Their Criminal Histories. In D.J. West (ed.) *Problems of Drug Abuse in Britain.* Cambridge: Institute of Criminology.

Nicol, A., Gunn, J., Griswood, J., Foggitt, R., and Watson, J. (1973) The Relationship of Alcoholism to Violent Behaviour Resulting in Long-Term Imprisonment. *Brit. J. Psychiat.* **123**: 47–51.

Noble, P.J. (1970) Drug Taking in Delinquent Boys. *Brit. Med. J.* 10 January 1970: 102–05.

Ogborne, A.C. and Melotte, C. (1977) An Evaluation of a Therapeutic Centre for Former Drug Users. *Brit. J. Addict.* **72**: 75–82.

Parr, D. (1962) Offences of Drunkenness in the London Area – A Pilot Study. *Brit. J. Criminol.* **2**: 272–77.

Phillips, G.F. (1973) The Legal Description of Cannabis and Related Substances. *Med. Sci. Law* **13**: 139–42.

Pierce–James, I. (1969) Delinquency and Heroin Addiction in Britain. *Bit. J. Criminol.* **9**: 108–24.

Power, D.J. (1974) Illicit Drug Taking. *Med. Sci. Law* **14**: 250–67.

Prins, H.A. (1973) *Criminal Behaviour.* London: Pitman.

Rathod, N. (no date) What is Addiction? In *Where on Drugs.* Advisory Centre for Education.

Rix, K.J.B. (1974) Evening Class on Alcoholism: An Experiment in Alcoholism Education. *Brit. J. Addict.* **69**: 33–4.

Rix, K.J.B. and Buyers, M. (1976) Public Attitudes Towards Alcoholism in a Scottish City. *Brit. J. Addict.* **71**: 23–9.

Rix, K.J.B., Buyers, M. and Finchman, D. (1976) Alcoholism and the Drunkenness Offender in a Scottish Burgh Police Court. *Med. Sci. Law* **16**: 188–92.

Rosenberg, C.M. (1971) The Young Addict and His Family.

Brit. J. Psychiat. **118**: 469–70.

Rubington, E. (1969) Types of Alcoholic Offenders. *Fed. Pbn.* **XXXIII**: 28–35.

Scott, P.D. and Willcox, D.R.C. (1965) Delinquency and the Amphetamines. *Brit. J. Addict.* **61**: 9–27.

Scott, P.D. and Buckle, M. (1971) Delinquency and Amphetamines. *Brit. J. Psychiat.* **119**: 179–82.

Smith-Moorhouse, P.M. and Lynn, L. (1966) Drinking Before Detention. *Prison Serv. J.* **V** (July): 29–39.

Spring, J.A. and Buss, D.H. (1977) Three Centuries of Alcohol in the British Diet. *Nature* **270**: 567–73.

Stevens, B.C. (1978) Deaths of Drug Addicts in London during 1970–74: Toxicological, Legal and Demographic Findings. *Med. Sci. Law* **18**: 128–37.

Sunter, J.P., Heath, A.B., and Ranasinghe, H. (1978) Alcohol Associated Mortality in Newcastle-upon-Tyne. *Med. Sci. Law* **18**: 84–9.

Vaillant, G.E. and Rasor, R.W. (1966) The Role of Compulsory Supervision and Compulsory Parole in the Treatment of Addicts. *Fed. Pbn.* **XXX**: 53–9.

Voegele, G.E. and Dietze, H.J. (1963) Addiction to Gasoline Smelling in Juvenile Delinquents. *Brit. J. Criminol.* **4**: 43–60.

Voigt, J., Dalgaard, J., and Simonsen, J. (1975) Fatalities Among Drug Users in Denmark in the Period 1968–1972. *Med. Sci. Law* **15**: 265–69.

Washbrook, R.A.H. (1977) Alcoholism versus Crime in Birmingham, England. *Int. J. Off. Ther.* **21**: 166–73.

Watson, J.M. (1978) Clinical and Laboratory Investigations in 132 cases of Solvent Abuse. *Med. Sci. Law* **18**: 40–4.

West, D.J. (1963) *The Habitual Prisoner.* London: Macmillan.

Wiepert, G.D., D'Orbán, P.T. and Bewley, T.H. (1979) Delinquency by Opiate Addicts Treated at Two London Clinics. *Brit. J. Psychiat.* **134**: 14–23.

Wilkinson, R. (1970) *The Prevention of Drinking Problems: Alcohol and Cultural Influences.* New York: Oxford University Press.

Willett, T.C. (1964) *The Criminal On the Road.* London: Tavistock.

Wilson, S. and Mandelbrote, B. (1978a) Drug Rehabilitation and Criminality. *Brit. J. Criminol.* **18**: 381–85.

—— (1978b) The Relationship between Duration of Treatment in a Therapeutic Community and Subsequent Criminality. *Brit. J. Psychiat.* **132**: 487–91.

World Health Organisation (1952) *Expert Committee on Mental Health, Alcoholism Sub-Committee, Second Report.* Tech. Rep. Ser. 48. Geneva: WHO.

—— (1964) *Expert Committee on Addiction Producing Drugs. Fifteenth Report.* Tech. Rep. Ser. 273. Geneva: WHO.

—— (1974) *Expert Committee on Drug Dependence. Twentieth Report.* Geneva: WHO.

Wright, J.D. (1976) Knowledge and Experience of Young People Regarding Drug Abuse Between 1969 and 1974. *Med. Sci. Law* **16**: 252–63.

Zacune, J. and Hensman, C. (1971) *Drugs, Alcohol and Tobacco in Britain.* London: Heinemann Medical Books.

FURTHER READING

Bean, P. (1974) *The Social Control of Drugs.* London: Martin Robertson.

Cockett, R. (1971) *Drug Abuse and Personality in Young Offenders.* London: Butterworths.

Edwards, G. and Grant, M. (eds.) (1977) *Alcoholism. New Knowledge and New Responses.* London: Croom Helm. (This recent work is highly recommended as it brings together many research studies. It is divided into three sections: I. Scientific Understanding. II. The Varieties of Harm. III. Treatment and Education.)

Glatt, M.M. (1974) *A Guide to Addiction and Its Treatment: Drugs, Society and Men.* Lancaster: Medical and Technical Publishing.

Jellinek, E.M. (1960) *The Disease Concept of Alcoholism.* Connecticut: Hillhouse Press.

Phillipson, R.V. (ed.) (1970) *Modern Trends in Drug Dependence and Alcoholism.* London: Butterworths.

Royal College of Psychiatrists (1979) *Alcohol and Alcoholism: The Report of a Special Committee.* London: Tavistock.

Zacune, J. and Hensman, C. (1971) *Drugs, Alcohol and Tobacco in Britain.* London: Heinemann Medical Books.

CHAPTER TEN
Female offending

If to her share some female errors fall,
Look on her face, and you'll forget 'em all.
POPE

The large shop, with its manifold
various seductions, betrays a woman into
crime.
LOMBROSO

Women are not the same as men; Their
physiology is different: Their instincts
and many of their basic attitudes to life
are different: Their psychological needs
are different.
ANN D. SMITH

Some readers may query the inclusion of a chapter on female offending in a book that has dealt mainly with socio psychiatric problems and aspects of the relationship between mental disorder and criminality. Is the reader to deduce from this inclusion that most female offenders must be considered to be psychiatrically disordered? Whilst the answer to this must generally be in the negative, it also has to be said that a large number of studies have found a high proportion of psychological disturbance in female offenders. Some aspects of this have already been touched upon in previous chapters in this book and it therefore seemed appropriate to try to give as complete a picture as possible by devoting a specific chapter to female offending. There are two other, but closely associated, reasons for so doing. First, until very recently, female offending had received scant attention in the criminological, penal, and socio-forensic literature.* Second, it has been the subject of a somewhat polemical debate between those who see female offending mainly in deterministic terms and those (particularly feminists, such as Smart (1976)) who see the phenomenon not only from a more broadly based perspective, but who also suggest that a male view of female criminality will inevitably be distorted.

In this chapter I will try to demonstrate that the truth about female offending probably lies somewhere between the extreme psychological deterministic interpretation and the excessively sociological. I shall place the problem of female offending within a brief perspective of male-female differences. I shall then derive what I can from the statistics and forms of female criminality, examining also one or two offences that are 'female-specific'. I shall then comment upon the degree of psychiatric morbidity in female offenders and upon some studies that have been made of other aspects of the aetiology of female crime. Finally, some treatment considerations will be touched upon.

Male and female differences

Although some might not agree with the apparent dogmatism expressed in the quotation from Ann Smith at the beginning of this chapter, there is quite incontrovertible evidence that there are vital physiological and psychological differences between men and women and that it is very unwise to ignore these. However, it is also true that some of these fundamental differences are exacerbated by socially determined attitudes that may well be heavily prejudiced in favour of men. There is good anthropological evidence that sex roles may be reversed,

---

* Two recent examples illustrate this point. The revised edition of *The Work of the Prison Service in England and Wales (Prisons and the Prisoner*, Home Office 1977) devotes five and a half out of its one hundred and eighty-eight pages specifically to the problems of women and girls in prison. The Butler Committee (Home Office and DHSS 1975) stated in a footnote (p.7): 'throughout the report, we refer to offenders as male except where specific reference to women is appropriate. Apart from convenience, this is justified by the statistics, for women are a small minority of offenders.'

but as Gibbens (1971) says this may only be a tribute to the adaptability of men and women. He goes on to state that 'in animals it seems clear that males are more aggressive and that pre-natal endocrine development prepared them for this.' He adduces evidence that if the females of the species receive male sex hormone before birth, their behaviour is likely to be altered quite markedly and that sex hormones may operate by selectively enlarging the amygdala and the centres of aggressive response. He cautions us however that, 'Unravelling the bio-psycho-social components of female social behaviour is clearly far in the future . . .' Reference was made in Chapter 8 to the importance of attitudes towards human sexuality and sexual behaviour. These attitudes are of fundamental importance in understanding the more general differences that exist between the behaviours of men and women. Ford and Beach (1965) state:

'After reviewing the cross-species and cross-cultural evidence, we are convinced that tendencies towards sexual behaviour before maturity and even before puberty are genetically determined in many primates, including human beings. The degree to which such tendencies *find overt expression* is in part a function of the needs of the society in which the individual grows up, but some expression is very likely to occur under any circumstances [my italics].'

Walker (1968) in commenting for example upon the alleged differences in physical strength between men and women is inclined to be dismissive of concern as to causality. He says 'it hardly matters whether this is a physiological or a sociological fact. Whether with a different up-bringing girls would have the strength and dexterity of boys or not, in this society they do not.' In recent years, feminist writers, such as Smart (1976), have taken issue with this mode of thinking, which they suggest reflects a somewhat narrow and male-dominated point of view. We shall return to this theme, only adumbrated here, when we come to examine the characteristics of female offenders in a little more detail.

In discussions about female criminality much is made of the

more recent changes and developments in opportunities for women and the ways in which these may be reflected in changing patterns of female offending. Smith (1974) asks us to take note of an increase in female involvement in crimes of serious assault, hijacking, and other forms of terrorism. She also suggests that women's increasing involvement in the effects of modern technology may see them becoming increasingly involved in business frauds, forgeries, and other offences of deception. But as we shall see later, this may be a somewhat oversimplified view. Loewenstein (1978) makes the point that 'changing sex roles are bringing about profound changes in the way women and men interact, work together, rear children and live together in families.' It is important to remember that such changes have formed a take-off point for the theorizing and position of the feminist movement, and in particular the stance they have taken concerning female criminality; this is exemplified in the work of writers such as Adler (1975), and Kestenbaum (1977). However, more critical exponents of the feminist view have suggested that it is erroneous to link the rise in the feminist movement and female offending too closely. With this in mind we should now examine the statistics of female crime and the way the judicial and penal systems deal with women offenders.

Statistics relating to female offending

Numerically speaking, women constitute a very small proportion of the total offender population. Overall, the proportion of male to female offenders is about 8:1, though there is some variation in the figures depending upon type and seriousness of offence. It is also clear from an examination of the criminal statistics that there are differences between the sexes in respect of cautioning; but here the difference in ratios is not quite so high – about 4:1. In 1975, some 189,000 females were found guilty by the courts compared with some 1,800,000 males (Home Office 1976). In the last few years, the proportion of women found guilty of indictable offences has been about 15 per cent and for non-indictable offences about 8 per cent

(D'Orbán 1971). Although we shall be examining aspects of motivation for crime by female offenders later in this chapter, it seems appropriate to say something about these now since they will influence the published statistics of female criminality. Much thought and speculation has been devoted to the reasons for the differences in the proportion of male to female offenders. It has been suggested that women may be reported for criminal activity by the police less often on the grounds of 'chivalry' and because of a reluctance to prosecute the 'weaker' of the species. There *may* be some truth in this, because even when cases actually come before the courts for adjudication and sentence, it is frequently pleaded that the female involved was an unwitting or unwilling accomplice or that she was the victim of a Zvengali-like influence. The question of opportunity has already been mentioned, and recent reported increases in recorded female criminality seem to support the view that opportunities for criminal involvement by females have been changing. It has also been suggested that the law discriminates against men; as was pointed out in Chapter 8 the law (at least until fairly recently) has penalized the sexual misbehaviour of males far more than that of females – with the exception of soliciting for prostitution. It has been suggested that the delinquencies of women take mainly non-criminal forms such as promiscuity or that psychiatric explanations for criminal conduct may be invoked more frequently in women. This results in their diversion from the penal and judicial systems into psychiatric methods of disposal and care. (I shall return to this later.) However, in relation to female juvenile offenders we should note that 'girls who steal from home or from shops later tend to show disobedience at home, staying out late and making undesirable sexual relationships. Thus, there is considerable overlap between sexual misconduct and other forms of delinquency' (Gibbens 1959). Some writers, for example Pollak (1961), have suggested that the courts may tend to find fewer women guilty of offences. In general, the evidence for this seems to be conflicting. Jones (1965) noted a barely significant difference, but Mannheim (1965) suggested that the difference was more marked. D'Orbán (1971), using the criminal statistics for 1969, found some confirmation of Mannheim's view. Finally, we can note that in an American study by Kalven and Zeisel (1966) of spouse homicides, only ten out of seventeen wives were found guilty compared with twenty-two out of twenty-seven husbands (quoted by Walker (1968) .)

THE PRESENT POSITION

If we take them at their face value, it would seem that the criminal statistics do indicate that women are much less involved in identified crime than men. However, current figures also indicate that there has been a recent sharp increase in known female crime. Smart (1979) states that:

> 'the total of all indictable offences by women has virtually doubled in the ten years from 1965 to 1975 and the greatest proportionate increase has been in violent offences against the person. Indeed between 1965 and 1975 there has been an increase of 225 per cent in the numbers of women committing these offences, while offences against property with violence have increased by 149 per cent and offences against property without violence by 66 per cent.'

Similar increases have been reported in the United States. Kestenbaum (1977), using official statistics, asserts that the arrest rate for females doubled in the period 1960–1970, and that whilst the crime rate for men stood at about 25 per cent, for women it was 74 per cent. The arrest rate of women for violent crimes rose to 69 per cent in 1969–1970. She also states that a significant number of these persons were heads of households or single parents, suggesting that these facts had important implications for their families. However, Smart has several cautionary remarks to make concerning the interpretations that might be placed on these apparent increases and the degree to which they may be laid at the door of feminist activity for change in relation to social perceptions of women. No doubt her remarks could be applied to the American scene also, though we cannot consider this in detail here. Let us deal with the feminist position first. She rightly suggests that the movement itself may be an 'outcome of social processes and forces which may themselves be more directly related to changes in criminal behaviour than a social movement intent on improving the position of women in society.' She then links this position with the use of the criminal statistics to prove that an increase in female offending is not a *new* phenomenon. This is because extrapolations from the statistics usually quoted in support of a recent upsurge have often been confined to the last twenty years or so. By using the statistics for a much longer period, Smart demonstrates that, for example, for the period 1935–1946, there was an increase of some 365 per cent. In addition, she suggests that the interpretations of *current* statistics can be misleading. Taking the statistics of murder by women in England and Wales as one example, it would appear that there has been an increase of 500 per cent in the years 1965–1975, but in terms of actual numbers of *individuals* involved they are 1 and 5 respectively! Moreover, as she rightly points out, it is misleading to

> 'Compare proportionate increases in female crime with those in male crime because the *absolute* figures for the former are typically so small that an insignificant change distorts the percentage increase, while for the latter, the figures are so large that massive changes are required before the percentage increase changes noticeably.'
>
> (Smart 1979)

It would seem, therefore, that changes in the offence rates of women need to be seen not only in a perspective that is wider than that merely related to the specific activities of the feminist movement, but that they also need to be reviewed in a longer historical context than is usually the case. Such an examination reveals female criminality to be but one response by women to a number of forces that have been operating for change during the last forty to fifty years.

Sentencing policies and their effects

As we have seen, it had for long been observed that women

were prosecuted less often than men and stood a better chance of acquittal. Until very recently it was also thought that female offenders were treated more leniently by the courts. However, recent research has begun to call this latter assumption into question. May (1977) found, in a study carried out in Aberdeen, that the courts showed a slight tendency to deal more severely with juvenile female offenders. 'Girls aged 14 years or more were much more likely to be severely dealt with than younger girls, as too were those girls charged with a juvenile status offence, more than half of whom (52 per cent) were either placed on supervision or sent to an institution for a short spell.' He suggests that his findings confirm recent trends observed by workers in America. Mawby (1977) has also examined this problem. He suggests, as have others, that girls are more likely to be institutionalized than boys for 'non-criminal' reasons – no doubt for their own protection. He found that court sentencing policies in respect of young persons *under* twenty-one seems to be broadly similar, but above the age of twenty-one the females apprehended by the police have noticeably fewer previous convictions than males. He also suggests that statistics indicate that males going to prison and Borstal are considerably more recidivist than females. Females are more likely than males to be remanded in custody but *not* subsequently sentenced to a term of imprisonment. Mawby concludes that

> 'when *previous record* is taken into consideration, females are more likely to be imprisoned than males [my italics]. More precisely, for adults, females with no previous convictions make up five times the proportion of receptions than do males with no previous convictions. Put another way, if, of women with no previous convictions sentenced to imprisonment, 80 per cent were sentenced to non-custodial treatment, the proportion of female receptions with no previous convictions would *still* be greater than for adult male receptions. The fact that women are being sentenced to short terms of imprisonment where men are handled outside the penal system is illustrated by the large proportion of female offenders serving short sentences.'

Generally speaking, women respond better than do men to many of our penal treatment measures. Thus, they seem to respond better to probation, to fines, or to a term in prison, or care in a psychiatric institution* (Goodman and Price 1967; and Walker and McCabe 1973). The reasons for this are hard to discern. It may be that women respond better as individuals to measures of deterrence, or they may have a greater regard for, and are able to make better use of, social work, supervision, and support. Perhaps, overall, they are more sensitive to acquiring and maintaining the good opinions of others or it may be that later transgressions and breaches of the law are overlooked.

Some offences peculiar to women

There are one or two crimes which are only committed by women and for which the law makes specific provision. The crime of infanticide is one such example. The implications of this offence in relation to issues of criminal responsibility were considered in Chapter 2. There are certain other offences that are found to be committed by women more than by men – examples are the procuration of criminal abortion,** shoplifting, and prostitution. In recent years, the offence of baby (child) stealing has figured fairly prominently in the media. Instances of non-accidental injury to children tend to be attributed more frequently to mothers than to fathers, but in many cases it is often hard to discern who really struck the first blow or to what extent one partner was covering up for the other. (The problem of non-accidental injury to children and family violence is too large a topic to embark upon here and is the subject of a considerable body of specialist literature. Several references to overviews of the literature on the subject are

---

* At least as far as reconviction is concerned, but they seem harder to manage while actually in the institutions – see later discussion.

** Since the Abortion Act, 1967 the number of men and women engaged in the procuration of illegal abortions has of course declined, though there will of course still be the occasion case. In 1975, there were only two such cases recorded (Home Office 1976).

listed at the end of this chapter.) I now give fairly brief consideration to four of these offences; infanticide, shoplifting, prostitution, and baby (child) stealing.

INFANTICIDE

The number of prosecutions for infanticide in any year is very small. In 1975, eight women were found guilty of this offence. All except one were dealt with by a non-custodial penalty (Home Office 1976). In Chapter 2, I indicated that when the legislation concerning infanticide was first enacted more weight was attached to the relevance of formal psychiatric illness than is now considered to be justified (Bluglass 1978). More often than not, infanticide occurs as a result of a combination of adverse social and psychiatric features. In a detailed Israeli study of thirteen cases, Winnick and Horowitz (1961) found that the average age of the defendant was nineteen years. Ten out of the thirteen mothers were unmarried and only one out of the thirteen had a previous conviction. Of particular interest is the fact that only two of the group were considered to come from stable family backgrounds. In a brief follow-up of this small group, the authors found that seven of the mothers had subsequently married within a few months of the court proceedings. Although the sample in this detailed Israeli study is very small, its results seem reasonably representative of the situation obtaining elsewhere (D'Orbán 1971; Bluglass 1978). In the light of current knowledge the offence can perhaps best be regarded as a form of non-accidental injury to children.

SHOPLIFTING

It has been clearly established that when women steal, they tend to steal from shops. Much of the research that has been carried out on shoplifters seems to support the opportunity theory; that on the whole women have greater access to shops and stores and are thus more prone to succumb to the temptations offered. This opportunity theory can be seen in the eighty-year-old quotation from Lombroso cited at the heading to this chapter. However, as Smart (1976) shows, proportionately *more men* than women have been convicted of shoplifting in recent years. It is very easy to assume that shoplifting is in the main a female activity, because, as Smart points out, the numbers of women officially recorded as involved in shoplifting 'far exceed the numbers of women involved in any other type of crime, which makes shoplifting quite unique in terms of female offences'.

The major work in this field was carried out by Gibbens and Prince (1962) and by Gibbens, Palmer, and Prince (1971) in which they examined the cases of 532 shoplifters. They found that whereas 42 per cent of the women stole clothes only, the tendency among men shoplifters was to steal books. (In point of fact, one very rarely comes across a female book-stealer.) They suggested that the following broad generalizations could be made about shoplifting:

(1) It is committed with unusual frequency by women over the age of forty. When committed by women under this age it is often committed by foreign born nationals, students, or 'au pair' girls.

(2) If further offences are committed, they are likely to be of shoplifting.

(3) Children and teenagers convicted of shoplifting tend not to be convicted of it in later life.

(4) A fairly high proportion of female shoplifters show psychiatric disorder in one form or another (20 per cent of first offenders and nearly 30 per cent of recidivists.) In their follow-up study (1971), in which they looked specifically at the mental health aspects of shoplifting. Gibbens, Palmer, and Prince concluded that 'it is tempting to suppose that in a fair proportion of cases, shoplifting is the first symptom of a frank depressive illness.' They also identified a group of chronic neurotic shoplifters, who steal small objects of value impulsively, often to the risk of a well-established career or family situation. They tend to deny anxieties or the existence of stresses, though these are readily observable in their total life-styles.

(5) 10 per cent of the sample studied had had a major physical illness, half of these had occurred in the last year before the survey. 8 per cent had chronic ill-health or permanent disability. One third of the psychiatric cases had gynaecological conditions, sometimes menopausal symptoms, but more often pre-natal and post-natal conditions, post-hysterectomy symptoms and so on.

The authors point out that recidivist shoplifters are sometimes 'professionals', but it should not necessarily be concluded from this that they are mentally normal. They found that a number of these 'professionals' had several mental hospital admissions. As we shall see later, writers such as Smart (1976) suggest that we tend to assume that because delinquent behaviour in women is seen as 'abnormal or unnatural' we are not necessarily justified in designating them as mentally ill or sick. However, for many people, it is perhaps more comfortable to think of a woman who deviates from the norm as being 'mad' rather than 'bad'. (See also the discussion in Chapters 2 and 3.)

PROSTITUTION

Prostitution in itself is not a criminal offence. The only unlawful elements are soliciting in public and keeping a brothel. Since the passing of the Street Offences Act, 1959 far fewer prostitutes have been arrested, but the number sentenced to imprisonment has risen. At any one time, some 10 per cent of women in prison are there because of prostitution offences. (The figures for the number of convictions were given in Chapter 8.) The association between juvenile delinquency and promiscuity referred to earlier in this chapter is again apparent when we examine populations of older female offenders. Gibbens (1971) reports that 'among women over 21 admitted to prison on remand or sentence, between a quarter and a third of every age group are or have been prostitutes, whether they have been admitted for theft, assault, drunkenness or drug taking . . .' Gibbens supports Lombroso's dictum that prostitution can in some respects be seen as the female equival-

ent of male criminality. Prostitutes tend to show a high concentration of personality and other mental disorder, 'multiple
social deviance' and physical abnormalities. Having said this, it
would be unwise to overemphasize the psychopathological
elements in the offence of prostitution. There seems to be
good evidence that such behaviour is also heavily culturally
determined. As Gibbens (1971) suggests "The strong family
and social pressures upon women to conform to acceptable
social and especially sexual standards stigmatizes the deviant
more heavily than in men, and selective association with
increasingly deviant men tends to keep them in this situation.'
Smart (1976), amongst others, also points out what appears to
be the double standard of morality for men and women. She is
rightly critical of the somewhat ambivalent conclusions of an
official Working Party set up to examine and revise the existing legislation (HMSO 1974). The Working Party concentrated their attention upon 'conduct which people find offensive precisely because it is committed by prostitutes in pursuing
their calling'. As Smart points out, the members of the Working Party were strangely unmindful of the offensive behaviour
indulged in by those men who 'kerb crawl' for 'service'. To be
fair, the Working Party did suggest the creation of a new
offence to deal with such behaviour. Despite this however, a
woman who persistently plies her trade will still be labelled as a
'common prostitute', though no such term of opprobrium is
reserved for her male counterpart, nor is there a similar one
for those who 'kerb crawl'. As Smart also points out, 'once a
woman is labelled a "common prostitute" the police are able to
cite her previous record in court in order to establish a fresh
offence of soliciting. In practice, therefore, the police do not
have to prove than an offender was soliciting on a specific
occasion once she has become identified as a known prostitute'.
One is forced to agree with Smart when she suggests that the
legislation renders prostitutes 'a very powerless section of the
community, having fewer rights to protection from the law
than ordinary citizens.' It is noteworthy that a prostitutes'
'collective' has now been established. This group seeks to redress what does appear to be an injustice. However, one must

have reservations as to the use of threatened exposure of the private behaviour of public figures by which this group is said to be attempting to bring about change. This does not enhance the legitimacy or the satisfactory future progress of their cause. In many ways, this aspect of the law relating to prostitution has much in common with that relating to 'suspected persons loitering with intent' – both seem to place the alleged offender at a singular disadvantage and both need revision.

Some of the posited characteristics of prostitutes will be considered when we examine the characteristics of female offenders more generally. However, it is worth noting here that very little work has been done on the *clients* of female prostitutes. A notable exception is the study by Gibbens and Silberman (1960). They examined the records of some 230 male patients suffering from VD, contracted mainly from consort with prostitutes. They found that 'those who went only with prostitutes tended to be passive men, often of good general character, living at home with a dominant mother, and a father either dead or of no account'. Those who went with prostitutes *and* a variety of other 'pick-ups' were considered to be more aggressive in temperament and came from more disturbed and unstable backgrounds. Their social relationships were considered frequently to be very shallow. Since many prostitutes are themselves said to come from similar backgrounds, we might conclude here that there was a certain mutuality of attraction and response.

CHILD (BABY) STEALING

Child, but particularly baby, stealing has come to prominence in recent years. D'Orbán (1972, 1976) has made an extensive study not only of the offence but also of the characteristics of those who engage in this behaviour. He is concerned to point out that we should distinguish between baby stealing – predominantly, but not exclusively, a female offence – and child stealing, which more often involves adult males in the abduction of young children of either sex. (See also Hunter (1973).) D'Orbán reminds us there are Victorian examples of this type of offence when children were stolen in order to obtain their clothes.* He remarks on an increase in its more pathological form in the last twenty years or so. During the years 1950–57 he notes that there was an average of nine cases, but in 1973 sixty-one cases were reported. On the whole, he and other workers do not seem to consider that the widespread publicity arising from such cases results in an increased incidence due to 'copying'. However, Hunter (1973) wonders whether prosecution may not make matters worse for all concerned. D'Orbán suggests the following classification which he bases on the twenty-four cases of baby stealing he studied:

(1) girls of subnormal intelligence who stole a baby to play with;

(2) psychotic patients whose offence was motivated by delusional ideas;

(3) psychopathic personalities preoccupied with a desire to have children;

(4) a manipulative group in which the motive for baby stealing was an attempt to influence a man by whom they had become pregnant and with whom their relationship was insecure. These offences were precipitated by crises (such as miscarriage) or the threat of desertion. These women presented the stolen baby to their partner pretending the child was his.

D'Orbán concluded that the offence seemed usually to be an attempt to 'compensate for emotional deprivation or frustrated maternal feelings, and a real or imaginary miscarriage may be a predisposing or precipitating factor. The offence rarely seems premeditated, though there was evidence of previous planning in some cases, particularly in the manipulative group'. However, the 'stolen babies were well cared for and were usually quickly recovered' (D'Orbán 1972). All in all,

* Child stealing in varied forms figures prominantly in folklore and legend; there are numerous stories of a 'changeling' left in place of another child taken by fairies. In Shakespeare's *A Midsummer Night's Dream,* the quarrel between Titania and Oberon centres around the changeling, being brought up by Titania, whom Oberon covets for his page.

D'Orbán's researches suggest that in these cases we are likely to be dealing with highly psychopathological factors, though of course this is not to say that social factors are of no account in relation to both understanding and management.

Psychiatric morbidity in female offenders

The difficulties in establishing causal relationships or connections between mental disorder and criminality were stressed in Chapter 3. These difficulties should be borne in mind in our consideration of psychiatric morbidity in female offenders. D'Orbán (1971) has usefully reviewed a number of studies made earlier in the century and these need not be recapitulated here. The more recent work of Guze (1976) has been referred to elsewhere in this book. He included sixty-six convicted females among his sample of offenders and made the following psychiatric diagnoses: sociopathy – 65 per cent; alcoholism – 47 per cent; hysteria – 41 per cent; drug dependence – 26 per cent; homosexuality – 6 per cent; anxiety neurosis – 11 per cent; depression – 1 per cent; schizophrenia – 1.5 per cent; mental subnormality – 6 per cent. The low incidence of depresssion is of interest since this is one of the mental disorders most commonly found in women. It may be that there were a number of depressive elements in Guze's other diagnoses or that depressive components were 'masked'. The finding concerning anxiety neurosis is of interest. In a recently reported study, Barack and Widem (1978) administered the Eysenck Personality Questionnaire to a group of American women awaiting trial. They found that, compared with a control group, these women scored significantly higher on the Eysenck neuroticism and psychoticism scales. The high proportion of cases of hysteria is also of interest. I commented in Chapter 5 on the possible association between hysteria and psychopathy. Guze suggests that the differences between the two conditions may be limited to the overt manifestations and that 'underlying etiologic and pathogenetic processes are similar'. He asks whether sex differences can be used to identify the most important features of culture and family life related to the development of the two conditions. Sociologists would certainly suggest that the view men take of the behaviour of women will markedly affect the extent to which they are regarded as sick or criminal (see Smart 1976: Chapter 6). There may be a tendency for women offenders to be regarded as so unusual because of their small numbers, that they are therefore regarded as 'abnormal' (Walker 1968). There is evidence that there are more female than male in-patients in ordinary psychiatric hospitals and units and that in the special hospitals the proportion of women to men is about ten times higher than in the prisons. Gibbens (1971) takes note of the views of sociologists who concentrate their attentions upon the means by which society labels forms of social deviance in various ways and who also suggest that the finding of mental abnormality in female offenders may be due to a culturally induced 'set' on the part of the psychiatrist. Gibbens refutes these views to some extent by pointing out that they underrate the objectivity of psychiatric evaluation of symptoms and pathology. 'Women offenders are more often depressed than men, and with quite specific symptoms, such as phobias.' Whilst I have some sympathy with those who point to the problems that may stem from the labelling process, my own practical experience over the years has led me to the view that clinical depressive and other symptoms are in fact not infrequently overlooked – sometimes with tragic consequences. (I referred to this problem at some length in Chapter 6.)

Whatever the reasons, there is certainly concern about the proportion of female offenders in custody who are considered to be suffering from some form of mental disability. As long ago as 1967, Goodman and Price (1967) reported that a very high proportion of psychiatrically disturbed girls were sent to Borstal and that the staff were not equipped to deal with them. They considered that this just compounded their problems. They also drew attention to the need for psychiatric hospital facilities. The Governor and staff of Holloway Prison in their evidence to the Butler Committee gave the following account of the incidence of mental disorder among female prisoners.

'The ratio of disturbed against non-disturbed offenders is

much higher for females than for males. There are very few "mentally ill" women in Holloway, but there are many who may be considered "mentally abnormal" according to our definition (below) in that there is a great deviance from sociological and psychological norms.' They used the term 'mentally abnormal' to indicate:

'(a) people with a defined psychiatric diagnosis, e.g. schizophrenia, which can be treated psychiatrically or medically;

(b) those people with the broad psychiatric diagnosis of "personality disorder" or "behaviour disorder", which might be helped with medical, psychiatric, psychological or sociological methods;

(c) those people who are classified as "psychopaths" or "sociopaths", whose condition cannot be treated medically or psychiatrically, but might be more appropriately treated by psychological or sociological methods.'

They indicated that the majority of their population would come under categories (b) and (c) above (Home Office and DHSS 1975: 41–2).

The Governor and staff of Holloway also suggested to the Butler Committee that 'social enquiry reports should be obtained in relation to all women appearing before the courts, as a means of both discovering any signs of psychiatric disorder and of avoiding unnecessary custodial remands which may have a seriously damaging effect on the women themselves and on their families' (Home Office and DHSS 1975: 163). The Committee considered that to have accepted this suggestion in its entirety would have provided too great a workload for the probation service. They did stress, however, that the probation service should keep a 'watchful eye throughout the proceedings for any sign of mental disorder and they should no doubt be specially vigilant in the case of a woman defendant.' (See also my comments in Chapter 4.)

There does not appear to have been any diminution in the number of women in custody considered to be mentally abnormal. The daily average prison population of women offenders for 1977 was 1,358; the highest recorded figure was 1,440 in September of that year. On 31 December 1977, 127 women and girls in custody were considered to be suffering from mental disorder of a nature or degree warranting their detention in hospital for medical treatment under the provisions of the Mental Health Act, 1959. Eighty-one women had a history of being detained in mental hospital at some time before being received into Prison Department custody. The report comments on the time that it takes to care adequately for these women offenders, many of whom require single accommodation. This, and the general pressure upon Holloway in providing reports to courts meant that many inmates who would normally have been housed in the south had to be dispersed to prisons further north, thus making family visiting and other arrangements for personal contacts extremely difficult. This has obviously exacerbated an already difficult situation (Home Office 1978). However, Holloway can no doubt continue to expect this concentration of difficult women since its ongoing rebuilding programme envisages a hospital orientation. In addition, it seems unlikely that ordinary psychiatric hospitals will depart readily from their reluctance to receive difficult female offender/patients. (See also Chapter 11.)

OTHER CHARACTERISTICS

So far I have referred mainly to psychiatric morbidity, but some other associated aspects must now be considered. In many ways, the distinction between psychiatric and other factors is an arbitrary and artifical one, but the distinction has been made merely in order to achieve clarity of presentation.

Chromosomal factors

These were mentioned in Chapter 3. Although no specific chromosomal abnormalities *in relation to crime* have been found in women, Gibbens (1969) has indicated that women show a very high proportion of both autosomal and sex chromosomal abnormalities. However, as D'Orbán (1971) indicates 'the whole question of chromosome abnormalities in female offenders has only recently been raised and requires further investigation'.

Physique

It has been noted by various workers (e.g., D'Orbán 1971) that delinquent girls tend towards physical overdevelopment and are above average in height and weight for their age. Epps and Parnell (1952) compared female delinquents and undergraduates, finding the delinquents to be more mesomorphic – a finding incidentally that also holds good for young *male* offenders (Prins 1973). Smith (1962), in her study of women in prison, observed that precocious sexual development, when not accompanied by equal development of personality, may encourage restless or rebellious behaviour and may tempt a girl into promiscuity and antisocial conduct.

Physiological factors

The extent to which factors such as the menstrual cycle influence criminality has been much debated ever since the late nineteenth century. The major work in this area is that undertaken by Dalton (1961, 1964). In her earlier study, she found that nearly 50 per cent of a group of women offenders in prison had been convicted in the menstrual or immediate pre-menstrual period. This was against an expected incidence of 29 per cent. She also studied women reported to the prison authorites for bad behaviour, finding that 54 per cent had been reported during their menstrual or pre-menstrual period. Of those who were reported *on more than one occasion*, 70 per cent had misconducted themselves during this time. A later study is reported by Hands, Herbert, and Tennent (1974). They found some association between phases of the menstrual cycle and aggressive behaviour among women detained in a special hospital. However, the writers urge caution in drawing conclusions as to a close association, suggesting that the strains and stresses of a closed institutional community were probably of equal importance. Another piece of somewhat negative evidence is reported in an earlier piece of work by Epps (in Gibbens and Prince 1962). She could not find any association between shoplifting offences and any particular phase of the menstrual cycle. All in all, the evidence seems to be somewhat conflicting, though many women will provide anecdotal evidence of increased irritability, unpredictability, and perhaps a tendency towards some acts of negligence (e.g. in driving) during the pre-menstrual period. Pregnancy and its associated changes in physiological functioning is sometimes suggested as a possible causative factor in female offending – particularly in some cases of infanticide (referred to earlier) – and also in non-accidental injury to children ('baby battering'). Likewise, the menopause has also been implicated, but again, the evidence is not conclusive. More recently, Skynner (1976), in a textbook of family therapy, has summarized some research findings by Bardwick (1974). These seem to show that sex hormones influence differentially the level of certain enzymes that control the balance of excitatory and inhibitory functions in the nervous system between men and women respectively. Skynner suggests that this research explains the need for some women to wish for male domination and partially also the way in which they may persistently provoke their marital partner if this domination is not forthcoming. Although the research only offers somewhat slender evidence of the influence of physiological factors on social behaviour, it cannot be dismissed lightly. In summary, we can say that there *may* be instances in which physiological factors are of importance in a particular case, and this is why it is wise to keep an open mind. By being aware of all the possibilities, courts and other social institutions may be properly advised. (The remarks made about mental disorder at the end of Chapter 3 apply with the equal force here.)

Sexual difficulties

A high proportion of prostitutes have been said to be lesbian or bisexual. Gibbens (1971) puts the figure as high as 16 per cent.

It has also been suggested that many other female offenders have sexual problems and the comments made in Chapter 7 concerning female arsonists are relevant here. It has frequently been observed that many prostitutes have curious love-hate relationships with their ponces in which sado-masochistic trends can be discerned and in which mutual violence seems more or less acceptable. However, we should remember that the whole area of female homosexuality has been subjected to study only comparatively recently; the work of Kenyon (1968, 1975) and Hopkins (1969) in this field will repay study.

Special hospital populations

In addition to the studies that have been made of women in prison, a number of studies have also been made of female offenders detained in the special hospitals. Mitchell and Murphy (1975) and Brooks and Mitchell (1975) have described the characteristics of the female population in Carstairs State Hospital in Scotland. These female offender/patients were predominantly young, single, and with a history of significantly more previous psychiatric admissions than their male counterparts. Before admission to Carstairs, they showed a greater degree of violence towards themselves and other patients. Tennent *et al.* (1976) conducted a large-scale survey of female admissions to the three English special hospitals. 82 per cent of the Broadmoor patients, 38 per cent of the Rampton patients, and 27 per cent of the Moss Side patients, had been admitted directly or indirectly because of the commission of offences. The tendency was for the Broadmoor patients to have had more violent records, to have had a disturbed upbringing, to have been in social class III or IV occupations and to have been nearly always admitted as the consequence of an act of violence. The main diagnoses will have been of schizophrenia or of psychopathy. Patients in Rampton and Moss Side will be broadly similar. They will have come from poor backgrounds, be single, and have spent considerable periods of their lives in mental and subnormality hospitals. The reasons for their admission will most likely have been because of an attack on staff at another hospital. On the whole, the Moss Side inmate will be assessed as of slightly higher intelligence than her Rampton counterpart and the diagnoses in her case may not be clear cut. She is more likely to have been in employment than her Rampton sister and stands and even chance of discharge after five years.

Other background factors

Many workers have described the unstable and impoverished backgrounds from which younger female offenders are drawn (Epps 1951, 1954; Cockburn and Maclay 1965; Goodman and Price 1967; Cowie, Cowie, and Slater 1968). From the evidence in these studies one is forced to conclude that psychopathological elements appear to be more florid and traumatic than in the backgrounds of young male delinquents. It may be, for some of the reasons given earlier, that reactions to female delinquency within the home are more melodramatic and that the memories of these tend to persist in recollections of those most closely involved. One interesting (though not altogether surprising) factor which emerges from a number of studies is the extent to which an impoverished relationship with father or his absence seems to be significant. Riege (1972) compared the attitudes towards parents of twenty-five delinquent girls with those of a matched group of non-delinquent controls. She found, amongst other things, that delinquent girls see their fathers as deficient in giving love and praise. She also found that a significant proportion of the delinquent girls had experienced separation from their fathers, especially during their early adolescent years. Gilbert (1972), in another comparative study of delinquent and non-delinquent girls, also found that affection from father seemed to be a key factor in determining the delinquent girl's self-image and the extent to which this influenced her relationships with the opposite sex.

Finally, we may note a useful study by Felice and Offord (1972) in which they postulated three developmental pathways to delinquency in girls. They examined three groups of girls (eighty in all) in two independent institutions in the United States. On the basis of their investigations they suggest three aetiological typologies (Groupings). *Group I*. The girls in this group would be of average IQ, coming from a small lower-middle-class family showing severe parental psychopathology and family disruption. *Group II*. These would be girls of slightly below average IQ, living in a small town and coming from a poor family containing approximately four siblings. In about half of these cases one of the parents (usually the father) would be alcoholic. (See the comments made earlier about the significance of the role of fathers.) The girls in this group would have 50 per cent chance of having a sibling with some psycho-social difficulty. *Group III*. Would contain the black girl of low IQ. She would come from a very large, very poor family, live in a metropolitan centre, would most likely be illegitimate and have been raised by mother alone or by other relatives. Other siblings would show marked disturbance and would probably be sisters rather than brothers.

General treatment considerations

Even though there may be division of opinion as to causes, few would dispute that a large number of female offenders come from very unstable and unhappy backgrounds and show marked signs of disturbance. There is an important and infrequently mentioned consequence of these facts, namely, that as Gibbens (1971) points out, 'maladjusted women may not come to notice themselves, but they have a powerful influence in producing the next generation of delinquent boys.'

It is well known that women do not respond well to incarceration; in fact they seem to take to it less amenably than men. Smith (1974) notes how imprisonment of women is complicated by the not infrequent accompaniment of pregnancy and traumatic sequelae for children and spouse. Gibbs (1971), whilst noting that the *shorter*-term effects of imprisonment on the family did not seem to be as serious as had been anticipated, considered that the *long*-term effects were very damaging. Even though admission to ordinary or special psychiatric hospitals may, for some observers, seem to be merely compounding the worst aspects of labelling, this, and the possibility of some form of constructive treatment, must seem better than the incarceration of highly disturbed women in penal institutions where the staff, however much they may wish to be helpful, have not the facilities for the intensive care required. It has been observed that in comparison with the little that is done in prison for male offenders, even less seems to be done to provide women with industrial rehabilitation to enable them to compete in the outside world. Hall Williams (1970), in noting the lack of work opportunities in prisons, such as Holloway, acknowledges that the staff, in evidence to the Royal Commission on the Penal System (interestingly, now defunct), argued for the introduction of factory-type conditions. Such opportunities do now exist for men, in prisons such as Coldingley. The young female offender is likely to find herself in much the same position as her older counterpart. Richardson (1969) commented upon the concentration on domestic tasks in what were then girl's Approved Schools (now Community Homes). Smart (1976) observes that these attitudes reflect the still widely held view that, on the whole, girls and women should only be trained for domestic and similar roles. She suggests that female offenders 'experience all the disadvantages of the traditional female role (i.e. drudgery, boredom, limited horizons) without the "advantages" (i.e. romance, flirtation, and sexual encounters)'. Though one may not entirely agree with what she implies are universally held feminine aspirations, nevertheless her point is worth noting. Because the regimes in many institutions for women seem to lack imagination and purpose, it is hardly surprising that when they return from these institutions to the community they are as ill equipped to cope with our complex and changing society as when they entered them. A useful account of some of the practical and emotional difficulties encountered and how these may be alleviated is given by my colleague Mark Monger (Monger 1967). The conclusions contained in a number of studies, that a large proportion of female offenders have experienced very poor relationships with fathers or father figures prompts the suggestion that we probably do not capitalize sufficiently on the use of male staff for work with them. Happily, attitudes are changing. A male governor has now been appointed to a girls' Borstal, and reciprocally, a woman has been appointed to be in charge of a remand centre whose population is largely male. In Scotland, a similar female appointment has recently been made. Parsloe (1972), in an important article on cross-sex supervision in the probation service, reminds us that originally, in the days of the old Police Court Mission, men did supervise women and children. As early as 1909, it had been noted that male probation officers had successfully supervised women offenders. Gradually this flexible and sensible arrangement came to be eroded, and it was not until amending legislation was introduced in 1967 that male probation officers were again enabled to supervise women offenders. It has of course been the practice for many years for men to deal with women clients presenting with marital problems. One wonders why this curious anomaly was sustained for so long? Arguments against male officers being involved with female offenders under statutory supervision tended to rely on the problems of blackmail or sexual advances. This seems to be a curious belief and a weak position in the light of their freedom to work with non-statutory clients. Parsloe has some perceptive things to say about the positive use of such male-female relationships, but at the same time alerts us to the possibilities of harmful phantasies. 'Women clients, however, who make advances to male officers tend to be seen as seductive, dangerous, scheming women, and because the stereotype of the passive little woman dies hard, these women who so unnaturally make the advances are regarded with some fascination but also with fear.'

In this important area of sexuality, Parsloe suggests that 'achieving the purpose of the relationship may involve the use of sexual feelings, but the purpose in itself is not a sexual one . . . Whatever the problems of the arousal of sexual feelings between officer and client, such feelings are real, are appropriate to two adults, and provide a spur for growth.'

It would seem that Parsloe's comments have applicability to a

wide range of female offenders, but particularly those damaged in their early lives as a result of poor *paternal* relationships. It is worth noting here that a number of studies have
recorded a very high incidence of such poor relationships in
the backgrounds of prostitutes. As Glover put it many years
ago in his seminal paper on *The Psychopathology of Prostitution*
(1957): 'There exists an acute disappointment with the father,
while the relation to the mother is in its own way strongly
impregnated with hostility. These facts will be found of some
significance when we come to estimate the unconscious
homosexual factor in prostitution.'

We know, therefore, that many women offenders are much
in need of a relationship with someone of the opposite sex – a
relationship that is in Parsloe's words, 'caring, reasonably persistent and non-exploitive'. This element of persistence is
developed further by Scott (1977). He says that the

> 'hostile female makes the male therapist a ready target for
> past abuses from males, which often include: father, step-
> fathers (usually sexual abuse), brothers, boyfriends, hus-
> bands (common law), pimps, judges and policemen . . . it is
> naive for the therapist to assume a friendly, warm, positive
> regard approach will be sufficient . . . the period of testing
> can take several months, before a realisation that personal
> interest of the therapist is genuine . . . my firm impression is
> that for the most female offenders, a male therapist is pref-
> erable to a female therapist, since the negative relationships
> are the principal hurdle to be circumvented or "taken
> down".'

As with a number of other persistent offenders – for example psychopaths, we must be prepared for failure and the
need to go on trying (see Elder 1972).

Concluding comments

It would seem that apart from a minute proportion, few
female offenders need to be kept in conditions of maximum
security; and even in circumstances where this is necessary it

should be possible to try to rebuild and promote relationships along the lines suggested above. This relationship building should of course be attempted as often as possible in the community, and institutional care used only as a last resort. In addition, incarceration in all-female communities can surely only serve to compound these relationship problems? One can easily see how pervasive can be the 'bitchiness' that exists in some 'total' institutions for females. It may be that the feminist movement will continue to work for change in this as in other areas; in this respect some shift towards parity with men is all to the good. From time to time, however, the more strident, dogmatic, and emotional utterances of the less well-informed feminists probably does the movement more harm than good. There is the danger that the best critical work of the movement (as evidenced in the analyses by Smart for example) could be lost with the result that attitudes (both male and female) towards female offenders could harden and even become worse than they are.

When one surveys all the literature and takes opinion, one concludes that there is no single, simple theory that can adequately account for the sex differences in female/male offending. There is a complex web of bio-psycho-social forces that impinge to bring about these differences. It would therefore be unwise in the present stage of our knowledge to take an entrenched and blinkered position on either side of the psychological (determinist) – sociological (feminist) fence. It is just because female offending is such a complex and emotive subject that there are good arguments for studying it as a topic in its own right.

References

Adler, F. (1975) *Sisters in Crime. The Rise of the New Female Criminal.* New York: McGraw Hill.

Barack, L.I. and Widem, C.S. (1978) Eysenck's Theory of Criminality Applied to Women Awaiting Trial. *Brit. J. Psychiat.* **133**: 452–56.

Bardwick, J.M. (1974) *The Sex Hormones, the Central Nervous*

System and Affect Variability in Humans. In V. Franks and V. Burtle (eds) *Women in Therapy.* New York: Brunner-Mazel. Quoted in Skynner (1976).

Bluglass, R. (1978) Infanticide. *Bulletin Roy. Coll. Psychiatrists* August: 139–41.

Brooks, P.W. and Mitchell, G. (1975) A Fifteen-Year Review of Female Admissions to Carstairs State Hospital. *Brit. J. Psychiat.* **127**: 448–55.

Cockburn, J.J. and Maclay, I. (1965) Sex Differentials in Juvenile Delinquency. *Brit. J. Criminol.* **5**: 289–308.

Cowie, J., Cowie, V., and Slater, E.T.O. (1968) *Delinquency in Girls.* London: Heincmann.

Dalton, K. (1961) Menstruation and Crime. *Brit. Med. J.* **2**: 1752–753.

—— (1964) *The Premenstrual Syndrome.* London: Heinemann.

D'Orbán, P.T. (1971) Social and Psychiatric Aspects of Female Crime. *Med. Sci. Law* **11**: 104–16.

—— (1972) Baby Stealing. *Brit. Med. J.* 10 June 1972: 635–39.

—— (1976) Child Stealing: A Typology of Female Offenders. *Brit. J. Criminol.* **16**: 275–81.

Elder, P.D. (1972) House for Ex-Borstal Girls – An Exploratory Project. *Brit. J. Criminol.* **22**: 357–74.

Epps, P. (1951) A Preliminary Survey of 300 Female Delinquents in Borstal Institutions. *Brit. J. Delinq.* **1**: 187–97.

—— (1954) A Further Survey of Female Delinquents Undergoing Borstal Training. *Brit. J. Delinq.* **4**: 265–71.

—— (1962) In Gibbens and Prince (1962).

Epps, P. and Parnell, R.W. (1952) Physique and Temperament of Women Delinquents Compared with Women Undergraduates. *Brit. J. Med. Psychol.* **25**: 249–55.

Felice, M. and Offord, D.R. (1972) Three Developmental Pathways to Delinquency in Girls. *Brit. J. Criminol.* **12**: 375–89.

Ford, C.S. and Beach, F.A. (1965) *Patterns of Sexual Behaviour.* London: Methuen.

Gibbens, T.C.N. (1959) Supervision and Probation of Adolescent Girls. *Brit. J. Delinq.* **10**: 84–103.

—— (1969) The Delinquent and His Brain. *Proc. Roy. Soc. Med.*

62: 57–60.

—— (1971) *Female Offenders*. In T. Silverstone and B. Barraclough (eds) *Contemporary Psychiatry*. Ashford: Headley Brothers.

Gibbens, T.C.N. and Prince, J. (1962) *Shoplifting*. London: ISTD.

Gibbens, T.C.N. and Silberman, M. (1960) The Clients of Prostitutes. *Brit. J. Vener. Dis.* **36**: 113–17.

Gibbens, T.C.N., Palmer, C. and Prince, J. (1971) Mental Health Aspects of Shoplifting. *Brit. Med. J.* **3**: 612–15.

Gibbs, C. (1971) The Effect of the Imprisonment of Women upon Their Children. *Brit. J. Criminol.* **11**: 113–30.

Gilbert, J. (1972) Delinquent (Approved School) and Non-Delinquent (Secondary Modern School) Girls. *Brit. J. Criminol.* **12**: 325–56.

Glover, E. (1957) *Psychopathology of Prostitution*. London: ISTD.

Goodman, N. and Price, J. (1967) *Studies of Female Offenders. Home Office Studies in the Causes of Delinquency and the Treatment of Offenders*. Home Office Research Unit. London: HMSO.

Guze, S.B. (1976) *Criminality and Psychiatric Disorders*. Oxford: Oxford University Press.

Hall Williams, J.E. (1970) *The English Penal System in Transition*. London: Butterworths.

Hands, J., Herbert, V., and Tennent, G. (1974) Menstruation and Behaviour in a Special Hospital. *Med. Sci. Law* **14**: 32–5.

Home Office and DHSS (1975) *Report of the Committee on Mentally Abnormal Offenders. (Butler Committee)*. Cmnd. 6244. London: HMSO.

Home Office (1976) *Criminal Statistics for England and Wales. 1975*. Cmnd. 6566. London: HMSO.

—— (1977) *Prisons and the Prisoner. The Work of the Prison Service in England and Wales*. London: HMSO.

—— (1978) *Report on the Work of the Prison Department. 1977*. Cmnd. 7290. London: HMSO.

Hopkins, J.H. (1969) The Lesbian Personality. *Brit. J. Psychiat.* **115**: 1433–436.

Hunter, J. (1973) The Problem of Baby Stealing. *Soc. Wk.*

Today. **4**: 266–68.

Jones, H. (1965) *Crime and the Penal System* (3rd edition). London: University Tutorial Press.

Kalven, H. and Zeisel, H. (1966) *The American Jury*. Boston: Little Brown.

Kenyon, F.E. (1968) Studies on Female Homosexuality. *Brit. J. Psychiat.* **114**: 1137–150.

—— (1975) *Homosexuality in the Female*. In T. Silverstone and B. Barraclough (eds) *Contemporary Psychiatry*. Ashford: Headley Brothers.

Kestenbaum, S.E. (1977) Womens' Liberation for Women Offenders. *Soc. Casework.* **58**: 77–83.

Loewenstein, S. (1978) An Overview of Some Aspects of Female Sexuality. *Soc. Casework* **59**: 106–14.

Mannheim, H. (1965) *Comparative Criminology (Vol. II)*. London: Routledge and Kegan Paul.

Mawby, R.I. (1977) Sexual Discrimination and the Law. *Probation* **24**: 39–43.

May, D. (1977) Delinquent Girls before the Courts. *Med. Sci. Law* **17**: 203–12.

Mitchell, G. and Murphy, J.B. (1975) A Survey of Female Patients in Carstairs State Hospital. *Brit. J. Psychiat.* **127**: 445–47.

Monger, M. (1967) *Casework in After-Care*. London: Butterworths.

Parsloe, P. (1972) Cross-Sex Supervision in the Probation and After-Care Service. *Brit. J. Criminol.* **12**: 269–79.

Pollak, O. (1961) *The Criminality of Women*. New York: S.A. Barnes.

Prins. H.A. (1973) *Criminal Behaviour*. London: Pitman.

Richardson, H. (1969) *Adolescent Girls in Approved Schools*. London: Routledge and Kegan Paul.

Riege, M.G. (1972) Parental Affection and Juvenile Delinquency in Girls. *Brit. J. Criminol.* **12**: 55–73.

Scott, E.M. (1977) Therapy with Female Offenders. *Int. J. Off. Ther. and Comp. Criminol.* **21**: 208–20.

Skynner, A.C.R. (1976) *One Flesh: Separate Persons*. London: Constable.

Smart, C. (1976) *Women. Crime and Criminology. A Feminist Critique.* London: Routledge and Kegan Paul.

—— (1979) The New Female Criminal: Reality or Myth? *Brit. J. Criminol.* **19**: 50–9.

Smith, A.D. (1962) *Women in Prison.* London: Stevens.

—— (1974) The Woman Offender. In L. Blom-Cooper (ed.) *Progress in Penal Reform.* Oxford: Oxford University Press.

Tennent, G., Parker, E., McGrath, P., McDougall, J., and Street, D. (1976) Female Patients in the Three Special Hospitals: A Demographic Survey of Admissions 1961–65. *Med. Sci. Law* **16**: 200–08.

Walker, N. (1968) *Crime and Punishment in Britain* (2nd edition). Edinburgh: Edinburgh University Press.

Walker, N. and McCabe, S. (1973) *Crime and Insanity in England. (Vol. 2).* Edinburgh: Edinburgh University Press.

Winnick, H. and Horowitz, M. (1961) The Problem of Infanticide. *Brit. J. Criminol.* **2**: 40–52.

Working Party on Vagrancy and Street Offences (1974) London: HMSO.

SUGGESTED FURTHER READING

On violence towards children and violence in the family

Borland, M. (ed.) *Violence in the Family.* Manchester: Manchester University Press.

Franklin, A.W. (ed.) (1975) *Concerning Child Abuse.* Edinburgh: Churchill Livingstone.

Helfer, R.E., and Kempe, C.H. (eds.) (1974) *The Battered Child* (2nd edition). Chicago: Chicago University Press.

Martin, J.P. (ed.) (1978) *Violence and the Family.* London: John Wiley.

Renvoize, J. (1978) *Web of Violence.* London: Routledge and Kegan Paul.

Smith, S. (1975) *The Battered Child Syndrome.* London: Butterworths.

On Women and mental illness

Chesler, P. (1974) *Women and Madness.* London: Allen Lane.
Miller, J.B. (1973) *Psychoanalysis and Women:* Harmondsworth:
  Penguin.

Aspects of the imprisonment of women

Arrowsmith, P. (1970) *Somewhere Like This.* London: W.H.
  Allen.
Giallombardo, R. (1966) *Society of Women: A Study of a Woman's
  Prison.* New York: John Wiley.
Kassebaum, G. (1966) *Women's Prison.* London: Weidenfeld
  and Nicolson.

CHAPTER ELEVEN

Conclusions and some thoughts on reforms

Attempt the end, and never stand to doubt;
Nothing's so hard, but search will find it out.
ROBERT HERRICK

Life is the art of drawing sufficient conclusions from insufficient premises.
SAMUEL BUTLER

In preceding chapters I have attempted to outline some
aspects of the relationship between mental disorder and
criminality from a clinical and judicial point of view. I have also
examined in some detail certain characteristics of those variously labelled as offenders, deviants, or patients. It will have
become clear that such individuals may be dealt with in a
variety of ways and that their disposal through the penal or
hospital system may more often than not rely on chance factors
than on any real planning that has regard for society's, and
their own, best interests. Their almost serendipitous disposal
throws into sharp relief issues of treatment versus punishment, some of which were adverted to in Chapter 2. Walker
(1976) makes an important point in this connection. He suggests that the current indulgence in discrediting treatment

> 'owes its appeal to a mixture of accusations – compulsion,
> pseudo-consent, indeterminacy in sentencing, spurious-
> ness, ineffectiveness, inhumanity, degradation, interfer-
> ence with the integrity of the personality – not all of which
> can be levelled at all kinds of treatment *but all of which can be*

conflated into an ambiguous indictment [my italics].'

They are also exacerbated by the fact that we do not question often enough the meaning of treatment. Do we merely mean ease of management (for ourselves – running an 'easy nick'?). In this connection, Scott (1975) suggests that 'we must learn the gentle art of controlling without punishing, and at the same time helping without being afraid of unpopularity and without needing immediate gratification.' Should we be asking more frequently is this form of treatment likely to be effective, and if so what resources do we require to implement it? I shall comment on some of these issues under three headings: legislative and administrative reforms; resources; remedies and issues arising.

Legislative and administrative reforms

In the conclusion to Chapter 2, I referred to the dilemma inherent in determining the best interests of the individual as against the best interests of the community. Many people now consider that in recent years the rights of the individual have been overridden by the needs of the community, especially the rights of those mentally disordered offenders found to be in need of long-term detention. The Butler Committee (Home Office and DHSS 1975) showed a keen awareness of some of these problems and some of their proposals for remedy were referred to in Chapter 2. Gostin (1977), on behalf of MIND (NAMH), is even more critical and cites numerous cases in which he considers that offenders' rights have been abrogated. However, some of his proposals for advocacy and for surveillance of patients' rights, though necessary, will not change public attitudes of apathy and fear towards those who are dually labelled as 'mad' and 'bad'. As I have suggested elsewhere, it would be 'a matter of much regret if MIND in the furtherance of its campaign for patients' rights paid less attention to its long-standing and well-known interest in the promotion of education and understanding in the mental health field' (Prins 1977). This recent growing concern has been recognized by the Government in its White Paper: *Review of the*

Mental Health Act, 1959 (DHSS 1978). The main proposals for reform concerning offender/patients are contained in Chapters 2, 5, and 6; the most important of these are now summarized.

POLICE POWERS

The Government is in favour of the retention of Section 136 of the Mental Health Act, 1959. They emphasize, however, that a police station should only be used as a 'place of safety' as a last resort. They also recommend that its use should be monitored mainly through the use of a statutory form which would require reasons to be given for the use of the section in any particular case. Such a form is already in informal use in one police area.

DEFINITIONS AND COURTS' POWERS UNDER SECTIONS 60 AND 65*

(1) For patients said to be suffering from psychopathic disorder or mental handicap there should be a requirement, both on admission to hospital and at renewal of detention, of likelihood of benefit from treatment. This proposal arises from the opinion expressed elsewhere in the White Paper that the term *psychopathic disorder* should be retained in the Act. (See discussion in Chapter 5.) However, the White Paper does suggest that the words 'and requires or is susceptible to treatment' should be omitted from the *definition* but that the requirement that there is likelihood of benefit from treatment should be incorporated into the *criteria* for compulsory admission and renewal of detention for persons suffering from psychopathic disorder. This would in some ways get round the often cited 'circular argument' problem in relation to the definition of psychopathy and it would shift the emphasis on to issues of possible treatability. Some may consider that this is merely a tinkering with a fundamental problem, but it seems to me to be a fair compromise given the realities and constraints

---

* The current provisions are set out briefly in Chapter 4.

of the present state of knowledge and skill in the area of psychopathy. In passing, we should also note here, that the Government propose that alcohol and drug dependence *in themselves* and sexual deviancy *in itself* should be excluded from the terms of the Act. The White Paper does recognize, however, that in certain instances it may be appropriate to detain a person on the grounds of mental disorder arising from, or suspected to arise from, alcohol or drug dependence or from the withdrawal of alcohol. It also acknowledges that when a mentally disordered person commits a *sexual offence* it should still be open to the court to make a hospital order if the normal conditions for making such an order are satisfied. These proposals, if implemented, would help to remove some of the ambiguities and uncertainties in the current classification of alcohol, drugs, and sex offending referred to in Chapter 3.

(2) The present periods of detention under Section 60 (in respect of both admission and renewal) should be halved. They are currently for one year.

(3) Medical recommendations made for the purpose of Section 60 should *not* be made by two doctors from the *same* prison, hospital, or other institution.

SECTION 65

(1) Section 65 should be reworded in order to make the essential purpose of a restriction order more clear – namely to protect the public from serious harm. This is a helpful proposal and would go some way towards making a clearer distinction between the offender who is really dangerous and the offender who merely has a high nuisance value. (See discussion in Chapter 6.)

(2) The present powers that afford flexibility in relation to the duration of restriction orders should be retained.

(3) Responsible medical officers (RMOs) should be required *by Statute* to make an annual report on each of their restricted patients (my italics).

(4) New arrangements should be introduced to enable receiving hospitals to make representations to a court against the

making of a restriction order, if the hospital considers that such an order would make for particular difficulties. Guidance should also be issued followlng legislation to encourage hospital staff and supervising officers to keep in close contact in cases where restricted patients have been recalled to hospital. These two aspects involve questions concerning resources and team work and will be the subject of further comment.

SECTIONS 72, 73, AND 74

(1) Restriction under Section 74 should cease to apply on what would have been the earliest date of release of a prisoner transferred to hospital under Section 72.

(2) Prisoners transferred to hospital under Section 72, who are thought to require detention after what would have been their earliest date of release from prison, should be treated as if admitted to hospital on that date under Section 26, but with the usual procedures for the making of a Section 26 order being waived.

POWERS OF MENTAL HEALTH REVIEW TRIBUNALS IN RELATION TO DETAINED PATIENTS

The opportunities for patients detained under Section 60 and 65 to refer their cases to a Tribunal should be increased in line with the proposed restrictions in the periods of detention, except that patients detained under Section 65 should not have the right to request reference to a Tribunal within the first twelve months. Automatic reviews by Tribunals for unrestricted patients should take place after six months, then within three years of admission and at three-yearly intervals thereafter. The Home Secretary should be required to refer the case of a restricted patient automatically to a Tribunal at the end of any three-year period in which the case has not been otherwise referred.

REMANDS TO HOSPITAL AND INTERIM HOSPITAL ORDERS

I noted in Chapter 4 that the Butler Committee wished to see a more flexible system of remands to be available. The White Paper contains no firm proposal on this issue but refers to the Consultative Document *Remands in Hospital and Interim Hospital Orders* that has recently been circulated to a wide range of interested parties. The implementation of such a proposal has resource implications and throws up the whole question of the use of prison or hospital for the observation, detention, and treatment of offender/patients. I referred to these difficulties briefly in Chapter 4, but will now consider them here in more detail.

Resources

THE PRISON OR HOSPITAL ISSUE

Parker and Tennent (1979) examined the operation of *Part V* of the Mental Health Act, 1959 for the periods 1962–64 and 1972–74 and in particular the part the courts, the ordinary psychiatric and subnormality hospitals, the Special Hospitals, and the prisons play in the disposal of mentally abnormal offenders. They show that the intention built into the Act of vesting the care of such offenders in the NHS is currently not being met. The Courts have been making much less use of the Act for these offenders during the last few years. In 1966, 1,440 hospital orders were made by courts under Section 60, whereas in 1976, there were only 924 (DHSS 1978). In 1977, the number of hospital orders made without restriction on the recommendation of prison medical officers fell by about 13 per cent and the number with restriction fell by over 43 per cent.

> 'These figures illustrate the increasing difficulty being experienced by medical officers in finding hospitals willing to receive and treat their mentally disordered patients, particularly in those cases where courts consider an order restricting discharge from hospital to be necessary. Where a

suitable hospital place cannot be found, courts often feel that there is no alternative to a custodial sentence, and the burden of caring for the persons concerned falls on the prison medical officer and his or her staff.'

(Home Office 1978)

In the light of this concern it is of interest to note that Pope and Gibbens (1979) have recently published their survey of the problem in four maximum security prisons during the period 1972–73. They concluded that these mentally disordered inmates did not constitute any more than their fair share of 'all those seen as either disruptive or presenting management problems, probably less'. They suggest that the problem is more complex than might appear at first sight and is largely influenced by the extent of mental disorder in the prisons at any one time, the action taken to deal with it, and the way the disruptive behaviour is viewed by staff. It seems likely that staff reaction is probably the most influential factor. In those institutions where there are good staff support facilities and an easy flow of information it would seem likely that even quite seriously disruptive behaviour can be tolerated and dealt with.

It is possible to account for the dimunition in the number of hospital orders in the following way.

(1) *Changes that have occurred in the long-term care of mental hospital patients in the last twenty years.* More patients are now admitted informally and for much shorter periods. Very few hospitals now operate locked wards, or if they do, they use them very occasionally (Bluglass 1978).

(2) In the light of these developments, *staff have become increasingly reluctant to treat patients they fear may be violent or disruptive and for whom they have not the necessary secure facilities.* Some of this reluctance springs from a genuine concern amongst the nursing staff that they may not have the skills required to deal with such patients, but it is also true to say that refusal has also been used as a springboard for arguments for improvements in general pay and working conditions. Gunn (1977) puts the matter in context: 'The truth is that most mental hospitals are demoralised . . . they have

an air of doom and decline. To suggest, as many staff feel is being suggested, that they should go back to a custodial role is too much for them to bear.'

(3) *In addition, some consultants are reluctant to accept restricted patients because of the additional controls they are expected to exercise over home leave or discharge.* They also consider that such orders result in their having to continue to be responsible for offender/patients for whom they feel they can offer no effective treatment (Gostin 1977; Bowden 1977).

(4) *Difficulties in obtaining beds in the Special Hospitals.*

THE ROLE OF THE SPECIAL HOSPITALS

The historical development of the Special Hospitals in England and Wales has been well documented (Greenland 1969; Walker and McCabe 1973; Gostin 1977). (Some aspects of the development of the State Hospital for Scotland at Carstairs may be found in the report of an enquiry into that institution published in 1977 (Scottish Home Department 1977).) In England and Wales, the Secretary of State for Social Services is responsible under Section 40 of the National Health Reorganisation Act, 1973, for providing and maintaining 'establishments for persons subject to detention under the Mental Health Act, 1959, who, in his opinion, require treatment under conditions of special security on account of their dangerous, violent or criminal propensities'. It is important to note here that approximately one third of all patients in Special Hospitals are *not* offenders but have been admitted under compulsory powers under *Part IV* of the Mental Health Act; most of these admissions are from other psychiatric hospitals because of difficult or disruptive behaviour (Home Office and DHSS: para. 2.33). The Special Hospitals, unlike all other hospitals, are provided and managed directly by the Department of Health and Social Security. Because of this (and for other reasons to be discussed shortly) they tend to suffer from a certain degree of insularity and isolation. Gostin (1977) quotes evidence from reports of the Hospital Advisory Service

(HAS) that Broadmoor (for example) 'has an isolated and inward-looking culture' and that relationships between the consultant staff and referring or receiving local psychiatric hospitals have not been as open and cooperative as they might have been.

There are at present three long established Special Hospitals which serve the whole of England and Wales – Broadmoor in Berkshire, Rampton in Nottinghamshire, and Moss Side in Lancashire. A fourth – adjacent to Moss Side – is under construction and is partly occupied. Broadmoor caters mainly for mentally ill and psychopathic patients, accommodating some 750 at the present time. In recent years a number of public statements have been made expressing much concern about Broadmoor's gross overcrowding and antiquated accommodation (Gostin 1977). Rampton caters mainly for subnormal and psychopathic patients. It has been in the public eye recently because of widely publicized allegations of physical abuse of patients. These are currently the subject of investigation by the authorities and further comment, even conjectural, would be quite inappropriate as the matter is best regarded as *sub judice*. Rampton suffers from the problems inherent in trying to provide a regime of both containment and rehabilitation for a very mixed patient population: from the severely subnormal patient at one end of the spectrum to the fairly intelligent psychopath at the other. A large proportion of the subnormal patients and some of the psychopathic do not really need to be in Rampton, but ordinary subnormality hospitals and the local authorities are reluctant to make provision for them. The nationwide catchment areas of all the Special Hospitals makes contact with relatives and other interested parties very difficult. This is likely to compound an already difficult situation where relationships between patients, relatives, and others may be fraught or have broken down.

Moss Side Hospital houses some 1,100 mainly subnormal residents and the fourth hospital, Park Lane, which at present houses some 70 patients (mainly from Broadmoor), will eventually take around 400, mainly mentally ill and psychopathic patients (Locke 1978).

Even the most severe critics of the special hospitals would admit that they have a tremendously difficult task in trying to combine containment, clinical treatment, and rehabilitation. It is probably no exaggeration to suggest that as a community we have yet to decide whether these institutions are hospitals or prisons. Certainly, to the uninitiated observer, the atmosphere and regime would appear to be more indicative of a prison than a hospital. The nursing staff are members of the Prison Officers' Association and formal uniforms of one kind or another are usually worn. Keys are much in evidence and nursing staffs quite naturally see a large part of their role as being that of custodians. Inevitably, stresses arise when they are also asked to act as agents of therapy and rehabilitation. There is no doubt that the Special Hospitals have to contain some highly dangerous individuals, but it is important to emphasize once again that they also have to contain a not inconsiderable number of offender/patients whose potential for dangerous behaviour is minimal. As already indicated, this is because the ordinary psychiatric and subnormality hospitals are reluctant to accept patients carrying an 'offender' label. Parker and Tennent (1979) quote a written Parliamentary answer which indicates that in 1977, of the 184 special hospital patients awaiting transfer at the beginning of May, 99 had been waiting less than twelve months, 57 had been waiting between one and two years, 17 had been waiting two and three years, and 11 had been waiting longer than three years.

I have already referred to the isolated position of the Special Hospitals. There is a further and very important point to be made in this connection, namely that their geographical isolation renders them particularly vulnerable to the possibilities of staff in-breeding. It is not uncommon to find that some families have served the hospitals as nurses or other workers for two or more generations. Although this may give the advantage of continuity of service, there is also the danger of prejudice, complacency, and narrowness of outlook developing, to say nothing of the possibilities of a too-ready acceptance of possible abuses of privilege. From the point of view of management, the Special Hospitals have tended to move from being essentially autocratically or idiosyncratically run institutions to what might best be described as 'faceless' democracies. For example, it has been said that in order to find the person accountable to the DHSS for the management of Rampton, one has to seek him in an office at that Department's headquarters in London! In recent years, in many psychiatric and subnormality hospitals, there has been a move to abolish the position and role of medical superintendent and to substitute a flexible and shared democratic management structure. In many cases this has followed the pattern adopted in some 'therapeutic communities'. Unfortunately, the flow of information between all parties that is so essential for the success of such enterprises has not always been forthcoming. Indeed, the report of the enquiry into the escape of two patients from Carstairs Hospital, referred to earlier, highlights a lack of information flow and interdisciplinary staff communication as one of the important factors in the background to the patients' escape plans.

It is interesting to note in Special Hospitals where the position of medical superintendent has been maintained (for example at Broadmoor) that despite overcrowding and the occasional protest from patients, their relatives, and/or pressure groups, it has proved possible to provide some kind of therapeutic regime. The reason for this may be that Broadmoor's inmate population is reasonably homogenous and that treatment regimes based upon a degree of homogeneity are easier to establish and maintain. Despite this, it seems clear that the ethos of large 'total' institutions like our Special Hospitals militates against easy communication flow and patient self-help. Maxwell Jones (1979) puts it very succinctly when he says:

> 'Virtually everyone in the mental health field knows that the latent potential of "patients" to help themselves is not a high priority; . . . It is quite sickening to see the administration, both medical and non-medical, deciding what is "best" for "patients" – often not even consulting the staff who are in daily contact with "patients" far less the "patients" themselves.'

It would of course be quite unrealistic to attempt to graft a therapeutic community model on to our Special Hospitals 'wholesale' because there are obvious limitations to a completely open democratic process in such institutions. However, it is possible to facilitate within limits a more democratic regime. As Morrice (1979) puts it: 'It is facilitated by opening channels of communication vertically and horizontally, encouraging face to face encounters and by sharing in a relevant way the responsibility for decisions.' A good example of what can be achieved, albeit in a maximum security *prison* setting, can be seen in the work of the special unit at Barlinnie prison in Glasgow. From the few accounts that are available it would seem that inmates hitherto considered to be intractably violent, disruptive, and beyond rehabilitation could not only become model prisoners but could also develop highly creative talents.

> 'Prisoners and staff lived, worked and played together, without bossiness and all the other barriers to interpersonal relationships. Not only did violence disappear but rehabilitation became a reality . . . The experiment was unbelievably successful and, being successful, damned itself. Introduced initially as a method of removing violent and disruptive individuals from other prisons, it demonstrated that the whole prison system was wrong . . .'
>
> (Whitehead 1979)

The experiment was terminated in its original format largely as a result of what appears to have been a single incident of drug smuggling. One cannot but feel that this single incident was used to end a regime which, by its success, had proved the ineffectiveness of more harsh and traditional methods of incarceration.

It would seem then that even those considered to be the most violent and disruptive of inmates can be handled humanely within large maximum security institutions in small 'therapeutic community' type units. Morrice (1979) reminds us of Schumacher's advice that 'small is beautiful'; it may be that some of the proposals I make shortly for smaller 'transitional communities' would give support for Schumacher's view. Smaller units offering secure or semi-secure accommodation within the ordinary hospital system would also go some way towards meeting the needs of some of these offender/patients. The need for this type of provision is now considered in some detail.

SECURE ACCOMMODATION

In July 1974, the Bulter Committee produced an *Interim Report* (Home Office and DHSS 1974) which reiterated suggestions made by a committee some thirteen years earlier (Ministry of Health 1961). These were to the effect that urgent consideration should be given to the establishment of regional secure units located in some regional psychiatric hospitals and that regional health authorities should also make provision for a variety of units allowing for flexibility of treatment. It also recommended the setting up of special diagnostic centres which would provide assessment and advice on the management of especially difficult cases. Although these recommendations were accepted by the Government, only one such centre was established (The Northgate Clinic at Hendon in North-West London, but this centre has tended to concentrate its work mainly on the problems of adolescents). The Butler Committee in its *Interim Report* recommended that urgent priority should be given to establishing NHS Regional Secure Units offering some 2,000 places overall. A year earlier an internal DHSS working party, chaired by Dr J. Glancy, had presented its own report on the need for secure accommodation in NHS Hospitals; they also recognized the need for secure *units* for a small proportion of the psychiatric hospital population and calculated that the need would be for some 1,000 beds in England and Wales (DHSS 1973). In 1974, the Government accepted the proposals of both these committees and allocated specific funds for their construction. They also gave a clear indication that health authorities should have promoted them by 1976 or 1977. In the meantime, until these new long-term units were established, interim security arrangements should be made.

It is sad to report that, to date, little progress has been made in establishing either the regional secure units or interim secure facilities. Bluglass (1978) reports that 'some six or seven units are in a planning stage but no building has yet started, and most are probably a long way from this position.' The reasons are not hard to find. As already indicated, there is considerable reluctance on the part of hospital staffs at all levels to deal with such patients, and the greatest pressure against implementation has tended to come from the nursing unions. Union pressure has severely restricted the functioning of the interim unit at Prestwich Hospital; see *The Guardian* 14 November 1977 and discussion above. There is, however, a potentially more serious implication. This concerns the nature of the relationship between central and local government. It would appear that despite the provisions of clearly earmarked funds, some health authorities have contrived not to use them at all and in some areas they have been made available for other purposes. The relationships between central and local authorities have always been delicate and finely poised. Their history shows a reluctance on the part of central authorities to overcontrol. However, it would seem that there may be considerable dangers in this element of 'laissez-faire' in the mental health field and there are good grounds for suggesting that central government should be more directive. Support for this contention comes from the sadly recurring theme in recent years of the serious faults and weaknesses which have been revealed as a result of a number of enquiries into the working of psychiatric and subnormality hospitals. The problems faced by the Special Hospitals have already been mentioned and recently the gross overcrowding at Broadmoor has received renewed publicity. This occurred as a result of four patients (aided by the National Association for Mental Health (MIND)) taking their cases to the European Commission on Human Rights. The Commission admitted their applications under those articles dealing with inhuman and degrading treatments and the lawfulness or otherwise of detention. In the meantime, the Commission agreed to send an investigation team to examine conditions at Broadmoor.

Temporary relief might have been afforded by the establishment of interim secure accomodation units but their progress has not fared any better. To date, some three or four
hospitals have established such units but their functioning has
to some extent again been vitiated by the opposition of the
unions and by staff conflict (see earlier discussion). However,
Higgins (1979) and Faulk (1979), in recent accounts of units at
Rainhill, Merseyside, and in Hampshire respectively, indicate
that some little progress has been made. Their accounts of the
likely difficulties to be encountered in running such centres
serve as useful models for the problems that might be met in
establishing Regional Secure Units. A further and equally
important difficulty that has emerged in thinking about the
regimes of interim secure units concerns misunderstandings
as to the types of patients they should receive. This is because
the guidelines given in various reports have been interpreted
in a variety of ways by those concerned in establishing them.
The major misunderstanding seems to be that these units are
for dangerous patients, whereas they are intended to cater for
the *disruptive* rather than the dangerous individual. Moreover,
the general public on hearing that such accommodation is to be
provided are filled with apprehension and 'Fantasies of murderers and rapists on the rampage in local housing estates have
not always been relieved by good public relations and education' (Bluglass 1978).

Remedies, and issues arising

We can now identify two distinct but overlapping groups of
offender/patients for whom provision needs to be made. First,
there are the patients who need secure conditions for their
management because they exhibit dangerous behaviour or
potential for such behaviour. The Butler Committee considered that a number of these would need to be detained in
prison and they suggested a new form of indeterminate sentence (see Chapter 6). The case of Mawdsley quoted in Chapter
1 would no doubt come under this category. However, the

indeterminacy of the sentence permits the possibility of allowance being made for changes in behaviour so that flexible discharge procedures can be used. Some of the difficulties inherent in the discharge of such offenders were examined earlier in this book. Second, there is, as already suggested, a much larger group of offender/patients who are not dangerous, but who are often difficult and disruptive. These are the patients that the late Doctor Scott called 'embarrassing' or 'unrewarding'. These would include a number of those with alcohol and drug abuse problems (see Chapter 9). As Bluglass (1978) suggests, many of these were 'previously given asylum by mental hospitals but now they are increasingly rejected, and they form the basis of much of the present problem.' A number of people consider that we need to return to the concept of 'asylum' in its original 'caring' sense. Admittedly this is important, but it is not enough. We need also to provide a much greater degree of flexibility within the whole system in order to promote interchange between a range of facilitating environments such as hostels, halfway houses, and day centres. On the medical side, bringing the prison medical service within the NHS, as advocated in Chapter 4, would be a step in the right direction, as it would, one hopes improve standards and decrease professional isolation. However, I fear that isolationist attitudes may well prevail against such changes being introduced. As things stand at the moment we operate a more or less 'one-way' system with few staging posts between full-time incarceration and freedom in the community. I have represented this position in *Figure 11(1)*.

A more flexible 'two-way traffic' system is suggested in *Figure 11(2)*.

Admittedly, such a system would require a much greater investment of funds than has currently been available, but in the end, such short-term investment would have long-term benefits as has been demonstrated for example in the work of one or two detoxification units (see Chapter 9). In addition, more community-based projects might help to lessen public anxiety, one hopes through the accompanying familiarity with the needs and problems of offender/patients that would fol-

Figure 11(1)   *Present system of 'one-way traffic' within the hospital and penal systems*

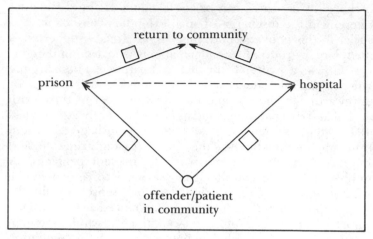

Note to Figure 11(1)

The dotted line represents the occasional formal transfer opportunities between prison and hospital.

The squares represent the very few hostels and other centres that are available as intermediate 'staging posts' (transitional communities).

low. Such schemes would also depend for their success upon a much greater flexibility of outlook among all those professionals most directly concerned. This aspect will be considered before bringing this chapter to a close.

TRAINING IMPLICATIONS

One of the main premises of this book has been that the understanding and management of offender/patients rests upon a multi-disciplinary approach; the arguments for this need not be recapitulated here. Very few opportunities exist for these most directly concerned with the management of such offender/patients to share common training experiences and it is unlikely that there will be any major increase in these opportunities in the immediate future. However, opportunities can be sought for a sharing of experiences at *post-*

Figure 11(2) *Alternative model of planned 'two-way traffic' within the hospital and penal systems*

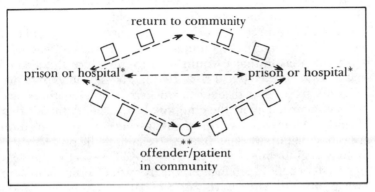

Notes to Figure 11(2)

*This model is suggested on the assumption that the prison medical service would become part of the NHS and that disposal of offender/patients would be dependent upon how need could best be met in any particular case – for example because of security or the availability of specialist treatment facilities.

**The dotted lines represent my conception of a 'two-way' scheme in which offender/patients could be moved more flexibly through the system according to need. Ideally, I would wish to see more opportunities for formal and informal recall and return to prison if required, particularly at crisis points. However, I doubt if our present penal philosophy could embrace this, though current thinking about young adult offenders shows some possibilities in this direction (Home Office 1978). The squares indicate the provision of a flexible system of hostels, day centres, and half-way houses. Goldmeier, Sauer, and White (1977) have produced some evidence showing lower recidivism rates for mentally ill offender/patients discharged into the community through such half-way houses. Such provision would be dependent not only upon funds for new buildings or the adaptation of old premises, but on the availability of appropriately trained residential and field staff in sufficient numbers.

professional qualifying level and I referred to one such experiment in Chapter 1. In one or two areas in the country we now have centres for forensic psychiatry. For example, the Maudsley Hospital has an established tradition and a Chair in the discipline; the Midlands Centre for Forensic Psychiatry at Birmingham – under Professor Robert Bluglass – is another good example of a lively unit which has also done much to foster education and research in this field.

Much as I respect the work of such centres, I would like to see studies in this area becoming rather more broadly based. It is for this reason that I would wish to introduce the idea of *socio-forensic studies* (see Prins 1979). My recent experience leads me to suggest that social workers, amongst others, are much concerned about the emotional and other demands that offender/patients make upon them. One or two probation areas have set up working parties to examine the problem and to suggest guidelines for work in this area. One such example is an excellent report produced recently by the Nottinghamshire Probation and After Care Service (1978). Other probation areas have also expressed concern (the West Midlands for example) as has the National Association of Probation Officers more generally. The Butler Committee had some interesting and thought-provoking things to say about the exchange of information and collaboration between medical and non-medical personnel. The importance of after-care was evidenced in a small study carried out specifically for the Committee by one of its members – Doctor Douglas Acres (Appendix 3 of the Report). He reports a follow-up of the careers of seventeen women and seventy-five men released from the three Special Hospitals during 1971 who were discharged directly into the community and not transitionally to NHS hospitals. Those patients who received after-care were considered likely to fare better than those who did not. Those supervised by probation officers did marginally better (from the point of view of reconviction) than those supervised by local authority social workers. The explanation for this may well be that probation officers have a longer record of experience in dealing with offenders and offender/patients than their colleagues in a social services departments. Indeed, Acres refers specifically to the skills that some social workers had acquired. Despite this, he obtained evidence that they would welcome more support in carrying out their task. 'There appeared to be meagre facilities for training and supporting these officers, a matter which merits some consideration, for some felt very unsupported in their demanding task, even though 67 per cent appeared to have enjoyed a good relationship with the Special Hospital.' The opportunities to develop further skills in this area and to share the discussion of mutual problems with other personnel would go a long way to solving some of the difficulties to which Acres refers. It is my hope that educational institutions – particularly the universities, with their legal, medical, social work, and forensic-psychiatry departments – together with the Royal College of Psychiatrists, the British Psychological Society, the Royal College of Nursing, and the Central Council for Education and Training in Social Work will actively encourage the promotion of multi-disciplinary training for work with this least attractive and difficult group of individuals – labelled variously as offenders, deviants, or patients. It may be that a university or institution of comparable status would consider setting up a *Centre for Socio-Forensic Studies*. This would not necessarily entail the expenditure of vast sums of money as such a Centre would merely seek to coordinate and rationalize existing resources using a federal rather than a departmental model. It would have the advantage not only of culling expertise from various sources, but helping to cross the many boundaries in this interdisciplinary field. (At an informal level, organizations such as the British Academy of Forensic Sciences, the National Association for the Care and Resettlement of Offenders and the Institute for the Study and Treatment of Delinquency (ISTD) already seek to do this to a limited but useful extent.) If this book has increased the reader's understanding of this group of our fellow citizens and has stimulated a challenge to try to help them, then the decision to write it will have been well worthwhile.

References

Bluglass, R. (1978) Regional Secure Units and Interim Security for Psychiatric Patients. *Brit. Med. J.* **1**: 489–93.

Bowden, P. (1977) The NHS Practice of Forensic Psychiatry in One Region. *Psychol. Med.* **7**: 141–48.

DHSS (1973) *Report on Security in NHS Psychiatric Hospitals. (Glancy Report).* London: DHSS.

DHSS, Home Office, Welsh Office, Lord Chancellor's Department (1978) *Review of the Mental Health Act, 1959.* Cmnd. 7320. London: HMSO.

Faulk, M. (1979) Regional Secure Units. 2. The Lyndhurst Unit at Knowle Hospital, Fareham, Hants. *Bulletin of the Royal Coll. Psychiatrists* March.

Goldheimer, J., Sauer, R.H. and White, E.V. (1977) A Halfway House for Mentally Ill Offenders. *Amer. J. Psychiat.* **134**: 45–8.

Greenland, C. (1969) The Three Special Hospitals in England and Patients with Dangerous, Violent or Criminal Propensities. *Med. Sci. Law* **9**: 253–64.

Gostin, L.O. (1977) *A Human Condition. (Vol. 2).* London: MIND (NAMH).

Gunn, J. (1977) Management of the Mentally Abnormal Offender: Integrated or Parallel. *Proc. Royal. Soc. Med.* **70**: 877–80.

Higgins, J. (1979) Regional Secure Units. 1. Rainford Ward, Rainhill Hospital, Merseyside. *Bulletin Royal Coll. Psychiatrists* March.

Home Office and DHSS (1974) *Interim Report of the Committee on Mentally Abnormal Offenders.* Cmnd. 5698. London: HMSO.

—— (1975) *Report of the Committee on Mentally Abnormal Offenders (Butler Committee).* Cmnd. 6244. London: HMSO.

Home Office, (1978) *Report on the Work of the Prison Department.* Cmnd. 7290. London: HMSO.

—— (1978) *Youth Custody and Supervision. A New Sentence.* Cmnd. 7406. London: HMSO.

Jones, M. (1979) The Therapeutic Community, Social Learning and Social Change. In R.D. Hinshelwood and N. Manning (eds) *Therapeutic Communities: Reflections and Progress.* London: Routledge and Kegan Paul.

Locke, J. (1978) The Special Hospitals. *Social Work Service* (DHSS) May 1978

Ministry of Health (1961) *Treatment of Psychiatric Patients Under Security Conditions.* HM (61) 69. London: HMSO.

Morrice, J.K.W. (1979) *Basic Concepts: a Critical Review.* In R.D. Hinshelwood and N. Manning (eds) *Therapeutic Communities: Reflections and Progress.* London: Routledge and Kegan Paul.

Nottinghamshire Probation and After Care Service (1978) *Report of Departmental Working Party on the Mentally Abnormal Offender and Psychiatric Hospital Liaison.* Nottingham.

Parker, E., and Tennent, G. (1979) The 1959 Mental Health Act and Mentally Abnormal Offenders: A Comparative Study. *Med. Sci. Law.* **19**: 29–38.

Pope, P.J. and Gibbens, T.C.N. (1979) Medical Aspects of Management Problems in Maximum Security Prisons. *Med. Sci. Law* **19**: 111–17.

Prins, H.A. (1977) Review of Gostin's 'A Human Condition' (Vols. 1 and 2). *Brit. J. Soc. Work* **7**: 367–68.

—— (1979) Socio-Forensic Studies: A Promising Field for Future Development. *Med. Sci. Law* **19**: 108–10.

Scott, P.D. (1975) *Has Psychiatry Failed in the Treatment of Offenders? The Fifth Denis Carroll Memorial Lecture.* London: ISTD.

Scottish Home Department (1977) *State Hospital, Carstairs Report of Public Local Inquiry into the Circumstances Surrounding the Escape of Two Patients on 30 November, 1976 and into Security and Other Arrangements at the Hospital.* Edinburgh: HMSO.

Walker, N. and McCabe, S. (1973) *Crime and Insanity in England (Vol. 2)* Edinburgh: Edinburgh University Press.

Walker, N. (1976) *Treatment and Justice in Penology and Psychiatry. The Sandoz Lecutre, 1976.* Edinburgh: Edinburgh University Press.

Whitehead, J.A. (1979) *Violence in Mental Hospitals and Prisons. Int. J. Off. Ther. and Comp. Criminol.* **23**: 21–4.

Name index

Abarbanel, G., 248
Abrahamson, D., 149
Adler, F., 300
Alcoholics Anonymous, 277–78
Alexander, F., 140
Allen, C., 218
Amir, M., 244–45
Anne, Princess, 65
Anthony, H.S., 151
Arnold case (1724), 16
Ashley, Jack, 247
Ashley, M.C., 48
Atkin Committee (1923), 19
Avison, N.H., 48

Bagley, C., 241
Baker, T.B., 278
Ball, Ian, 65
Ball, J.C., 289
Ball, M., 189
Banay, R.S., 47
Bancroft, J., 236
Banks, C., 46, 210
Barack, L.I., 312
Bardwick, J.M., 317
Barnett, I., 229
Bartholomew, A.A., 131, 225, 269, 270
Bateman, R. v., (1925), 12
Baxstrom, Johnnie, 177
Baxter, *see Hill* v. *Baxter*
Beach, F.A., 215, 299

Bebbington, P.E., 278
Bell, D.S., 287
Bellingham case (1812), 17
Bender, L., 207
Bennett, D.H., 158
Bewley, T.H., 287
Blackburn, R., 150
Blacker, E.J., 47
Blair, D., 24, 80, 81, 83, 145–46, 179
Bleechmore, J.F., 139
Blom-Cooper, L., 127, 169
Bluglass, R.S., 348; hospitals, provision of 336, 343, 344, 345; infanticide, 306; psychiatrists' reports, 113; studies of prison populations, 45, 46, 47
Boatman, B., 238
Boggis, J.J., 200
Bonn, J., 84
Bottoms, A.E., 164
Bowden, P., 122, 337
Bracton, 14–15
Brandon, D.H., 218
Bratty case, 25
Brewer, C., 80, 82–3
Brill, H., 48
British Academy of Forensic Sciences, 349
Brittain, R.P., 185, 253–54
Bromberg, W., 45, 46

Bronowski, Jacob, 195
Brown, G.W., 54
Browning, D.H., 238
Brownmiller, S., 245
Buckle, M., 288
Burkitt, family, 5
Burt, J.L., 248
Buss, D.H., 266
Butterworth, *see Kay* v. *Butterworth*
Buyers, M., 265, 276
Byrne case (1960), 34

Camps, F.E., 272
Canterbury Tales, 225
Cantley, Judge, 4
Card, R.I.E., 21, 198
Carlisle, J.M., 236
Carroll, Lewis, 8
Cass, J., 236
Chambers, E.D., 200
Champion, R.A., 287
Christie, J., 256
Clarke, M.J., 14
Clark, T., 145, 149
Cleckley, H., 34, 139, 141, 145,
    146, 147–50
Cleobury, J.R., 144
Clouston, G.S., 107
Cobb, S., 52–3
Cockburn, J.J., 319
Cocozza, J.J., 177
Coddington, F.J., 111
Cohen, L.H., 48
Coke, Sir Edward, 15
Concise Oxford Dictionary, 9, 11
Cook, T., 273
Coope, G., 270
Cooper, J., 47
Coutselinis, A., 283
Cowie, J., 319
Cowie, V., 319
Cox, M., 186
Craft, M., 139, 141, 156, 158, 189
Cramer, M.J., 47

Croft, J., 43–4
Crown, J., 43–4
Cullens, M., 230
Curran, D., 138
Cushman, P., 285
Cuthbert, T.M., 182
Cutting, J., 80

Dacre, A.J.I., 203
Dalgaard, J., 282
Dalton, K., 316
Davidson, A.F., 278
Davies, T.S., 236
Dawtry, F., 280, 289
De Berker, P., 107
De Lint, J., 265
Dell, S., 113
Devlin, Lord, 10
Dietze, H.J., 281
D'Orban, P.T., 287, 301, 306,
    310–11, 312, 315–16

Eacott, S.E., 226
East, N., 113, 128, 130, 138, 214,
    217, 218
Edwards, G., 269, 271, 278, 280,
    290
Elder, P.D., 323
Ellis, Havelock, 215
Epps, P., 316, 317, 319
Esterson, A., 42
European Commission on
    Human Rights, 343–44

Faulk, M., 45, 64–5, 69, 78, 115,
    182, 350
Feldman, M., 44
Feldman, M.R., 152
Felice, M., 319
Fenton, G.W., 24
Ferrers case (1760), 16
Field, L.H., 236
Finch, John, 9–10
Finchman D., 276

Fish, Prof., 72
Fitch, J.H., 235
Foldes, P.A., 273
Ford, C.S., 215, 299
Forssman, H., 93
Foucault, M., 103–04
Fox, L.W., 112
Freeman, H., 48
Frie, D., 230
Freud, S., 197, 207, 237–38
Friedman, S., 45, 46
Fry, J.F., 200, 201, 203, 204
Fulcher, G., 61

Galbally, F., 255
Ganser, S.J.M., 74–5
Gath, D., 273
George III, King of England,
    16–17
George, R., 232
Gibbens, T.C.N., and alcohol,
    269; incest, 239–40; prison,
    336; prostitution, 308–09,
    310, 317; rape, 244, 249;
    reports, 113, 114, 119, 121,
    122; sexual differences, 299;
    shoplifting, 70, 307;
    specialization, 1; studies of
    prison population, 46, 47;
    women offenders, 301, 313,
    135, 320
Gibbs, C., 320
Gibson, E., 107
Gibson, H.B., 90
Gilbert, J., 319
Gillies, H., 45, 46, 47
Gittleson, N.L., 226
Glancy, J., 342
Glatt, M.M., 268, 269, 271, 272,
    280
Glossary of Mental Disorders, 86
Glover, E., 323
Glueck, B., 45, 46
Goodman, N., 305, 313, 319

Gordon, A.M., 285, 286
Gordon, R., 231
Gossop, M., 287
Gostin, L.O., 331, 337, 338
Gough, H.G., 143
Grant, M., 278
Gray, W.J., 128
Greenland, C., 177, 190, 337
Grimes, J.A., 286
Grossbard, H., 156
Grossman, G., 266
Grotius, 15
Grunhut, M., 105
Guardian, The, 3–6, 166–68, 184,
    249, 276, 343
Gunn, J., on depression, 59, 72;
    epilepsy, 83, 84–5; mental
    disorder, 42–3; mental
    hospitals, 336; prisoners, 45,
    47, 48–9, 50, 127, 128–29,
    132; psychopathy, 144
Gurvitz, M., 139, 140
Guttmacher, M.S., 14
Guze, S.B., 45, 48, 144, 269, 312

Hadfield, James, 16–17
Haigh case, 73
Haines, D., 270
Hale, Sir Matthew, 15
Hall, J., 248
Hall-Williams, J.E., 94, 239, 240,
    249, 321
Hamblin-Smith, Dr., 128
Hamilton, J.R., 276, 277
Hands, J., 316
Hardgrove, G., 248
Hare, R.D., 150, 152, 154, 156
Harper, M.J.R., 103
Harrington, A., 156–57
Harris, T., 54
Hart, H.L.A., 10, 13, 22
Havard, J.D.J., 272
Hawkins, G., 242
Hawks, D.V., 285

Hays, P., 76
Head, Henry, 148
Heath, A.B., 266
Heath, Neville, 67, 253
Heilbron, Judge, 246
Henderson, D.K., 34, 139, 140, 144
Henriques, B.L.Q., 112
Hensman, C., 269, 271, 278
Herbert, M., 153
Herbert, V., 316
Hershon, H.I., 273
Hertoft, P., 216
Higgins, J., 344
Hill, Sir Denis, 257
Hill v. *Baxter* (1958), 22
Hogan, T.B., 11–12
Holden, A., 165
Holmes, Richard, 179
Home Office; Committee on Mentally Abnormal Offenders, 1; *Habitual Drunken Offenders*, 275
Hopkins, J.H., 318
Horowitz, M., 306
Howells, K., 244
Hubert, W.H., 128, 130
Hunter, J., 310, 311
Hurley, W., 209
Hyatt-Williams, A., 252–53

Iliffe, Terence John, 164, 165–66, 183
Inciardi, J., 203
Ingram, Fr M., 233
Institute for the Study and Treatment of Delinquency, 349

Jack, A., 244
Jackson, Hughlings, 84
Jacobs, F.G., 12, 15, 16
Jacoby, B., 277
Jahoda, M., 51

James, T.E., 219, 225
Jellinek, E.M., 266
Johns, J.H., 148
Johnson, Kenneth, 166
Johnson, V., 215
Johnson, W., 232
Johnston, W.C., 181
Jones, Barry, 167
Jones, I.H., 230
Jones, H., 301
Jones, M., 141, 340
Jones, P.E., 21, 198
Jordan, B., 187
Jung, C.G., 197

Kahn, J.H., 104, 107
Kalven, H., 302
Karpman, B., 141
Kaufman, A., 82
Kay v *Butterworth* (1954), 83
Kelley, M.F., 271
Kennedy, A., 113
Kennedy, L., 256
Kenyon, F.E., 318
Kessel, W.I.N., 266
Kestenbaum, S.E., 300, 302
Kinsey, A.C., 215
Kittrie, N.M., 154
Kloek, J., 64
Knuller case (1973), 220
Koch, I.L., 140
Kolvin, K., 113
Kozol, H.L., 177
Kyle, E., 271

Laing, R.D., 42
Lambert, K., 231–32
Lancaster, N.P., 256
Landon, P.B., 154
Lassen, G., 48
Law Commission, 13
Law, S.K., 231
Le Couteur, N.B., 200, 201, 203, 204

Leicester University, School of Social Work, 2
Lemon, N., 112–13
Levine, D., 173
Lewis, A., 139
Lewis, N.D.C., 206, 207
Ley, John, 65
Lidberg, L., 82
Lightfoot, W., 107
Lindner, R.M., 141
Lion, J.R., 87, 186
Lipman case, 25, 282
Litauer, W., 107
Locke, J., 338
Loewenstein, S., 300
Lukianowicz, N., 239

MIND, 331, 343
McCabe, C., 139, 177, 305, 337
McClintock, F.H., 48
McCord, J., 139
McCord, W., 139
McCulloch, J.W., dependency, 279; drugs, 282; mental disorder, 55, 60, 62, 69, 71, 72, 86, 87, 92
Macdonald, J.M., 182, 183, 184, 201, 203, 206, 225, 245
MacGrath, P.G., 180–81, 189
McGuire, R.J., 236
McKenna, Judge, 166
McKerracher, D.W., 203
Macht, L.B., 207
Mack, J.E., 207
Mackay, Patrick, 145, 149, 163
Maclay, D.T., 227, 228
Maclay, I., 319
M'Naghten, Daniel, 16, 17–20, 24, 65
Mahar, D., 45
Maisch, H., 239–40
Malinowski, B., 215
Mallinson, P., 138
Malzberg, B., 48

Mandelbrote, B., 294
Mannheim, H., 301
Martin, Jonathan, 205
Masters, W.H., 215
Mather, N.J. de V., 203, 236
Mathis, J.C., 229–30
Maughs, S.B., 139
Maule, H.G., 47
Mawby, R.I., 304
Mawdsley, Robert John, 3–4, 344
Mawson, A.R., 151–52
Mawson, C.D., 151–52
May, D., 304
Mead, Margaret, 215
Measey, L.G., 270
Mechanic, D., 51
Megargee, E.I., 177
Mehta, B.M., 226
Melotte, C., 290
Mendels, J., 57
Menninger, K., 51
Mercier, D.J., 140
Midlands Centre for Forensic Psychiatry, 348
Miles, A.E., 156, 158
Mills, Harry, 229
Milo, B., 230
Milte, K.L., 255
Mitchell, G., 318
Modestinus, 15
Monahan, T.M., 209
Monger, M., 321
Moorhouse, P.M. Smith-, *see* Smith-Moorhouse
Morgan, DPP v., 245–46
Morrice, J.K.W., 341
Morris, N., 242
Mortimer, Barry, 3, 4
Mott, J., 285–86, 287
Muller, D., 236
Munro, A., 55
Murphy, J.B., 318

Nakashima, I.J., 238

National Association for the Care and Resettlement of Offenders, 349
National Association for Mental Health, *see* MIND
National Association of Probation Officers, 348
Neustatter, W.L., 61, 70, 73, 76, 77, 81, 82, 113
Newton, J., 204
Nichol, A.R., 177
Nichols, F.L., 245, 250, 251, 256
Nicholls, P., 271
Nicol, A., 270
Noble, P.J., 288–89
Northgate Clinic, 343
Nott, Lyndon, 167
Nottinghamshire Fire Service, 200
Nottinghamshire Probation and After-Care Service, 348
Nursten, J., 107

O'Connell, B.A., 76
Offord, D.R., 319
Ogborne, A.C., 291
Oltman, J.E., 45, 46
Orr, J.H., 130
Orthner, H., 236
Ounsted, C., 113

Packman, J., 187
Page, L., 111–12
Palmer, C., 307
Parker, E., 335, 339
Parker, T., 229, 232–33
Parnell, R.W., 316
Parr, D., 273
Parrott, Michael William, 168–69
Parsley, *see Sweet* v. *Parsley*
Parsloe, P., 322, 323
Partridge, M., 140
Paul, D.M., 234
Payne, C., 177

Peel, Sir Robert, 17
Penrose, L.S., 50, 93
Penycate, J., 145, 149
Perceval, Spencer, 17
Peto, J., 271
Phillips, G.F., 283
Pichot, P., 139
Pinel, P., 139
Pitcher, D.R., 93
Podola case (1959), 29, 75
Pollak, O., 301
Pollock, C.B.R., 228
Pollock, H.M., 48
Pope, P., 114, 119, 121, 122, 210
Pope, P.J., 336
Power, D.J., 76, 81, 234, 248, 279
Prewer, R.R., 127
Prichard, J.C., 139–40
Price, J., 70, 305, 307, 313, 319
Prins, H., on arson, 201; crime, 43; dangerousness, 171, 172, 316; dependency, 279; drugs, 282; inquiries, 164; MIND, 331; mental disorder, 60, 62, 69, 71, 72, 78, 86, 89, 92; police discretion, 27; psychiatrists, 105; psychopaths, 156; remand for report, 114, 115; sexual deviation, 218; socio-forensic studies, 348
Prison Commission, 127
Prometheus, 195

Quay, H.C., 148
Quick case (1973), 81

Ranasinghe, H., 266
Rappeport, J., 48
Rasor, R.W., 290
Rathod, N., 265, 286
A Review of the Mental Health Act (1959), 141–42, 332–35
Richardson, H., 321

Riege, M.G., 319
Rix, K.J.B., 265, 276
Roberts, D.F., 238
Robertson, G., 144
Robins, Lee N., 153
Robinson, Barry, 167–68, 184–85
Robitscher, J., 105
Roeder, F., 236
Rollin, H., 49, 66
Rooth, F.G., 224, 225–27, 230
Rosenberg, C.M., 287
Roth, M., 68
Rousseau, J.J., 225
Roy, A., 287
Roy, C., 245, 250, 251, 256
Rubington, E., 269
Rupp, J.C., 254
Russell, C., 185
Russell, W.M.S., 185

Samuels, A., 26, 34–5
Sapsford, R.J., 210
Sarbin, T.R., 172, 188
Scacce, A.M., 249
Schalling, D., 150, 154
Schipkowensky, N., 58
Schmideberg, M., 154–55
Schofield, M., 215
Schorer, C.E., 75
Schultz, L.G., 245
Scott, D., 196, 201, 202, 203, 205
Scott, D.F., 84
Scott, E.M., 323
Scott, P.D., 15; on children protection, 21; dangerousness, 172; disruptive patients, 345; drugs 288; Ganser syndrome, 75; history-taking, 179; occupation and violence, 185; offenders, 2; prisoners, 45; psychiatrists' report, 113; psychopaths, 147, 156; sexual

deviation, 218; treatment, 331
Sedley, Sir Charles, 225
Selling, L.S., 46
Senior, R. v., (1899), 12
Shapiro, A., 90, 92
Shaw, R., 252
Shaw case (1962), 220
Silberman, M., 47
Silberman, N., 269, 310
Simcox, Christopher, 169–70, 183
Simon, F.H., 177
Simonsen, J., 282
Skynner, A.C.R., 317
Slater, E., 68
Slater, E.T.O., 142, 319
Smart, C., 299, 302–03, 307, 308, 309, 313, 321, 324
Smith, Ann D., 298, 300, 316, 320
Smith, D., 45
Smith, D.D., 210
Smith, Dr Hamblin-, *see* Hamblin-Smith
Smith-Moorhouse, P.M., 269
Soothill, K.L., 114, 119, 121, 122, 210, 239–40, 244, 249
Sparks, R.F., 107, 112, 114
Spring, J.A., 266
Steadman, H.J., 177
Stekel, W., 207
Stevens, B.C., 282
Stone, R. v., (1977), 12
Stott, D.H., 79
Streatfeild Committee (1961), 112
Stürup, G., 155–56, 189
Suedfield, L.P., 154
Sunter, J.P., 266
Sweet v. *Parsley* (1969), 11
Szasz, T., 42

Taylor, M., 285–86, 287
Tennent, G., 113, 236, 316, 318,

335, 339
Tennent, T.G., 163, 171, 207, 208
Thompson, C.B., 45, 46
Tidy, Pauline, 168
Tollinton, H.P., 128
Toner, Barbara, 245
Topp, D.O., 67, 127, 129, 132, 196, 197, 204
Trafford, P.A., 115
Trethowen, W.H., 52, 83
Treves-Brown, C., 141
Tupin, J.P., 45
Tutt, N., 92

Usdin, G.L., 181–82

Vaillant, G.E., 290
Valentine, M., 53
Vallance, M., 236
Vandersall, T.A., 207–08
Victoria, Queen of England, 17
Virkkunen, M., 233, 239
Voegele, G.E., 281
Voigt, J., 282

Walker, N., on dangerousness, 171, 175–76, 177, 183, 184; law, history of, 14, 15, 16, 17, 27; mental disorder, 48; psychopathy, 139; special hospitals, 337; treatment, 330; women offenders, 299, 302, 305, 313
Waller, Judge, 167
Washbrook, R.A.H., 270
Watson, J.M., 281
Watts, F.N., 158
Way, C.K., 239, 249
Webb, D., 186
Weber, H., 91
West, A.C., 113
West, D.J., 45, 58, 64, 90, 93, 245, 250, 251, 256, 269

Whitehead, J.A., 341
Whitehouse, Mary, 214
Whiteley, S., 141
Whyte, M.B.H., 105
Widem, C.S., 312
Wiener, J.M., 207–08
Wiepert, G.D., 287
Wiggins, Mrs, 166–67
Wilkinson, R., 265
Willcox, D.R.C., 288
Willett, T.C., 272
Williams, A. Hyatt-, see Hyatt-Williams
Williams, Barry, 3, 4–6
Willaims, J.E. Hall-, see Hall-Williams
Williams, M., 236
Wilson, S., 290
Windle, R. v., (1952), 18
Wing, J.K., 51–2
Winnick, H., 306
Woddis, G.M., 46, 59–60, 64, 69–70, 78
Wolff, C., 216
Wood, S., 48–9
Woods, S., 187
Woodside, M., 113
Woodward, M., 90
Woolf, P.G., 204
Wootton, B., 141
World Health Organisation, 54, 279
Wright, E., 244
Wright, J.D., 280, 288

Yarnell, H., 206, 207
Young, B.G., 236
Young, Francis Graham, 164–65, 183, 185, 190

Zacune, J., 278
Zakus, G.E., 238
Zeegers, M., 105
Zeisel, H., 302

Subject index

Aarvold Committee, 164–65,
170, 257
Abnormality of mind, 34, 41n; of
personality, 85–7
Abortion, illegal, 305
Act, 12
actus reus, 12
Addiction, 265, 285; *see also*
Dependence
Aetiology of mental disorder,
42–3, 50–4
Affective disorders, 55–7; and
crime, 57–61; endogenous,
57; exogenous, 57; treatment,
57
After-care, 348
Aging process, and mental
disorder, 85
Alcohol, 263–78; and arsen, 205,
209; classification of offences,
271–76; and crime, 268–71;
and death, 266; dementia, 24;
dependence, *see* Alcoholism;
and incest, 239; and the law,
273, 274–75; offences,
271–76; and organic states,
80; and rape, 244, 250; and
responsibility, 23, 24–6; and
society, 264–65, 276;
treatment of offenders,
276–78; and violence, 270
Alcoholism: and crime, 268–71;

definition, 266;
detoxification, 274, 275–76;
habitual drunken offenders,
273–76; stages, 266–68;
treatment, 276–78
Amentia, 87
Amnesia: and crime, 75–6;
hysterical, 76–7; organic, 82
Amphetamines, 281, 288
Anoxia, 89
Anxiety states, 68, 71–2; and
crime, 71; symptoms, 71
Arousal, and psychopathy,
151–52
Arson, 195–211;
attention-seeking, 206–07;
characteristics, 203–10;
classification of arsonists,
202–08; definition, 197–98;
financial gain, 201, 203;
increase, 201–02;
investigation, 200;
pathological, 203–08;
revenge, 205–06, 209; and
sexuality, 77, 197, 207, 210;
and social dysfunction, 209;
statistics, 198–201
Automatism: epileptic, 84; and
responsibility, 23–4
Autonomic nervous system, and
psychopathy, 151

Baby-battering, 305, 317
Baby-stealing, 305, 310–12
Bail, and psychiatric reports, 106–08, 121–22
Barbiturates, 281
Barlinnie Prison, 341
Bible: fire in, 196; justice in, 14
Bisexuality, 216
Brain damage, 81–3, 144; and responsibility, 16
Brain tumours, 81, 83
Broadmoor Hospital, 4, 5–6, 204, 338, 343, 344; security, 6; therapeutic regime, 340; women in, 318
Buggery, 215–16, 219, 222, 248–49
Butler Committee (1975), 37–8, 164; and assessment, 178; automatism, 24; collaboration, 348; dangerousness, 171, 173–74, 344; diminished responsibility, 35–6; fitness to plead, 29–30; guardianship orders, 111; Homicide Act, 20; Iliffe, 165–66; infanticide, 36; intoxication, 26; M'Naghten Rules, 20; probation officers, 114; prosecution, 27–8; psychiatric reports, 107–08; psychopathy, 141; remands, 335; rights, 331; secure accommodation, 342; severe illness, 32–3; special verdicts, 32–3; women offenders, 298, 313–14

Cannabis, 282–83
Capacity, 11
Carstairs State Hospital, 318, 337, 340
Cerebral status, assessing, 82–3

Children: and alcoholic parents, 268–69; and arson, 206, 207–08; homosexual stage, 233–34; offences against, and report, 117; and pornography, 220; remand for report, 123–25; and responsibility, 21; sexual assaults on, 231–37
Child-stealing, 305, 310–12
Chorea, 23, 79, 140
Chromosomal abnormalities, 89, 93–4, 315–16
Cognition, faculties of, 18
Coldingley Prison, 321
Communication: inter-agency, 190; and subnormality, 90, 91–2
Concussion, 82
Cortical studies of psychopathy, 150–51
Courts: expectations of psychiatric help, 111–13; hospital orders, 109–11; psychiatric reports, 106–08; *see also* Law
Criminal Damage Act (1971), 197, 198
Criminality: and affective disorders, 57–61; and alcohol, 268–71; and amnesia, 75–6; and anxiety states, 71; defined, 43–4; and depressive illness, 57–60, 69–70; and drugs, 284–89; and epilepsy, 84–5, 140; and intelligence, 90; and menstruation, 316–17; and mental disorder, 1, 6, 14, studies, 41–2, 42–50; and physique, 316; in psychiatric populations, 47–50; and schizophrenia, 64–7; and sub-normality, 89–93; women, 299–300

Criminal Justice Act: (1967), 106, 275; (1972), 275
Criminal responsibility, *see* Responsibility
Crown courts, 110; and arson, 199
Culpability, 11
Cyproterene acetate, 230, 236, 252

Dangerousness, 163–90; assessment, 6, 65–6, 166, 169, 176–86; dealing with, 187, 188–90, 344–45; definition, 171–72; on discharge, 165–70, 177; ethical issues, 174–76; and the law, 173–74; and mental disorder, 163; premonitery signs, 167, 168, 169, 178, 182, 183–85, 190; psychological, 174–75; sentencing, 174–76
Death: and alcohol, 266; and drugs, 282; and sexual offences, 252–57
Defence, and psychiatric report, 126
Delinquency, girls, 319–20
Demeanour in court, 118–19, 121
Dementia: pseudo, 72, 74; senile, 85, 205
Dependence, drug, 265, 279, 281, 282, 283; treatment, 289–91
Depressive disorder, 55, 57; assessing, 59–60; and crime, 57–60, 69–70; definition, 70; and fire, 205; mild, 61, 68, 69–70; psychotic, 57, 58; severe, 57–61; symptoms, 69
Detoxification centres, 274, 275–76, 344
Deviation, sexual, 217

Discharge, 339; and dangerousness, 165–70, 177; and supervision, 165–66, 176, 348–49
Disease, defined, 51–2; organic: and arson, 204; and mental disorder, 78–85
Disruptive patients, 345
Down's syndrome, 89, 93
Drinking, *see* Alcohol
Driving: and alcohol, 271–72; offences, 272
Drug offences, 284, 285–89; classification, 284; and psychiatrists reports, 117, 121; studies, 285–88; treatment, 289–91
Drugs: abuse, 285; and crime, 284–89; and death, 282, 290; dependence, 265, 279, 281, 282, 283; hard, 280, 287, 288–89; and hostility, 287; obtaining, 284; pushing, 284; and responsibility, 24–6; and sex offenders, treatment, 230, 236, 252; and society, 280; soft, 288–89; types, 281–83; users, types, 283, 288–89
Drunkenness, *see* Alcohol
Durham rule, 19, 32

Encephalitis, 78–9, 140, 144
Endocrine disorders, 81
Enuresis and arson, 207
Epilepsy, 22, 23, 24, 83–5; and crime, 84–5, 140; and fire, 204, 205, 209; types, 83–4
Exhibitionism, *see* Exposure
Exposure, indecent, 104, 224–30; cause, 228–29; classification, 226–28; exhibitionism, 225–26; and prosecution, 27, 222; repeated, 178; treatment, 229–30

Fantasies, violent, 168, 180, 184–85, 254
Feltham Borstal, 129
Female offending, *see* Women
Fetishism, 77–8, 221
Fire, 210; attraction of, 195–96, 210; death by, 67, 196, 203, 204; in mythology, 195–96; and sexuality, 197, 207; *see also* Arson
Fitness to plead, 28–31
Flexibility of treament, 345
Fugues, 72, 73
Functional psychoses, cause, 55; classification, 55–67; and crime, 57–61, 64–7; definition, 55

Ganser syndrome, 72, 73, 74–5
Gender, 216
General paralysis of the insane (GPI), 79–80, 205
Genitals, exposure, *see* Exposure
Girls: and the courts, 304; delinquency, 319–20; paternal relationships, 319, 320, 321–22
Glue sniffing, 281
Grendon Underwood Psychiatric Prison, 128–29, 209
Guardianship orders, 109, 111
Guilt, legal, 12

Habitual Drunkard's Act (1879), 275
Habitual drunkenness of offenders, 273–76
Hallucination, 60, 62–3
Harm, psychological, 174–75; *see also* Dangerousness
Health & Social Security, Department of, and special hospitals, 337–38

Heroin, 282, 286
Hero syndrome, 206
Herpes virus, 79, 248
Herstedvester, Denmark, 155, 189
Holloway Prison, 321; mental disorder in, 313–15
Homicide Act (1957), 19, 20, 25, 33–4
Homosexuality, 220; and death, 254–55; offences against children, 234; phase, 233–34
Hormone treatments, 230, 236
Horton Hospital, 66
Hospital Orders, 108, 109–11, 335, 336–37
Hospitals; *see* Mental Hospitals; Special Hospitals
Hostels: for addicts, 291; for alcoholics, 278
Hostility, and drugs, 287–88
House of Lords, judgements, 11–12, 16, 17
Huntington's Chorea, *see* Chorea
Hyperglycaemia, 24
Hypoglycaemia, 81, 228
Hypomania, 56; and arson, 205; and crime, 60
Hysteria, 68, 72–7, 312; amnesia, 75–7, 82; assessment, 73–4; definition, 72; and malingering, 73; and psychopathy, 144, 312–13; symptoms, 72–3

Illness: behaviour, 51–2; defined, 51–2, 60; and responsibility, 22–3
Illusion, schizophrenic, 63
Immoral earnings, living on, 222
Imprisonment, effects, 44, 312–15, 320–22
Incendiarism, 202; *see also* Arson
Incest, 218, 222, 231, 237–42;

and alcohol, 239;
classification, 240–41; in law,
238, 242; prosecution,
238–40; and social conditions,
238–40, 241; and society,
237–38, 242; taboo, 237–38,
242; treatment, 241–42
Indecent assault, 222, 223,
242–43
Indecent exposure, *see* Exposure
Inebriate's Act (1898), 275
Infanticide, 36, 305–06, 317
Infections, viral, 78–9
Insanity, *see* Mental disorder
Intelligence and crime, 90
Intent, 11, 12, 22; exculpation,
13, 22
Intoxication, *see* Alcohol
Involuntary conduct, 22–3
Irresponsibility, *see*
Responsibility

Jealousy, 206
Juveniles, remand, 123–25

Kleptomania, 77, 104, 218

LSD (lysergic acid diethylamide),
281–82
Labelling, 2–3, 154, 313, 321,
330
Law: and alcohol, 273; and
dangerousness, 173–74; and
incest, 238; and morality,
9–10, 37; and psychiatry,
102–27; and rape, 245–47;
and responsibility, 9–20; and
the sexes, 301
Learning, and psychopathy, 152
Lesbianism, 317
Liability, 11–12; strict, 11, 13
Licensing Acts, 273
Local authorities and secure
units, 343–44

M'Naghten case, 17–20, 24;
Rules, 18–20, 31, 32, 33
Magistrates: attitudes towards
psychiatric services, 115–27;
expectations of psychiatric
help, 111–13; and offences,
types, 116–18; and other
factors, 117, 118–19, 121–23;
training, 112–13
Magistrates' Courts: arson in,
199; powers, 109–10; remand
for report, 106–07
Magistrates Courts Act (1952),
106
Malingering and amnesia, 73–4
Mania, extreme, 56; and crime,
60–1
Manic-depressive illness, 55
Manslaughter, 12; and murder,
19–20, 34
Maudsley Hospital, 348
Medical reports, *see* Reports,
psychiatric
Medicines Act (1968), 284
Melancholia, involutional, 57;
irrational, 56
Meningitis, 78, 144
Menopause, effects, 70, 317
mens rea, 12, 32
Menstruation and crime, 70,
316–17
Mental Deficiency Act (1913),
140
Mental disorder: assessment,
114; cause, 42–3,
50–4; classification,
54–94; and criminality, 1, 6,
14, 41–50; and
dangerousness, 163;
definition, 41n, 42–3, 51;
feigned, 73–4; and fire,
204–05; and fitness to plead,
28–31; interdisciplinary
approach, 1, 52, 133, 346,

349; organic, 78–85, 88–9; and philosophy, 103; and prosecution, 26–8; and responsibility, 14–26; and rights, 331; serious, 28–9, 32–3; and verdicts, 31–3
Mental health, defined, 51
Mental Health Act (1959): alcohol dependence, 333; courts powers, 332–34; definitions, 332; drug dependence, 333; guardianship orders, 111; hospital orders, 109; Part IV, 49; Part V, 335–36; and police discretion, 27; and police powers, 332; probation orders, 110, psychopathy, 141–42, 332; remand, 335; restriction orders, 333–34; *Review*, 141–42, 332–35; sentencing, 31, 109–10; Special Hospitals, 29, 173, 337; sexual offences, 220, 333, subnormality, severe, 32, 88; treatment, 164
Mental Hospitals. and restricted patients, 335–37; secure accommodation, 342–44
Mental subnormality, 32, 87–94; assessment, 88; cause, 88–9; classification, 88; and communication, 90, 91–2; and crime, 89–93
Moebius syndrome, 204
Molestation, sexual, of children, 231–37
Mongolism, 89, 93
Morality and the law, 9–10, 37; private, 10
Morphine, 282
Moss Side Special Hospital, 318–19, 338
Murder: early defence, 16–20;

mandatory life sentence, 35–6; and manslaughter, 19–20, 34; sexual, 252–54

National Health Services: and prison medical staff, 129–30, 131, 345; and secure units, 342; treatment of offenders, 335–36
Necrophilia, 104, 255–56
Negligence, 12
Neuroses, 67–78; mild, 68
Notification of addicts, 286

Obsessional states, 68, 77–8
Occupations, and violence, 185
Offences, types and report, 116 18, 123–27
Offenders, demeanour in court, 118–19, 121
Old Testament, and justice, 14
Omission, 12
Onomatopoiesis, 149
Opiates, 282, 285, 286, 290
Organic mental disorders, 78–85, 88–9

Paedophilia, 214, 231–37, 249; classification, 234–35; treatment, 235–37
Painting, as indicator, 168, 184–85
Panic reaction, 186–87, 188
Paralysis, general, of the insane (GPI), 79–80, 205
Paranoia, severe, 65–6
Parkhurst Prison, 129
Park Lane Special Hospital, 338
Pederasty, 231, 235, 236–37
Penal establishments: cross-sex supervision, 322; effects of, 44, 312–15, 320–22; medical services, 127–8, 129–32, 345; and mentally disturbed, 336;

and psychiatry, 127–32; studies of mental disorder, 44–7; women in, 312–15, 320–22

Personality disorders, 85–7

Perversion, 214

Phantasy, 168, 180, 184–85, 254

Pharmacy Act (1933), 284

Phenylketonuria, 89

Phoenix, the, 195

Physique, and criminality, 316

Plead, fitness to, 28–31

Police, discretion, 27, 109

Powers of Criminal Courts Acts (1973), 109, 110

Pregnancy and crime, 317

Pre-menstrual tension, *see* Menstruation

Premonitory signs of dangerousness, 167, 168, 169, 178, 182, 183–85, 190

Prestwich Hospital, 343

Prison, *see* Penal establishments

Prisoners, mental disorder, studies, 44–7

Privacy, right to, 180

Probation officers: and after care, 348; assessment of mental disorder, 114; and offences, types, 118; and other factors, 119, 121–23; and psychiatric services, 115–27; and remand for report, 114

Probation Orders, 110

Prosecution; iniation of, 26–8; police discretion, 27, 109

Prostitution, 219, 222, 305, 308–10, 317, 323; clients, 310; double standards, 309

Provocation, by victim, 183, 233, 244–45, 247

Pseudo-dementia, 72, 74

Pseudo-psychopathy, 143, 144, 154

Psychiatric hospitals, *see* Mental hospitals

Psychiatric populations, criminality, 47–50

Psychiatry: and classification, 131; and diagnosis, 131; forensic, 348; history of, 103–04; and the law, 102–27; and magistrates, 111–13, 115–27; and the penal system, 127–32; role, 104–05, 123

Psychoneuroses, *see* Neuroses

Psychopathy, 18, 34, 138–58; cause, 143–45, 150–52; characteristics, 147–50, 156–57; classification, 145, 154; diagnosis, differential, 145–47; essential, 144, 145, 146, 147–50, 154; history of concept, 138–42; hysteria, 144, 312–13; and infection, 79, 144; management, 141, 152–57, 158; as personality disorder, 86, 143–45, 158; and recidivists, 146, 147, 157; pseudo-, 144, 154; and sex, 144–45; semantic disorder, 148–49; as a term, 142, 153, 157–58; treatment, *see* management; true, 145, 147, 148

Psychoses, *see* Functional psychoses

Punishment, early views on, 14, 15–20

Pyromania, 197, 202, 219; *see also* Arson

Rampton Special Hospital, 90, 203, 338, 340; women in, 318–19

Rape, 218, 221, 222, 242–52; classification, 249–51; and consent, 246; effects of, 248;

and indecent assault, 242–43; legal aspects, 245–47; marital, 245; repeated, 244; reporting, 248; sentencing, 246–47; statistics, 243–44; studies, 244–45; treatment, 251–52; victims, 243, 244–45, 247–48; and virility, 243

Recidivists, 280; and alcohol, 268, 269, 271, 280; arson, 202, 210; psychopaths, 146, 147, 157

Remands for psychiatric report, 106–08, 111; on bail, 106–08, 121–22; in custody, 106: frequency, 114–27; improper use, 115; and region, 114, study of, 114, 115–27, and type of crime, 114

Reports, psychiatric, 106–08; on adults, 125–27; on children, 123–25; courts act on, 107; and defence, 126; and magistrates, 115–27; and offences, types, 116–18; and other factors, 117; and probation officers, 115–27; remands for, *see* Remands

Responsibility, 8–38; definition, 9–13; diminished, 19, 33–6; erosions of, 20–6; in history, 14–20; lack of, 10; and special verdicts, 31–3; and subnormality, 90

Restriction orders, 110

Retardation, mental, 87

Revenge, 205–06

Rights, and mental disorder, 331

Ritualism, *see* Obsessional states

Roman law and responsibility, 14, 15, 37

Royal Commission on Capital Punishment (1953), 19

Rubella, 88

St Vitus Dance, 23

Saxon law, and responsibility, 14

Schizophrenias, 55, 61–7; assessment, 65, 67; cause, 61; characteristics, 61–3; classification, 63–4; and crime, 64–7; feeling, lack of, 66–7; and fire, 204; insidious, 66–7; and violence, 65–6

Secure accommodation, 342–44

Self-immolation, 67, 196, 203, 204

Semantic disorder, 148–49

Senile dementia, 85, 205

Sentencing, discretion, 31, 33, 34, 109; for psychiatric treatment, 109–11; and sex, 303–05; to Special Hospitals, 37, 108

Sexes, differences, 298–300, 301; sentencing, 303–05

Sexual behaviour, normal, 217; variations in, 213, 214–15

Sexual deviation, 214, 216, 217; clinical classification, 217–19; legal classification, 219–21

Sexual disorder, 214

Sexual dysfunction, 214–15, 217

Sexuality, 216

Sexual offences: classification, 219–21; and death, 252–57; emotive nature, 213–14, 256; history-taking, 256; liberal view, 216; multi-method approach, 257; prosecution, 221; and psychiatrist's report, 117, 121; sentencing, 221; statistics, 221–24; terminology, 214–17; therapy, 230, 256; witnesses, 223; *see also* specific offences

Sexual Offences Act (1956), 238, 245; (1967), 216, 220;

(Amendment) Act, (1976), 245, 246
Shoplifting, 305, 306–08, 317; and depression, 69, 70; and mental disorder, 27, 66, 69, 307–08; and prosecution, 27; and psychiatrist's report, 117, 121; and schizophrenia, 66; and senile dementia, 85; type, 307
shoteh, 14
'Shunting' of offenders, 2–3, 66
Sin, *see* Morality
Social Workers: and after-care, 348–49; assessment of patients, 178–79, 180, 181; attributes, 186–90, 349; history-taking, 178–80; and the mentally ill, 179; and offenders, 176, 186; and psychiatry, 180–81; training, 248–49; types, 187
Socio-forensic studies, 348, 349
Special Hospitals, 173, 337–42; detention, 29, 37, 108, 170, 176; discharge, 165–70, 176, 177, 339, 348–49; isolation of, 337–38, 339–40; role, 338, 339; structure, 340; and therapeutic community, 341; women in, 318–19
Stealing, of children, *see* Child-stealing; compulsive, 77; and depressive illness, 69–70; *see also* Shoplifting
Street Offences Act (1959), 308
Subnormality, *see* Mental subnormality
Suicide: by fire, 67, 196, 203, 204; and sex offenders, 254–55
suttee, 196

Talmud, 14
Thresholds, stress, 57
Time, sense of, 157
Town Police Causes Act (1847), 224
Toxic compounds and behaviour, 80
Training: magistrates, 112–13; workers, 346–48
Transexualism, 216
Transvestism, 216
Treatment: flexibility, 345–46; general methods, 6; legislative and administrative reforms, 331–35; meaning of, 331; or punishment, 330; resources, 335–44; and training, 346–48
Tumours, *see* Brain

Unlawful intercourse (under-age), 222

Vagrancy Act (1824), 224
Verdicts, special, 31–3
Victim-precipitated violence, *see* Provocation
Violence, 172; and alcohol, 270; assessing, 6, 65–6, 188–90; and concussion, 82; and dangerousness, 172; dealing with, 187, 188–90; own, 187, 188, 190; repeated, 178; victim-precipitated, 183, 233, 244–45, 247
Voluntary conduct, 22

Wakefield Prison, 3–4, 129
Warlingham Park Alcoholic Unit, 278
Wolfenden Committee (1957), 10
Women: and arson, 206–07, 208–09, 318; attitudes to, 301,

313, 319; baby-stealing, 305, 310–12; background and crime, 319–20; criminality, 300, 302–03; chromosomal factors, 315–16; depression, 54, 312; drug offences, 284, 287; and feminism, 298, 300, 302–03, 324; infanticide, 36, 305–06, 317; and the law, 301–02, 304; and men, differences, 298–300; and mental disorder, 297–98, 307–08, 312–15; offending, 297, 300–24; paternal relationship, 319, 320, 321–22, 323; physiological factors, 316–17; physique and crime, 316; in prison, 312–15, 320–22; prostitution, 219, 222, 305, 308–10, 317, 323; psychopathy, 144–45; psychiatric morbidity, 312–15; relationships, therapeutics, 322, 323, 324; role, 300; sentencing, 303–05; sexual difficulties, 317–18; in Special Hospitals, 318–19; treatment, 320–23, 324; type of crime, 305–06; and violence, 302

Wormwood Scrubs Prison, 129
Wrong, interpretation of, 18

Y chromosones, 93